IMPERIAL RUSSIA

NEW HISTORIES FOR THE EMPIRE

EDITED BY
Jane Burbank
AND
David L. Ransel

INDIANA UNIVERSITY PRESS
Bloomington and Indianapolis

This book is a publication of

Indiana University Press
601 North Morton Street
Bloomington, Indiana 47404-3797 USA

www.indiana.edu/~iupress

Telephone orders   800-842-6796
Fax orders   812-855-7931
Orders by e-mail   iuporder@indiana.edu

The paper used in this publication meets the minimum requirements of
American National Standard for Information Sciences—Permanence of
Paper for Printed Library Materials, ANSI Z39.48-1984.

Manufactured in the United States of America

Library of Congress Cataloging-in-Publication Data

Imperial Russia : new histories for the Empire / edited by Jane
Burbank and David L. Ransel.
   p.   cm. — (Indiana-Michigan series in Russian and East
European studies)
Includes index.
ISBN 0-253-33462-4 (cloth : alk. paper). — ISBN 0-253-21241-3
(pbk. : alk. paper)
1. Russia—History—18th century.   2. Russia—History—19th
century.   I. Burbank, Jane.   II. Ransel, David L.   III. Series.
DK127.I475   1998
947'.06—dc21   98-17132

1 2 3 4 5 03 02 01 00 99 98

Contents

Acknowledgments

———•◦∞◦•———

THE EDITORS THANK several institutions and many scholars for the support, research, and stimulating discussions that made this project possible. We begin with our sponsors. The Joint Committee on the Soviet Union and Its Successor States of the Social Science Research Council and the American Council of Learned Societies provided the material, logistical, and personal support for three workshops for the project as well as seed money for the volume itself. We are particularly grateful to Susan Bronson, historian of imperial Russia and former Program Officer at the SSRC, who has seen this project through from beginning to completion; to Robert Huber, former Program Director of the Joint Committee, who gave superb advice on both intellectual and financial matters; and to Jill Finger, Program Assistant, who directed everyone to the right place at the right time. The organizers of the SSRC-ACLS project were Jane Burbank, Nancy Shields Kollmann, Richard Stites, and Reginald Zelnik, members of the Joint Committee.

A planning meeting was held at the University of Iowa in November 1991, supported in part by the Center for International and Comparative Studies there. We thank the Center and in particular Steven Hoch, our host on the steppe in a snowstorm, for the warm reception and gracious adjustments to weather worthy of Russia.

The papers in the volume were produced for two workshops, entitled "Visions, Institutions, and Experiences of Imperial Russia." The first workshop was held at the Kennan Institute of Advanced Russian Studies in Washington, D.C., in September 1993. We thank the Institute and above all its director, Blair Ruble, for hosting us and especially for our splendid meeting place in the Smithsonian castle.

The second workshop was cosponsored by Portland State University at its lovely urban campus. Our historian host, Louise Becker, made this an ideal location.

The discussions at all three meetings focused on the issues of interpretation, analysis, and categorization that inform this volume. We are grateful to all the participants in the meetings, including the authors of the chapters presented here, for their many contributions to the project. A big thank you, then, to Thomas Barrett, Sarah Berry, Jeffrey Brooks, Daniel Brower, Michael Confino,

ix

James Cracraft, Laura Engelstein, Lee Farrow, Gregory Freeze, Manfred Hildemeier, Steven L. Hoch, Isabel Hull, Austin Jersild, Colin Jones, Andrew Kahn, Andreas Kappeler, Allison Katsev, Michael Khodarkovsky, Valerie Kivelson, Nathaniel Knight, Nancy Shields Kollmann, Gary Marker, Louise McReynolds, Harriet Murav, Daniel Orlovsky, Irina Paperno, Priscilla Roosevelt, David Schimmelpeninck, Yuri Slezkine, Douglas Smith, Michael Stanislawski, Richard Stites, Willard Sunderland, Frank Sysyn, Kevin Thomas, Donald Thumin, William Wagner, Cynthia Whittaker, Richard Wortman, and Reginald E. Zelnik.

The editors are especially grateful to Michael Confino for his supportive engagement with this project, which was inspired in the first place by his splendid and provocative studies of imperial Russia.

Jane Burbank
David L. Ransel

Introduction

——⟨∞⟩··——

THE GOAL OF this volume is to raise questions and to encourage scholars to re-envision imperial Russian history liberated from schools, parties, and single story lines. The essays incorporate new research and new topics, results of a revitalized attention to Russia's past that has engaged historians and others in recent years. The volume has a specific genealogy: it is based upon a series of three workshops at which scholars from different universities, disciplines, and generations discussed new research and encouraged each other to imagine how imperial history might be reconceptualized. This introduction will sketch the intellectual and social context of this project and highlight the themes, questions, and methods represented in the book's separate subsections and chapters. With an eye toward future projects, Jane Burbank's "In Place of a Conclusion" takes a critical look at the blank spots, open questions, and unfilled plans that are likely to shape histories of imperial Russia still to come.

Reconceptualization of imperial Russian history was inspired by two recent changes: the collapse of Soviet power and with it the conventional framework for narratives of Russian history, and a new turn in historical writing about other places and times. The sudden appearance in 1917 of Soviet Russia with its claim to be the first socialist society had oriented much of the historical study of Russia in the twentieth century toward the problems and possibilities of Soviet-style organization, and, of particular relevance to this volume, toward the origins of the Russian revolution. This emphasis upon the Bolshevik revolution relegated Russian history before 1917 if not to the dustbin, then to the morgue. Many studies of the imperial era were scholarly autopsies, performed in confident awareness of the body's chronic ailments; the overriding question concerned the disease or combination of illnesses that had caused the organism's long-overdue demise. This perspective was a matter of form, if not faith, for most Soviet historians, but it figured, too, in many other interpretations. Nicholas Riasanovsky placed the blame for the revolution of 1917 on the rigidity of the system created by Nicholas I in the first half of the nineteenth century; Richard Pipes, following Petr Struve, pushed the beginnings of the empire's illnesses back into the early eighteenth century.[1]

The dissolution of the Soviet Union was accompanied by a reversal of evaluations of imperial Russia. In Russia, challenges to official history became weapons in the political offensives of *perestroika* and the subsequent struggles for control over the new polities emerging after 1991. Much of the history published in the popular press in the last years of the Soviet Union and the early years of the new Russian Federation described the whole Soviet period as a perversion of "normal" development. From this partisan perspective, imperial Russian history was refigured to represent the natural order. The corpse was exhumed and the autopsy performed again, this time to reveal the body's robust growth and strength before an untimely, tragic, perhaps criminal death.

For historians eager to move out from the long shadow cast over the tsarist period by the Soviet project and, at the same time, willing to investigate revisionist narratives before proclaiming them, the 1990s offered a chance to re-excavate the historic site of imperial Russia with new imagination and attentiveness. If the "road to revolution" and "crisis of the old regime" could be jettisoned as blueprints for research, and if metaphors of normalcy and organicism could also be challenged, historians could then ask a variety of new questions, and produce fresh, even if explicitly tentative, interpretations of the imperial past. The late perestroika years and the first years of post-Soviet experiments were exhilarating for scholars who were beginning new projects. The archives, libraries, and other repositories of the Soviet Union became accessible beyond the wildest dreams of even the most dedicated researchers. For a time, historians could see almost any file.

New politics in Russia meant not only generous access to materials, but also radical shifts in the way that history was produced. Russian historians could drop their five-year plans for scholarly research, break with the institutionalized and interpretive boundaries of "feudalism," "capitalism," and "socialism," and work on topics of their own choosing. Equally important, a different kind of international collegiality flourished. New opportunities arose to organize joint projects, to invite faculty to teach courses abroad, and to move historical debates out of the protected privacy of Soviet apartments and into public and professional arenas in Russia and abroad. These transnational discussions between "native" scholars and their foreign friends and colleagues have accelerated and enriched the reconceptualization of the imperial past.

A different kind of inspiration for the new Russian history of the 1990s has been the ferment in historical studies generally. The most evident change, and one whose impact can be registered in this volume, has been a gradual turn toward cultural studies and a move away from social history as it had been defined and revised in the 1970s and 1980s.[2] Two approaches have been particularly productive for historians of imperial Russia: interdisciplinary inquiry and cultural analysis.

The arts, and especially literature, have long had a place in Russian history taught in American universities. But this attention to culture, with its roots in the practices of Russians both in the emigration and at home, seldom reached beyond the obligatory, and immensely valuable, readings of Russian novels as historical sources.[3] A strong disciplinary divide marked most published research on Russia. Slavic departments fostered the domain of *belles lettres*, while historians produced books that adhered to conventional typologies of intellectual, political, or social history. The mainstream of historical study was further bifurcated in the 1970s and 1980s into investigations either of political thought (the intelligentsia and the cultural elite) or of society (social structure and class mobilization). By the 1990s, however, a major shift was perceptible. The growing enthusiasm for interdisciplinary and cultural studies produced a reintegration of literature into historical studies of Russia as well as innovative projects joining history with anthropology, art history, and history of science.[4]

This surge of transdisciplinary scholarship is in many instances an outgrowth of the social history of Russia developed in the 1970s and 1980s. In those decades, the most visible interdisciplinary interaction in Russian and Soviet history was between sociology and history, as a generation of social historians trained in the 1960s moved into faculties at American universities and challenged the then dominant approaches of political and diplomatic history.[5] Attracted to the generalizing power of quantitative methods popular in American social science, as well as by the dynamism of working-class history after E. P. Thompson, these scholars concentrated on labor, class, and revolution as preferred subjects of Soviet or late imperial history. The new social history of the Soviet Union was nourished by a series of seminars sponsored by the Joint Committee on Slavic Studies of the Social Science Research Council and American Council of Learned Societies. In the perestroika and post-Soviet years these seminars underwent significant intellectual restructuring, as social historians of Russia, attuned to the shifts in research focus in other fields, incorporated investigations of gender, ethnicity, and culture into their projects.[6]

The history of imperial Russia as a whole was not the subject of similar collective analysis or synthetic interpretation, even as excellent monographs were available on specific topics and eras. For example, a number of pathbreaking studies appeared on issues or institutions in the reigns of Peter I and Catherine II.[7] Substantial attention was also given to the era of the Great Reforms, including its prelude and aftermath.[8] But apart from Marc Raeff's essays, which covered only about half of the imperial period, and Pipes's provocative *Russia under the Old Regime*, no large-scale efforts were made to describe the structures, transformations, and continuities of the imperial period.[9] Historians continued, in their few syntheses and many research monographs, to examine imperial Russian history for clues to the great conflagrations of the early twentieth century.

The study of imperial Russia on different terms was the aim of the Imperial Russian History Initiative that led to this book. The Initiative consisted of three meetings sponsored by the Social Science Research Council and held at the University of Iowa in 1991, the Kennan Institute in 1993, and Portland State University in 1994. Participants in the first meeting engaged in wide-ranging and speculative discussions of how imperial Russian history might be reimagined; the two subsequent workshops focused on a series of research papers based on less-studied periods and topics.[10] The goal of these meetings, in contrast to some post-Soviet retrospectives, was not to find a usable past, but to explore and craft new narratives and interpretations. Although only twelve of the twenty-nine research papers and none of the fourteen speculative essays discussed at these meetings are reproduced in this volume—many will appear elsewhere—the volume as a whole reflects the collective explorations of these workshops.

Imperial Russia: New Histories for the Empire is pluralist in methods, interpretations, and topics. Contributors to the volume and participants in discussions of this project did not seek to recast the field by fixing its elements in a particular mold, but rather to extend new thinking on problems big and small. The collection does not privilege a particular kind of history—cultural, social, institutional, economic, political, or intellectual—but instead juxtaposes essays that either adhere to one or another of these approaches, purposefully blend them, or refuse some compartments altogether. Nor do the contributors promote a particular method. Demography, micro-history, discourse analysis, semiotics, new institutionalism, and history of ideas all find a place here. This intentional heterogeneity is true of topics, too. The main characters of these essays are a varied and mostly understudied lot: lesser nobles of the provinces and the capitals, reform-minded clerics, peasant resettlers in the process of migration, soldiers on the frontier, scholar-founders of the Russian Geographic Society, amateur ethnographers, a luxury-loving merchant and his extended family, among others.

The histories of these people of imperial Russia and their institutional, material, and informational cultures, are arranged in roughly chronological order within each of the four sections of the volume. Part One, "Autocracy: Politics, Ideology, Symbol," devotes attention to conceptions—both historiographical and historical—of autocratic rule. We begin with Valerie Kivelson's reconsideration of political agency after the death of Peter I, move on to Cynthia Whittaker's exploration of absolutist ideologies penned by eighteenth-century historians, and conclude with Richard Wortman's analysis of the tsarist regime's appropriation of familial symbolism in the early nineteenth century. Part Two focuses on two stretches of imperial imagination in the first half of the nineteenth century. Kevin Thomas analyzes two pioneering projects for a national museum, and Nathaniel Knight explores the emergence of pluralistic and incorporating conceptions of ethnic identity.

Part Three, "Practices of Empire," includes both the center and the periphery. Thomas Barrett's essay presents the Caucasian frontier as a place of cultural interactions; Willard Sunderland foregrounds peasant agency in expanding the empire and stirring ethnic competition on the periphery. Steven Hoch analyzes the land distribution practices of serfs as constitutive of both economic survival and an enduring type of noncapitalist agrarian production. Gregory Freeze discusses the Orthodox Church and its relationship to popular religious activities from the mid-eighteenth to the mid-nineteenth centuries. The chapters in Part Four explore different sites of "culture" and question the stereotype of a "weak" Russian society. David Ransel's essay focuses on the social and family life of a late-eighteenth-century grain merchant. Douglas Smith reconsiders the meaning of Masonic secrecy in Russia through an analysis of late-eighteenth-century debates. Irina Paperno relates this engagement with public discourse to the reform-era press and its preoccupation with suicide.

The period covered by this volume is the early eighteenth century to the 1880s. The framers of the project sought to devote attention to eras underrepresented in historiography, particularly the early nineteenth century. The decision not to go beyond the 1880s was deliberate: many excellent scholarly studies of the last decades of imperial Russia are available. In addition, our chronology reflects a desire to examine the empire's history before a period that is conventionally interpreted through the thick lens of revolutionary hindsight.[11] As for geographic space, we deliberately rejected the strategy of isolating subjects associated with colonial aspects of the empire in a special section, a practice that tends to exoticize non-Russians as "others" and normalize Russianness. The volume instead treats the institutions and practices of central Russia as part of imperial history and explores their relationship to the aspirations and opportunities that shaped life in the frontier regions.[12]

While the essays offer a variety of approaches and produce different glimpses of the past, several shared concerns and themes are evident. Common to almost all the essays is the choice to examine specific episodes or situations, rather than long-term processes. None of the contributors tell their particular stories with the aim of illuminating the centuries-long trajectory of the empire or prefiguring imperial Russia's "fate" as a political project. They try instead to escape the established frame of imperial decline that so often structured research projects and final paragraphs. This shift constitutes an important step toward more open-ended historical investigation. The focus is on the past as past and not on the future of the past.

The disconnection of mini-stories of politics, culture, or family life from the long story of the historical development of imperial Russia has significant advantages. Much Russian history produced in the twentieth century was influenced by the harshly critical attitudes of Russian scholars who wrote during the late imperial and early Soviet periods, in the bitterness of opposition and later defeat. Their animus against both the tsarist autocracy and its successor cast a long shadow over the history of the empire. This anti-Whiggish tendency was especially marked in historical accounts of the revolution of 1917, which, in both heroic and tragic variants, was attributed to the intractabilities of imperial Russia. Whether the topic was high politics, bureaucratic culture, or economic development, historians emphasized Russia's failures, usually to live up to some kind of European model. In contrast, our contributors have tried to assess imperial Russian government and society as going concerns.

Many essays in this volume investigate the people and institutions that kept imperial Russia functioning over a long period of time. Our contributors make clear that elites often cooperated effectively to defend and advance their interests; peasants practiced a form of production well suited to the risk-prone environment in which they lived; intellectuals organized clubs and salons conducive to lively discussion; publishers produced a wide array of newspapers for engaged readers; the autocracy changed its public face to find favor with society. At least through the early decades of the nineteenth century, Russian government and society functioned in concert and constituted a strong polity; this self-correcting absolutism emerged victorious from an era of revolution and war that overturned other European social and state orders. Despite government surveillance and periodic repression, Russian society continued through the nineteenth and early twentieth centuries to foster a vigorous intellectual, business, and civic life.[13]

Two sets of oppositions have long dominated Russian historiography: state and society, and Russia and the West. The essays in this book move away from these analytical categories, reconfigure them, and, in some cases, challenge their accepted meanings.

Common to most of the essays is a reconceptualization of agency. Rather than fitting the activities of "society" into a dialectic with the "state," most of the contributors attempt to analyze society as composed of distinct groups and individuals acting on their own behalf and not necessarily working for or against the state. This shift is particularly clear in Part Two, on practices of empire. Of interest to Barrett and Sunderland in the borderlands and Hoch in the central regions is how rural people made their lives within constraints established by ecological conditions and by local social institutions rather than how they responded to state power. Freeze, who in earlier studies has looked at unexpected points of conflict between church and state in Russia, here extends his analysis to conflict between church and society. He examines the activism of hierarchs, expressed in their efforts to establish institutional control over religious practice, but also assesses the ability of ordinary people to resist church interference in their localized versions of Orthodoxy.

Another new emphasis is the contributors' focus on institutions at the intersection of state and society rather than on central government ministries. Knight looks into the founding debates of the Russian Geographical Society and describes the different perspectives on Russian science and nationalism defended by individuals within this one organization. Thomas addresses the diverse and contested designs for displaying the empire through artifacts in proposed national museum collections. Freeze's study tells of the church's conflict with the financial and political claims of central ministries, but this time the story is told from the point of view of the church. In other words, not the central administration itself but institutions that functioned on its generous margins are the concern of our contributors, as they explore the interconnectedness of social practice and governance.[14]

Two categories that relate to social organization take the place of "society" as a location of inquiry in this volume. These are the public and the family. Despite a number of pathbreaking recent studies on the Russian public,[15] this concept is making only slow inroads into the conventional and highly politicized category of "society." The historiography on the prerevolutionary and revolutionary periods elides the public with the professional or middle classes and, usually, with liberalism. In addition, while most treatments of modern Russian history rightly place the rapid expansion of education and economic opportunity in the late nineteenth century, this emphasis has obscured the lively, if embryonic, public culture of the early imperial period. The intellectual circles of the 1830s and 1840s have received adequate attention, but not the larger public sphere that lent their exclusiveness significance.[16]

Smith's essay describes shifts in conceptions of "the public" in the eighteenth century as well as the appearance of a wide range of institutions that nurtured sociability and discussion. His reassessment of the controversy over Freemasonry allows us to see that, to many Russians, the Masonic lodges represented a threat to public activism, not a defense of it. Paperno takes on a different aspect of public life in her analysis of journalism in the reform period. By revising assumptions about a secularized, rationalist culture in this era, she deciphers a metaphoric and organic way of thinking, widely shared by educated people. Many of the other essays likewise imply that the concept of a "public" may have a brighter future than the generalizing notion of "society."

Family constitutes a second category that makes multiple appearances in this book. Primary units of social organization everywhere, families had exceptional importance in imperial Russia. Essays here describe how noble families played a key role in political action and negotiation; peasants worked as families to sustain production in the serf economy; an eighteenth-century merchant's ambitions and his fall-back strategies were directed toward security for his extended family; the Romanov dynasty revised its public image to highlight its internal nuclear bonds and turned this model of family loyalty to the service of state ideology. What do these various manifestations of family suggest?[17]

First, the influence of families represents another dislocation of power from its unitary position in the autocracy; attention is turned to power located in groups and individuals with immediate control over much of daily life. For both the peasant and the privileged, the family was a sustained organizing principle of politics and economics. Hoch argues that the power of male heads of households to exploit the labor of their family members was key to the long-term productivity of Russian peasant agriculture. Kivelson identifies the elite's concern for family interests as central to the renegotiation of autocratic authority in 1730. Ransel's merchant operated a family firm that built its wealth on marriage alliances and economic arrangements, within a large network of consanguineal and affinal relations.

Family also provided the symbolic framework for imperial rule. Whittaker notes that Vasilii Tatishchev and others employed family metaphors to describe the relation of the monarch (the father, the bridegroom) to the people, analogic reasoning common to European monarchies of the time and important in reinforcing the authority and self-regard of fathers and husbands at all levels of society. In the early nineteenth century, however, the monarchy recast this metaphor of vertical ties: the eighteenth-century father (or mother) of the fatherland now became the father of the imperial family. Wortman describes this semiotic shift from personalized mastery to a different kind of familial ethos, in which dynastic continuity and national unity were ritually represented through the domestic harmony of the imperial spouses and the heir's devotion to his father and the people.

Wortman's analysis is exemplary of the ways that essays in this volume revise the conventional oppositions of "Russia and the West." In Wortman's description of Russian imperial culture, Nicholas I adopted the family scenario of empire under the influence of his mother, the dowager empress Maria Fedorovna, who had come to Russia from Württemberg. Nurtured in the values of German sentimentalism, Maria Fedorovna tried to inculcate in her children the virtues of marriage, fidelity, and family love—no small task in view of the sexual infidelities of her older sons, not to mention the fact that her husband, Paul, was murdered to put his son on the throne. This story of the adoption of a new imperial symbolism based on European middle-class models of affective nuclear family ties suggests the close links between European political culture and developments in Russia. Wortman does not treat Russia and the West as separate civilizations.

Most of our other contributors read shifts in Russian political theory and institutions as examples of cultural intersection rather than borrowings from an alien source. Our authors play down the assumption of underlying differences between Russians and Europeans. Kivelson contends that Russian nobles adapted to their Western contemporaries' notions of meritocracy and efficiency and did not find them out of place. Paperno shows that Russian professionals and journalists shared the nineteenth-century European fascination with social statistics, and mounted many independent investigations of their own in which they compared Russian conditions with the experiences of other European countries. Suicide, the subject of Paperno's chapter, was only one of many subjects of transnational discussion and comparison.

"Europe" or "the West" were shorthand descriptors used by Russian elites in their writings and conversations, but these terms did not necessarily imply antagonism or inequality. Scholars interacted with European scientific culture on terms they set themselves. Thomas's essay on proposals for a Russian National Museum and Knight's on the founding of the Russian Geographic Society make this point. Thomas shows that national museums were under discussion across Europe in the early nineteenth century; scholars who proposed a museum for the Russian empire thought of their task as representing Russia within the emergent culture of European national displays. Later in the century, the founders of the Russian Geographic Society may have disagreed about which kind of European science—abstract or descriptive—was appropriate for the study and discovery of the Russian empire, but when they did so, they were echoing Europe's own debates and thus giving further evidence of Russia's integration into European intellectual and cultural life. The search for a distinctive cultural identity was common to European polities, not unique to Russia.

The contributors to this book regard Russia as a European absolutism yet reject the imposition of "Western" models (England, France, Germany) as measures of Russia's success. This stance, which recognizes particularity, while refusing to see it as alien, is consistent with the ways in which the authors draw upon a wide range of historiography to inform their research but not to prefigure their results. Many of the essays ignore or reject interpretive strategies traditional to Russian historiography, and instead use methods, theories, and topics introduced in the study of other national settings.

For Ransel, the essential move is from narrations about large groups to the perspective of a single individual on his life and social networks. Ransel grounds his merchant's story in a discussion of microhistory, an approach that has had a growing influence on history writing in recent years in Western Europe and America.[18] Smith omits the category of "intelligentsia" in his analysis of the place of Freemasonry in eighteenth-century public discourse. He throws out the state-vs.-society opposition as well, and instead makes reference to recent historiography on European publics of the same period, several of whose defining characteristics can be identified in the publics of Russian cities. Thomas rejects Soviet historians' assumption of nineteenth-century progress toward the modern goal of "rational" museology and engages instead the literature on European museums to highlight the particular kind of knowledge scholars hoped to produce through a Russian National Museum. Barrett's analysis of the colonial experience of the Caucasus draws on ideas from revisionist studies of the North American frontier. This literature gives attention to the power of the environment, to a "middle ground" of cultural mixing, and to the production of nationalized myths.

For the most part, our contributors avoid analysis of identity, despite the popularity of this issue in current scholarly work. This may be because, as Thomas and Knight argue, urban elites in Russia usually considered the multiethnicity of the empire a source of greatness and less often as evidence of conquest or as a rationale for racialized hierarchies. They assumed ethnicity to be primordial, and this assumption offered both rulers and the ruled the opportunity to exploit the exclusions and inclusions assigned to particular groups. From this standpoint, Barrett and Sunderland focus on what people did with their and others' ethnic categorizations, not on how these identities came to be. Ethnicity did not need to be negotiated; it was already there. What was negotiated was money, goods, marriages, enslavements, fines, land—sometimes using convenient and accepted notions of ethnicity to advance one's interest. The emphasis in these essays is on how individuals could maneuver in a social environment where ethnicity was a given. In accord with the shift away from locating action in abstractions such as classes or institutions rather than people, no contributor to this collection makes the mistake of assigning agency to an identity.

Although academic rituals privilege claims of innovation, historical scholarship is a collective and constructive endeavor that builds upon past work. This volume draws on research models borrowed from colleagues working in non-Russian areas as well as on the powerful inspiration of predecessors in our own field. The novelty of *Imperial Russia: New Histories for the Empire* is self-conscious exploration. The contributors ask readers to reconsider the framework of Russian history: to give more attention to specific episodes and their immediate historical contexts, to be sensitive to the difference between the immediate intentions of historical actors and the long-term fate of the empire, to consider new standards of success and failure. Individually, the essays represent shifts in perspective; collectively, they emphasize the intersection, rather than the conflict, of state and social institutions, the power of family organization and of other small communities both religious and secular, and the autocracy's resort to a series of changing symbolic practices. The volume accepts Russia's European-ness, defined by its imperial and absolutist status, and invites attention to Russia as a variety of European empire that boasted a cosmopolitan elite, multiethnic peripheries, and confident diversity.

Jane Burbank
David L. Ransel

Notes

1. *Nicholas I and Official Nationality in Russia, 1825–1855* (Berkeley, 1961), 270–71. In *Russia under the Old Regime* (New York, 1974), Richard Pipes dates the critical deviation of imperial Russia from the desirable Western path at the time of the 1730 succession cri-sis, which led eventually to the creation of a modern police state in the 1880s.

2. On the transformation of historical study, see Geoff Eley, "Is All the World a Text? From Social History to the History of Society Two Decades Later," in Terrence J. McDonald, ed., *The Historic Turn in the Social Sciences* (Ann Arbor, 1996), 193–243.

3. Among the few exceptions to this rule, the best known are probably Hans Rogger, *National Consciousness in Eighteenth-Century Russia* (Cambridge, Mass., 1960) and James Billington, *The Icon and the Axe* (New York, 1966).

4. The interest in cultural studies drew attention to innovative works written ear-lier, such as Vera S. Dunham, *In Stalin's Time: Middleclass Values in Soviet Fiction* (New York, 1976) and Iurii M. Lotman and B. A. Uspenskii, *The Semiotics of Russian Culture*, ed. Ann Shukman (Ann Arbor, 1984). Much of the innovative work in the 1980s and 1990s addressed the Soviet and the late imperial periods; outstanding examples are Svetlana Boym, *Common Places: Mythologies of Everyday Life in Russia* (Cambridge, Mass., 1994); Yuri Slezkine, *Arctic Mirrors: Russian and the Small Peoples of the North* (Ithaca, N.Y., 1994); Jeffrey Brooks, *When Russia Learned to Read: Literacy and Popular Literature, 1861–1917* (Princeton, 1985); Bruce Grant, *In the Soviet House of Culture: A Century of Perestroikas* (Princeton, 1995); Laura Engelstein, *The Keys to Happiness: Sex and the Search for Modernity in Fin-de-Siècle Russia* (Ithaca, N.Y., 1992); Reginald E. Zelnik, *Law and Disorder on the Narova River: The Kreenholm Strike of 1872* (Berkeley, 1995); and Douglas Weiner, *Models of Nature: Ecology, Conservation, and Cultural Revolution in Soviet Russia* (Bloomington, Ind., 1988).

5. Eley, "Is All the World a Text?," 198–99.

6. Diane P. Koenker, William G. Rosenberg, and Ronald Grigor Suny, eds., *Party,*

State and Society in the Russian Civil War: Explorations in Social History (Bloomington, Ind., 1989); Sheila Fitzpatrick, Alexander Rabinowitch, and Richard Stites, eds., *Russia in the Era of NEP: Explorations in Soviet Society and Culture* (Bloomington, Ind., 1991); William G. Rosenberg and Lewis H. Siegelbaum, eds., *Social Dimensions of Soviet Industrialization* (Bloomington, Ind., 1993).

7. A small selection from a large number of works might include: Robert O. Crummey, *The Old Believers and the World of Antichrist: The Vyg Community and the Russian State, 1694–1855* (Madison, 1970); James Cracraft, *The Church Reform of Peter the Great* (1972); Claes Peterson, *Peter the Great's Administrative and Judicial Reforms: Swedish Antecedents and the Process of Reception* (Stockholm, 1979); Marc Raeff, *Origins of the Russian Intelligentsia: The Eighteenth-Century Nobility* (New York, 1966); Brenda Meehan-Waters, *Autocracy & Aristocracy: The Russian Service Elite of 1730* (New Brunswick, 1982); Isabel de Madariaga, *Russia in the Age of Catherine the Great* (New Haven, 1981); John T. Alexander, *Bubonic Plague in Early Modern Russia: Public Health & Urban Disaster* (Baltimore, 1980); Robert E. Jones, *The Emancipation of the Russian Nobility, 1762–1785* (Princeton, 1973); David L. Ransel, *The Politics of Catherinian Russia: The Panin Party* (New Haven, 1975); Michael Confino, *Domaines et seigneurs en Russie vers la fin du XVIIIe siècle* (Paris, 1963).

8. Again a small selection: Terrence Emmons, *The Russian Landed Gentry and the Peasant Emancipation of 1861* (Cambridge, 1968); Daniel Field, *The End of Serfdom: Nobility and Bureaucracy in Russia, 1855–1861* (Cambridge, Mass., 1976); S. Frederick Starr, *Decentralization and Self-Government in Russia, 1830–1870* (Princeton, 1972); Richard Wortman, *The Development of a Russian Legal Consciousness* (Chicago, 1976); Ben Eklof, John Bushnell, and Larissa Zakharova, eds., *Russia's Great Reforms, 1855–1881* (Bloomington, Ind., 1994).

9. See Marc Raeff's *Imperial Russia 1682–1825: The Coming of Age of Modern Russia* (New York, 1971), and *Understanding Imperial Russia: State and Society in the Old Regime* (New York, 1984), tr. from French edition, 1982. Richard Pipes, *Russia under the Old Regime*. John P. LeDonne's *Absolutism and the Ruling Class: The Formation of the Russian Political Order, 1700–1825* (New York, 1991) provides a structural account, but again, not of the whole imperial period.

10. On the planning meeting and its outcomes, see Jane Burbank, "Revisioning Imperial Russia," *Slavic Review* 52, no. 3 (Fall 1993): 555–67.

11. Although, as Michael Confino has pointed out, many studies have extended the idea of crisis of the old regime a whole century and more. "Present Events and the Representation of the Past," *Cahiers du monde russe*, 35:4 (October-December, 1994), 851–53.

12. For recent explorations of the frontier and its relation to the history of the empire, see Daniel R. Brower and Edward J. Lazzerini, eds., *Russia's Orient: Imperial Borderlands and Peoples, 1700–1917* (Bloomington, Ind., 1997), and Paul Werth, "Big Candles and Internal Conversion: The Mari Pagan Reformation and the Emergence of Faith," unpub. manuscript.

13. See George Yaney's comments on the need to analyze a society as a set of "going concerns" and not to assume it had to fail because it eventually did so (perhaps for reasons that were highly contingent): *Slavic Review*, 24:3 (September 1965), 521–27. Some other writers share this more optimistic view of the possibilities for an evolutionary de-

velopment of imperial Russia. See, for example, Michael Karpovich, *Imperial Russia, 1801–1917* (New York, 1932); Seymour Becker, *Nobility and Privilege in Late Imperial Russia* (DeKalb, Ill., 1985); and Adele Lindenmeyr, *Poverty Is Not a Vice: Charity, Society, and the State in Imperial Russia* (Princeton, 1996).

14. An earlier work that takes this approach is David Ransel's study of foundling homes, *Mothers of Misery: Child Abandonment in Russia* (Princeton, 1988). For an early study of a central institution of the imperial state, see Daniel Orlovsky, *The Limits of Reform: The Ministry of Internal Affairs in Imperial Russia, 1802–1881* (Cambridge, Mass., 1981). Gregory Freeze's best-known works examine the clergy as a distinct estate: *The Parish Clergy in the Nineteenth Century: Crisis, Reform, and Counter-Reform* (Princeton, 1983) and *The Russian Levites: Parish Clergy in the Eighteenth Century* (Cambridge, Mass., 1977). Biographical approaches to institutions and their personnel are taken by Cynthia Whittaker in her *The Origins of Modern Russian Education: An Intellectual Biography of Count Sergei Uvarov, 1786–1855* (DeKalb, Ill., 1984) and Richard Wortman, *The Development of a Russian Legal Consciousness* (Chicago, 1976). For the last half of the nineteenth century and the beginning of the twentieth, the historiography on institutions at the intersection with society—the State Duma, the zemstvo, the professions, political parties—is robust.

15. See especially Gary Marker, *Publishing, Printing, and the Origins of Intellectual Life in Russia* (Princeton, 1985); Jeffrey Brooks, *When Russia Learned to Read*; Edith W. Clowes, Samuel D. Kassow, and James L. West, eds., *Between Tsar and People* (Princeton, 1991).

16. A few examples: Isaiah Berlin, *Russian Thinkers* (New York, 1978); Peter K. Christoff, *An Introduction to Nineteenth-Century Slavophilism: A Study of Ideas* (4 vols., various publishers, 1961–1991); Martin Malia, *Alexander Herzen and the Birth of Russian Socialism, 1812–1855* (Cambridge Mass., 1961); Nicholas Riasanovsky, *A Parting of Ways: Government and the Educated Public in Russia, 1801–1855* (Oxford, 1976).

17. For treatment of various aspects of family history, see David Ransel, ed., *The Family in Imperial Russia: New Lines of Historical Research* (Urbana, Chicago, London, 1978). For the power of noble families in the eighteenth century, see Brenda Meehan-Waters, *Autocracy and Aristocracy: The Russian Service Elite of 1730* (New Brunswick, N.J., 1982), and John LeDonne, "Ruling Families in the Russian Political Order 1689–1825," *Cahiers du monde russe et soviétique* 28:3/4 (1987), 233–322; for the late imperial period, see William G. Wagner *Marriage, Property, and Law in Late Imperial Russia* (Oxford, 1994).

18. For a discussion of microhistory's intersection with cultural studies, see Sarah Maza, "Stories in History: Cultural Narratives in Recent Works in European History," *American Historical Review* 101, no. 5 (December 1996): 1493–1515.

PART I

AUTOCRACY:
POLITICS, IDEOLOGY, SYMBOL

STANDARD ACCOUNTS OF Russian history usually treat autocracy as an unchanging element in the country's politics. The personal characteristics of rulers have always been granted significance, and attention has been paid to the social constituents of power, the nobility and bureaucracy. But only now are historians beginning to consider the relationship of absolutist rule in Russia to the cultural practices and symbolic systems within which it functioned. The three essays in this section offer new formulations of Russian politics that take into account changing cultural and symbolic contexts and their influence on the articulation of power.

Valerie A. Kivelson examines the evolving political culture of seventeenth- and early-eighteenth-century Russia, the background for the constitutional crisis that erupted in 1730. She rejects the common view of the lesser nobility of that era as tradition-bound, unthinking supporters of autocracy, incapable of sharing or even understanding the aspirations of some of their prominent members to place limits on tsarist power in 1730. Kivelson contends that throughout the seventeenth century the lesser nobility acted flexibly and opportunistically. They either opposed or supported the extension of state power as it suited their economic and social needs. These noblemen understood the time-honored practices of tsarist consultation with advisers and the need for approval of major decisions by "all the land"; they became skillful in organizing petition drives to articulate their desires. During Peter I's reign, the nobility deployed imported concepts of government as well, incorporating those that resonated with their own political experience and discarding others. Kivelson demonstrates that this evolving political culture was expressed in the efforts of ordinary nobles to achieve protection of their persons and interests during the events of 1730. While the outcome in favor of unlimited autocracy was due to the peculiar configuration of antagonisms that arose at the time, the nobles who participated

3

in the events of 1730 had a mature understanding of political action, an awareness of their own interests, and sought new means to advance them.

Cynthia Hyla Whittaker addresses political culture of another kind: the
definitions offered by contemporary Russian history writers of their country's
proper political order and destiny. The forty-seven writers studied by Whittaker
looked to Russia's history for a clarification of the contents and limits of political expression; their writings form an elite imaginary of their political world.
Whittaker finds three patterns of interpretation and labels them the dynastic,
the empirical, and the nondespotic. The first two represent secular rationales
for what was a rhetorically updated but essentially unchanged regime of unlimited one-person rule. The "nondespotic" orientation argues for the difference
between despotism and monarchy and reflects a position not unlike that Kivelson attributes to the rank-and-file nobility: namely, that autocracy was de facto
limited (recontracted at each new reign) and eventually would be so de jure.
This interpretation was a product of the reign of Catherine II (she was one of
the history writers who contributed to it), a response to European criticisms of
Russian autocracy, and a sign of the Europeanization of elite political thought.

Richard Wortman takes an altogether new approach to autocracy by analyzing the symbolic representations of the Russian monarchy. He first describes
the attributes of the eighteenth-century monarchs, represented as transcendent ideals, godlike figures who lived by their own rules. They took lovers. They
failed to nurture a bond with their children. The nineteenth century saw a radical shift to what Wortman calls the "creation of a dynastic scenario." This new
form represented the imperial family not as transcendent beings but as mor-
tals of an exemplary kind, bound to one another in family love and loyalty and
bound to the nation as embodiments of national feeling. They appeared as immanent ideals, models of virtuous conduct to be admired and imitated by their
subjects. This change was part of a long trend toward desacralization of European monarchy, but that process now took on special features of the sentimental
or early Romantic family ethos that arose in the aftermath of the French revolution. Wortman credits Maria Fedorovna, the wife of Emperor Paul, with setting the course for this family ideal of monarchy in Russia. Its first consistent
articulation accompanied the reign of Nicholas I, during which key ritual moments were depicted in terms of family devotion accompanied by displays of
emotion such as rapture and weeping. This ideal then became a model for the
expression of political loyalty. This sentiment-laden representation of autocracy
remained the dominant symbolism of Russian monarchy to the end.

1

Kinship Politics/Autocratic Politics

A Reconsideration of Early-Eighteenth-Century Political Culture

Valerie A. Kivelson

————◦∞◦————

WHILE MANY SCHOLARS of the Petrine era have sensibly resolved either to avoid the hackneyed debate over continuity or change altogether or to adopt a measured middle ground that allows elements of each, the problem still shapes discussions of the eighteenth century, often in unacknowledged ways. For this reason, a nuanced understanding of Russia's Muscovite heritage may be of value in an effort to reassess imperial history. This essay examines Russian political culture as it emerged from the Muscovite era and developed in the early eighteenth century. More specifically, it explores what politics signified and how it was experienced, shaped, and questioned by those who lived under the aegis of Russian autocracy in an era of rapid and deliberate cultural change. Two closely related sets of questions arise in the course of this discussion. The first concerns the ways in which Muscovite tradition shaped early-eighteenth-century political actions and ideas. Instead of measuring indicators of continuity or change, I hope to provide a contextual and variegated sense of pre-Petrine political culture and its particular reverberations and alterations in the first thirty years of the eighteenth century. Such an approach illuminates the ways in which certain Muscovite traditions elided with innovations of the Reforming Tsar while others conflicted with his reforms. It also permits an appreciation of what was genuinely new in the political vocabulary of the early eighteenth century.

The second set of questions addressed here involves the rather newer and more specific problem of defining the role and nature of kinship and patronage in early imperial notions of the political. This focus on kinship and patronage derives from recent historical debates over the nature of eighteenth-century politics. While most traditional scholarly treatments of noble political activities in the early eighteenth century conceived of the various reform movements as efforts to introduce Western-style rule of law and constitutional limitations on monarchical power and evaluated them as such, in recent decades historians have stressed the importance of noble clans and their competitive patronage networks rather than western political philosophies in defining and limiting the political ambitions of the nobility.

Frequently kinship politics appears in these more revisionist scholarly analyses as the antithesis of "real" politics, or politics defined by doctrinal or ideological content. According to such an interpretation, Muscovite boyars, and imperial Russian noblemen after them, merely elbowed each other to gain proximity to the tsar, the source of all bounty. Russian nobles, in this view, were concerned with family advancement, material security, and social status, not with politics per se.[1]

The consistent interweaving of high political and personal/familial issues in the political imaginary of Russian nobles in both the pre- and post-Petrine periods, however, suggests that the family was in fact a highly political site, and that the vocabulary of politics and the sense of political urgency that mobilized the lesser nobility from time to time to take action on the high political stage derived precisely from its concerns about clan and family. High politics and kinship politics, then, were mutually constitutive and fundamentally linked in conceptualization, motivation, and practice. The family lay at the heart of both Muscovite and early imperial political culture, and thus the ways in which family politics intersected with autocratic politics makes one of the most fascinating historical puzzles of the early eighteenth century.[2] The evident centrality of kinship politics and the contentiousness of policies regulating family life in both pre- and post-Petrine political culture suggest that the relationship between clan politics and high politics was integral rather than antithetical.

The "Constitutional Crisis of 1730"

The so-called "Constitutional Crisis" that accompanied the accession to the throne of Empress Anna Ivanovna in 1730, the focal point of this study, exposes a good deal about the underlying political culture and variegated political outlook of the nobility, that is, of the group in society most critical for determining the reception and execution of imperial policy in the early post-Petrine period. Appropriately in the context of a discussion of the intermixing of kinship and politics, the crisis began when the young emperor Peter II died suddenly on January 19, 1730, the day planned for his wedding to the daughter of one of his leading noblemen. Responsibility for selecting a successor fell in the breach to the Supreme Privy Council, a high council of eight members, which had effectively ruled the country under the weak leadership of the previous two monarchs. The council, comprised primarily of members of the two leading families of the land, selected Duchess Anna of Courland, niece of Peter the Great. Under the direction of Prince Dmitrii Mikhailovich Golitsyn, the council also took the radical step of issuing a set of conditions under which the new empress would rule. The conditions limited her right to declare war, conclude peace, impose new taxes, spend state revenues, or deprive members of the nobility "of their life, honor, and property without trial." In effect, the conditions would have created a limited monarchy under the authority of the Supreme Privy Council. Anna signed the conditions before beginning her journey from Mittau to Russia. However, in the meantime, rumors about the attempt to limit monarchical authority leaked out to the large numbers of nobles who had gathered in Moscow for the intended wedding of the late emperor and had stayed on for the funeral. United in opposition to the oligarchical grab for power on the part of the council, groups of noblemen formulated numerous counterproposals, which floated an array of reformist schemes. Over 400 noblemen affixed their signatures to the various plans. The council attempted to work up its own compromise proposals in response to noble dissatisfaction, but kept its plans veiled in secrecy, hence succeeding only in alienating the mass of the nobility still more. By the time Anna appeared before a general assembly of the nobility on the morning of February 25, the noble opposition was ready to submit a petition (the Cherkasskii Petition) begging her to arbitrate between them and the council. When the assembly reconvened in the afternoon, Prince Ivan Iur'evich Trubetskoi submitted yet another petition, backed by the cries of the guards, imploring her "graciously to resume such Autocratic power as Your glorious and praiseworthy ancestors possessed and abrogate the article sent to Your Imperial Majesty by the Supreme Privy Council and signed by You."[3] The new empress called for the copy of the conditions that she had signed and dramatically ripped them up.

The events of 1730 have long served as a testing ground for theories about the political culture of the Russian nobility. Although the basic outlines of the incident are more or less clear, the evidence has proved malleable to a wide variety of interpretations. The year 1730 appears to offer the intellectual's ideal moment: a historical event ambiguous enough to prove the validity of everyone's favorite theories, supporting even the most radically divergent interpretations. Traditionally viewed as a tragically missed moment in Russian history, when the nobility had and bungled an opportunity to create a limited monarchy, the events of 1730 have been subjected to serious revisionist scrutiny in the past two decades. The newer historical consensus stresses the continuity of more traditional forms of politics, the politics of kinship, patronage, and personal feud, and questions the truly "constitutional" content of the proposed conditions. These recent reinterpretations suggest that neither the members of the council nor the rank-and-file nobility that opposed them had much genuine interest in establishing a constitutional monarchy, but rather each group pursued its own personal vendettas and self-interest in the guise of political reform.[4]

The key figures in the 1730 events are generally understood to have been nobles of two stripes: the *verkhovniki* or the eight most powerful magnates who sat in the Supreme Privy Council; and the *shliakhetstvo*, the rest of the nobility, which encompassed the *Generalitet* or top four ranks of the Table of Ranks, plus the guards regiments, composed of young nobles of both high and lesser noble families. Those of the *shliakhetstvo* are often distinguished from the *verkhovniki* by use of the labels "rank-and-file" or "lesser" nobility. These terms are somewhat deceiving, because actually this "rank-and-file" included many of the leading families—the top four ranks were, after all, not to be sneezed at—but I will use these conventional terms nevertheless.

Much of our understanding of political behavior in the early imperial period flows from an assumption that the rank-and-file nobility stuck to the tenets of traditional Muscovite political culture.[5] In arguing for the continuity of Muscovite tradition, historians have applied the concept of political tradition or political culture with varying degrees of subtlety, some using them as ironclad determinants of political behavior and attitudes, others as providing a historically shaped, mutable framework within which political actors and observers operated.[6] More or less across the board, however, the lesser nobility is cast as the bearer of tradition, the iceberg that sank any and all progressive plans for reform. And yet, arguments about the continuity of Muscovite political culture generally rest on an imperfect sense of what that political culture was, and how this broad swath of the nobility understood it.

Muscovite Political Ideology and
Official Representations of Legitimacy

Most discussions of political life in Muscovite Rus' center on the role of the tsar, describing his unlimited autocratic power and his status as divinely appointed father-tsar ruling over meek and unresisting subjects. This is the image that foreign visitors took home with them, the image of tsarist despotism that has retained such a hold on the historical imagination. For the Muscovite gentry as well as for later historians, the tsar occupied the pinnacle of power and authority and served as the organizing focus of political order. Thus, an examination of Muscovite political culture necessarily begins at the top, with the role of the tsar and the image of his rule that the tsarist regime propagated. The kow-towing of the country's highest nobles, the claims of sanctity for previous tsars, the absence of any legal or constitutional limits on the tsar, all fostered the image of the tsar-autocrat, an image confirmed in the tsar's official title: "Sovereign, Tsar and Grand Prince, Autocrat of All Russia." Autocracy was, indeed, a powerful and pervasive current in Muscovite political life. It spawned and was supported by a culture of supplication, in which relations of power were broadly understood as personal, intimate ones, and political might was exercised in the form of intercession and protection.

Yet, it is important to note that these were not the only images advanced in official representations.[7] The image of absolute autocrat was diluted by imagery promoting several other, equally significant and equally official facets of political legitimacy. First, as Nancy Shields Kollmann and others have stressed, the tsar was often represented as functioning in conjunction with his boyars and kinsmen. Another important theme advanced in official representations of tsarist power, the theme of religious obligation, also serves to mitigate the image of unlimited autocracy. The tsar, legitimized both by his dynastic descent from ancestors "of blessed memory" and by his selection by God on high, was to rule as patriarchal autocrat, but was constrained to rule justly and piously. In moments of doubt he was obligated to confer in righteous brotherhood with his boyars and other worthy advisers.[8]

Through the mode of advice and consultation, a rough conception of popular participation also entered Muscovite political thought. State propagandists and ideologists praised consultation not only with the inner circle of boyars and royal kinsmen, but also with "all the land," meaning the Russian people as a whole. Ritualized deference to public opinion is evident in the importance of the ceremony of popular acclamation at the accession of new tsars, who had to be presented to an assembly of people of many different ranks for their approval before their coronation. The ritual acclamation was often pro forma or even completely orchestrated, as in the case of Boris Godunov, who drummed up a claque of supporters to back his unconventional candidacy in 1598. The fact that he bothered with staging this particular ritual, however, demonstrates that popular acclaim, not just birth and divine selection, held weight as a plausible basis of legitimacy. In public memory, as expressed in collective petitions, the first Romanov tsar was chosen to reign by will of God "and of all the land."[9] Dark rumors plagued the reign of Aleksei Mikhailovich (1645–1672) because he had forgone the crucial step of popular acclamation in his haste to solemnize the coronation.

The tsarist administration found many ways to display its respect for

and responsiveness to popular opinion. In its legislation, the administration
stressed that it was responding to complaints and suggestions raised by "all the
land." Numerous official decrees opened with conspicuous references to the collective petitions that had spurred the tsar to adopt particular measures. Assemblies of the Land were the most pronounced manifestation of this tradition of
official salutes to popular opinion. In a particularly well publicized instance,
in 1648 Tsar Aleksei Mikhailovich and "his spiritual father and intercessor, the
most holy Iosif, Patriarch of Moscow and all Russia decreed and the boyars affirmed" that an assembly of men of all ranks from all over the land should con-
vene in Moscow to hear the terms of the newly compiled *Ulozhenie* law code.

> [Those sent] were to be worthy and prudent men so that his sovereign tsar-
> ist and civilian business might be affirmed and put into effect with [the
> participation of] all the delegates so that all these great decisions, [prom-
> ulgated] by his present royal edict and the Law Code of the Assembly of
> the Land, henceforth would in no way be violated.[10]

The public introduction of the law code, thus, stressed the importance of
popular participation and affirmation through the delegates to the Assembly of
the Land. The text implied that their participation and assent in some way guaranteed the efficacy of the new legislation, which it otherwise would lack.

W hether these obeisances were merely formalities or popular input was actually seriously taken into account in formulating policy, the publicity granted
to public involvement shows that official ideology placed great value on at least
the appearance of a responsive, interactive relationship between tsar and
people. In formulating its public facade, the self-proclaimed autocracy (*samoderzhavie*) in the Muscovite variation chose to include many participatory and inclusive elements that contributed to legitimizing and solidifying the rule of the
autocrat.[11]

Transformations of Political Culture
in the Second Half of the Seventeenth Century

When Russian historians talk about traditional or Muscovite political culture, they often tend to discuss an exaggerated version of the personalized, patrimonial, Orthodox autocracy, ignoring the other currents that formed an important part of the political order. However, even when all of the various aspects
of Muscovite concepts of political legitimacy and conduct are taken into account, there is a danger of casting Muscovite Rus' culture as an unchanging
monolith, standing firm through time. A highly personalized, patrimonial order indeed shaped a major part of Muscovite political thought and action in the

high Muscovite period, between the mid-sixteenth and mid-seventeenth centuries. But by the middle of the seventeenth century, a single set of practices and expectations no longer lent coherence to Muscovite political interactions. Traditional political culture collided sharply with creeping routinization, and local autonomies encountered redefined boundaries as the self-aggrandizing state extended its ambitions and its control into previously untouched reaches. The gentry's collective petition campaigns of the second half of the century reflect a realistic appraisal of the changed conditions of political life and an appreciation of the advantages to be gained by embracing the new avenues of regulated and impersonal administration.

In the second half of the century, new Western ideas of government and state slowly percolated into the highest educated Moscow circles, gradually but significantly changing the appearance, language, and rhetoric of Muscovite court life. Little of this early wave of cultural Westernization touched the broader Muscovite society at all. The provincial gentry showed little interest in the German-style clothing or richly adorned palaces of the tiny Moscow avant-garde. What touched the gentry far more directly were the *homegrown* changes in the ambition, scope, and outreach of the state. Relations with the administration became increasingly regularized and depersonalized as the bureaucratic machine of the state grew.[12] In addition, in a qualitative change of tack, the state launched a far more activist, interventionist agenda in the second half of the century. Its legislation aimed at maintaining public order and regulating conduct in all of its smallest manifestations. The *Ulozhenie* included four articles on pet dogs.[13] In addition to regulating church attendance, proper conduct during mass, tobacco use, card playing, alcohol manufacture and consumption, in 1686 the state prohibited littering on public streets.[14] The growing regularization and institutionalization that the gentry had detected with alarm already in the first half of the century assumed increasingly concrete form. The number of chancelleries and chancellery officials grew steadily through the end of the century.[15] Procedures within the chancelleries and in all branches of government became ever more routinized.

In its collective petitions addressed to the tsar, the gentry demonstrated its ability to adapt itself creatively and productively to the changing practices of the state and to its own changing circumstances. With the promulgation of the new *Ulozhenie* law code in 1649, mid-century marked a relatively clear-cut change in the issues of concern to the gentry and its relation to the state. The *Ulozhenie* satisfied the gentry's primary demand, the abolition of the statute of limitations on the recovery of runaway peasants, thereby confirming landlords' ownership of their laborers. After 1649, the most pressing issue that confronted the gentry was the problem of enforcement. The law now supported the absolute right of the petty landholder to keep his or her serfs, but as long as the law remained only on paper, it would have no more effect on the "powerful people" than had any previous legislation. Landed magnates still could abscond with peasants and hide them on their scattered estates beyond the reach of the impoverished gentry. Moreover, the court system was utterly corrupt, and between searching for peasants and fighting with hassles and delays in court, the time and money involved in the process of recovering a runaway could far exceed the resources available to a small landholder.

In a series of petitions beginning in the 1650s (one perhaps dating as early as 1649), the gentry proposed a novel solution to the problem of enforcement.[16] Earlier petitions had agitated for diminishing the presence of the centralized chancelleries as much as possible, in an attempt to leave local administration and justice in local hands. The petitions of the second half of the century adopted precisely the opposite stance. They begged the state to take the responsibility for searching for runaways out of the hands of the individual landlord and to assume that burden itself. They envisioned a total process, in which state agents would take all initiative and responsibility, conducting ongoing searches for runaways.

> Order, Sovereign, investigators sent to all of your Sovereign towns, and to villages and districts . . . and order, Sovereign, the investigators to search for our runaway slaves and serfs without our [having to] investigate and petition and without judicial red tape.[17]

In a complete change of course, the gentry now insisted on handing responsibility over to outsiders in the employ of the central state. Displaying an acute attentiveness to and ability to understand Moscow politics, the gentry observed carefully and kept track of exactly what the policy on recovery of runaway serfs involved at any given time, and what loopholes remained. Upon noticing a chink in the law, the gentry promptly would submit a new petition drawing the government's attention to the problem and recommending a practical policy solution.[18]

The gentry very practically sized up the situation and incorporated the growing chancellery system as an effective component in an effort to turn governmental regulation to its own advantage. As E. P. Thompson says of laws, once ostensibly universal and egalitarian forms and rules are developed in a society, no matter whose interests they are initially developed to serve, they can be appropriated by the less powerful and deployed to serve their interests. The gentry, subject to the depredations of state officials and powerful magnates in spite of its relatively privileged status, now saw the functional utility of tailoring laws to its own purposes.[19]

The petitions of the second half of the century demonstrate that the gentry's attitude toward state intervention and regulation evolved pragmatically in conjunction with the explosive growth of state control. Peter the Great's innovations did not come out of thin air, nor did he have to impose his interventionist, bureaucratizing agenda on a stagnant, inflexible society. Specifically Western styles and manners had affected only a very small and very elite circle in Moscow prior to Peter's reforming crusade, but administrative routinization, depersonalization of relationships, and centralized regulation had all left their traces in the political culture of the broader provincial gentry. Out in the provinces, the gentry had been prepared for the Petrine reforms by fifty years of intensive bureaucratic buildup. The top-down reforms introduced by late-seventeenth- and early-eighteenth-century rulers encountered a society engaged on its own project of reshaping its political contours.

A good example of this kind of parallel activity from above and below is found in the abolition of *mestnichestvo*, the clan ranking system whereby rank and standing had been calculated according to genealogical seniority. In 1682 a small circle of reformers at the court of Tsar Fedor Alekseevich drew up a radical plan for restructuring both secular and ecclesiastical administration. They strove to put status and advancement on an entirely new basis, replacing precedence based on birth with advancement based on merit. "Honors, in particular, and administrative [posts] will be given to knowledgeable and requisite people according to [the degree of] reason and merit [that they have displayed] while serving in all kinds of state business."[20]

Resentment of those who garnered plum jobs on the basis of birth alone betokened a change in attitudes toward what constituted "merit."[21] The value of conscientious labor had not been unknown in earlier Muscovite sources, but generally it had been framed in terms of generations' worth of patient endurance and dutiful service, not in terms of earthy toil or individual accomplishment. Conventional formulations had appealed to the tsar's mercy in consideration of "the blood of our fathers, and our wretched little service, and endurance."[22] New notions of merit and honor, based on hard work and personal achievement (as opposed to birth order and blood ties) began to develop among the gentry in the second half of the century. An odd gentry petition from 1658 stressed honest labor as a fundamental virtue, asserting that in the ideal world, "people feed themselves by their own labor according to God's commandment." In the petitioners' eyes, runaway peasants inverted the practices of honest folk when they "drink and eat sweetly without labor, and dress and shoe themselves with other people's possessions" while virtuous peasants "with their honest labor feed themselves and pay both your sovereign taxes and our quit-rent payments."[23] This new respect for hard work, perhaps ahead of its time, anticipates (at a lower level and under different influences) the abolition of *mestnichestvo* in 1682, and the associated reform projects.

In the context of these new concepts of merit and accomplishment, the abolition of *mestnichestvo* reflected and fostered a shift in the meaning of kinship politics at court. The end of *mestnichestvo* did not in any way signal the end of kinship politics. On the contrary, the dramatic public burning of the genealogical books of the court elite was followed immediately by an order requiring all noble clans to submit new, authenticated genealogical records, certifying their claims to nobility through birth. Bloodlines, as documented through official state records, retained their centrality in defining the court elite, but those privileged people with the requisite degree of nobility now had to earn rank, status, and advancement through meritorious performance.

Kinship and personal politics, the practices of deference and influence all continued strongly throughout the Muscovite period, and, in fact, throughout the imperial period, as studies not only of the eighteenth century, but even of the Duma elections in the early twentieth century demonstrate. But traditional reliance on familial and patronage links did not continue unchanged, in a vacuum, and the growth of the state bureaucracy worked its effects on Muscovy well before the advent of Peter. Through a dynamic process of accretion and fusion Muscovite political culture incorporated and reacted to changing legal, international, cultural, and administrative conditions and produced its own autocratic bureaucratism, long before the attempted reforms of 1682 or the more successful ones of Peter the Great. Let us return, then, to the nobles' visions of reform in 1730.

"Between Slavery and Freedom:"
Noble Projects for Reform in 1730[24]

In 1730 Russian nobles were not novices when it came to assessing and articulating their own interests in the broader scheme of things. They could already draw on a century-long tradition of active participation in national-level politics and of vociferous opposition to oppression by the members of the highest elite circles. As David Ransel has pointed out, "the nobles quite consciously acted in their best interests as they perceived them and pursued these interests in a way defined by their historical experience as most effective."[25] The lesser nobility's experiences in the Muscovite era contributed to forming its reaction in 1730. Ransel highlights in particular the lesser landlords' hostility to boyar oligarchy as experienced during Ivan the Terrible's minority and during the *Semiboiarshchina* (Seven-Boyar Rule) during the Time of Troubles, and their economic competition with the boyar aristocrats for control of land and peasants throughout the seventeenth century. These historical memories added to the traditional Muscovite skew toward monarchism and against oligarchical rule by "evil boyars." The Supreme Privy Council's scheme fit that latter description all too well. In opposing the council's conditions, the rank-and-file nobility acted on solid, historically based experience, and "did not act lightly or from ill-considered motives."[26] The nobility did not rally in active support of autocracy, nor was their opposition directed against constitutionalism. Rather they mobilized against aristocratic oligarchy.

However, there was more to noble politics than the bitter memories of boyar rule in centuries past and more than knee-jerk hostility to oligarchy. Historical experiences had not stopped short with the Muscovite era. The dramatic innovations introduced by Peter the Great had not simply slid off the backs of noblemen and women. They had been effectively incorporated into a new autocratic culture, just as earlier generations had adapted to the growth of the administrative machine.

For a group that was supposedly steeped in naive monarchism, the rank-and-file nobility accepted the entire project of limiting autocratic rule with astonishing alacrity. Except for Vasilii Tatishchev's defense of autocracy, which G. A. Protasov has shown to have been written after the failure of the constitutional move was already clear, none of the nobiliary projects questioned the three fundamental premises of the council's efforts: that monarchy was the appropriate form of rule; that Anna was the appropriate choice of ruler; that her authority should be sharply limited.[27] When the council initially announced Anna's acceptance of the conditions at a meeting of high-ranking military and civil officials, some anonymous individual exclaimed, "I am utterly amazed and don't know how the sovereign could have got it into her head to write such a thing," but after this initial and fully understandable moment of confusion and wonder, the general response among the nobility was neither amazement nor denial.[28] Rather the assembled nobles greeted the moment with enthusiastic interest in refining the conditions under which the monarchy would be reformed.

Foreigners reported that all the nobility had been swept up in the movement to limit the autocracy, and that everyone was busy formulating plans. The French envoy Magnan wrote, "It is on this important project (the regulations that will be made for a new form of government) that everyone is currently working, but at the present moment it is still impossible to say what the new form of government will be, whether it will be based on that of England or rather on that of Sweden."[29] John Lefort noted, "The idea of the form of government has set spirits in motion here. The speculations of the great and lesser nobility are infinite."[30] The only people programmatically identified with a return to autocracy were those clearly on the outside of the Russian political tradition: mainly foreigners and some clergy, who did not share the bonds of kinship and tight patronage links that the Russian nobility enjoyed.[31]

Some observers at the time recorded that the lesser nobility was interested in blocking rather than furthering governmental reform. In a famous passage, Lefort noted:

> The new form of government that the magnates have devised gives material to the lesser nobility to agitate in the meanwhile. They speak as follows: the magnates claim to be limiting despotism and absolute power; this power would be tempered by a council which little by little would appropriate to itself the reins of the empire, to which we respond that by that time instead of a sovereign we would have nothing but tyrants in the person of each member of that body, which by their impositions would render us a hundred times more enslaved. We have no established laws which could serve as a basis for this body, which would make the laws itself, and at any moment could abolish the law and Russia would become a land of brigandage.[32]

Elsewhere Lefort claims that the petty nobility "want no change [in the form of government] and are already forming factions."[33] But, although these comments would tend to support the idea that the lesser nobility reacted to the Supreme Privy Council's reforms either factionally or in a purely traditional, pro-monarchist, and anti-aristocratic fashion, other evidence suggests that the rank-and-file nobility was well able to appreciate the benefits of sweeping political reform. Lefort himself reports that the lesser nobility's anti-aristocratic stance "doesn't interfere with their efforts to prevent certain abuses of sovereign authority, such as leaving an entire nation dependent on the whims and caprices of a favorite."[34]

Widespread support for political reform and limitation of sovereign power found expression in the plans formulated by the broader nobility in response to the conditions issued by the Supreme Privy Council. The various projects and plans submitted by groups of the nobility in late January and early February fully endorsed the idea of limited monarchy and went beyond the initial conditions in elaborating the terms of limitation. The documents of the time speak clearly about what it was that participants thought they were doing: Nobles submitted proposals for nothing less than a "new form of government." In large assemblies members of the nobility debated what form the government would take in the future.[35] The conditions and various later proposals tackled fundamental questions about how important state decisions would be made, what institutional bodies would govern, and how high officials would be selected. The outpouring of interest in governmental reform is clear in reports such as that of the English envoy Claude Rondeau on February 2: "I cannot yet acquaint your lordship with certainty what form of government the russ design to settle. . . . As yet they are not very well agreed amongst themselves how to settle it, but they have gone too far to go back, which obliges most people to think that they certainly will make some considerable alterations."[36]

Many of the nobles' counterproposals went even farther than the initial conditions drafted by the erudite Golitsyn with his knowledge of Western constitutionalism. All of the nobles' counterproposals developed mechanisms for including a broader segment of the nobility in important political decisions than the Privy Council had imagined. Some utilized Peter the Great's system of choosing high officials by ballot, demonstrating familiarity with and acceptance of this relatively new custom. Most called for some sort of diet that would share responsibility for ruling the land with the senate, "High Government," and monarch. For instance the "Society Project," which Protasov dates to late January, called for a diet that should "devise, and society confirm, whatever is necessary for the reform and welfare of the state."[37] The Project of the 361 worked out a complicated structure of representative bodies and set forth a vague system for electing representatives. The plan proposed creating a high government of twenty-one people, who would share the burden of rule with a senate of eleven (or one hundred in an alternate version) members. Government should be based on broad consultation within the elite: "Important affairs of state and necessary additions to the statute pertaining to the government of the state should be drafted and approved by common consultation between the High Government, Senate, general officers, and the nobility."[38]

What made the traditionally subservient Russian nobility suddenly so receptive to the idea of limited monarchy and legislative assemblies in 1730? Why did the nobles, who had called themselves slaves of the tsar a few short generations earlier, suddenly presume to limit the power of their sovereign? In part this shift may be attributed to the creeping secularization of conceptions of society and state, some of which were imported from the West. The distancing of the divine from the process of governance helped to make limiting the sovereign's will imaginable. However, in light of the reading of the Muscovite heritage given above, the shift was not so abrupt as all that. Indigenous Russian political traditions contained strong antecedents for the nobles' commitment to representing the popular will and limiting autocracy. The fact that the nobles' plans in 1730 emphasized the need to consult with a broad slice of noble society, particularly if "additions" were to be made "to the statutes pertaining to the government of the state," recalls Muscovite practice of summoning assemblies of the land, consultative bodies, or at least the leading boyars to approve anything new: a change in foreign policy; a declaration of war; a new law code. When the boyars invited the Polish Prince Wladislaw to assume the Muscovite throne in 1610, among the conditions they set for his accession were that only the boyars had the right to alter the judicial system, and increases in taxes could be approved only "with the consent of the boyars and other influential people."[39] In this condition they drew on the somewhat more ambiguously phrased precedent of the 1550 Law Code, which stipulated that any additions to the code should be made by the sovereign but approved by the boyars.[40] The Russian nobles' ideas about formal limitation of autocratic rule thus reflected Muscovite precedent as well as imported Western ideas about constitutional order.

What then was the meaning of limited monarchy in autocratic Russia? Here it would be useful to remember that even in Western Europe "constitutionalism" had a very difference valence in the first half of the eighteenth century than it would in the second. The truly limited monarchies, Poland and Sweden, were plagued with difficulties.[41] France, where monarchs ruled through elaborate institutional systems, and Britain, where an ever-growing set of settlements and precedents checked royal power in favor of parliament, nevertheless retained immensely powerful royal centers.[42] The politics of patronage combined easily with the electoral politics in eighteenth-century England, where aristocratic families saw to it that their clients filled the seats of the House of Commons and laws of entail guaranteed the preservation of a very small, privileged landed elite.[43]

In a wide array of reassessments of 1730, historians have scrutinized every aspect of this issue, and many have questioned the truly "constitutional" impulses of the early-eighteenth-century reformers, portraying them instead as pursuing traditional clan politics masquerading as fancy Western legalism. The nobility at large has been described as demonstrating little interest in any aspect of the matter other than securing its own civil privileges and economic well-being. Otherwise it has been relegated to a largely passive role, as simple dupes of clever foreigners' propaganda or as dutiful followers of aristocratic patrons and superior officers who in turn had personal axes to grind.

The excitement that foreign witnesses recorded in their journals and the enthusiasm and daring with which the nobility gathered together to formulate plans and suggestions without any encouragement from above offers quite a different picture. Limits on autocratic power apparently appealed to the nobility and made sense to them at a number of different levels of political understanding. Russian nobles would have had long been familiar with the idea of written terms constraining the sovereign's actions, primarily from the coronation oaths sworn by rulers to their subjects. The "constitutional" direction of the reform movement followed an ancient, though ineffectual, tradition of codifying customary restraints on tsarist power. The Privy Council's conditions began with the traditional insistence on the ruler's obligation to preserve the Orthodox faith and to take the counsel of leading advisers before making major policy decisions. The nobiliary proposals drew on other aspects of Muscovite tradition as well. In its demands for broadening the franchise (to include them) and expanding the legislative bodies of state (slightly), the rank-and-file nobility expressed its abhorrence of oligarchy, and its sense that autocratic rule was the best antidote for tyranny by the few, the oppression of the weak by the strong.[44] Preoccupation with just and merciful rule surfaced in some of the most vaguely worded articles, such as: "as to the peasants, upon adequate investigation, give them some tax relief."[45]

Yet neither in the seventeenth century nor in 1730 did "tradition" or faith in a good monarch define the limits of the nobles' political vision. In 1730, the nobility demonstrated its continuing understanding of the benefits of benevolent paternalism but also strikingly displayed its enthusiasm for improving the institutional design of the state and its understanding of the new developments in political life and theory. The formalizing of institutional power apart from the monarch's will was a logical extension of the institutional checks and balances and the ethos of service to the nation so energetically introduced by Peter I, who styled himself first servant of the state. As Cynthia Whittaker discusses in the following essay and elsewhere, the concept of autocracy itself was changing in the eighteenth century, and its justification shifting from eternal salvation to earthly well-being.[46] These incipient changes prepared the nobility to accept the radical idea that the sovereign should be stripped of effective power, including the power to tax or spend, to marry or to declare an heir, to wage war or conclude peace. That the final sentence in the council's conditions provoked no objections from the rank-and-file nobility shows how far the concept of autocracy had altered: "And if I do not fulfill or keep any of these promises, *I shall be deprived of the Russian Crown.*"[47]

The Cherkasskii Petition, submitted directly to Empress Anna on the morning of February 25, is generally considered the beginning of the end of the effort at constitutional reform. It is condemned in historical retrospect as the lesser nobility's retreat to the known and comfortable forms of autocracy, its willing acceptance of a return to tyranny. The document proves to be a treasury of ambivalence and contradiction contained within a single framework. It begins as a traditional supplication, in the mode of Muscovite petitions, reminding the empress of her duty before God and people, who had jointly chosen her to rule:

Most glorious and most gracious Sovereign Empress! Although You have been elevated to the throne of the Russian Empire by the will of the

Almighty *and the unanimous consent of all the people,* in testimony of Your high favor to the whole State, Your Imperial Majesty has deigned to sign the articles presented by the Supreme Privy Council, and we thank You most humbly for this gracious intent.

Compare this with the address to Tsar Aleksei Mikhailovich from "people of all ranks" in 1648, which explains that the tsar had been chosen by joint decision of God and the people of Muscovy:

your royal majesty, like your majesty's deceased father the Sovereign Fedorovich [Mikhail] . . . was raised up and chosen as Sovereign and Great Prince by God *and the entire people.*[48]

In traditional manner the Cherkasskii Petition then lightly chided the ruler for being overly kind and generous, to the point of benefiting the wicked with her mercy: "However, most Gracious Lady, some of these articles raise such doubts that the majority of the people is in fear of future disturbances." Once again, the parallel to the traditional Muscovite tropes used to censure tsarist rule are striking. In 1648 petitioners blamed the sovereign's excessive kindness as the source of the nation's troubles: "But today, as a consequence of the fact that your tsarist highness is so patient, evil people . . . accrue all sorts of advantages and riches from serving on state business, regardless of the fact that through them the entire people comes to ruin."[49]

The Cherkasskii Petition closed on a submissive note, agreeing to submit any plans for reform "for Your Majesty's approval," a direct parallel to the old Muscovite closing, "In this, Sovereign, as you decree." To this point, the petition clearly resembled its forebears and drew upon old Muscovite traditions. The concrete proposals offered in the petition, however, reflect anything but a traditional monarchist outlook. This petition, supposedly marking noble capitulation to autocratic rule, goes far beyond anything produced in the previous century. The petitioners asked the Empress to "permit an assembly" broadly composed of "all general officers, [other] officers, and nobles, one or two from every family," whose task would be no less than "to devise a form of government for the state." The constituent assembly's decisions would be reached not by traditional consensus, nor by weight of rank and power, but "on the basis of the majority's opinion," after examination of all of "the opinions submitted by us and others," and investigating "all circumstances."

In broad terms, the vision of the goal and purpose of government expressed in the Cherkasskii Petition demonstrates a marked change from Muscovite days. The traditional tsar had been responsible for maintaining piety in his earthly realm and herding his flock to eternal salvation. In 1730, the petitioners endorsed quite a different understanding of the state's mission. They planned that there should "be devised a safe system of government for the peace and welfare of the state."[50] Notions of society as a collective entity and of governance "for the common good" had made their first tentative appearances in Muscovy in the late seventeenth century, but their impact and acceptance at that time had been very limited.[51] Already by 1730, those feeble first shoots had taken firm root. The petitioners during the Constitutional Crisis had no doubt about the social goals of good government. The Orthodox vision of statecraft had faded quickly from noble memory, and had been replaced by a concept of political legitimacy based on popular will and the good of the nation.

All this evidence of changed political attitudes and expectations is partially undercut by the submissive closing of the Cherkasskii Petition, which promises to submit the results of the future assembly's deliberations "for Your Majesty's approval." By phrasing its demands as a supplication and by giving the empress the ultimate say in deciding which plan to implement, the nobility handed all real power back to her sovereign hands. This turned out to be a tactical error for those nobles who were genuinely committed to political reform. Sedov explains that "Evidently the *dvorianstvo*, in giving autocracy to the empress, poorly understood that with this they had already established a form of governance and discussion of other forms could go no further."[52]

Muscovite political culture exerted a powerful influence on noble behavior in 1730, but it cannot and should not be understood as an immutable force that led the nobility around by the nose. Muscovite political culture reflected a malleable, evolving cultural tradition, developed by historical actors, set in historical time. By 1730 the people who had lived in and whose experiences were shaped by ongoing Muscovite traditions had also experienced the revolutionary changes introduced by Peter the Great. They had donned Western clothing and had somehow or other imbibed at least the minimal education required by law. Many of the elements generally ascribed to Western political theory, such as the ideas of popular will and public good and the principles of formalized limits and legislative assemblies, resonated with Muscovite traditions and, therefore, were immediately comprehensible and relevant to early imperial nobles. Confluence of Muscovite and Petrine traditions did not always produce friction. The forced shaving of Old Believers' beards does not tell the whole story. Important elements of the two traditions combined easily, creating a composite political culture. In the seventeenth century, some limitations were part of what was understood as good autocratic rule. By the eighteenth century, there was a new awareness that there were limited and unlimited forms of autocracy, and that reasonable limits could be enshrined in some kind of written form, still without impinging on the autocratic nature of the monarch.

Family Politics or Families in Politics?

Recent Western scholarship has inverted the inherited wisdom that maintained that the attempt in 1730 represented a break with ancient patterns of patrimonial autocratic culture. Instead, following Brenda Meehan-Waters's lead, the current trend views 1730 as yet another manifestation of traditional clan interest at work. Indeed, kinship and patronage bonds and antagonisms played a significant role in determining the alignments of key actors. The nobles' proposals themselves place matters of kinship in the foreground. What the passages about kinship reveal, however, is the same kind of creative adaptation of traditional clan politics to new political circumstances that characterized the nobles' understanding of other aspects of the process of governmental reform.

As the Project of the 361 envisioned it, in the governing assembly "there should be no more than one candidate from any one [noble] family, and no more than two persons from one family participating in the election; and the quorum for voting should be no less than one hundred persons, and no members of the candidates' families may participate in the vote."[53] This careful formulation indicates that family still remained the primary political unit and category of political solidarity, but that the principle of kinship was now skillfully interwoven with other guiding principles: relatively broad representation within the nobility, majority rule, public and class interests. The leading families should now be explicitly limited in their control over powerful state bodies. The various proposals for governmental reform were all quite short, so the very fact that the nobles bothered to include elaborate discussions of the number of delegates allowed per family demonstrates the inextricable link between family politics and national politics in their minds. The individuals involved in court policy making would inevitably come from leading noble families, and those particular families would benefit in any number of ways. Hence the imperative to control family representation, not by barring favoritism and patronage, but rather by spreading the benefits of power broadly among noble families.

Actually, the limitation on the number of delegates per family fits well with the Muscovite clan system described by Kollmann, in which leading families carefully shared power and the spoils of the system, never allowing one family to garner all the plums. It also fits nicely with John LeDonne's vision of eighteenth-century politics as a balance of power among three sets of noble families.[54] Muscovite political culture again ran parallel to more modern, eighteenth-century developments, facilitating the easy assimilation of new organizing concepts into an older, adaptable framework. The content was quite new, but its resemblance to traditional forms made the transformation of noble political culture a smooth process.

Throughout the eighteenth century kinship continued to play a defining role in determining membership in the inner circle of those eligible for important, remunerative posts conferring high status on their holders. Peter's Table of Ranks did more to perpetuate noble elite than to open it to newcomers; Meehan-Waters has shown that the same noble families dominated the top posts in 1730 as in the late Muscovite era.[55] Terrible proof of the lasting force of kinship in political life came with the harsh retribution meted out by Anna's regime to the extended families (women and children included) of the insolent members of the Supreme Privy Council who had dared to limit her sovereignty.[56]

Yet, kinship ties and the ability to call on family connections assumed a somewhat different significance in an era in which merit rested on individual rather than ancestral performance. Well-placed patrons could advance their kinsmen, but they would be leery of expending political capital on someone incapable of filling a post credibly or reflecting well on their benefactor.[57] The struggles of the nobility to guarantee entrance for their sons into the Cadet Corps and other educational institutions in the early eighteenth century illustrate the ways in which kinship continued to confer advancement, but now the best way to forward one's relatives' careers had changed. Instead of simply flaunting one's family tree, it was now expedient to procure educational benefits and technical skills, guaranteeing successful performance on the job. C. H. von Manstein, a general in Russian service, reported that some sense of the right to advance by merit rather than by birth mobilized the nobles' anti-oligarchical sentiments in 1730, but he understood advancement by merit as a recent Petrine innovation. He wrote that the nobles were given to understand that "none of them stood any chance of obtaining preference of the least consequence, while the council of state should have all power in its own hands; . . . whereas if the empress were declared sovereign, the least private gentleman might aspire to the first posts of the empire, as easily as the princes; that there were examples of this under Peter I when the greatest regard was paid to true merit."[58] The emphasis on education and qualifications was certainly new with Peter, but the notion of work and ability underlying it traces its roots tangentially to the changing attitudes toward merit discussed above. With just cause (although perhaps somewhat overreading the past), writers of the eighteenth century admired the abolition of *mestnichestvo* as an antecedent of their own commitment to rewarding merit rather than birth. The playwright Alexander Sumarokov wrote in praise of Tsar Fedor Alekseevich: "he abolished the prerogatives of families who drew their pride from their ancient genealogies alone and not from services rendered to the fatherland."[59]

Apart from their commitment to limited monarchy and governmental reform, the rank-and-file nobility in 1730 displayed intense interest in a few issues touching more directly on their civil status, the "bread and butter demands of the majority of noble servicemen."[60] Many scholars distinguish between what they categorize as truly political matters, such as determining a new form of government, and civil matters, involving private life and family politics. Marc Raeff stresses that the "noblemen's political horizon did not extend beyond an expression of hope that the worst abuses and hardships would be alleviated in time."[61] Meehan-Waters asserts that articles in the nobles' proposals concerning service and inheritance were "matters neither of dispute nor of great political importance," and were tossed in to win signatures from among retired officers, soldiers, and the Guards regiments.[62] The distinction between "civil" and "political" in this context obscures yet another ongoing feature of Muscovite political culture in imperial politics: family politics were not distinct from high politics; indeed family concerns drove participants into what might be recognizable as political activism in a more modern context.

Chief among the "apolitical" matters raised in the projects were complaints about the grueling and degrading effects of the service system established by Peter the Great and the Table of Ranks. The proposals expressed dissatisfaction with the demands of lifelong service and the requirement that nobles begin service at the bottom ranks just like everyone else. In a characteristic formulation, the Grekov Project (Project of the 361) specified: "Devise the best system of service for the nobility, so that no one is compelled to serve more than twenty years against his will, and in order not to oblige any noble to serve as sailor or artisan against his will."[63] Another proposal specified that "Noblemen should not be appointed to the military ranks of private and artisan, but special companies should be established for them."[64] These proposals again accept the basic premise set out from above, that service should be required and that it should be regulated by the Table of Ranks. What they attempt is to refine the existing conditions to suit noble interests and to preserve noble distinction at a time when the characteristics of nobility had become dangerously unclear. Shoring up noble identity and exclusivity was more than a private matter.

The second civil demand that recurred in almost all of the noble proposals was the abolition of Peter's deeply hated law requiring that nobles practice unigeniture. "The seniority rule in matters of inheritance should be abrogated and complete freedom given to the parents; and, if there are no parents left, the inheritance is to be divided in equal shares."[65] In addition to the problem of disinheriting younger sons and brothers, as Lee Farrow has shown, one of the most irksome aspects of Peter's inheritance law was that it barred all women from inheriting land.[66] Resistance to such inequitable division of property grew from the traditional Muscovite practice of dividing property equally among all sons and allotting generous portions, sometimes in land as well as in moveable property, to widows, daughters, and sisters. Official regulation had discouraged the bequeathing of land to females from the late sixteenth century on, but Muscovite landowners had nonetheless persisted in their practice, while the administration apparently closed its eyes.[67] When Peter's decree simultaneously made the prohibitions more stringent and put teeth into enforcement, the nobility viewed this as a serious incursion into their business. Inheritance and landholding meant more than just economic standing; they connoted social status, facilitated social and service advancement, and contributed to a person's marriageability. Noble family interests thus assumed explicitly political form and expression, and played themselves out on the national political scene.

These proposals echo the concerns of the provincial gentry of the seventeenth century, when the political content of these familial and personal matters was beyond dispute, when kinship politics *was* politics and autocratic culture meant clan maneuvering under the carapace of tsarist rule. By weaving these particular issues of civil concern into proposals for remodeling the entire state, the nobility continued its ancient pattern of conceiving of family and politics on the same plane. As in the Muscovite era, family politics became the substance of political debate, while evolving political conceptions gave shape to the way that politics played out. Making use of a novel opportunity for reforming the governmental order, the nobility placed its deepest concerns, those of family, inheritance, status, service, and wealth, at the forefront. Focused on the particular and the familial, Russian nobles understood how to play those issues out on the national political scene.

Ultimately, of course, the constitutional efforts of 1730 failed. The nobles endorsed instead what they evidently viewed as an equally attractive option, an unlimited monarch grateful to and reliant on the general nobility. With this alternative configuration of government as an acceptable possibility, more radical constitutional plans were undermined by the corrosive infighting of kinship groups. But the constitutionalist language of the nobles' proposals had not arisen simply as a mask for apolitical family feuding. In the particulars of their civil demands, if not in the establishment of a limited monarchy, the nobles did in fact gain a good deal. Upon ascending to the throne, Empress Anna immediately disbanded the unpopular and discredited Supreme Privy Council. Soon thereafter she established special cadet corps for the sons of nobles, so that they could avoid demeaning service in the lowest ranks, and in 1731 she abolished Peter's law of single inheritance. As in 1648, the sovereign conspicuously demonstrated that she listened attentively to the voice of "all the land" and took very seriously her obligation to rule justly and responsively. She responded favorably to all requests except those that encroached upon autocratic authority. Wearing the new mantle of the Reforming Tsar (to use Whittaker's term), the eighteenth-century sovereigns obviated the perceived need for constitutional limitation on their power by renegotiating the traditional consultative relations between a mutually dependent tsar and nobility. Yet, the nobles' willingness to reinstate full autocracy in no way vitiates their earlier enthusiasm for establishing a strictly limited monarchy and a government based on a broad noble franchise. In the terms of the day, the two outcomes were not dissimilar: either solution obligated the autocrat to hear noble complaints and meet noble needs; either prevented the consolidation of a hated oligarchy.

The events of 1730 provide a vivid illustration of the amalgamation of levels and understandings of political and social life that had been characteristic of Muscovite political culture and that came to characterize noble political culture in the eighteenth century. The nobles' plans expose the interpenetration and dynamic interplay of various planes of state and society, culture and politics. The significance of family politics did not preclude the participation of families in broader political endeavors. The rank-and-file nobility's focus on service, family, and inheritance in fact propelled that group onto the national political scene and forced the nobles to express an abstract political vision. Although the traditional Muscovite framework of parental rule, stern yet merciful, continued to shape Russian understandings of relations of power as fundamentally personal, informal, and intimate, it would be misleading to describe a unidirectional attraction on the part of the lesser nobility toward the old, or an obstinate nostalgia for bygone ages. Instead of facing "a choice between two models of political authority—the European-rational-bureaucratic, and the native-Russian-traditional," the Russian nobility maintained both, often expressing a preference for the latter but making good use of the former when the need arose.[68]

The Russian nobility, as participants in a vibrant autocratic culture, saw no contradiction between an interest in rationalizing and institutionalizing administrative function and a commitment to personal service to the sovereign. Nor did the nobles remark on any contradiction between constitutional monarchy and representational institutions on the one hand, and autocracy and kinship politics on the other. Kinship politics and high politics were similarly linked in the noble political imaginary and in noble political action. In each case, the two aspects were equally legitimate and equally central to their definitions of "the political." Muscovite political culture exerted a strong influence on the behavior, visions, and understandings of politics expressed by the early-eighteenth-century nobility, but it facilitated rather than hindered the introduction of new ideas and the evolution of a very new politics of the imperial age. The various successes and failures of eighteenth-century reform efforts and cultural innovations may be explained in significant part according to how they resonated with existing Russian practice. Instead of reflexively resisting any new ideas, the Russian nobility easily incorporated those innovations that made sense within its cultural framework, while rejecting those that were incompatible with strongly rooted practices. A surprising number of supposedly radical Western ideas already had parallels, in form if not in substance, in traditional Muscovite ideology. The ongoing dynamism of noble political culture resulted from the interplay of new ideas and practices as they were assimilated and reworked to fit local understandings, and as noble understandings themselves modified upon extended contact with novel practices and ideas.

Notes

I would like to thank Jane Burbank, Kali Israel, Gary Marker, Cynthia Whittaker, and Elise Wirtschafter for their readings and generous assistance in working through various aspects of this argument.

1. For instance, D. A. Korsakov, *Votsarenie Imperatritsy Anny Ioannovny* (Kazan', 1880) discusses the constitutional politics, derived from Swedish models, that informed the reformers of 1730, and O. A. Omel'chenko, *"Zakonnaia monarkhiia" Ekateriny II: Prosveshchennyi absoliutizm v Rossii* (Moscow, 1993) provides an account of an ongoing, cosmopolitan discussion of reform and rulership in mid-century. An example of the alternative view, John P. LeDonne writes of eighteenth-century court politics that "the lack of issues of principle reduced political struggles to conflicts over personal and group preeminence and often destroyed the better men in calculated acts of collective vindictiveness." "Ruling Families in the Russian Political Order, 1689–1825," *Cahiers du monde russe et soviétique* 28 (1987): 306.

2. This eighteenth-century intersection has been examined in a number of excellent works: LeDonne, "Ruling Families in the Russian Political Order"; Brenda Meehan-Waters, *Autocracy and Aristocracy: The Russian Service Elite of 1730* (New Brunswick, N.J., 1982); David L. Ransel, *The Politics of Catherinian Russia. The Panin Party* (New Haven, 1975). For a very convincing investigation of the ways in which private concerns constituted a public sphere in eighteenth-century France, see Sarah Maza, *Private Lives and Public Affairs: The Causes Célèbres of Prerevolutionary France* (Berkeley and Los Angeles, 1993). Maza elaborates on ideas about the domestic and the public sphere drawn from Jürgen

Habermas, *The Structural Transformation of the Public Sphere: An Inquiry into a Category of Bourgeois Society*, trans. Thomas Burger and Frederick Lawrence (Cambridge, Mass., 1989).

3. Marc Raeff, *Plans for Political Reform in Imperial Russia, 1730–1905* (Englewood, N.J., 1966), 51; Korsakov, *Votsarenie*, 275.

4. Richard Pipes makes the case for the tragically missed moment in *Russia under the Old Regime* (New York, 1974), 184–85. Other proponents of the constitutionalist reform view include Ia. Gordin, *Mezh rabstvom i svobodoi: 19 ianvaria–25 fevralia 1730 goda* (St. Petersburg, 1994); Korsakov, *Votsarenie*; G. A. Protasov, "Dvorianskie proekty 1730 goda (istochnikovedcheskoe izuchenie)," *Istochnikovedcheskie raboty* 2 (1971): 61–102; S. A. Sedov, "Plany ogranicheniia samoderzhaviia v 1730 godu i pozitsiia dvorianstva," *Sosloviia i gosudarstvennaia vlast' v Rossii. XV-seredina XIX vv. Mezhdunarodnaia konferentsiia Chteniia pamiati akad. L. V. Cherepnina. Tezisy dokladov* (Moscow, 1994), vol. 2, 91–98. The newer approach was initially formulated in Meehan-Waters, *Autocracy and Aristocracy*, 132–48, esp. 147–48. See also LeDonne, "Ruling Families in the Russian Political Order," 296: "The issue, then, in February 1730, was not so much 'constitutionalism' as whether the Saltykovs and the Naryshkins would agree to be displaced by the Dolgorukovs and Dmitrii Golitsyn as the regulators of the political system and the chief dispensers of patronage."

5. This view unites historians who otherwise propound very disparate views. For instance, Raeff, *Plans*, 43–44; David L. Ransel, "The Government Crisis of 1730," *Reform in Russia and the USSR: Past and Prospects*, ed. Robert O. Crummey (Chicago, 1989), 65, 67; Meehan-Waters, *Autocracy and Aristocracy*, 13; Pipes, *Russia under the Old Regime*, 184–85.

6. David L. Ransel offers an unusually nuanced understanding of gentry political attitudes. He attributes more rationality and agency to the lesser nobility than most studies have done, and he sees attitudes deriving from historical experience. "Political Perceptions of the Russian Nobility: The Constitutional Crisis of 1730," *Laurentian University Review*, no. 3 (1972): 32–33.

7. For a superb overview of Muscovite autocratic culture, see Nancy Shields Kollmann, "Honor and Society in Early Modern Russia," chap. 5, unpublished manuscript, 1995. I would like to thank her for permission to cite her unpublished work.

8. Daniel Rowland, "The Problem of Advice in Muscovite Tales about the Time of Troubles," *Russian History* 6 (1979): 271–72.

9. P. P. Smirnov, "Chelobitnye dvorian i detei boiarskikh vsekh gorodov v pervoi polovine XVII v.," *Chteniia v Imperatorskom Obshchestve Istorii i Drevnostei Rossiskikh pri Moskovskom universitete (ChOIDR)*, 254 (Moscow, 1915), no. 3, 54.

10. *The Muscovite Law Code (Ulozhenie) of 1649. Part I: Text and Translation*, trans. and ed. Richard Hellie (Irvine, Calif., 1988), 2.

11. On this subject, see my *Autocracy in the Provinces: The Muscovite Gentry and Political Culture in the Seventeenth Century* (Stanford, 1997), chaps. 7–8.

12. Hellie, *Muscovite Law Code*, chap. 10, art. 2, 23; Kollmann, "Honor and Society in Early Modern Russia," chap. 6, 13–14.

13. Hellie, *Muscovite Law Code*, chap. 10, arts. 281–84, 84–85.

14. Kollmann, "Honor and Society in Early Modern Russia," chap. 6, 38.

15. N. F. Demidova, *Sluzhilaia biurokratiia v Rossii XVII v. i ee rol' v formirovanii abso-lutisma* (Moscow, 1987); A. A. Zimin, "O slozhenii prikaznoi sistemy na Rusi," in *Doklady i soobshcheniia Instituta Istorii (Akademii Nauk)* 3 (1955): 164–76.

16. A number of petitions are published in Novosel'skii, "Kollektivnye dvorianskie chelobitnye o syske beglykh krest'ian i kholopov vo vtoroi polovine XVII v.," in N. I. Pavlenko, et al., eds., *Dvorianstvo i krepostnoi stroi Rossii XVI–XVIII vv. Sbornik statei, pos-viashchennyi pamiati Alekseia Andreevicha Novosel'skogo* (Moscow, 1975), 303–43. Novosel'skii reprints two petitions found in V. N. Storozhev, "Dva chelobit'ia (K bibliografii materia-lov dlia istorii russkogo dvorianstva)," *Bibliograficheskie zapiski*, 1892, pt. 1 (1892): 7–15.

17. Storozhev, "Dva chelobit'ia," 11.

18. For instance, a 1658 petition notes that the law set no penalties for harboring those peasants who had been recorded in the previous census but omitted from the most recent one. Novosel'skii, "Kollektivnye dvorianskie chelobitnye o syske beglykh krest'ian i kholopov," 309.

19. E. P. Thompson, *Whigs and Hunters: The Origin of the Black Act* (New York, 1975), 265–69.

20. A. Prozorovskii, "Sil'vestra Medvedeva Sozertsanie kratkoe let 7190, 91 i 92, v nikh zhe chto sodeiasia vo grazhdanstve," *ChOIDR*, 1884, *kn.* 4, *otd.* II, 19; quoted in M. Ia. Volkov, "Ob otmene mestnichestva v Rossii," *Istoriia SSSR* no. 2 (1977), 57.

21. On the development of concepts of honor and merit in France in the same pe-riod, see the exemplary work of Jay Michael Smith, "The Culture of Merit in Old Regime France: Royal Service and the 'Old' Nobility, 1600–1789." Ph.D. diss., The University of Michigan, 1990. On the shift from "honor (*chest'*)", derived from birthright, to "glory (*slava*)," derived from personal achievement, see David Das, "History Writing and the Quest for Fame in Late Muscovy: Andrei Lyzlov's *History of the Scythians*," *Russian Review* 51 (1992): 502–509.

22. Storozhev, "Dva chelobit'ia," 12; Novosel'skii, "Kollektivnye dvorianskie chelo-bitnye o syske beglykh krest'ian i kholopov," 335.

23. Storozhev, "Dva chelobit'ia," 12, 13, 14.

24. I take this heading title from the recent book of the same title: Gordin, *Mezh rabstvom i svobodoi.*

25. Ransel, "Political Perceptions," 20.

26. Ibid., 34.

27. Raeff, Ransel, and others have noted this immediate acquiescence by the nobility to the fundamental assumptions.

28. Feofan Prokopovich, "Prilozhenie," *Russkii arkhiv*, 1909, no. 1, 437.

29. Magnan, "Doneseniia frantsuzkago poverennago po delam pri russkom dvore za 1727–1730 g.," *Sbornik imperatorskogo russkogo istoricheskogo obshchestva (SIRIO)* (St. Pe-tersburg, 1891), 75, 458.

30. John Lefort, "Diplomaticheskie dokumenty, otnosiashchiesia k istorii Rossii v XVIII stoletii," *SIRIO* (St. Petersburg, 1870), vol. 5, 348.

31. Even among this group of monarchists, the identification may be questionable, as James Cracraft has indicated. His work on Feofan Prokopovich, purportedly a die-hard

defender of Peter's absolutist legacy, shows that Prokopovich envisioned a monarchy tempered by the political reforms discussed and approved by a general assembly. "The Succession Crisis of 1730: A View from the Inside," *Canadian-American Slavic Studies* 12 (1978), 81–82.

32. Lefort, "Diplomaticheskie dokumenty," 347.

33. Ibid., 348.

34. Ibid.

35. Prokopovich, "Prilozhenie," 436; Magnan, "Doneseniia frantsuzkago poverennago," 487–88.

36. C. Rondeau, *Doneseniia i drugiia bumagi angliskikh poslov, poslannikov i rezidentov pri russkim dvore s 1728 goda po 1733 god,* vol. 66 of *SIRIO* (St. Petersburg, 1889), 134.

37. Raeff, *Plans,* 50; from V. Kashpirev, *Pamiatniki novoi russkoi istorii. Sbornik istoricheskikh statei i materialov* (St. Petersburg, 1871), vol. 1, pt. 2, 7–8.

38. Raeff, *Plans,* 48–49, from Kashpirev, *Pamiatniki,* 4–5.

39. *Akty, otnosiashchiesia k istorii Zapadnoi Rossii, sobranye i izdannye Arkheograficheskoi Kommissieiu* (St. Petersburg, 1846–1853), 4:314–17.

40. *Rossiiskoe zakonodatel'stvo X–XX vekov v deviati tomakh* (Moscow, 1985), 2: 120, art. 98. See also an excellent discussion in Kollmann, "Honor and Society in Early Modern Russia," chap. 5.

41. Thanks to Cynthia Whittaker for this observation.

42. On France, see William Beik, *Absolutism and Society in Seventeenth-Century France: State Power and Provincial Aristocracy in Languedoc* (Cambridge, Mass., 1985). On England, see John Brewer, *The Sinews of Power: War, Money, and the English State, 1688–1783* (London and Boston, 1989).

43. Sir Lewis Bernstein Namier provides the classic description of this phenomenon. Although considered dated in his approach, he still has much to offer. Namier, *The Structure of Politics at the Accession of George III* (London, 1929). See also H. J. Habakkuk, "Marriage Settlements in the Eighteenth Century," *Transactions of the Royal Historical Society,* 4th ser., vol. 32 (London, 1950): 15–30.

44. For instance, see the broadsheet quoted in Ransel, "The Government Crisis of 1730," 57.

45. Raeff, *Plans,* 47; from Korsakov, *Votsarenie,* Appendix, 9–11.

46. Cynthia Whittaker, "The Reforming Tsar: The Redefinition of Autocratic Duty in Eighteenth-Century Russia," *Slavic Review* 51 (1992): 77–98.

47. Raeff, *Plans,* 47; from Korsakov, *Votsarenie,* 18 (emphasis mine).

48. Smirnov, "Chelobitnye," 54 (emphasis mine).

49. Smirnov, "Chelobitnye," 54.

50. Raeff, *Plans,* 50–51; from Korsakov, *Votsarenie,* 271–72.

51. Nancy Shields Kollmann, "Concepts of Society and Social Identity in Early Modern Russia," in Samuel H. Baron and Nancy Shields Kollmann, eds., *Religion and Culture in Early Modern Russia and Ukraine* (DeKalb, Ill., 1997).

52. Sedov, "Plany," 96.

53. Raeff, *Plans,* 48; from Kashpirev, *Pamiatniki,* 4.

54. Nancy Shields Kollmann, *Kinship and Politics: The Making of the Muscovite Political System, 1345–1547* (Stanford, 1987); LeDonne, "Ruling Families in the Russian Political Order," 233–322.

55. Meehan-Waters, *Aristocrats and Servitors*.

56. See the portrait of the suffering of an unfortunate bride: N. B. Dolgorukaja, *The Memoirs of Natal'ja Borisovna Dolgorukaja*, trans. C. E. Townsend (Columbus, 1977).

57. This is suggested in David L. Ransel, "Character and Style of Patron-Client Relations in Russia," in Antoni Maczak, ed., *Klientelsysteme in Europa der frühen Neuzeit* (Munich, 1988), 219–20.

58. C. H. von Manstein, *Contemporary Memoirs of Russia from the Year 1727 to 1744* (London, 1770; rept. 1968), 33.

59. Quoted in Hans Rogger, *National Consciousness in Eighteenth-Century Russia* (Cambridge, Mass., 1960), 53.

60. Meehan-Waters, *Aristocrats and Servitors*, 139.

61. Raeff, *Plans*, 44.

62. Meehan-Waters, *Aristocrats and Servitors*, 139–40.

63. Raeff, *Plans*, 49; from Kashpirev, *Pamiatniki*, 5.

64. Raeff, *Plans*, 50; from Kashpiev, *Pamiatniki*, 7–8.

65. Raeff, *Plans*, 50; from Kashpiev, *Pamiatniki*, 7–8.

66. Lee A. Farrow, "Peter the Great's Law of Single Inheritance: State Imperatives and Noble Resistance," *Russian Review* 55 (1996): 430–47.

67. Kivelson, *Autocracy in the Provinces*, chap. 3.

68. Wilson R. Augustine, "Notes toward a Portrait of the Eighteenth-century Nobility," *Canadian Slavic Studies* 4 (1970), 384.

2

The Idea of Autocracy among Eighteenth-Century Russian Historians

Cynthia Hyla Whittaker

————··◦⟨∞⟩◦··————

THE IDEA OF autocracy changed profoundly in eighteenth-century Russia. Among the educated elite, secular justification for power replaced religious sanction. Dynamic change legitimized the office rather than maintenance of stability. Rationalist arguments superseded acceptance based on tradition. The figure of the Russian autocrat as the equivalent of other European absolutist monarchs supplanted the image of an isolated and unique Orthodox ruler. The vast majority of Russians clung to the older views, but the Petrine reforms and Enlightenment ideals propelled a movement among the educated elite toward greater participation in political discourse and prompted an unprecedented reappraisal of its central feature, the autocracy. Diplomats, clergy, bureaucrats, journalists, scientists, professors, men and women of letters, army officers, court personnel, even autocrats themselves joined the public discussion, causing a political watershed: for the first time, Russians engaged in sustained and relatively widespread discourse about their form of government and thus transformed the political environment.[1]

The official documents, political treatises, histories, and various literary genres in which this discourse unfolded reveal attitudes that ran contrary to current assumptions, since historians over the past century focused either on oppositional individuals and groups or on the alienation of society from government. A fresh reading of the materials indicates widespread support for autocracy and demonstrates its function as a source of integration and cohesion among the educated elite.[2] These Russians discussed autocracy's legitimacy, debated its feasibility, and elaborated sophisticated arguments, drawn from the Enlightenment arsenal of ideas, to arrive at a critical and rational endorsement. Furthermore, they perceived autocracy as a dynamic form of government, not as reactionary or even static, and therefore saw themselves as part of a progressive polity. The interpretation of autocracy itself became an enterprise that reflected shifts in domestic politics, changing Enlightenment criteria for good government, and varying public values, attitudes, and expectations.

Many groups participated in this new discourse, but among the most characteristic were eighteenth-century Russians who wrote histories of Russia. Leaving aside historiographical issues, this study will use these works as evidence for charting public attitudes toward autocracy in the course of the century. Histories constitute an illustrative set of sources for this purpose since their authors include a cross section of politically attuned Russians and since the writing of history throughout Europe in the eighteenth century centered on interpretations of rulership.

Russian historians in this epoch were nearly all amateurs and thus more typical of the educated public than the monastic annalists who were their forebears or the trained academics who were their successors.[3] The historians under analysis—all those who wrote interpretations of large segments of Russia's past and perforce of its rulers—came from a variety of political milieus, each affording a different perspective on autocracy. Their amateur status makes these authors doubly representative because they mirror the intellectual world both of writers of history and of their actual professions. Aleksei Mankiev (d. 1723) was a diplomat who wrote *The Kernel of Russian History* while imprisoned during the Great Northern War.[4] Vasilii Tatishchev (1686–1750), an expert administrator in the areas of mining, manufacturing, and minting, spent thirty years writing his multivolume *Russian History* "at night" and between assignments.[5] Mikhail Lomonosov's (1711–1765) fame rests on his position as the father of modern Russian literature and of modern Russian science, but he also found time to author *Ancient Russian History*.[6] Mikhail Shcherbatov (1733–1790), the court historiographer, confessed that he wrote the many volumes of *Russian History from Ancient Times* "more for my own personal pleasure" and spent a lifetime in state service.[7] Ivan Boltin (1735–1792) published historical critiques while serving as an army officer and administrator.[8] Timofei Mal'gin (1752–1819) wrote *A Mirror for Russian Sovereigns*, alongside his duties as a translator with the civil service rank of collegiate assessor.[9] And, Catherine II (1729–1796), while somewhat better known for her achievements as empress, published "Notes Concerning Russian History."[10] Six literary figures, who wrote less ambitious works about Russia's past, complete the list of thirteen published amateur historians.[11] The works of thirty-two anonymous writers remain unpublished (deservedly) in the archives.[12] Since only forty-five authors were involved in writing histories of Russia, observations and conclusions about this body of evidence can be based upon complete coverage. Eighteenth-century historians thus constitute a useful historical source because they include a wide but manageable sample of the Russian educated public.

Moreover, this group guarantees material for gauging attitudes toward autocracy since eighteenth-century Western and Central European histories centered on rulers, and Russians consciously adopted the genre.[13] As Iurii Lotman and Boris Uspenskii have pointed out, the emergence of people who could "think historically . . . was one of the basic innovations of post-Petrine culture" and an example of "real, not mythological Europeanization."[14] Full-fledged participants in their century's trends, Russians wrote history *en philosophe*, which demanded the formulation of an idea of progress, the demonstration of secular causation, and the display of interpretive sweep and didactic intent. Enlightenment histories intertwined each of these features with monarchical activity—understandably, as nearly all European countries were monarchies— and hence insured Russian authors' placing their own rulers at center stage.

Yet another reason why European eighteenth-century histories were bound to center on monarchs was that the majority were written at their behest. Fedor Emin noted that "all over Europe, Christian monarchs are trying to assemble accurate histories that document reigns, actions, attitudes, morals, various changes."[15] In Russia, this turned history into an exercise in national self-consciousness since autocrats also wanted historians "to do battle" with foreign detractors of the country and its leaders.[16] Peter the Great appealed for a national history to counteract "Polish lies";[17] Empress Elizabeth (1742–1761) summoned historians to refute German scholars who described the early Slavs as "barbarians, resembling beasts";[18] Catherine urged denunciation of the "falsehood . . . slander . . . and insolence" of the "frivolous Frenchmen" who wrote histories of Russia.[19]

Whatever the need to please a sponsor, philosophes genuinely regarded monarchs as high priests of the new secular morality. Eighteenth-century thinkers were not interested in stabilizing society but in improving it, and the linchpin in these plans for making progress toward secular salvation was the enlightened ruler.[20] Voltaire (1694–1778), who dominated historical thinking in the century, replaced Providential with royal causality and claimed that it was "the great actions of kings that have changed the face of the earth." He enshrined monarchs as those rare examples of human genius who brighten a historical landscape otherwise filled with struggle, folly, and crime.[21]

For eighteenth-century Russian historians, the most vivid example of the necessary connection between progress and the royal person was close at hand. The full-scale reform program of Peter the Great (1682–1725) made him the prototype of enlightened monarchs in Europe and prompted Russian historians to advance a dynamic interpretation of autocracy that became a hallmark of the century. After Peter, rulers were expected to justify their enormous power by being "reforming tsars," activist agents of change and improvement.[22] Mal'gin deprecated do-nothing tsars by giving them epithets such as Rostislav the Prayerful, Vsevelod I the Quiet or Fedor III the Sickly, since "they made no important changes."[23]

The activity expected of a dynamic tsar went far beyond the centuries-old functions of warrior and judge and superseded the old primary role of defender of Orthodoxy. According to Lomonosov's typical list, the new duties included increasing the population, eradicating idleness, fostering prosperity, raising the cultural level, battling superstition, encouraging geographical exploration, and, more traditionally, expanding borders.[24] Autocrats were to provide moral, if not necessarily spiritual, leadership: Catherine II claimed that a monarch was needed to save people "from envy," the vice most prominently mentioned by eighteenth-century Russian historians; Mankiev lauded autocrats who tried to eliminate drunkenness; Mal'gin looked to them to banish anti-Semitism from the realm.[25] Tatishchev portrayed Peter as an ideal monarch since he enabled his country to thrive in everything from the tool industry to the administration of justice—despite a long and costly war.[26] As the century wore on, not only the traditional image of Orthodox Tsar but even that of Warrior-King receded in the wake of the perceived need for reform. Alexander Sumarokov deemed "domestic improvements . . . the greatest tasks of monarchs"; Mal'gin agreed that "domestic accomplishments are infinitely more precious than all victories and conquests."[27]

With monarchs considered the ultimate causal factor in the state, not only their personal virtues or triumphs but also their vices or failures acquired significance. Tatishchev concluded: "With the good judgment and proper behavior of a sovereign, a state is enhanced, enriched, and flourishing, but laziness, love of luxury, and cruelty [in a sovereign] are ruinous, and our history is filled enough with such examples."[28] Similarly, Boltin and G. T. F. Raynal (1713–1796) argued that a populace tends to "remain on its sovereign's [moral and cultural] level."[29] For this reason, Enlightenment historians felt duty bound to instruct monarchs on their tasks and to provide them with textbooks of political morality. The very first statement about writing secular history in Russia offered the hope that it would demonstrate to autocrats the "results of good and evil acts."[30] Lomonosov expected his history to "give sovereigns examples of governing,"[31] while Tatishchev claimed that history's "use" was providing rulers with "a knowledge of the past" so that they may "wisely discuss the present and future."[32] Nicholas Novikov suggested that a "Philosopher-King . . . could inculcate, spread, implant . . . support, encourage, and patronize knowledge"—using the entire litany of hortatory verbs typical of eighteenth-century writers in spurring or motivating their monarchs into enlightened action.[33]

The image of "reforming tsars" and the appearance of pragmatic didacticism announce the new secularism of Enlightenment history and its reaction against the providential or religious interpretations of monarchical rule that had reached their climax in France with the writings of Jacques Bossuet (1627–1704). Although a strict theory of divine right was never prominent in Russia, there did exist the tradition of ecclesiastical histories, really chronicles, that originated in medieval Kiev.[34] They stressed the autocracy's biblical origins and its ties with the House of Palaeologus, but especially its role in the expansion of the Orthodox Church.[35] About a dozen eighteenth-century historians continued the tradition, but only one was published.[36] However, the seventeenth-century *Synopsis* by Innokenti Gizel' (d. 1683) retained an audience and was one of the most popular books in the eighteenth century.[37] This short work possessed an appealing triumphal quality with its emphasis on religious feats: the glorious conversion of the Russians to Orthodoxy under Vladimir I (980–1015) and the equally glorious victory of the Orthodox over the Tatar Horde under Ivan III (1462–1505). The rest of the book, though, consists of brief descriptions of princes and tsars whose quiescence was their paramount feature; they seemingly did little more than come to the throne, build a church or monastery, and then go to their heavenly reward. The abandonment of both this image of a passive ruler and of a religious teleology marked the major innovations of eighteenth-century Russian historians.

Another similarity among these historians was their use of a common vocabulary but lack of precision when speaking about autocracy. They equated Russian autocracy (*samoderzhavie*) and European absolutism (*edinovlastie*) and used them interchangeably along with the generic monarchy (*monarkhia*) and invested all the terms with the notion of the "independent and unrestricted power of one ruler, under God."[38] The historians also subscribed to the widely held opinion of the time that there existed three equally valid forms of government, each with its own corrupt form: monarchy (autocracy)/despotism; aristocracy/oligarchy; and democracy/anarchy.[39] Their discussions therefore centered on whether autocracy, despite the risk of despotism, might still be preferable in Russia to aristocracy or democracy, with their threat of becoming oligarchic or anarchic.

Despite these similarities among the historians, their differences in interpreting autocracy remain their single most prominent characteristic. These differences lend them what John B. Bury would call their "permanent interest," the fact that each arose "at a given epoch and is characteristic of the tendencies and ideas of that epoch"[40] and especially, one may add, in an era when histories were unabashedly subjective. While proclaiming the value of Baconian methodology in the search, compilation, analysis, and publication of major historical documents,[41] interpretive history was more prized in the eighteenth century and was still viewed throughout Europe as a branch of literature or as a practical extension of philosophy—philosophy teaching by example—and was expected to reflect the writer's own perceptions.[42] Thus, historians consciously and purposefully expressed the attitudes of their era, and, in Russia, the differences among them offer ideal gauges for charting the much broader discourse about the autocratic idea.

A close reading of the fifty-two extant histories reveals a discourse that falls into three distinct patterns of interpretation, which I am calling the dynastic, the empirical, and the non-despotic models; they are categorized according to what authors understood as the basis for the legitimacy and feasibility of autocracy in Russia. Each interpretation resulted in its own version of historical events, often contradicting the others, and had its own candidate for the worst episode in Russian history, which I call the Antithetical Event. The first two emerged in the Petrine and immediate post-Petrine eras (c. 1710s–1750s), while the third was prevalent in Catherinian Russia (1762–1796). The interpretations neither replaced nor argued against each other but instead accumulated, overlapped, and offered complementary assessments of autocracy's legitimacy, feasibility, and preferability. By the end of the century, all three coexisted, thus producing a rich and nuanced understanding of the idea of autocracy that provided the intellectual context for political attitudes in modern Russia.

The Dynastic Interpretation

The early years of the eighteenth century marked the first break with the Orthodox approach of Gizel''s *Synopsis*. Peter the Great's radical moves to modernize the country and secularize the state coincided with the Early Enlightenment's movement away from Medieval structures of knowledge and value systems based on tradition and religious authority. This atmosphere gave rise to a secular and dynamic interpretation of autocracy. It originated with Mankiev, who was motivated to write history precisely because he wanted to bear witness to the accomplishments of the Petrine era in which he lived and to place it in the context of Russia's past; in other words, he was writing history backwards, influenced by a seminal epoch. Lomonosov, Vasilii Trediakovskii, Ivan Barkov, and a dozen unpublished historians repeated this approach, since they shared Mankiev's secular sensibility and the conviction that lay at the base of his work, namely that Peter's reign represented the culmination of all Russian history, and, given the lackluster character of post-Petrine rulers, that view remained strong until Catherine II ascended the throne.

The dynastic interpretation remained old-fashioned and wedded to the chronicle tradition in its premise that "the genealogy of monarchs forms the

basis of Russian history"[43] and in the polite attitude that any legally born monarch "deserves praise," even an Ivan the Terrible (1533–1584).[44] Its novelty lay
in its emphasis on secular events and material progress, and its replacement of
religious with dynastic sanction and causality. For example, Lomonosov's enor-
mously popular *Short Russian Chronicle* devoted only six lines to the Christiani-
zation of Russia.[45] Previous works equated the history of Russia with the history
of Orthodoxy in Russia, but the new histories equated it with the fortunes
of Russia's two dynasties. The secular leadership of the Riurikids (862–1598)
and the Romanovs (from 1613) was celebrated for causing the country's past
strength and greatness and guiding it toward an even more glorious future.

Dynastic historians presented to the Russian educated public an autocracy
the equal of any ruling house in the rest of Europe, an important desideratum
when the country was just entering the Western family of nations. Legitimacy
rested on resplendent lineage and constant efficacy, traits the historians accentuated even at the dawn of Russian history. The eighteenth-century public generally accepted the idea that "Russia" originated when discordant Slavic tribes
summoned Riurik (?862–?873) and his kin from some distant land to rule over
them. The dynasts, however, wanted to downplay the foreign origin of Russia's
first dynasty and to heighten its grandeur. Embellishing a then dubious and
now discredited chronicle, they upgraded Gostomysl'—the legendary last
leader of ancient Novgorod—into an internationally renowned prince whose
advice was sought by rulers from "distant countries." They then claimed that
his daughter, Queen Umila of Finland, was Riurik's mother; this genealogy resulted in a happy intersection (*peresechenie*) of bloodline that connected the new
dynasty with the family of the last Slavic "prince."[46] To further underscore that
Riurik was "of the highest blood and lineage," these historians resurrected the
old myth that he descended from a long imperial line that stretched from
Assyrian and Egyptian monarchs to David and Solomon, Alexander the Great,
Julius Caesar, Augustus, and Prus.[47] For the dynastic school, the invitation to
Riurik demonstrated that, like any proper people, the Russians recognized the
need for an illustrious ruling clan, which, "by dint of a single blood and for the
common good," could "unite the Slavic peoples into a single tribe under single
rule." Once Riurik "established autocratic power," simultaneously Russia came
into being and immediately "flourished," to use the most common verb (*tsvesti*)
attributed to dynastic leadership.[48]

These authors, rooted in classical learning, depicted autocracy as preferable
to the frequently idealized democratic republics. Having that form of government before Riurik, Russians were portrayed as living in an Hobbesian state
of "envy, feuding, discord, and enmity."[49] Lomonosov rued that medieval
Novgorod's "free charters resulted in a not small cause for the division of Rus-

sia"; he claimed delight when finally Ivan III "abolished the republic ... and brought it under his own autocracy."[50] Since it was popular to recognize a similarity between Roman and Russian history,[51] Lomonosov felt forced to admit that Rome thrived when a republic but concluded: "On the contrary, with difference of opinion and freedom Russia nearly fell into total ruin; autocracy from the beginning strengthened her and, after the unfortunate times, restored, fortified, and made her illustrious." Indeed, an anonymous historian elaborated, under autocratic leadership Russia's history had become "greater than even that of Greece or Rome." Thus, dynasts cast freedom and republicanism in a negative light, associating them historically in Russia with anarchy, civil war, and bloodletting. However, this did not imply that Russians had settled for slavery or despotism, since their autocrats were not tyrants but legitimate and dynamic rulers in whom breathed "the spirit of Numa, the ancient Roman law giver."[52]

Peter the Great—despite his abrogating hereditary succession, something the dynasts chose to ignore—provided final proof of the benefits of hereditary autocracy for Russia. He was the "culmination" of the dynasty, indeed of all dynasties; one history allowed half of its nearly 700 pages for recounting Peter's day-to-day activities and recognized him as the best issue of an ancestral line traced back to Noah. Mankiev saw in Peter's reign a demonstration of the intimate connection between autocracy and progress: "He enlightened all Rus' ..., and it was as though reborn."[53] Lomonosov, likewise awed by Peter's dynamism, pioneered a progressive but cyclical view of Russian history, whose fortunes rose and fell depending on the strength of dynastic leadership. Each stage arose from the ashes of the previous, more glorious than before: "Farsighted sovereigns" ensured that "each misfortune was followed by a prosperity greater than before, each fall by a greater renewal."[54] Thus, the dynastic historians, inspired by Peter's achievements, celebrated his long line of Riurikid and Romanov ancestors. By no longer anchoring legitimacy in divine prescription or merely in bloodline, they announced a dynamic and secular definition of the autocracy, pronouncing it the one form of government with proven historical capacity to avoid anarchy and to bring Russia stability, grandeur, and progress.

The Empirical Interpretation

While the dynastic model became a standard way of viewing autocracy among the educated public, Tatishchev originated a second more theoretical interpretation in the 1730s and 1740s, a view later repeated in the works of three unpublished historians and Emin.[55] Mankiev's formation as an historian resulted from Peter's Westernizing reign, but Tatishchev's arose from his participation in the "Events of 1730," when some members of the aristocracy and nobility had a passing flirtation with placing "conditions" or limitations on the monarch's power.[56] Tatishchev's *History* directly responded to the perceived threat of aristocratic government and to the succession of post-Petrine rulers whose weakness lessened their prestige and political control. Arguing within the intellectual context of the Enlightenment and focusing on the era's two most cherished traits, Tatishchev sought to demonstrate that, nevertheless, autocracy represented the most "rational" and therefore "natural" form of government for Russia.

In the empirical model, history became a laboratory for those abstract principles and natural laws of politics, "which we comprehend . . . through our senses and our reason,"[57] and which could be "scientifically" observed and tested. Tatishchev especially valued the teachings of Christian Wolff (1679–1754) and Christian Thomasius (1655–1728), two leaders of the German Enlightenment. Basing their observations on reason and experience, they concluded, like most European thinkers, that democracies are appropriate only in small states, aristocracies only where there are an educated population and protected borders, and limited monarchy of the British variety only where people are both enlightened and well acquainted with notions of individualism. None of these characteristics applied to Russia. Without such conditions, these thinkers supported a state headed by a willful ruler who would wield unlimited powers and work through a bureaucracy to effect the common good. Logically, Tatishchev denied the feasibility of any form of government except autocracy in a country of Russia's size, location, and cultural level: "Large regions, open borders, in particular where the people are not enlightened by learning and reason and perform their duties from fear rather than an internalized sense of right and wrong must be an [unlimited] monarchy." Anything less than absolute power would invite anarchy and invasion. Hence, Tatishchev reasoned, Peter's unlimited power gave him the right to choose his own successor without regard to bloodline; on this issue, the rationalists stood alone since the other historians respected the overwhelming sentiment in favor of hereditary monarchy.[58]

Unlimited monarchy in Russia was not only the sole rational choice, Tatishchev asserted; experience further suggested that it was also the most natural or innately correct form of government since it functioned like society's most natural and basic institution, the family. The source of autocratic power flowed from the proposition that "the monarch is like a father," with the state a family writ large; thus, the child's or subject's lack of freedom was natural and just until the father or monarch could guide his charges to maturity. This paternal structure also implied an ethical foundation for autocracy, which had been missing with the retreat of the previously dominant religious sanction. Tatishchev believed that there existed natural prohibitions against arbitrary or despotic behavior since fathers and monarchs had no reason and "no power to harm or ruin" their children or subjects, only to promote their "welfare, happiness, [and] security"; at any rate, "natural law will always dictate what is useful or harmful." Thus, Tatishchev embraced the optimistic Enlightenment belief in the necessary functioning of laws that accorded with man's innate sense of morality and could conclude that unlimited power was not only necessary but by nature benevolent. This argument, of course, put a modern patina on the centuries-old paternal view of monarchical stewardship and gave it double resonance.

Switching similes, Tatishchev and Emin also based the legitimacy of autocracy upon its contractual origin, an argument that was considered empirical in the eighteenth century and that was made popular in Russia with the introduction of the writings of Samuel Pufendorf (1632–1694).[59] While the individual (*poddannyi*) is like a child of the ruler, the people as a whole (*narod*) are like a spouse. The contract between ruler and ruled was equated with a marriage contract: it is entered into "fully and rationally" and is "freely made."[60] The dynasts wrote simply that Riurik "established autocratic power" to bring order to the tribes, but Tatishchev and Emin emphasized that a contract had been forged between him and the people. It was the people who recognized the disaster of "freedom," of "each living according to his own will," and it was the people who concluded "that autocratic rule was preferable to anarchy."[61] Then, it was the people who besought "Riurik to take all the power alone" and "firmly establish absolutism"; they "deemed it best to submit to a single rule and, after unanimous agreement, they called Riurik."[62] Thereafter, his descendants signed themselves "tsar and grand prince and autocrat of Russia,"[63] again in keeping with popular consent since the people reasoned that without an unlimited monarch "there existed neither order nor justice." Locke (1632–1704) and his followers excepted, most thinkers in the first half of the eighteenth century, including Tatishchev, believed that such a contract "can be destroyed by no one."[64]

Tatishchev was so convinced of the continuing necessity for unlimited monarchy in Russia that, throughout his *History*, he judged tsars almost solely on their maintenance and increase of autocratic power. For instance, he had no trouble applauding Ivan IV's supposed strengthening of monarchical power, even through a policy of terror; he recognized that Boris Godunov (1598–1605) was a "despoiler of the throne," but at least he ruled autocratically. Like the dynasts, the empirical school extolled Peter, however not as the culmination of the dynasty but of unlimited power; by ending the Patriarchate and denying the need for boyar assent in legislation, Peter finally established full autocracy.[65]

This school thus presented to the Russian educated public an autocracy whose unlimited power was empirically necessary by dint of physical and cultural circumstances, conformity to natural law, and force of contract. Nonetheless, while Tatishchev believed that autocracy alone was suitable in Russia for the foreseeable future, he also believed in progress. He defined it as the gradual accumulation of knowledge—under the leadership of a firm autocrat/father—with each generation building on the achievements of the previous until a fully enlightened population developed; then, and only then, could he envision a lessening of the autocracy's unlimited power and, presumably, only when both tsar and people agreed to renegotiate their contract.[66]

The Nondespotic Interpretation

The dynasts presumed unlimited power on the part of the autocrat and the empiricists regarded it as a necessity; indeed, throughout Europe, philosophes uncritically applauded absolutist monarchs for their capacity quickly to enact enlightened reforms. However, beginning in the 1770s, the focus shifted from the benefits of unlimited power to the danger of its becoming despotic, with power wielded in an oppressive, unjust, cruel, and arbitrary manner and with little concern for the common welfare. In Russia, the *Bironovshchina* during the reign of Anna Ivanovna (1730–1740), the alleged tyranny practiced by Peter III during his brief six months of rule in 1762, and Catherine II's assiduous contrast between her own "rule of law" and the "despotism" of her husband also encouraged discussion of the nature of autocratic power and prevention of its dangers. In this atmosphere, historians gave birth to a new model for interpreting autocracy; they include the remaining seven published authors and a half dozen unpublished ones whose histories were written in roughly the last third of the century. They can be called the nondespotic school since its members strove to validate Russia's form of government as a monarchy and to fight its equation with despotism. These historians absorbed the established image of a dynamic and secular tsar of glorious lineage, proven competence, and empirical necessity. However, the dynasts and empiricists applauded unlimited power. The nondespotic group denied its existence and based the legitimacy and feasibility of autocracy on the grounds that its power had always been *de facto* limited and on the assumption that *de jure* limitations were close at hand.[67]

This school of historians took a defensive posture vis-à-vis Europe in describing autocracy. Probably this stemmed in part from their feeling that they were full-fledged not just fledgling participants in the Enlightenment, but that Russia was not yet recognized as having come of age. Certainly, they were angry that some Europeans regarded autocracy not as the Russian variant of absolutism but as a separate form of "primitive despotism." Boltin, for instance, was incensed by the statement of a French historian that "from ancient times they [the Russians] lived in slavery and always recognized bondage as their natural condition"; Boltin penned two volumes of uninterrupted spleen trying to refute such conceptions.[68] But it was Catherine II who led the attack by beginning her famous *Instruction* (*Nakaz*) to the Legislative Assembly of 1767 with the dictum, "Russia is a European state"; also in her "History," she reminded Enlightenment thinkers of their precept that "humankind everywhere and forever has the same passions, desires, inclinations and for achieving them not rarely uses the same means."[69] In this spirit, Boltin was willing to admit that Ivan IV was a tyrant but only while insisting that he was little different from other rulers of the era, such as Louis XI (1461–1483) of France.[70] In other words, the nondespotic school was intent on defining autocracy as limited in nature, in the same way, *mutatis mutandis*, that other European monarchies were limited by customs, intermediary bodies, or fundamental laws and thus precluding any equation with despotism. Most went further and postulated a firm connection between autocratic government and security of person and property, a commonly held definition of "freedom" in the late eighteenth century, hence bringing the idea of autocracy—sincerely "reinvented"—even more in step with Enlightenment ideals and Russian aspirations.

Prince Shcherbatov, himself a member of one of Russia's oldest aristocratic families, was unique among this group in propounding an aristocratic limitation. His depiction of autocracy centered on its necessity in Russia and on its need to cooperate with the aristocracy; both aspects resulted from the weakness of human nature. Shcherbatov greatly admired David Hume (1711–1776), especially his emphasis on the psychology of both rulers and ruled as causal factors in history. Shcherbatov believed that people in general lack moderation; they act either like "wild beasts after blood" or "like lambs" and eternally engage in a contest between passion and reason and virtue and vice. While Tatishchev marshalled cool abstractions to prove a natural need for autocracy, Shcherbatov stressed that humans' natural beastiality required the guidance of an authoritarian ruler. He believed, like most Enlightenment thinkers, that monarchs were the primary causal factors in state and society, but he deviated in viewing the people as inert or passive under their dominance. A more enlightened population would make more freedom possible, he agreed, but, until then, the people were tabulae rasae upon whom the monarch impressed his mark. The ruler's psychological makeup, intelligence, and character informed the level of laws and these in turn informed the level of morals and manners among the people. In Russia, Shcherbatov warned, whenever the people prematurely tried to control the government, for instance in the Republic of Novgorod, freedom "turned into an evil and one of the causes for Russia's ruin."[71]

While arguing the necessity of autocracy in Russia, Shcherbatov recognized that monarchy, too, had an inherent weakness: rulers themselves were human and hence tempted by such vices as "ambition and despotism." In a theory reminiscent both of premodern Russian conceptions of a "good tsar" and of Montesquieu's *thèse nobiliaire*, he averred that Russian autocrats had avoided these weaknesses by acting in harmony with a council of wise aristocratic elders or boyars; from the time of Riurik, only this "holy union" had provided Russia's defense against despotism. In other words, for Shcherbatov there were two collective actors on the historical stage: rulers and aristocrats. He alone of all the historians made the causal connection that "the state flourishes and its prosperity increases where there is fidelity, honor, unity, and strength in the hearts of the aristocracy," not just of the monarchs. For instance, Shcherbatov directly blamed the dim and childless Tsar Fedor (1584–1598) for the rise of despotism during the Time of Troubles (1598–1613) since he relied on the upstart Boris Godunov for advice rather than on "the most worthy, most farsighted true servants of the fatherland," the old boyars. The problem was compounded by Boris's psychological makeup; he demonstrated a capability for ruling, but his fatal vice, "lust for the throne," led to his hostility to the boyars and thus to his "becoming despotic." The causal flow led, in turn, to the collapse of the economy and autocracy and near extinction at the hands of Sweden and Poland.[72]

Shcherbatov's treatment of Peter the Great was more equivocal. The emperor committed Shcherbatov's trio of mortal sins: he was a man of passion; he failed to consult with boyars; he used despotic measures. However, Shcherbatov forthrightly admired Peter and forgave his sins as normal in the era and because backward Russia needed a forcible thrust into the modern age. While Shcherbatov agreed that Peter "raised despotism to a new extreme," he brought "Russia out of weakness into strength, out of disorder into order, and out of ignorance into enlightenment." In the end, "from his despotism, we received enough enlightenment to criticize that despotism"[73]—a theme that lay at the heart of political discourse in post-Petrine Russia.

Shcherbatov's sponsorship of his own small group's ability to curb despotism had limited appeal among the educated public. In addition, the fact that the boyars were powerless to prevent Ivan IV's despotism weakened Shcherbatov's own confidence in the aristocratic limitation. By the last volume of his *History*, which extends to the year 1610, he seemed to concede that formal guarantees offered more certainty, a solution that grew ever more popular as the century wore on. Vasilii Shuiskii (1606–1610), the "unlucky" boyar-tsar who ruled during the Time of Troubles, was adjudged "glorious among all earthly rulers" since he wanted to take an oath "in keeping with the institution of monarchical power" but with guaranteed legal protection at least of boyar life and property. Shcherbatov, in the dedication of his history to Catherine, prodded her to follow suit: "Since the people have been oppressed for so many centuries already, they await from Your hand their happiness and freedom . . . , the most precious gift of mankind."[74]

Other writers reexamined the historical evidence for curbs on despotism and discovered a Russian political tradition rooted in a traditional elective principle, thus completely contradicting the dynasts' picture in which Riurik imposed autocracy and Tatishchev's concept of a contract in which the people once and forever gave Riurik and his descendants unlimited power. Ivan Elagin emphasized that among the early Russians, "we do not find the slightest sign of autocracy, and even less of despotism, and neither an hereditary throne," but rather "examples of the free election of Leaders or Princes." Other historians of this epoch claimed that Riurik was "never given unlimited power," and that is why his descendants never took a kingly title or crown.[75] Russian rulers, they contended, were never "considered the image of God or earthly gods," and hence "princes, boyars, and the people took part in government and the power of the Grand Princes was not autocratic"; in fact, from the beginning, "the Russian people were free." Boltin cited the people of the city of Vladimir saying: "We are a free people. We chose the princes ourselves, and they kissed the cross to us." Professor Khariton Chebotarev of Moscow University, Catherine's mentor on history, confirmed that "autocratic government in Russia . . . was founded on free and voluntary election" but added that over the centuries people had constantly renewed the election since autocratic rule was consonant with the common good.[76] The motif of autocracy being "chosen" time and again dominated histories in the last third of the century.

The nondespotic school was also anxious to prove that, throughout Russian history, autocracy better guarded freedom, or security of person and property, than the other two forms of government. Medieval Novgorod, according to Chebotarev, demonstrated "the natural and ruinous results of a democracy": "It is not strong enough to uphold and defend the freedom and rights of its citizens." Boltin agreed: "Experience demonstrates that a democratic government cannot preserve the security and tranquility of individual people" as "freedom turns into wilfulness or lack of restraint." For this reason, he explained, Russians long ago understood that "the rule of a single person is incomparably better, profitable, and useful both for society and especially for the individual than the rule of many," where "envy, squabbling, and hatred reign." In addition, "monarchy in a large state is preferable to aristocracy, which normally wastes time in argumentation and is not given to daring views; only a Monarch can launch and carry through actions of great purport." Boltin concluded: "Monarchical government occupies the middle ground between despotism and republics and is the most reliable safeguard of freedom."[77]

In their association of freedom and autocracy, the nondespots tended to be critical of Peter the Great for his use of force in promulgating legislation. Boltin, unlike Shcherbatov, believed that the people, not the tsars, should ultimately make the laws because "laws conform to behavior rather than behavior to laws." He thus preferred Catherine the Great as a "model of wise and great sovereigns" since, in her "golden age," Peter's use of force was no longer employed. But serfdom remained a problem. After agreeing with Rousseau (1712–1778) that slavery is "the primary sin against nature," Boltin temporized and took the position that became standard among moderate and enlightened Russians until the eve of emancipation: only after the soul is freed through education could the body be freed and, then, only "by degrees and gradually." He depicted Catherine the Great as pushing the process forward since she understood how "to teach each subject how to use freedom for the benefit of himself as well as of his neighbor and the fatherland." Himself the owner of 900 male "souls," Boltin hoped that soon legislation would be passed "to limit the powers of landowners over their serfs"[78] and trusted that full freedom, even for the serfs, would be harvested as the "fruit of Catherine's labors." Elagin was equally optimistic. While he was nearly alone among the Russian historians in ruing the "beating down of Novgorod's freedom," that "indubitable beginning of Russian history," he was confident that under Catherine, Novgorod's form of government would be resumed in Russia.[79] Another instance of history being written backwards, Elagin's ideal government not so mysteriously resembled the balance of power and rule of law attained by the eighteenth-century British monarchy.

Thus, this pattern defined autocracy as inherently nondespotic since its power had always been limited *de facto* by aristocratic counsel, fundamental laws, and an elective principle that offered continuous validation. Furthermore, while always protecting freedom, autocracy offered the best hope for evolving *de jure* limitations and guarantees of freedom in the future—especially under the guidance of the "ever-wise legislator," as Catherine the Great liked to be called.[80]

The Antithetical Event

Underscoring their differences, stylistic analysis of the historians' texts discloses their unconscious fixation on what can be called the Antithetical Event. The Antithetical Event was that moment in history when the autocracy as interpreted, legitimized, justified, or defined by a given group was undermined or confronted with its negation. In describing this occurrence, the historians wrote at greater length and used emotional and hyperbolic language in contrast to their usual dry and factual presentation, which more often than not consisted in a ponderous rephrasing of old chronicles. In effect, during narrations of the Antithetical Event, history was transformed into a morality play or cautionary tale. Since this appears to be an unconscious process, it attests to the sincerity of the authors' professed interpretation of the autocracy. In addition, the negative portrayal of certain tsars implied the opposite positive characteristics and confirmed the didactic purpose of Enlightenment history.

Mankiev's *History* is a calm, rather dull, dynastic tale. The author treated the legitimate Ivan the Terrible with gentle courtesy. He even recognized Shuiskii as a legal monarch since he could trace his lineage back to Riurikid grand princes; the boyar-tsar's problems were attributed to "the envy and lack of unity among Russians themselves." The tone dramatically altered when the "illegitimate" Boris Godunov ascended the throne. The dynasts maintained that Fedor, the last of the Riurikid rulers, wanted the throne to go to his cousin, a Romanov; there would then have been yet another "intersection with Riurikid blood" since Anastasia Romanovna had been married to Ivan IV during the "good" part of his reign.[81] Instead Boris, Fedor's brother-in-law, conspired to seize the throne, and the "illegitimacy" of his reign caused the Time of Troubles—not the failure to consult with boyars as Shcherbatov insisted. Mankiev described Boris as odious and personally responsible for flood, famine, inflation, widespread crime, smoking, and drunkenness; in addition, he stood accused of arresting and robbing boyar clans; supposedly, his policies in Astrakhan resulted in such poverty that parents were forced to sell their children into slavery; of course, he had Dmitrii of Uglich, the last of the Riurikids, killed. With a sigh of relief, Mankiev welcomed the return of legitimacy: "And thus, although Boris Godunov, having wanted to rule himself, killed the Tsarevich Dmitrii and sought to kill others, nonetheless, he could not kill the legitimate successor to the Muscovite throne," Mikhail Romanov. Since legitimate, the first Romanov was able to undo Boris's damage and "save Russia from the Swedish and Polish wolves." For dynasts, tirades against Godunov for "alienating the whole people," as Barkov put it, often filled more pages than the deeds of good rulers and occupied as much as one third of the narrative.[82]

Other dynastic historians indicted Sophia Alekseevna for trying to interrupt normal laws of succession. Relying on the support of streltsy or guards regiments, her regency—an attempt to keep her half-brother Peter I and her brother Ivan V (1682–1696) from the throne—lasted from 1682 until 1689 when she finally "lost her lust for the autocracy." Lomonosov's *Chronicle*, while popular, could not be duller in presentation; it consisted of columned tables with the names and dates of rulers, their degrees of removal from Riurik, and pithy descriptions of their years in power. But when confronting the usurper Sophia, Lomonosov wrote a separate essay that depicted confiscation, terror, pillage, heresy, and ill-gotten gains that resulted from this illegitimate rule. While "the boyars, the nobility, and the people loved their sovereigns and ardently desired that they take the reins of government into their own hands," they were filled with "fear." Lomonosov even condoned Peter's personally taking on the role of executioner to finally undo the power of the streltsy: "He made silent his mercy in order to render the justice due."[83]

In a revealing contrast, Sumarokov, who anchored the true legitimacy of an autocrat in both "inheritance and laws," likewise found his Antithetical Event in Sophia's regency but for reasons stemming from the nondespotic interpretation. He considered Sophia a usurper not because of bloodline (she herself was a Romanov) but because "the public had elected" Peter tsar. With the support she received from those "most vile and venomous" armed guards, the government became the tyranny that the nondespotic school feared. Indeed, Sumarokov rendered an exceptional portrait of a good monarchy's antithesis, one similar to the rule of a Caligula or Nero: "the love and warm feeling between monarchs and subjects" disappeared; subjects were turned into "slaves who trembled day and night;" "weapons and wilfulness" replaced regularity of rule; there was a disregard of law, "the foundation on which the prosperity of all the Russian people is based." Sumarokov ended with the didactic peroration that the streltsy episode was "our disgrace!" and Russians should "know the truth and learn."[84]

For Tatishchev and Emin of the empirical school, the Antithetical Event occurred not once but whenever unlimited autocracy was replaced by aristocracy. Darkness and disgust clouded their otherwise arid prose until joy emerged at the return of autocracy. For instance, monarchical power disintegrated in the eleventh and twelfth centuries and in part paved the way for the Mongol Yoke of the thirteenth and fourteenth centuries. Tatishchev sorrowed: "Thus arose aristocracy, but it was without decency. . . . and there was a great bloodletting; and all this gave free reign to the Tatar invader to destroy everything and subjugate everyone to its power and, because of this, autocracy, the strength and honor of Russian sovereigns, was extinguished. . . . as was church learning, and the people were plunged into superstition. . . . And thus it continued for 130 years. . . . until the restoration of the ancient monarchy."[85]

Concerning the Time of Troubles, Boris did not trouble the empiricists since he ruled autocratically, but Shuiskii, Shcherbatov's hero, was accused of overseeing "a pure aristocracy" of seven families and "because of this wayward government, soon the state fell into such extreme ruin and collapse that it barely escaped partition or Polish overlordship." The same seven families attempted to substitute aristocratic rule in 1730, and in Tatishchev's circles open comparisons were made between the two episodes. "A great many" of these "vindictive grandees. . . . were power-hungry, others money-hungry, and others filled with uncontrollable spite against their opponents," and none had any concept of working for the common good or the enlightenment of the people, "the true aims of government," according to Tatishchev.[86] Indeed, a motivation for Tatishchev's writing his history was to discredit forever proponents of aristocracy in Russia by propounding a convincing denunciation drawn from these two historical events.

Shcherbatov defined a good autocrat as one who took boyar advice, and thus his Antithetical Event was the reign of Ivan IV, against whom he directed 1,223 pages of diatribe. When Ivan first began to reign, Shcherbatov asserted, "the conduct of the ruler was completely praiseworthy, as he did nothing of importance without the advice of his relatives and boyars";[87] it should be noted that most other historians, regardless of "school," attributed Ivan's problems to the "envy, bribery, and hypocrisy" he witnessed while under boyar care as a youth.[88] At any rate, for Shcherbatov, when the union between tsar and boyar was broken, "good spirit, love for the fatherland, and fidelity to the ruler were extinguished with fire and sword and in their places were put fear and trembling"; this resulted in the "unbridled power," or despotism, "which autocrats so desire" and can obtain unless restrained by their best and brightest boyars.[89]

In the nondespotic school, Boltin and Mal'gin considered Ivan an aberration and recognized that Boris Godunov had been elected to the throne by a legal assembly. Their Antithetical Event occurred during the reign of Anna Ivanovna, who was herself not a despot—leaving Ivan IV as "the only one" in Russian history—but was dominated by her German favorite, Biron, "an ignoble tyrant" who "robbed the people blind." To heighten their accusation, they contrasted the era of Ernst Johann Biron with the golden age of Catherine when "everyone expresses his opinion freely." But, in the 1730s, "a wife was afraid to speak with her husband, a father with his son, a mother with her daughter about their disastrous condition for fear they would be overheard by servants and denounced." Boltin treated Biron's control of the government and subsequent weakening of monarchical power as a *de facto* aristocracy: "There you have the fruits of aristocratic power. . . . The evil will incessantly multiply and its politics will turn into intrigues, into conspiracies, into confrontations, into discord . . . while ambition and cupidity profit from its disorder."[90]

Thus, inflation of prose, character, and incident occurred whenever arguments in favor of the legitimacy and feasibility of autocracy were refuted by an actual event that betrayed its weaknesses as a form of government: the possibility of rule by favorites; the chaos that might ensue if the line dies out; the incapacity or youth of a monarch that leaves an opportunity for usurpers; the tragic results of a monarch who wields power despotically. Nonetheless, the historians rejected the alternatives. After all, aristocracies and democratic republics were held in low repute or deemed unworkable throughout most of Europe, especially in a large state, and it would seem wisest to take a chance with autocracy. As a dynast, Lomonosov feebly claimed that "the insolence" of a tyrant would be "cut short by death." Tatishchev, the empiricist, considered Ivan IV the single despot and judged that "it would not be sensible to change the former order for such an extraordinary situation." After intense analysis, Boltin concluded: "The ills of a monarchy are ephemeral and light" but "weaknesses in republics are never rectified and remain heavy and lasting"; indeed, "all things considered, it is better to leave things the way they are."[91] Such conclusions were neither reactionary nor even defensive of the status quo. The hope gleamed among these historians that once Russia had achieved an enlightened population, an enlightened autocrat would establish institutionalized limits on absolute power so that, in the words of an often-quoted political aphorism, the ruler would "have all the power to do good and none to do evil." Such a government was the "last, best hope" of most eighteenth-century Europeans, not just Russians, as they moved from adulation of absolutism to a desire for its constitutional limitation.

Overall, the more the critical spirit of the Enlightenment induced eighteenth-century Russian historians to analyze autocracy, the more they became persuaded that it best suited the country's interests. Their message reached a small but influential audience among the educated elite, who all breathed the same rarefied intellectual air and spoke the same "language."[92] The rulers also shared this climate, and this resulted in a dialogue between autocrat and historian never equalled in Russian history. Peter inspired Lomonosov and Tatishchev with his modernizing, Westernizing vision, and they, both as historians and in their other positions, in turn tried to communicate it to his successors. Historians writing during Catherine's era were all as anxious as she to cooperate in making Russia as "civilized" and up to date as the rest of Europe. Throughout the century, the historians' negative pictures of antithetical tsars and positive pictures of ideal rulers fulfilled the didactic purpose of Enlightenment history and invited autocrats to apply current Enlightenment standards to their own reign.

In the next century, historians no longer enunciated a coherent message concerning autocracy. Nicholas Karamzin (1766–1826) urged rulers to stand fast and not follow the path of constitutional monarchy. Sergei Soloviev's (1820–1879) State School of historiography, on the contrary, inherited the eighteenth century's emphasis on evolutionary change from above. Vasilii Kliuchevskii (1841–1911) shifted the focus of history almost entirely away from autocrats to socioeconomic issues. The often reactionary nature of late imperial politics led to the negative portrayals of autocracy that have dominated the twentieth century and once again resulted in its equation with despotism.

In contrast, eighteenth-century histories provide evidence that a representative sample of the educated public engaged in a political discourse that reflected a broad consensus. The idea of autocracy had long been central to Russian political thought and maintained by silent and iconic support based on tradition and religion. But the more modern and secular political context of the eighteenth century fostered a rush to redefine the bases of support. Russians, autocrats included, transformed the idea of autocracy from a static concept into a vital force that could absorb waves of Enlightenment thinking and project a dynamic, rational, and Western image. This constant redefining, reinterpreting, perhaps even reinventing of the idea of autocracy was not necessarily cynical or opportunistic; the scope and quality of discourse suggest sincere belief and serious conviction. Moreover, in this process, autocracy served as a centripetal force in society and was seen to embody its ideals and aspirations.

Revolutionary doctrine remained aberrant in the eighteenth century since the educated public, like the historians, believed that fundamental reforms—emancipation and a limited monarchy—were still premature. An activist and enlightened autocrat engineering gradual change seemed to provide a lucid and pragmatic plan for the present and the future. This program was also consonant with the highest political expectations since, translated to Central and Eastern Europe, the French Enlightenment offered a prescription for modernizing and centralizing a state, not liberating mankind. But by the end of the eighteenth century, autocrats began to show signs of falling behind the times and failing to satisfy newer values and visions, and the educated public itself developed into a more disparate and less accommodating group. While these eighteenth-century thinkers may seem naively optimistic, their identification of autocracy with progress and enlightenment became the fundamental problematic of future political thought—the hope of some, the despair of others.

Notes

The opportunity to examine primary sources for this article was afforded by grants from the National Endowment for the Humanities, the Rockefeller Foundation, IREX, the City University of New York and the Harriman Institute of Columbia University. The first draft of the article was presented at the SSRC Workshop on Imperial Russia (Washington, D.C., 1993) and benefited greatly from suggestions made by participants.

1. The attitudes of all these groups will be analyzed in my forthcoming book, *Autocracy and Progress: The Justification of Absolutism in Eighteenth-Century Russia*. This article, like its companion piece, will focus on the autocrat as a domestic ruler not as an emperor; please see C. H. Whittaker, "The Reforming Tsar: The Redefinition of Autocratic Duty in Eighteenth-Century Russia," *Slavic Review* 51 (Spring 1992): 77–98.

2. The studied manner in which the Russian monarchy worked to elicit such support is a theme in Richard S. Wortman's *Scenarios of Power: Myth and Ceremony in Russian Monarchy*, vol. 1, *From Peter the Great to the Death of Nicholas I* (Princeton, 1995).

3. The three professional historians who were at work in Russia in the century— Gottlieb Baier (1694–1738), Gerhard Müller (1705–1783), and August-Ludwig Schlözer (1735–1809)—are not included in this study since they were imported German academicians, and therefore their works would not necessarily reflect Russian perspectives on the autocracy, but see A. B. Kamenskii, "Akademik G.-F. Miller i russkaia istoricheskaia nauka XVIII veka," *Istoriia SSSR* 1 (1989): 144–59. Also consult S. M. Solov'ev, "Pisateli russkoi istorii XVIII veka," *Arkhiv istoriko-iuridicheskikh svedenii* 2 (1855): 3–82; P. N. Miliukov, *Glavnye techeniia russkoi istoricheskoi mysli* (Moscow, 1897): 17–19, 70–146; S. A. Peshtich, *Russkaia istoriografiia XVIII veka* 1 (Leningrad, 1961), 194, 222–62.

4. A. I. Mankiev, *Iadro rossiiskoi istorii* (St. Petersburg: published in 1770, 1784, 1791, 1799).

5. V. N. Tatishchev, *Istoriia rossiiskaia*, 6 vols. (Moscow, 1768–1784) and *Istoriia rossiiskaia*, 7 vols. (Moscow, 1962–1968).

6. M. V. Lomonosov: *Kratkii rossiiskii letopisets s rodosloviem* (St. Petersburg, 1759); *Drevniaia rossiiskaia istoriia ot nachala rossiiskago naroda do konchiny velikago kniazia Iaroslava Pervago ili do 1054 goda* (St. Petersburg, 1766), written from 1754 to 1758.

7. M. M. Shcherbatov, *Istoriia rossiiskaia ot drevneishikh vremen*, 7 vols. (St. Petersburg, 1774–1791); the quotation is located in *Pis'mo kniazia Shcherbatova k priiateliu* (Moscow, 1788), 140.

8. I. N. Boltin: *Primechaniia na istoriiu drevniia i nyneshniia Rossii Leklerka*, 2 vols. (St. Petersburg, 1788); *Kriticheskiia primechaniia na istoriiu Kn. Shcherbatova*, 2 vols. (St. Petersburg, 1793–1794).

9. T. S. Mal'gin, *Zertsalo rossiiskikh gosudarei ot rozhdestva Khristova s 862 po 1791 god* (St. Petersburg, 1791).

10. Catherine II is the only writer of history in this group who is not Russian-born. Ekaterina II, "Zapiski kasatel'no rossiiskoi istorii," *Sobesednik liubitelei rossiiskago slova* 1–11 (1783), 12–15 (1784). Published anonymously, the "Zapiski" take up roughly seventy pages of each issue of the journal; she followed an outline prepared for her by Professor Kh. A. Chebotarev (1746–1815) of Moscow University, *Vstuplenie v nastoiashchuiu istoriiu o Rossii* (Moscow, 1847).

11. In order of date of birth, they include V. K. Tred'iakovskii (1703–1769), *Tri razsuzhdeniia o trekh glavneishikh drevnostiakh rossiiskikh* (St. Petersburg, 1773); A. P. Sumarokov

(1718–1777), "Kratkaia Moskovskaia letopis' (1774)," "Kratkaia istoriia Petra Velikago (n.d.)" and "Streletskii bunt (1768)," *Polnoe sobranie sochinenii* 6 (Moscow, 1781): 161–79, 234–42 and 185–228; I. P. Elagin (1725–1794), *Opyt povestvovaniia o Rossii* (St. Petersburg, 1803); I. S. Barkov (1732–1768), "Sokrashennaia rossiiskaia istoriia," in Gilmar Kuras, *Sokrashennaia universal'naia istoriia* (St. Petersburg, 1762), 357–90; F. A. Emin (1735–1770), *Rossiiskaia istoriia* (St. Petersburg, 1767–1769); and N. I. Novikov (1744–1818), *Opyt istoricheskago slovaria o rossiiskikh pisateliakh* (St. Petersburg, 1772).

12. I have read, as far as I can judge, all the extant histories. The manuscripts are located in the Archive of the St. Petersburg Institute of History of the Russian Academy of Sciences (hereafter, using an acronym based on the Russian name, SOII), The Library of the Russian Academy of Sciences located in St. Petersburg (BRAN), the Manuscript Division of the Russian National Library located in Moscow (RO), and the Russian State Archive of Ancient Acts located in Moscow (RGADA). I have not included the hundreds of chronologies and genealogies since they offer little interpretation. I am grateful to Dr. E. B. Beshenkovskii, the Slavic bibliographer of Columbia University, for sharing with me his deep knowledge of these manuscript collections.

13. In the tradition of Pierre Bayle's *Dictionnaire historique et critique* (1697) and J. G. Walch's *Philosophisches Lexicon* (1726), Tatishchev attempted a compendium of knowledge but only reached the entry "kliuchnik": *Leksikon rossiiskoi. Istoricheskoi, geograficheskoi, politicheskoi i grazhdanskoi*, 3 vols. (St. Petersburg, 1793). Shcherbatov translated works on legal, ethical, and philosophical themes: M. D'iakonov, "Vydaiushchiisia russkii publitsist XVIII veka," *Vestnik prava* 7 (1904): 1–27. Boltin had a superb library of Enlightenment books and translated the *Encyclopédie* to the letter "k": V. Iushkov, *Ocherk iz istorii russkago samosoznaniia XVIII-go veka. Obshchie istoricheskie vzgliady I. N. Boltina* (Kiev, 1912). Elagin was typical in the sources he used and cited: Mably, Rousseau, Robertson, Hume, d'Alembert, Voltaire, and Pufendorf: *Opyt, passim*. Edward L. Keenan agrees that Western culture was rapidly assimilated in this century, while Stephen L. Baehr disagrees: "The Trouble with Muscovy: Some Observations upon Problems of the Comparative Study of Form and Genre in Historical Writing," *Medievalia et Humanistica* 5 (1974): 104; *The Paradise Myth in Eighteenth-Century Russia* (Stanford, 1991), xi.

14. Iu. M. Lotman and B. A. Uspenskii, "The Role of Dual Models in the Dynamics of Russian Culture," in *The Semiotics of Russian Culture*, ed. A. Shukman (Ann Arbor, Mich., 1984), 35.

15. Emin, *Rossiiskaia istoriia* 1:1–2.

16. The quotation is found in N. L. Rubinshtein, *Russkaia istoriografiia* (Moscow, 1941), 138. On the broader implications of this topic, consult Hans Rogger, *National Consciousness in Eighteenth-Century Russia* (Cambridge, Mass., 1960).

17. As quoted in Mankiev, *Iadro*, i. For similar injunctions, see "Istoriia rossiiskaia s 1450 po 1617 (c. 1711)," f. 115, n. 543:45, SOII; Tatishchev, *Istoriia rossiiskaia* 1 (Moscow, 1962): 81.

18. Lomonosov: "Report (21 Jun 1750)," *PSS* 6:79–80; "Zamechaniia na dissertatsiiu G.-F. Millera 'Proiskhozhdenie imeni i naroda rossiiskogo', *PSS* 6:17–79; *Istoriia*, 173–216.

This sensitivity was not confined to Russians; at this time, an historian, Fréret, was sent to the Bastille for maintaining that the Franks were not of the Gallic race: G. P. Gooch, *History and Historians in the Nineteenth Century* (Boston, 1959), 13.

19. Boltin, *Leklerk* 1:1; also see V. O. Kliuchevskii, "Lektsii po russkoi istoriografii," *Sochineniia* (Moscow, 1959), 426.

20. On this issue, consult Franco Venturi, "History and Reform in the Middle of the Eighteenth Century," *The Diversity of History*, ed. J. H. Elliott and H. G. Koenigsberger (Ithaca, N.Y., 1970), 225–44.

21. Voltaire, *Collection complète des Oeuvres* (Geneva, 1768–1777), 12:52 ("*L'Esprit des Lois* de M. de Montesquieu"); 30:455 ("Sommaire de l'Histoire"). When, in 1756, his *Essai sur les Moeurs et l'Esprit des Nations* went on sale in St. Petersburg, it sold an unprecedented 3,000 copies on the first day: Émile Haumant, *La Culture française en Russie* (Paris, 1910), 110.

22. Please consult: Whittaker, "The Reforming Tsar," *passim*.

23. Mal'gin, *Zertsalo*, 3.

24. G. Vasnetskii, *M. V. Lomonosov: Ego filosofskie i sotsial'no-politicheskie vzgliady* (Moscow, 1954), 14–18.

25. Ekaterina II, "Istoricheskoe predstavlenie iz zhizni Riurika: Podrazhenie Shekspiru," *PSS* 1 (St. Petersburg, 1893), 133; Mankiev, *Iadro*, 180–81; Mal'gin, *Zertsalo*, 28.

26. Tatishchev: "Kratkoe iz"iatie iz velikikh del Petra Velikogo, imperatora vserossiiskogo," in P. Pekarskii, "Novye izvestiia o V. N. Tatishcheve," *Zapiski Imperatorskoi Akademii nauk* 4 (1864): 18–19; *Istoriia* 1 (Moscow, 1962), 87. Also consult A. I. Iukht, "V. N. Tatishchev o reformakh Petra I," *Obshchestvo i gosudarstvo feodal'noi Rossii*, ed. V. T. Pashuto (Moscow, 1975), 209–18; in a similar vein, see Feofan Prokopovich, *Istoriia imperatora Petra Velikago, ot rozhdeniia ego do Poltavskoi batalii* (Moscow, 1788), written at the beginning of the century and not a history but a chronology.

27. Sumarokov, "Streletskii bunt," 179; Mal'gin, *Zertsalo*, 141–43. Mal'gin's entry for Peter the Great, for instance, devoted 50 percent to his domestic deeds, while Lomonosov devoted 95 percent to his military exploits; 95 percent of Mal'gin's entry on Catherine relates to domestic events and Peter III is condemned for being an "enthusiast for military affairs."

28. Tatishchev, *Istoriia* 2 (Moscow, 1773): 460.

29. V. Ikonnikov, "Boltin," *Russkii biograficheskii slovar'* 3 (New York: Kraus Reprint, 1962), 188.

30. "Predislovie k istoricheskoi knige, sostavlennoi po poveleniiu Tsaria Feodora Alekseevicha," in E. Zamyslovskii, *Tsarstvovanie Fedora Alekseevicha* (St. Petersburg, 1871), app. 4:xxxix.

31. Lomonosov: *Istoriia*, 171; "Posviashchenie k pervomu tomu 'Istorii rossiiskoi' V. N. Tatishcheva," *PSS* 6:15–16.

32. Tatishchev: *Istoriia* 1 (1768), i–iv; *Razgovor o pol'ze nauk i uchilishch* (Moscow, 1887): 65 (written in 1733).

33. Novikov, *Opyt*, 1–3.

34. See, for instance, Ellen Hurwitz, "Metropolitan Hilarion's *Sermon on Law and*

The Idea of Autocracy 55

Grace: Historical Consciousness in Kievan Rus'," Russian History 7 (1980): 322–33; and M. N. Tikhomirov, "Razvitie istoricheskikh znanii v Kievskoi Rusi . . . X–XVII vv.," *Ocherki istorii istoricheskoi nauki v SSSR,* ed. M. N. Tikhomirov (Moscow, 1955), 89–105.

35. "Istoriia o nachale russkoi zemle (1760–1761)," f. 735, n. 178:41–46, RO; "Nashestvie tatar v Rossiiu i rodoslovie velikikh kniazei rossiiskikh," f. 36, op. 1:451–61, SOII; "Letopisets, 1222–1555," f. 36, op. 1:129–440, SOII; "Letopisets kratkii do 1659 goda: Sbornik 1754 g.," Rumiantsev, f. 256, n. 374:252–57, RO; "Kratkii letopisets: Khronograf Dorofeia Monemvasiiskogo (1731)," f. 178, n. 1256:334–56, RO; "Vypiski iz letopistsa za 1154–1571 gg. (1784–1791)," f. 151:40–42, RO.

36. The exception was P. A. Zakhar'in (1750–1800), *Novyi sinopsis* (Nikolaev, 1798). But most, often lengthy and laboriously copied, remained in the archives, for instance, "Russkaia istoriia (1758)," Likhachev, f. 238, n. 1, SOII; "Letopisets rossiiskii (1756)," 16.4.1:1–660, BRAN.

37. Innokenti Gizel', *Sinopsis* (published in Kiev in 1674, 1678, 1680, and 1683; in St. Petersburg, published twenty times in the eighteenth century and in 1823, 1836, and 1861.

38. On the problems of translating these terms, consult Isabel de Madariaga, "Autocracy and Sovereignty," *Canadian-American Slavic Studies* 16 (Fall-Winter 1982): 369–87, definition on 374.

39. Montesquieu, in Book II of *The Spirit of the Laws,* defines the "three species of government" as republican (under which he subsumes aristocracy and democracy), monarchical, and despotic.

40. John B. Bury, *The Ancient Greek Historians* (New York, 1909), 252.

41. On Tatishchev's contributions, consult: S. N. Valk, "V. N. Tatishchev i nachalo novoi russkoi istoricheskoi literatury," *XVIII vek* 7 (1966), 71–72; Boltin, as another example, edited a model edition of *Pravda russkaia* (St. Petersburg, 1792).

42. See, for instance, J. B. Black, *The Art of History: A Study of Four Great Historians of the Eighteenth Century* (New York, 1965) and Preserved Smith, *The Enlightenment, 1687–1776* (New York, 1962), 202–30.

43. "Rodoslovie gosudarei rossiiskikh ot pervoi Riurika do tsaria Feodorova Ivanovicha (c. 1750)," f. 187, op. 2, ed.khr. 115:2, RGADA. In the archives, there are dozens of lengthy genealogical studies that examine every rivulet of the Riurikid clan, for example: "Sbornik: Otryvok iz rodoslovnoi velikikh kniazei i gosudarei do Ekateriny (1776)," f. 218, n. 695:1–114, RO; "Kniga rodoslovnaia (1765)," 4.1.36: 182 pages of graphs, BRAN; "Nachalo kniazheniia rossiskikh kniazei do Elizavetoi Petrovnoi," f. 218, n. 676:26–52, RO.

44. Mankiev, *Iadro,* 181.

45. D. D. Shampai, "O tirazhakh 'Kratkogo rossiiskogo letopistsa s rodosloviem'," *Literaturnoe tvorchestvo M. V. Lomonosova,* ed. P. N. Berkov & I. Serman (Moscow, 1966), 282–85 (it was published in a tirage of 2,400, the largest in the century).

For instance, while dynastic histories concentrated on the political struggle between autocracy and republicanism in fifteenth-century Novgorod, the ecclesiastical histories were concerned with its flirting with foreign faiths: "Gistoriia drevniaia rossiiskaia o kniazhei (1756)," 16.4.1:4, BRAN.

46. Catherine includes all these emendations to Russian history in her "Zapiski": 2:75, 78–79, 87–89 and in her play, "Istoricheskoe predstavlenie," 120–21. Riurik also began to "speak Slavic" by the end of the century: Zakhar'in, *Novyi sinopsis*, 26; Mal'gin, *Zertsalo*, 2. Also see A. S. C. Ross, "Tatishchev's 'Joachim Chronicle,' " *University of Birmingham Historical Journal* 3 (1951): 53–54.

47. "O tsariakh," f.36, op. 1, n. 644:5–31, SOII; "Letopisets ot nachala russkoi zemli do tsaria Alekseia Mikhailovicha," f. 310, n. 1283:5, RO; "Rodoslovnaia kniga velikikh i udel'nykh kniazei: 81 glava s tablitsami (1768)," f. 181, op. 1, ed.khr. 176:1–7, RGADA.

48. Lomonosov: *Letopisets*, 291–96; *Istoriia*, 214–16; an anonymous historian claimed that Riurik built "over 100 cities": "O prishestvii velikago kniazia Riurika na veliko novogorodskoe kniazhenie i o velikikh kniazekh i tsarei prezhde byvshikh v Rossii (1768)," 31.4.16:23, BRAN. See, for instance, the classic by I. K. Kirilov, *Tsvetushchee sostoianie vserossiiskogo gosudarstva*, ed. V. A. Rybakov (Moscow, 1977), reprint of version published in 1727–1730.

49. Mankiev, *Iadro*, xi–xii.

50. Lomonosov, *Letopisets*, 300, 319. Alexander Radishchev's preoccupation with Novgorod is evident in his historical jottings: "K rossiiskoi istorii," *PSS* 3:31–40.

51. "Razsuzhdenie o rossiiskoi i rimskoi pravitel'stvakh," f. 17, n.343; E. K. Putnyn', *Istoki russkoi istoriografii antichnosti: M. V. Lomonosov, A. N. Radishchev* (Saratov, 1968); Allen McConnell, "Radishchev and Classical Antiquity," *Canadian-American Slavic Studies* 16 (Fall-Winter, 1982): 469–90; Stephen L. Baehr, "From History to National Myth: *Translatio imperii* in Eighteenth-Century Russia," *Russian Review* 27, 1 (January 1978): 1–14.

52. Lomonosov, *Istoriia*, 171, 214–16, 220.

53. "Istoriia russkaia (c. 1750)," 32.13.1:372–671, BRAN; another allots 138 of its 213 pages to Peter: "Drevnaia rossiiskaia istoriia do 1710 goda (1786)," f. 11, ed.khr.19, SOII. One anonymous author began in the style of an ecclesiastical history but then, as if unable to suppress himself, spent the rest of the manuscript recounting Peter's deeds: "Russkaia istoriia svodnaia (c. 1750)," 25.1.3:42–179, BRAN. Mankiev, *Iadro*, 383–84.

54. Lomonosov is quoted in F. Ia. Priima, "Lomonosov i 'Istoriia rossiskoi imperii pri Petre Velikom' Voltera," *XVIII vek* 3 (1958): 183. On Lomonosov's political views, which were quite unsophisticated despite his being tutored by Christian Wolff, consult A. A. Morozov, "M. V. Lomonosov i teleologiia Kristiana Vol'fa," *Literaturnoe tvorchestvo M. V. Lomonosova*, ed. P. Berkov and I. Serman (Moscow, 1962), 163–96; M. I. Sukhomlinov, "Lomonosov, student Marburgskogo universiteta," *Russkii vestnik* 31 (1861), 127–65; Walter Gleason, "The Two Faces of the Monarch: Legal and Mythical Fictions in Lomonosov's Ruler Imagery," *Canadian-American Slavic Studies* 16 (1982), 399–409.

55. On his strange career, consult E. B. Beshenkovskii: "Zhizn' Fedora Emina," *XVIII vek* 11 (1976): 186–203; "Istorigraficheskaia sud'ba 'Rossiiskoi istorii' F. A. Emina," *Istoriia i istoriki* (Moscow, 1973).

56. Peter the Great, though, was Tatishchev's original inspiration as well for writing history: P. Znamenskii, "Tatishchev i ego istoriia," *Trudy Kievskoi dukhovnoi akademii* 1 (1862): 197–228.

57. Tatishchev, *Istoriia* 1 (Moscow, 1962): 359.

58. Tatishchev: *Razgovor*, 136–37; *Istoriia* 1 (Moscow, 1962), 362, 371. In *Russia under Catherine the Great* 1 (Newtonville, 1978), the editor, Paul Dukes, claims that Tatishchev influenced Montesquieu in this view: 18–19.

59. S. Pufendorf, *L'Introduction à l'histoire générale . . . où l'on voit . . . les interêts des souverains* (Amsterdam, 1743); translated into Russian and published in 1718, 1723, 1767, 1777.

60. Tatishchev: *Istoriia* 1 (Moscow, 1962), 359–61; *Razgovor*, 135–40; "Proizvol'noe i soglasnoe razsuzhdenie i mnenie sobravshegosia shliakhetstva russkogo o pravlenii gosudarstvennom," *Utro* (1859): 371. Also see Emin, *Istoriia* 1:x.

61. Mankiev, *Iadro*, 18–27; Tatishchev, *Istoriia* 2 (Moscow, 1963), 33–34; Emin, *Istoriia* 1:38–39.

62. "Drevnaia rossiiskaia istoriia do 1710 goda (1786)," f. 11, ed.khr. 19:35, SOII.

63. "Russkaia letopis' s drevneishikh vremen do 1700 g. (1741)," f. 181, op. 1, ed.khr. 358:707, RGAGA.

64. Tatishchev, *Istoriia* 2 (Moscow, 1963), 33–34; Emin, *Istoriia* 1:38–39; "Russkaia istoriia ot Riurika do Ekateriny (c. 1735)," 32.6.1:1–16, BRAN.

65. Tatishchev: "Razsuzhdenie," 369–79; *Istoriia* 1 (Moscow, 1962), 87; "Kratkoe iz"iatie," 18–19; Emin, *Istoriia* 1:27.

66. Tatishchev: *Istoriia* 1 (Moscow, 1768), 18 and 2 (Moscow, 1963), 137–43.

67. The question of whether or not there were limitations on the tsar's power has its own long history; see, for instance, Daniel Rowland, "Did Muscovite Literary Ideology Place Limits on the Power of the Tsar (1540s–1660s)?" *The Russian Review* 49 (April 1990): 125–55.

68. Boltin, *Leklerk*, II:471; also see V. S. Ikonnikov, *Istoricheskie trudy Boltina* (St. Petersburg, 1902), 18–20. He attacked Nicholas LeClerc, *Histoire physique, morale, civile et politique de la Russie ancienne et moderne*, 6 vols. (Paris, 1783–1794) which was based on P. S. Levecque, *Histoire de Russie*, 5 vols. (Paris, 1782–1783).

69. Ekaterina II: "Zapiski," I:105; "Mnenie Gosudaryni Ekateriny II o tom, kak dolzhno pisat' Russkuiu istoriiu," *Russkii vestnik* 5 (1816): 3–11. Boltin agreed: "Read through the past centuries of all kingdoms and of all republics and you will find the same behavior, conduct, and actions. . . . virtue and vice belong to all ages and to all nations," and to both sexes, he added, when someone tried to claim that female monarchs are more kindly and moderate than male ones: "Women are simply people and have the same virtues and the same vices." Boltin, *Leklerk* 2:1. 82–87, 172–73, 423–24.

70. Boltin, *Leklerk* 1:306–310; 2:17. Michael Cherniavsky makes much the same argument in "Ivan the Terrible as Renaissance Prince," *Slavic Review* 27 (1968), 195–211.

71. Shcherbatov, *Istoriia*: 1 (1794): xv, 280–81; 2 (1805): 257.

72. Shcherbatov, *Istoriia*: 2 (1783): 541–42; 5, pt. 2 (1786): 111; 6 (1790): 50–53; 7, pt. 1 (1790): 262–64; "Istoriia rossiiskaia (1766)," 45.8.268:9, BRAN.

73. Shcherbatov, "Razsmotrenie o porokakh i samovlastii Petra Velikago," *Chteniia v Imperatorskom Obshchestve istorii i drevnostei rossiiskikh* (1860): 8–9, 14, 19.

74. Shcherbatov, *Istoriia*: 7 (1790): 131; 1 (1794), n.p.

75. The quotations are Elagin's, *Opyt*, 1:81, 166–67. Similar sentiments are expressed

in "Istoriia rossiiskaia ot Ivana Groznogo do kontsa XVII veka," f. 115, ed.khr. 91:80, SOII; "Ob izbranii na tsarskii prestol Mikhaila Feodorovicha," f. 36, op. 1, n. 645:107–109, SOII; Boltin: *Shcherbatov* 1:230–31; *Leklerk* 1:250–51; 2:289–90, 464, 471–75.

76. Shcherbatov, *Istoriia* 1 (1794): 191–92, 225; 2 (1805): 5; Boltin: *Shcherbatov*, 1:176–78. Boltin on Vladimir: *Otvet general maiora Boltina na pis'mo kniazia Shcherbatova* (St. Petersburg, 1789), 129–30; E. A. Bolkhovitinov (Mitropolit Evgenii, 1767–1837), *Istoricheskoe obozrenie rossiiskago zakonopolozheniia* (St. Petersburg, 1826), v (originally published in 1797). Chebotarev, *Vstuplenie*, 19.

77. Chebotarev, *Vstuplenie*, 4; Boltin, *Leklerk* 2:476–78.

78. Boltin, *Leklerk* 1:316–18; 2:22–23, 104, 172, 206–09, 233–37, 251, 254–55, 330, 360–62.

79. Elagin, "Opyt povestvovaniia o Rossii (1790)," f. 181, ed.khr. 34, pt. 1:1–28, RGADA.

80. Zakhar'in, *Novyi sinopsis*, v.

81. This handing over of the scepter, with "Godunov looking on with envious eyes" is one of the great "moments in Russian history" that Lomonosov thought should be depicted in painting: Lomonosov, "Idei dlia zhivopisnykh kartin iz rossiiskoi istorii," *PSS* 6:371.

82. "Rodoslovie gosudarei rossiiskikh ot pervoi Riurika do tsare Feodorova Ivanovicha (c. 1750)," f. 187, op.2, ed.khr. 115:4, RGADA, Mankiev, *Iadro*, 210–31, 264, 271, 236, 328; "Russkaia letopis' s drevneishikh vremen do 1700 g. (1741)," f. 181, op. 1, ed.khr. 358:1117, RGADA; "Kratkoe ob"iavlenie o samoderzhavtsakh rossiiskikh (1759)," f. 1274, op. 1, n. 3016:20–30; Barkov, *Istoriia*, 372–75.

83. "Russkaia letopis' s drevneishikh vremen do 1700 g. (1741)," f. 181, op. 1, ed.khr. 358:1176–1255, RGADA; Lomonosov, "Opisanie streletskikh buntov i pravleniia tsarevy Sof'i," *PSS* 6:100–31.

84. Sumarokov, "Bunt," 192–97, 205, 218–19.

85. Tatishchev, *Istoriia* 1 (Moscow, 1962), 366–67; Emin, *Istoriia* 2:522.

86. D. A. Korsakov, "Artemii Petrovich Volynskii i ego 'konfidenty'," *Russkaia starina* 10 (1885): 28. Tatishchev made his argument in four places: *Istoriia* 1 (Moscow 1962), 366–68 and 4 (Moscow, 1964), *passim*; *Razgovor*, 138–39; and "Razsuzhdenie," 370–73. On his commitment to Enlightenment, see *Istoriia* 2 (Moscow, 1963), 78–81. In contrast, the older ecclesiastical histories were more concerned about the threat of Roman Catholicism replacing Russian Orthodoxy if Poland had succeeded in conquering Russia: "Istoriia rossiiskaia 1740 g.," 16.13.6: 396–419, BRAN; "Gistoriia drevnyia rossisskaia o kniazhei (1756)," 16.4.1: 81–96, BRAN; "Istoriia rossiiskaia (1715)," m.4698: 106–245, RO.

87. Shcherbatov, *Istoriia* 5, pt. 3 (1786): 217. Another historian who shared Shcherbatov's views devoted 312 pages of a 675-page narrative to the "Tsar-Tormentor": "O samoderzhavstve godudarei tsarei vseia Rossii (1768)," 31.4.16, II:45–367, BRAN.

88. Mankiev, *Iadro*, 190; "Istoriia rossiiskaia (1740)," 16.13.6:386, BRAN.

89. Shcherbatov, *Istoriia* 5: pt. 2:91, 287–89; pt. 3:222–23.

90. Boltin, *Leklerk* 2:467–71, 476–78, 522–23. Mal'gin quotes Boltin's condemnation word for word but adds that he was just as bad as Ivan the Terrible: *Zertsalo*, 117.

91. Lomonosov, *Istoriia*, 233; Tatishchev, "Razsuzhdenie," 373; Boltin, *Leklerk* 2:476–78, 355.

92. Their works began appearing in 1755 during the publication explosion of the last half of the century and were usually published in tirages of 600, 1,200, and 2,400; readership figures are not available, but they are probably small.

For a definition of "language" in semiotic terms, please see B. A. Uspenskii, "Historia sub specie semioticae," in Daniel P. Lucid, ed., *Soviet Semiotics* (Baltimore, 1977): 107–108.

3

The Russian Imperial Family as Symbol

Richard Wortman

—•—⟨∞⟩—•—

O N THE OCCASION of his coronation, Easter Sunday, April 5, 1797, Emperor
Paul I issued two edicts that drew a close connection between the flourishing of the imperial family and the well-being of the state.[1] He decreed his
Law of Succession, then had it placed "for preservation" in an ark in the
Assumption Cathedral. The law supplanted the Petrine rule of designation with
an order of hereditary succession. Paul sought to ensure "the tranquillity of
the State," to be "based on a firm law of inheritance upon which every right-
thinking person is certain." A Statute of the Imperial Family, issued the same
day, declared the "increase of the Sovereign family (*familiia*)" one of the grounds
for the "illustrious condition" of the state. Russia had experienced the principal
blessing, "seeing the inheritance of the Throne confirmed in Our Family, which
may the All-High perpetuate to eternity." The statute specified the estates and
revenues to go to members of the family, the titles they held, and the rules of
inheritance they would observe. It established an appanage department to manage the family's estates and income.[2]

The need to restore a reliable order of succession was widely understood in
Russia during the second half of the eighteenth century. Leaving the succession
to each ruler's discretion had put the throne at the disposition of the cliques
in the court, particularly the guards' regiments. The turmoil accompanying
each succession, it was clear, endangered the security of the state. Catherine II,
herself a beneficiary of this situation, composed projects for a new succession
law in 1766 and 1785. Both projects contended that such a law was necessary to
preserve the unity and indivisibility of the empire, the reason that Peter had
cited in justification of succession by designation.[3] But Catherine did not issue
a succession law. Indeed, hereditary succession, though preferable in principle,
hardly suited the interests or tastes of Russian monarchs of the late eighteenth
century. Even after Paul promulgated his law, it proved hard to follow, and neither he nor Alexander acted in a way to implant a firm or certain system of in-

heritance. A dynastic tradition could not be established by an edict alone; it required the elevation of family values and patterns of public conduct and these took hold in Russia only in the second quarter of the nineteenth century. The law could only have the desired effect when it corresponded to the principal symbols that the monarch used to represent his power. This paper will discuss the emergence of the imperial family as principal symbol of Russian monarchy as it was presented to the elite in ceremonies, literature, and visual representation—what I call a dynastic scenario.

The modes of behavior and representation that governed the imperial court until 1825 were consistent with the principles underlying Peter the Great's succession law of 1722. The law stated the fundamental incompatibility between the principle of inheritance and Peter's own conception and practice of monarchy. Petrine absolutism was grounded on a principle of utility; the monarch's dedication to the well-being of the state justified his extensive authority. Peter's statutes proclaimed the submergence of the past, and the principle of hereditary monarchy could hardly withstand this razor. An ineffectual or destructive son was an obstruction to the goals of monarchy. The succession took on the features of an oedipal drama recounted in Alain Besançon's account of the bitter struggle ending in the death of Alexei Petrovich. Peter's second-born son, Peter Petrovich, had died in 1719, thereby depriving him of a male heir. The succession law projected the father-son conflict into the next century. The son, possessed by "the malice of Absalom," was an ever-present threat to the throne, the greatest source of instability and a peril to the general good. These notions were formulated and elaborated in the *Pravda voli monarshei*, which has been generally attributed to Feofan Prokopovich.[4]

The results of the law are well-known to us from the series of coups and the constant fears of plots and usurpers that menaced the throne during the eighteenth century. But a law does not operate in a vacuum and in many respects it continued to reflect the dominant values of the rulers and the court. The utilitarian legitimation continued to dominate in the manifestos, odes, coronation orations, and the symbolism of the court in the eighteenth century. As Cynthia Whittaker has shown, the conception of the "reformer-tsar" defined the persona of each of the monarchs. In a more practical sense, the absence of a husband for the reigning empress ensured that the well-being of the noble elite would be observed. In either case, an heir was an incubus, menacing the claims based as much or more on achievements than hereditary rights. The heir represented a potential challenge to the claims of having ushered in an "age of gold" or paradise; his existence, posing the suggestion of an alternative, impugned the panegyric mystique.[5]

Thus, Elizabeth designated Peter of Holstein her successor, keeping him and his wife Catherine under close watch, but there was already an effort to remove him before she breathed her last. Peter III pointedly omitted mention of his son, Paul, in his decree of accession, which became one of the grounds cited by Catherine II when she deposed him seven months later. Catherine herself may have viewed hereditary monarchy as a necessity to maintain the stability of empire, and she called him "heir" in her accession manifesto, but confirming her son's rights was something that she never ventured to do, and rumors, probably without substance, suggested that she wished to replace him with her grandson, Alexander, in the last years of her reign.[6]

The utilitarian premise was not an abstract idea but a behavioral principle affirmed in the statements and ceremonies of the imperial court. The metaphor of a god, the performance of classical allegories in the court, were meant to set the ruler apart, to show him or her as the exemplification of eternal values of reason, beauty, and justice, achieved by the reign of a sovereign qua deity. The standard of conduct set by the courts of France and the German principalities hardly emulated the biblical image of the righteous and humble nuclear family. The word "virtue" was used to designate the type of civil behavior consonant with the conduct of the genteel servant of the state and not Christian probity. The escapades of the empresses were hardly matters for discreet silence. Indeed, for those following the example of Louis XIV, the display of lovers was a display of power, Eros, and wisdom, representing modalities of a classical symbolic of transcendence.

The members of the ruler's family were included in the realm of monarchical representation during the eighteenth century. Peter the Great designated the birthdays and name days of members of the imperial family *tabel'nye* or *vysokotorzhestvennye dni*, in the manner of German princes. But family members and particularly the heir were kept safely distant from center stage. Catherine II, who had no claim to the throne except her relationship to her son, included him in major ceremonies, but especially as he grew older and more threatening, tried to keep him away from the life of the court. The popularity he attracted when he visited Moscow in 1775 with his first wife, the Grand Duchess Natalie Alekseevna, so troubled Catherine that she forbade Paul and the Grand Duchess Maria Fedorovna from visiting Moscow after their wedding in 1781.[7]

It was Paul's intention to end this distrust and to introduce a feeling of reverence for the imperial family as dynasty. In the initial days of his reign, he set about restoring his father, Peter III, to the imperial genealogy, emphasizing his own descent from Peter the Great. Paul performed a macabre ceremony of disinterring Peter III and then crowning his coffin, staging the coronation that his unfortunate father had not hastened to arrange. To establish the spousal character of the monarchy, the corpse of Catherine was lifted from her coffin and crowned at the side of her dead husband's coffin. Paul, thus, made an initial gesture to restore the symbolic role of the imperial family.[8]

This was reflected in the unprecedented form of the new succession law, a covenant between him and the Empress Maria Fedorovna, which they had composed in 1788. The decree carried both signatures. The families of the German states often made such family agreements, but they did not issue them from the throne with only two signatures. It thus represented an element of private law given public force by the sovereign will. On the basis of their agreement, the emperor and empress designated their son Alexander heir, "by natural law." The statute introduced what was called the "Austrian system" of succession: male primogeniture of succession with women following in line only in the absence of a male heir. It required the permission of the ruler for marriages of all those in line for the throne. It also spelled out the organization and conditions of regencies in case the heir had not reached maturity, to prevent a recurrence of the events that had kept Paul himself from the throne in 1762.[9]

Just as Peter's succession law sought to deal with the peril of an incompetent successor, Paul's sought to ensure "the tranquillity of the State," which was "based on a firm law of inheritance upon which every right-thinking person is certain." If Peter's Succession Law was directed at the scheming and perfidious son, Paul's took care to support the claims of the son and to leave no room for the pretensions of an ambitious consort. Love now was to be defined in terms of the dedication and constancy to be exemplified by the members of the imperial family who identified their destinies with those of the fatherland. The conclusion of the law declared that it provided "proof before the whole World, of Our love for the Fatherland, the love and harmony of our marriage, and love for Our Children and Descendants."

Paul I introduced the legal and symbolic basis for the dynastic monarchy. He also fathered the children who represented and established the dynasty in the first half of the nineteenth century. But he had been raised in the ways of the eighteenth century and governed in the circumstances of a court in which such values held little respect. While he sought to restore the respect due to the father of the family, his behavior in this regard followed the pattern of absolute monarchs of the last century. Even before his accession, he had openly taken Catherine Nelidova as mistress, and during his reign continued to exhibit his infidelities, particularly with Anna Lophukhina, the daughter of his procurator-general, to whom his court had to show the proper signs of respect. Paul's relationship with his son, Alexander, also followed the eighteenth-century pattern. The distrust between father and son, fed by Catherine's infatuation with her grandson, only grew after her death. Paul suspected, possibly with some grounds, that Alexander was involved in conspiracies to oust him from the throne. In the last two years of his reign, he began to hint of plans to name a new heir.[10]

Neither Alexander nor his younger brother Constantine Pavlovich evinced a predilection for the family or married life. Both were married young, at Catherine's instance, to princesses who quickly wearied them. Constantine's spouse, the Grand Duchess Anna Fedorovna left Russia in 1801, only five years after their marriage, and his liaisons were numerous and well-known in the court. Alexander after the first years of their marriage paid little attention to the Empress Elizabeth Alekseevna, who spent most of his reign living a lonely, isolated life. His numerous dalliances became the subject of the talk of the European elite, for whose eyes, indeed, many of them were presented. The two daughters Elizabeth bore him died in infancy, and he left no heir.

The imperial family at the close of Alexander's reign provided no basis for the sure and reliable political continuity that Paul had envisioned in his law of succession. Constantine had shown reluctance to rule and in 1820, after divorcing the Grand Duchess Anna, contracted a morganatic marriage with a Polish aristocrat. While not a legal bar to the throne, the marriage made him an unlikely candidate to represent the future of the dynasty. Yet Constantine made no open statement of abdication. Alexander, in effect, was forced to act according to the Petrine law and choose his successor. He apparently informed his younger brother, Nicholas, of his decision to designate him heir. But he did so in so secretive and fumbling a manner that he virtually ensured a succession crisis at his death. The manifesto Alexander signed in 1823 was placed, with two letters from Constantine indicating his intention to abdicate, in the State Council, the Senate, the Holy Synod, and the Assumption Cathedral in Moscow. But it had not been promulgated, for reasons that remain inscrutable, and therefore had no legal force. At the moment of Alexander's death, it was known only to Alexei Arakcheev and A. N. Golitsyn, the Metropolitan Filaret, Maria Fedorovna, and possibly to Nicholas himself.[11] The succession crisis that ensued created the setting for the uprising of December 14, 1825.

Maria Fedorovna, Nicholas Pavlovich, and the Creation of a Dynastic Scenario

The verbal, visual, and ceremonial presentations of the reign of Nicholas I elaborated the themes of family and dynasty. As in the eighteenth century, Europe provided the model for these values, but Russian monarchy adopted and displayed them in their most consistent and uncompromising forms. The Russian court not only upheld family values but glorified them as attributes of Russian autocracy. Just as Catherine the Great sought to display the Russian empire as the most enlightened and progressive of states, Nicholas I would present it as the exemplar of the familial values of the West. In so doing, he created the dynastic ceremonies and symbolic forms that would rule Russia until the fall of the monarchy.

Clearly, the principal factor promoting an ethic of family solidarity was the specter of revolution: the threat of violent overthrow united father with son and brother, and encouraged shows of affection rather than caution. But as the examples of Paul and Alexander suggest, the threat was insufficient in itself to instill the norms and patterns of conduct necessary to make the imperial family a central symbol of monarchy. This awaited the reception of the sentimental or early romantic family ethos that arose after the French revolution.

The monarchies that reemerged on the ashes of Napoleonic Europe differed fundamentally from those of the previous century. Once restored to their dominant position in domestic and international affairs, monarchs had to adapt to take into account the new social and political forces awakened during the revolutionary period. The principle of popular sovereignty may have been defeated, but only by calling upon the principle of popular sovereignty itself in rallying national feeling against Napoleon's forces. Nineteenth-century monarchs began to develop ways to represent themselves as the embodiments of national feeling rather than as distant figures whose title to rule stemmed from other-worldly origins.[12]

In certain respects, this change was the next step in the ongoing "desacralization" of European monarchy during the eighteenth century. But the new imagery could be no less elaborate or fanciful than the old. The spinning of personal and historical mythology around the monarchs would continue over the next half-century, elevating them as figures revered or worshiped by the elite and uniting conservative elements of the nation during periods of rapid change. If the monarch could no longer be presented as a god, he or she could be idealized as a better kind of mortal, embodying the features that people admired. Francis II of Austria and especially Frederick William III of Prussia, exemplified what Heinz Dollinger described as the "leading-image of bourgeois monarchy." Self-effacing, modest, averse to elaborate public presentations, they preferred the comfort of their homes. An affectation of simplicity and equality replaced resplendent majesty as a royal ideal.[13]

While this image may have appealed to "bourgeois" values, European monarchs succeeded in divesting it of egalitarian connotations. They displayed a style of life that may have been bourgeois in its origins, but by the early nineteenth century took on the attributes of a cultural ideal that was portrayed in the literature and the art of the period. The new monarchs appeared as immanent rather than transcendent ideals: no longer gifts from the heavens, shedding benefactions on the land, they became exemplars of human conduct, of modest virtue, to be admired by their subjects. This virtue was demonstrated in his or her private life, and particularly in the realm of the family. European monarchs of the eighteenth century had hardly been encumbered by biblical strictures; their nineteenth-century successors were expected to provide models of probity for their subjects.

The increasing autonomy of European bureaucracies encouraged this change. Administrative reforms of the early nineteenth century in Prussia and Austria created a separation between court and bureaucracy, limiting the monarch's powers over administrative institutions and making his symbolic role all the more significant. The Prussian king and the Hapsburg emperor, as centers of aristocratic society and the emerging middle-class elite, epitomized common values of family and religion that appealed to both. The idealization of the monarch's family elevated the ruling dynasty as the historical embodiment of the nation. The sentimental family idyll, thus, was united with the national past to create a myth of the ruler as national ideal.

King Frederick William III was the model of the effacing king, who exemplified probity, constancy, and piety. In the austere tradition of Prussian royalty, he constructed no immense palaces. The single "palace" he built, at Paretz, hardly suited a court; he told the architect David Gilly, "Everything should be made very simple; just think that you are building not for a prince but for an ordinary landlord." He hated public appearances and preferred to walk alone in the woods. He disliked the etiquette of the court and would, unpredictably, ignore it. Only on the parade ground did Frederick William show a taste for show, but the symbolic value of his military leadership was destroyed by the debacle at Jena in 1806.[14]

Frederick William also differed from his predecessors in his preference for a virtuous and ideal family life. From the outset of his reign, he presented himself as a model of familial rectitude. At his accession in 1797, he banned his predecessor's mistresses and introduced "almost the style of a German burgher home" to his court.[15]

But he introduced more than strict morality. His family represented an ideal of romantic love to unite the nation. In the aftermath of the French Revolution, he sought to emphasize not the distance between king and nation but their common values. The first issue of the new journal, *Jahrbücher der Preussischen Monarchie unter den Regierung von Friedrich Wilhelm III*, published in 1798, identified the household of the king, which was "pervaded with the values of true domesticity," with the greater family of the people.[16]

The image of the family united the monarchs and subjects who "entered

The Russian Imperial Family as Symbol   67

into this beautiful sphere." The royal family now began to put on display the ideal of love in marriage. An essay in the June, 1798, issue *Jahrbücher der Preussischen Monarchie*, entitled "Belief and Love," averred "We have seen in our time that a marvel of transubstantiation has come to pass. Has not the court turned into a family, the throne into heaven, a royal marriage into an eternal union of the heart?"[17] Dispossessed of his kingdom after the battle of Jena, forced to accepted the reforms instituted by Baron Heinrich Stein, Frederick William indeed was left with the private realm as his only domain. He claimed no designation from above and even removed the words "by the grace of God" from his title. A painting of "Frederick William and Queen Louise with their Children" typified the Biedermeier style and became a model for subsequent royal family pictures.[18]

If Frederick William exemplified paternal feeling and morality, Queen Louise became the model of cultivated, selfless mother and spouse. She combined the elements of "true religiosity" and "true patriotism," epitomizing "the new Prussian wife." She participated in the German literary awakening of her day, though her first language remained French. From the pietism of Gerhardt, she acquired a faith in the spiritual perfectibility of mankind, and, influenced by the theories of Rousseau and Pestallozzi, she tried new approaches to the upbringing of her children. After her death in 1810, shortly after returning from exile to Berlin, she became the subject of a myth of the pure and holy woman. Poets sang her virtues; artists depicted her in terms of the transfiguration and with the features of the Virgin Mary. One adept of this myth was the queen's oldest daughter, Princess Charlotte, the future Empress Alexandra Fedorovna of Russia.[19]

Following the example of his father-in-law, Frederick William III, Nicholas I presented himself as a model of constancy, family values, and simple religious faith. The ruler's superordinate character now derived not from his Olympian achievements, but from the immortality of a dynasty consecrated by God and history. Nicholas created the illusion that the hereditary rights of the dynasty were identical to the historical destinies of the Russian state. Russian imperial presentation, however, did not permit the retiring, private lifestyle of the Prussian king. The monarch as exemplar of private virtue had to be presented in a scenario, an elaborate dramatic performance of domestic dedication, to be admired and imitated by his servitors. The Prussian manner of reserve had to be combined with the French model of constant representation of the monarch as supreme being. Nicholas as stern and righteous paterfamilias became the living manifestation of the moral preeminence of the dynasty.

It was the dowager empress, Maria Fedorovna, who shaped the new scenario and instilled familial values in Nicholas during the last decade of

Alexander's reign. Only forty-two years old at Paul's death, Maria Fedorovna retained precedence as the principal figure at the imperial court. While Alexander shunned public appearances, she presided over social functions, family dinners, and outings, enforcing the strict etiquette she had observed in Paul's reign. Her palace at Pavlovsk became the social and cultural center of the monarchy. She brought to Russia Protestant notions of the altruistic mission of women and the image of empress as protector of the poor and bereft. She developed the network of foster homes and women's training institutes that she had founded under Paul and encouraged other charitable activities. Maria Fedorovna initiated the tradition of secular charity as a woman's concern in Russia.

Maria Fedorovna shared the religious and ethical values of the Prussian royal house. Her father, a Duke of Württemberg, had been in Prussian service, and she had been educated both in stern patriarchal Protestant values and the French manners and tastes of the German courts of the eighteenth century. As grand duchess and empress, she maintained close family ties, intervening to ensure her parents and siblings marriage alliances, positions in Prussian and Russian service, and, when necessary, subsidies to avert financial disaster. Her attachment to her parents was encouraged by the sentimental literature of the late eighteenth century. She wrote to them in 1780 that she admired the stoics' ability to remain indifferent to everything, but had no desire to emulate them. "The closer I come to maturity, the more I become convinced that the ability to feel nurtures our soul: without it people become savage and cease being people."[20]

These sentiments remained with Maria Fedorovna and she strove to instill them in the members of the Russian imperial family. She introduced the practice of demonstrative mourning for the deceased members of the house and the sense that family bonds only grew stronger after death, aspects of "cult of memory" ascendant in the West. She hallowed the memory of her parents and her husband with two memorials built in the park at Pavlovsk, "To My Parents," and "To My Husband-Benefactor." Thomas de Thomon's "To My Husband-Benefactor," completed in 1810, is a monument in the form of a Greek temple to her grief for Paul, for whom her feelings had been less than tender. The interior is occupied by Ivan Martos's statue of a mourning wife, her head resting at the side of an urn. The motif of twenty-four weeping faces on the metopes expresses the feeling of sorrow due the father of the dynasty.[21]

Maria Fedorovna tried to show her children the importance of marriage and marital love, but her oldest sons remained deaf to her pleas. Maria Fedorovna became the family conscience, warning her children that they

Monument To My Husband Benefactor. Sculptor Ivan Martos. Photo by Richard Wortman.

served as personal models for their subjects. When, in 1803, the Grand Duke Constantine informed her that he wished to terminate his marriage to the Grand Duchess Anna Fedorovna with a divorce, the empress replied with an angry letter. After describing "wounds of the heart" he had inflicted on her, she pointed out the symbolic implications of such a step. It would bring "ruinous consequences for public morals as well as a lamentable and dangerous temptation for the entire nation." The humblest peasant far from the capital, noting the absence of the grand duchess's name next to his in church prayers, would lose respect for the sacrament of marriage and for religious faith itself.[22]

Maria Fedorovna's romantic vision of family relations and connubial love was set forth by her protégé, the poet Vasilii Zhukovskii. Zhukovskii's verse shifted the referent of imperial virtue from a civic ideal, personified in figures of the gods, heroes, or Roman emperors, to the private ideals of the nursery and the hearth. Zhukovskii announced the new poetic theme in an ode to Maria Fedorovna of 1813.

> And where is a more glorious subject for the poet?
> Tsaritsa, mother, spouse, daughter of tsars,
> The beauty of tsaritsas, the joy of the hemisphere,
> Who can find the language proper for it?

Zhukovskii concluded the ode with an evocation of Alexander's imminent return to Russia. He presented the moment as a family, not a mythical event, personal affection expressing imperial glory.

> Blessed hour! In the form of martial heroes,
> He bends his illustrious head,
> The Lord-son before the mother-tsaritsa,
> May their love bless this glory—
> And withal the saved world lies,
> At your sacred hand![23]

Maria Fedorovna's three youngest children, Nicholas, Michael, and Anna, grew up sharing strong feelings of family solidarity. Ignored by the court, they drew close to each other. They formed their own club, "triopathy," and wore special rings, one of which they gave to their mother as an honorary member. They maintained close ties throughout their lives, what Anna Pavlovna described as their *"family union."* Their later correspondence continued to express an intimacy of feeling and a common purpose that united the members of the house.[24]

Grand Duke Nicholas Pavlovich shared his mother's reverence for the institution of marriage and inclination to regard marital vows as lofty and sacred. When Nicholas showed an interest in Princess Charlotte of Prussia on his return from France in 1814, Maria Fedorovna's esteem for him, previously none too high, rose appreciably. She herself had dreamt of such a match and in 1809 had discussed the possibility with Queen Louise herself. Princess Charlotte worshiped the memory of the queen, whose bust she later kept in her boudoir. She made herself in her mother's image, adopting her romantic literary tastes and showing the same devotion to family and children. After Louise's death, which had occurred when Charlotte was thirteen, she took her mother's place at her father's side and learned at an early age the poise and confidence of a sovereign.[25]

The writers and artists of eighteenth- and nineteenth-century Russian monarchy employed the devices of their craft to present the acts and ceremonies of their sovereign in terms of the monarchical ideals of their age. These devices transformed the transitory appearances of the monarch and the presentations of the court into charismatic moments, expressing the sacred character of imperial rule. The metaphorical mode predominated in eighteenth-century texts and illustrations; metaphor transformed the rulers into heroes and heroines, gods and goddesses, establishing a distance between the monarch and his elite, and between the elite and the ruled. The nineteenth-century mode sought to create the illusion of immanence rather than transcendence. Nicholas's person expressed qualities and values integral to this world, or as was claimed, particular to Russia. In this respect, he adopted the manner of Frederick William III and other Western monarchs who appeared as exemplars of virtue and the private life for their subjects. The principal devices that produced the illusion of immanence was the metonym, or, more specifically, the synecdoche, which presented the emperor with his family as a concrete expression of the nation.

The texts of Nicholas's reign presented imperial display with new meanings. Rather than expressions of otherworldly spheres where godlike figures cavort and rejoice, ceremonies of the monarch served as microcosms of Russia, representing the attitudes towards authority and modalities of conduct, both official and private, that should prevail in the macrocosm of the empire.[26]

In this equivalence, the macrocosm was defined in terms of the microcosm. The emperor, his family, the dynasty, the army, and the state epitomized the principal qualities of Russia and represented the whole. Here we see a kinship between political and symbolic representation. Both, Kenneth Burke observed, invoke synecdoche to describe the identity between microcosm and macrocosm. All attempts to "represent" the general will of the people in parliamentary institutions involve a transfer of qualities to the representative body that stand for the people as a whole.[27] Likewise, the imagery of official nationalism claims to reflect the will of the people by making the tsar in his ceremonial appearances the representation of the whole. Nicholas was frequently described as "the embodiment of Russia." The ceremonies of the monarchy embodying Russia were presented to a broadened elite through the official and semiofficial press, which became an important medium during the Napoleonic Wars and expanded greatly during Nicholas's reign.[28]

The elevation of the family became apparent from the moment of Nicholas's victory over the Decembrist revolution. On the afternoon of December 14, Nicholas brought his eight-year-old son Alexander before the Sapper battalion, which had saved the imperial family from a threat from the Grenadiers' Regiment. Nicholas made clear that he and the heir were one. He asked the troops to love his son as they loved him. Then he placed Alexander in the arms of several Cavaliers of the Order of St. George and, at his command, the first officers in each line rushed to the boy and kissed his hands and his feet.[29]

This was the initial demonstration of the new importance of the principle of primogeniture in the life of the imperial house. Nicholas showed that the imperial family rather than the emperor alone represented the spirit and values of autocracy. The scene became an emblematic one for his reign. It was commemorated in popular pictures and on the bas-relief of the statue Alexander erected

Nicholas I Presenting His Son, Alexander, to the Sapper Battalion, on Senate Square, December 14, 1825. Bas Relief on Nicholas I monument by N. Ramazanov. Lithograph from *Russkii Khudozhestvennyi Listok*, 1859.

to his father in 1858. The fact that Alexander had stood at his father's side on the day of the rebellion was inscribed in his service list along with the military honors he received on that day.

The family as exemplar of autocracy was a central theme of the visual imagery of Nicholas's reign. An engraving by Thomas Wright after a painting by George Dawe completed not long after Nicholas's accession indicates the new importance of the emperor's family for the future of Russian monarchy. A portrait of the Grand Duke Alexander Nikolaevich is set in a large medallion surrounded by flowers, between medallions with portraits of the emperor in uniform and the empress in decolleté gown. The medallions are placed above and dominate a small sketch of the winter palace. It was the family of Nicholas that now represented the benefactions of monarchy, symbolized by the sun, emanating from the imperial residence.[30]

The domestic happiness of the imperial family was depicted in the mannered poses of English sentimental art by English artists at the Russian court. The paintings of Dawe, rendered into engravings by his compatriot, Wright, presented royal personages for the first time in intimate family groups. One of these shows the empress sitting with the infant Olga Nikolaevna in her right

Emperor Nicholas I, Grand Duke Alexander Nikolaevich, and Empress Alexandra
Fedorovna, 1826. Engraving by Thomas Wright. Artist, George Dawe. From N. K.
Shilder, *Imperator Nikolai Pervyi: ego zhizn' i tsarstvovanie* (St. Petersburg, 1903), Vol. 1.

arm, and the seven-year-old Alexander Nikolaevich grasping her gown on the
left. Another is a garden scene: Alexander Nikolaevich in sailor suit pushes
his little sister Maria, wearing a bonnet of flowers, on a swing. Both have the
innocent cherubic expressions of nineteenth-century beautiful children. Popular prints took up this theme and showed the emperor adjusting his son's pillow
and a family scene at Ekateringof.[31]

A large number of lithographs and paintings presented the heir at various stages of his education. Upon the death of the Grand Duke Constantine
Pavlovich in June 1831, Nicholas issued a decree declaring, that "Our most be-
loved son" should henceforth be called "Sovereign Heir, Tsesarevich and Grand
Duke" (*Gosudar' Naslednik, Tsesarevich i Velikii Kniaz'*). The decree was printed in
the press and a series of pictures executed that made Alexander's new title
known.[32] A *lubok* of 1831 shows him in stylized equestrian pose; he wears a
cuirassier's uniform and looks dashing and heroic. At the bottom among his
various titles the word tsesarevich is inscribed in bold capitals. Nicholas's family now held all of the titles and symbolic distinctions of the senior line, which
provided the occasion to issue new pictures of the heir as loyal son. In a water-
color by Alexander Briullov, the heir stands at the center of a group of cadets in

dress uniform at Peterhof in 1831. He is the tallest and most poised of the boys. His arm is on a staff; beside him is a waving standard. At his foot, sitting under the barrel of a cannon, is his younger brother, Constantine Nikolaevich not yet four years old. Behind, Karl Merder, the heir's governor, looks on, and an officer in a plumed hat sits on a horse. Lithographed copies of the painting were sent to all military schools.[33]

Most important, Nicholas made his family the principal subject of imperial ceremonies. Here I will focus on three of these: the coronation, the ceremony of the majority of the heir, and Alexander's initiation as the hereditary ataman of the Cossacks of the Don. These ceremonies presented the imperial family as the symbol of the monarchy and likened the types of political subordination to the bonds of dear kin. The paternalistic theme of the tsar as father, protecting his children, now took on a higher moral and literary meaning of sentimental love. The various estates of the realm were gathered to show loyalty as familial act. The "love" of the people became a way to absorb them into a greater family embracing all of Russia.

The coronation remained the central declaratory ceremony of Russian monarchy through the nineteenth century, consecrating and showing the character and goals of the monarchy as well as the character of each new reign. But the central theme of the ceremony had shifted markedly during the nineteenth century. Eighteenth-century coronations had celebrated the successful aspirant to the throne as the champion of the general good, legitimizing dubious claims to succession. Nineteenth-century coronations, beginning with Nicholas's, consecrated the monarchy itself, as it was incarnated in the ruling dynasty of which the enthroned emperor was God-chosen representative. Nicholas's immediate family became embodiment of a dynastic tradition that, in fact, had begun only with Nicholas's reign.

The principal account of Nicholas I's coronation, written by Pavel Svin'in in his journal *Otechestvennye Zapiski*, presented the entire imperial family as the object of popular affection. In the entry procession to Moscow, Nicholas rode down the avenue flanked by his brother Michael, his brother-in-law, Prince Karl of Prussia, the Duke of Württemberg, and his son, Alexander.[34] It was Alexander, not the emperor, who was endearing. "The kind Russian people admired the angelic charm of the Heir to the Throne with indescribable rapture." The author went on to point out that this "Royal Child" (*Derzhavnyi Mladenets*) was particularly dear to Muscovites because he had been born in the Kremlin. A lithograph issued at the time shows the entry into Moscow at the Tver gate. Nicholas is looking smart on a prancing horse next to his brother and the suite; the empress sits in an open carriage, under a parasol. Peasants stand on the buildings waving their caps; joyous people crowd the windows and the balconies.[35]

With Nicholas's coronation, great reviews and maneuvers became an integral part of the coronation celebrations. They assumed the character of ceremonial expressions of the devotion of the military to the imperial family. Military reviews took place frequently during the month between the entry procession and the coronation ceremonies. On July 30, a parade of over fifty thousand troops paid homage to the dowager empress. Grand Duke Alexander rode in his father's suite, on a magnificent steed. The eight-year-old galloped past the emperor, charged up and stopped before him to the delight of the spectators. The son had paid deference to the father. Then, Nicholas led a detachment before his mother and saluted her, giving recognition to her personal and ceremonial preeminence in the house."[36]

Nicholas took part in large-scale maneuvers of the Moscow regiments on August 15 and 16, which were summarized in Svin'in's articles. The maneuvers not only served as a useful exercise for the troops but provided the large numbers of foreigners and other spectators "a splendid spectacle rare for the residents of Moscow."[37]

The feeling of the unity of the dynasty was enhanced by the surprise arrival of the Grand Duke Constantine in Moscow. Constantine as usual was peevish, but Nicholas's deferential attention succeeded in calming him by the day of the ceremony. A broadsheet printed at this time shows the three brothers, Nicholas, Constantine, and Michael, riding side by side, with the heir on horseback at Michael's side. On the day of the coronation a manifesto was issued establishing the rules for a regency and designating Nicholas's "most kind" brother, Michael, regent should Nicholas die before the heir's majority.[38]

Svin'in's account of the ceremonies in the Assumption Cathedral focused on the members of the family; they and their German relatives are the only participants whom he identifies by name. Svin'in evoked the emotional response of the moment after the investiture of the emperor and empress with the regalia. "What rapture (*vostorg*) seized the hearts of those standing by and in general all the inhabitants of Moscow learning by the resounding of the bells and the salvos from the cannons that the Imperial Couple were invested with the purple and crowned!" He remarked how Maria Fedorovna overflowed with rapture, *vostorg*. "All of Her [Maria Fedorovna's] thoughts, all of Herself, it seemed, was in the heavens from which the blessing descended upon the Head of Her Crowned Son." He then marveled over the feeling with which Nicholas kissed her and his brothers, Constantine and Michael.[39] Svin'in described the anointment, communion, and recessional in similar terms.

The author of the official coronation album published in Paris, one Henry

Graf, also rhapsodized over the family drama. The embrace between the dowager and the young emperor was "with a visible emotion shared by all those present." But Graf focused primarily on the embrace with Constantine, thus confirming the solidarity of the dynasty for the European audience. "Few of those present could hold back their tears, especially when the Emperor embraced the Tsarevich Grand Duke Constantine, who gathered at this moment the finest fruit of his noble sacrifices." The illustration entitled "the Crowning" of Nicholas presented not the crowning but Constantine embracing Nicholas who was already crowned. An act of affection thus was used to show the tsarevich's homage to his younger brother and to dispel the uncertainties about his abdication. The same scene was depicted in a popular print of the time.[40]

The spectacle fulfilled the literary and mythical expectations of the foreign guests and the Russian official elite. The Duke of Raguse found the unity and devotion of the family "one of the most beautiful things the imagination can conceive."[41] Alexander Benckendorff recalled the family coming out of the cathedral, "The incomparable face of the sovereign shone with beauty under the valuable gems of the imperial crown. The young empress and the heir near the empress-mother also attracted everyone's gaze. It was impossible to imagine a more splendid family." Those in attendance also followed the sentimental scenario; they gave their sympathy to the family by weeping—shedding tears of joy to share in the pathos of the triumphant dynasty. Benckendorff remarked on the tears shed when Nicholas handed his sword to Constantine Pavlovich. State-Secretary Dmitrii Bludov wept unabashedly when Maria Fedorovna embraced the emperor. The ceremony confirmed his religious belief. "I was again assured of the sweetness and the necessity of Faith, that every passion, even the most noble love of Fatherland, not purified by religion, leads only to error and misfortune."[42]

Nicholas's coronation introduced scenes of family devotion and reconciliation to the solemn Byzantine rites. The family became a metonymic expression of the constant, devoted, and pure feelings that attach servitors and subject to the throne. The political bond was sustained by a mythical bond of affection for the imperial family, which the dignitaries of Nicholas's state would be expected to display at the proper occasions. The shedding of tears of joy, and when necessary grief, became obligatory at court ceremonies—a sign of loyalty and sharing in the family life of the tsar, which symbolized his moral and, therefore, political supremacy. The elite became absorbed in the family of the tsar, a family that exemplified the current European ideal of dynastic monarchy and the current Russian ideal of utter dedication to one's sovereign.

Paul's Law of Succession of 1797 had set the majority of the heir at the early age of sixteen in order to ensure a smooth succession in the event of the early

Alexander II as heir in dress uniform. Engraving by O. Keselev. Drawing by Gompelen Glukho-Nemoi. From *Stoletie Voennogo Ministerstva: Imperatorskaia glavnaia kvartira; istoriia gosudarevoi svity; tsarstvovanie Imperatora Nikolaia I* (St. Petersburg, 1908).

death of the ruling emperor. Alexander was the first heir to reach that age under the law, and to mark the event Nicholas staged a major ceremony of oath taking on April 22, 1834, introducing a new rite of passage into the life of the imperial court. Pronounced by all grand dukes, the oath made the maintenance of autocracy a filial obligation, consecrated by God. Metropolitan Filaret of Moscow composed an imposing ceremony in which the son pledged obedience to his father, the autocrat, and the laws of Russia before the assembled elite of the Russian state.

Alexander's oath, written by Michael Speranskii, gave emphatic statement to the principles of the unity of family feeling with autocratic government and the maintenance of the inviolability of the prerogatives of the father-sovereign. The purpose of the ceremony, Speranskii asserted, was to confer religious sanction on the heir's future obligations. An oath, he wrote, "is an act of conscience and religion, by which he who vows summons God in witness to the sincerity of his promises and submits himself to His wrath and vengeance in case of violation." The Archpriest G. P. Pavskii's instruction to Alexander before the ceremony summoned him to renew the vow to Christ that had taken place at his baptism. "Only a true follower of Christ and sound member of the kingdom of God can be a useful member of the human kingdom."[43]

Like the promulgation of the succession law, the first ceremony of majority took place on Easter Sunday, lending it an especially sacred character. It was an important rite of passage for the heir, from a child to his father's helper, joining his father at least symbolically in the exercise of autocratic power. At midnight of New Year's 1834, Nicholas and Alexandra had told him that the coming year would be the most important of his life. Alexander wrote in his diary, "I feel its importance and will try to prepare myself as much as I can for this moment, for I know that even after it is over, the main task awaits me, that is to complete what has been begun. I ask the All-Powerful Father to give me strength to follow the example of my father in a worthy manner."[44]

As the day approached, the solemnity of the occasion and its significance for Russia were impressed upon Alexander. On April 16, Nicholas took his son on a walk to the Peter-Paul fortress. He told him of the difficulties he would encounter and urged him to turn to his father and mother for advice. "I will never forget this conversation," Alexander wrote in his diary. Nicholas now initiated him in the cult of ancestors, the immortal unity of the dynasty. At the cathedral, father and son kissed the graves of Paul I and Alexander I and their spouses and the grave of Constantine Pavlovich. Nicholas kissed him and said, in French, "When I lie there, visit me sometimes." "These words touched me so much that I could not contain my tears, and I prayed to myself that the All-Powerful God allow a long life to my dear father."[45] The next day Alexander received the epaulette and braids of a Flügel-Adjutant of Nicholas's suite.

The ceremony of the oath on April 22, 1834 in the Great Church at the Winter Palace was a major state occasion, described in a detailed account published in *Russkii Invalid* and *Severnaia Pchela*.[46] The ceremony sought to involve the entire state in the family drama of the Russian house; the account referred to those present as "all of Russia." On one side, there stood arrayed the diplomatic corps, State Councillors and Senators. Behind them were Court Officials, members of the Emperor's Suite, Generals, State Secretaries, and others with the right of entry "behind the Cavalier Guards," and the mayor of St. Petersburg. They faced the wives of the diplomatic corps, and ladies of the court. Deputies representing art, science, commerce, and industry were also present. Officers of the guards and lesser civil officials awaited in the adjoining halls. From Alexander's teaching staff, Zhukovskii, Edward Collins, and possibly others attended.[47] The palace was so crowded that Pushkin had difficulty slipping through the back stairways to visit his aunt.[48]

The first part of the event, in the Great Church, was the recitation of the oath as heir to the throne. After the Metropolitan Serafim and other clergy met the imperial family with the cross and holy water, Nicholas led his son to the pulpit, before the life-giving cross and the gospels. Alexander, raising his right hand, delivered the oath. He vowed to serve and obey his father "in all respects" (*vo-vsem*). He promised that he would not spare his life, and would give his last drop of blood, the words of Peter the Great. He would defend the rights and power of "the autocracy of His Imperial Majesty" and would "assist the service of his majesty and the welfare of the state." He pledged to observe all the rulings of the throne and the Laws of the Imperial House. Finally, he called upon God "to guide and teach him in the great service" that had devolved upon him. At this point, he broke down in tears and it took several tries to continue. The emperor and empresses then embraced and kissed him.

Metropolitan Filaret in a letter to Prince D. V. Golitsyn described similar feelings. "Kisses and tears reunited father, mother, and son. When my own absorption in this inspiring spectacle ended, and my own tears dried, I could see that all present were in tears."[49] Pushkin indicated in his diary that those who did not weep made sure to wipe their eyes as well.[50] The ceremony was a reprise of the domestic scenario, and a display of feeling, whether real or feigned, showed participation in the spectacle of family solidarity.

After pronouncing the oath, the heir signed it and Count Karl Nesselrode, the foreign minister, removed the document for safekeeping in the State Archive. The first part of the ceremony concluded with the singing of a Te Deum, a 301-gun salute from the cannons of the Peter-Paul fortress, and the tolling of the church bells of the capital. Then after the prayer for the long life of the emperor, the imperial family received congratulations from the members of the Synod.

The tears and the family embrace were understood and presented in the sentimental idiom. The report published in *Severnaia Pchela* and in *Russkii Invalid*, following the sentimental ascription—and prescription—of emotion, described a general feeling of tenderness (*umilenie*), which "penetrated all hearts." It dwelled on the embraces of parents and son. First, Nicholas kissed Alexander three times. Alexander wanted to hug his mother, but Nicholas reached her first. Then the emperor clasped both of them to him in an embrace. "With this spectacle of all royal and human virtues, a reverent tremor of tenderness (*umilenie*) touched all hearts." The author of the newspaper accounts compared Alexander's tears to those of Michael Fedorovich when as a boy he had accepted the throne of Russia; the tears showed his understanding of the importance and greatness of the ritual. "May Your tears, Successor of the Great Tsars, be pleasing to God. May they be a guarantee of the goodness of Your soul and the happiness of Your Fatherland." The civil ceremony was followed by an equally imposing military ceremony, the heir's taking of the oath as military officer in the Hall of St. George. The subsequent celebrations, receptions, banquets, and balls continued through Holy Week.

The ceremony of the majority represented the first formal presentation of

Alexander as a dynastic symbol, expressing the unity of the governmental and social elite with the dynasty. The rhetoric of the writers close to the throne transformed him into a national symbol as well. A song Zhukovskii wrote for the occasion, set to music by Count Michael Viel'gorskii, presented Alexander's birth as a national event. From the heights of the Moscow Kremlin, the poem began, "the Russian Land" (*Russkaia zemlia*) had witnessed Alexander's birth. Years had passed quickly, and now, on the day of the resurrection, the "touching ritual" (*umilitel'nyi obriad*) was taking place in "Petrograd." Alexander embodied the unity between Moscow and Petersburg, the word now russified.

The ceremony revealed both generational and political solidarity. Father and son, dynasty and people were united in the person of the heir. The son enters the cathedral, raises his hands to heaven,

> Before him the father and ruler,
> The *tsar* receives the oath of his *son*.
> Hearken with a blessing,
> To the words of his young soul,
> And raise your arms to heavens,
> Faithful Russia, together with him.[51]

Another "Russian Song," by one B. Fedorov, appeared in *Russkii Invalid* on May 2. Fedorov used a group of boatmen, rowing up the Neva to the palace, as an expression of the joy of the nation as a whole. The boatmen he imagined provided the synecdochical voice of acclamation, on the birthday of "the kind son." They sang to the tsar,

> Great is your Imperial joy,
> It spreads through all Holy Rus.
> You have raised an Heir for Yourself,
> ALEXANDER, Your young son is Your hope!
> He is the comforting ray of the bright sun,
> Our dawn, our light from the great day!
> Glory to the Russian sun!
> Rejoice Father of the Fatherland![52]

Alexander's tour of Russia after his nineteenth birthday, from April through December 1837, brought the dynastic scenario to the far reaches of the empire. Accompanied by Zhukovskii and an adjutant of Nicholas, S. A. Iur'evich, Alexander covered a distance of over 13,000 miles. It was the longest tour of the empire by a tsar or tsarevich, and took him to regions, including parts of Siberia, never visited by a member of the imperial family. His charm in public appearances awakened sentiments that attached the population to the autocracy, drawing the local elites into the family's love as a trope for lofty and humane feelings.

Two events of Alexander's trip assumed especial importance for the role Alexander was to play in his father's scenario—the visit to Moscow in July and August, and his installation as Cossack Ataman in Novocherkassk in October. The Moscow visit linked his personal appeal as heir who was born in Moscow with Russia's historical past. The Metropolitan Filaret emphasized this theme in the welcome speech he delivered on Alexander's arrival, which was printed in *Severnaia Pchela*. Alexander, Filaret declared, had now reached Moscow, the resting place of his ancestors. "Here you will come even more into contact with the heart of Russia and its vital force, which is an inherited love for hereditary tsars, repelling in previous centuries so many enemy forces. You will see it in its free play, in those waves of people striving towards You, in those enraptured (*vostorzhennykh*) gazes and solemn cries." An inherited, historical affection was the source of the ruler's authority. "May the love of Russians make your task easy, inspired by love for Russia."[53]

According to Nicholas's instructions, Alexander slept in the room where he was born and took historical tours of the city that identified his and the family's fate with Russia's past. Andrei Murav'ev, a specialist on religion and Muscovite antiquities, published an account of his excursions with Alexander to the sites of Moscow and its vicinity. Murav'ev described the young heir's visit to the relics and shrines of his ancestors. In the Novospasskii Monastery, Alexander proceeded slowly beneath a painting of his family tree, "as if attaining at the end of this long genealogical chain that bright link to which he was predestined," Murav'ev wrote.[54]

Another dramatic moment of Alexander's visit to Moscow was his meeting with his mother on August 3, after a separation of three months. An account of the reuniting of mother and son by the popular children's writer Prince Vladimir L'vov appeared in the September 27 issue of *Russkii Invalid*. L'vov described the scene of a moving embrace. The sun shone with bright rays. The empress and one of his sisters embraced him. "Let foreigners envy us!" L'vov wrote. "Let all Russia enjoy this spectacle and let it be repeated many, many times. Happy is the people whose ruling family gives such an example of love and friendship. Can the tears of joy and the cries of the suffering fail to strike a chord in their hearts?"[55]

The trip culminated with the meeting of father and son at Novocherkassk in the steppes of New Russia with a new ceremony of initiation that expressed the allegiance of the elite of the Don host not only to the emperor, but to the heir, and the dynasty as a whole. Nicholas had prepared this when in October 1827 he had named Alexander honorary "Ataman of all the Cossack Hosts" and

"Chief of the Don Regiment." The position of honorary ataman was presented as a direct personal bond between the imperial family and the cossacks that brought the Host into the single great family of those loyal to the tsar. The ceremony on October 21 cemented this bond. It identified the devotion of the cossacks with the devotion of son to father, establishing a rite for all future heirs to the throne.[56]

Emperor and heir rode in ceremonial procession into Novocherkassk, the administrative center of the Don Host. The cossack leaders formed a circle around the cathedral; in the middle the "appointed" "*nakaznyi*" cossack ataman conferred the *pernach*, one of the maces constituting the cossack insignia of power, on Nicholas, who then conferred it on Alexander. Nicholas explained the significance of the event. He declared that by appointing his son his ataman, he was giving "the most valuable pledge (*zalog*)" of his goodwill to them. "May this serve as proof of how close you are to my heart. When he replaces me, serve him as loyally as you served my ancestors and me. He will not forsake you." In his diary, Alexander described the ceremony and copied down his father's address. *Russkii Invalid* reported that "these words were impressed on the heart of each and every one of those present. General, but silent tenderness (*umilenie*). This then passed into the joyous cries of pure enthusiasm (*vostorg*) from the people."[57] The next day, Alexander and Nicholas inspected a review of over 17,000 members of the Host and in the evening attended a ball where the heir took part in several dances.

The domestic scenario introduced in the reign of Nicholas II represented far more than a romantic embellishment to the image of the tsar. It made the family a central symbol of the moral purity of Russian autocracy, which purported to be the purest form of absolute monarchy. The association between domestic morality and autocratic government outlived Nicholas's reign and remained intrinsic to the image of the Russian monarch for the duration of the empire. To violate the principle of autocracy became tantamount to a biblical sin against the father, while violation of family morality would throw into doubt the moral foundations of autocratic rule. Nicholas introduced the forms of behavior, the ceremonies, the feelings of obligations that underlay the notion of Russian dynastic monarchy in the nineteenth century.

The family scenario served various functions in the adaptation of the monarchy to the political circumstances of nineteenth-century Europe. The attachment between father and son and between husband and wife elevated the concept of dynastic inheritance to a moral plane and made so elusive a goal appear as part of the national concept of Russian monarchy. The sentimental outpourings of family feeling described by numerous Russian and European writers reaffirmed the common values that identified the Russian sovereign with his Western counterparts. Finally, the display of family devotion became a model for the expression of political loyalty. The political bond was personalized. The allegiance to the monarch, no longer demonstrated in the mere witnessing of baroque allegories, now required shows of personal ardor, manifestations of the soul, such as rapture, tenderness, and profuse weeping—a public sharing of what purported to be the innermost feelings of the members of the imperial family.

Notes

1. This paper is partially drawn from sections and materials from my book *Scenarios of Power: Myth and Ceremony in Russian Monarchy, vol. 1: From Peter the Great to the Death of Nicholas I* (Princeton, 1995).

2. *PSZ*, 17,910, April 5, 1797; *PSZ*, 17,906, April 5, 1797.

3. Catherine's projects for a succession law are discussed in M. M. Safonov's unpublished manuscript "Zaveshchanie Ekateriny II."

4. PSZ, February 5, 1722; Alain Besançon, *Le tsarévitch immolé; la symbolique de la loi dans la culture russe* (Paris, 1967), 109–22; G. Gurvich, *"Pravda voli monarshei" Feofana Prokopovicha i eia zapadnoevropeiskie istochniki* (Iur'ev, 1915); Mikhail Zyzykin, *Tsarskaia vlast' i zakon o prestolonasledii v Rossii* (Sofia, 1924), 72–82; James Cracraft has thrown doubt on Prokopovich's authorship of the *Pravda*. See James Cracraft, "Did Feofan Prokopovich Really Write *Pravda Volei Monarshei*," *Slavic Review*, vol. 40, no. 2, (Summer, 1981), 173–94.

5. On the age of gold in Russia, see Stephen L. Baehr, *The Paradise Myth in Eighteenth-Century Russia* (Stanford, Calif., 1991), 38–40, 44–49, and "'Fortuna Redux': The Iconography of Happiness in Eighteenth-Century Courtly Spectacles," in A. G. Cross, (ed.), *Great Britain and Russia in the Eighteenth Century: Contacts and Comparisons* (Newtonville, Mass., 1979), 110.

6. PSZ, 11,390, December 25, 1761; Peter Bartenev, *Osmnatstaty vek; istoricheskii sbornik*, (Moscow, 1869), 4:217; the story of Catherine's reputed intention to remove Paul from the succession is the subject of Safonov's "Zaveshchanie Ekateriny II."

7. E. S. Shumigorskii, *Imperatritsa Mariia Fedorvna (1759–1828)* (St. Petersburg, 1892), 1:174.

8. Safonov, "Zaveshchanie Ekateriny II," chap. 8, 218–28; *Kamerfur'erskii tseremonial'nyi zhurnal*, 1796: 788–91, 821–24, 861–68.

9. *PSZ*, 17,910, April 5, 1797; B. Nol'de, "Zakony osnovnye v russkom prave," *Pravo*, 1913, no. 9, 524–26.

10. N. Ia. Eidel'man, *Gran' vekov; politicheskaia bor'ba v Rossii, konets XVIII-nachala XIX*

stoletiia (Moscow, 1986), 240–41; N. K. Shil'der, *Imperator Pavel Pervyi; istoriko-biograficheskii ocherk* (St. Petersburg, 1901), 287–94, 478–79; E. P. Karnovich, *Tsesarevich Konstantin Pavlovich* (St. Petersburg, 1899), 74.

11. S. V. Mironenko, *Stranitsy tainoi istorii samoderzhaviia* (Moscow, 1990), 74–85; W. Bruce Lincoln, *Nicholas I: Emperor and Autocrat of All the Russias* (Bloomington, Ind., 1978), 22–26.

12. See Heinz Dollinger's important article, "Das Leitbild des Burgerkönigtums in der europäischen Monarchie des 19.Jahrhunderts," in Werner, ed., *Hof, Kultur, und Politik im 19.Jahrhundert,* (Bonn, 1985), 325–62.

13. Ibid., 345–52.

14. Thomas Stamm-Kuhlmann, "Der Hof Friedrich-Wilhelms III. von Preussen 1797 bis 1840," Karl Möckl, ed., *Hof und Hofgesellschaft in den deutschen Staaten im 19. und beginnenden 20. Jahrhundert* (Boppard am Rhein, 1990), passim; Hajo Holborn, *A History of Modern Germany, 1648–1840* (New York, 1964), 2:375–76.

15. Ibid., 375.

16. Wulf Wülfing, Karin Bruns, Rolf Parr, *Historische Mythologie der Deutschen* (Munich, 1991), 59.

17. Ibid., 60.

18. Holborn, 2:396; Dollinger, 347.

19. Wülfing et al., 61–78; Stamm-Kuhlmann, 318; Bogdan Krieger, "Erziehung und Unterricht der Königen Luise," *Hohenzollern Jahrbuch* (1910), 117–73; A. Th. Von Grimm, *Alexandra Feodorovna, Empress of Russia* (Edinburgh, 1870), 1:51–54.

20. Shumigorskii, 1:149.

21. *Pamiatniki arkhitektury prigorodov Leningrada,* 248–49.

22. E. P. Karnovich, *Tsesarevich Konstantin Pavlovich* (St. Petersburg, 1899), 141–48; N. K. Shil'der, *Imperator Nikolai Pervyi; ego zhizn' i tsarstvovanie* (St. Petersburg, 1903), 1:128.

23. V. A. Zhukovskii, *Polnoe sobranie sochinenii* (St. Petersburg, 1902), 2:24–25

24. S. W. Jackman, *Romanov Relations* (London, 1969), 4, 107, and passim.

25. A. Th. von Grimm, *Alexandra Feodorovna, Empress of Russia* (Edinburgh, 1870), 1:52–55.

26. On the synecdoche as the expression of the identity of microcosm and macrocosm, see Kenneth Burke, "Four Master Tropes," in his *A Grammar of Motives and a Rhetoric of Motives* (Cleveland, 1962), 508.

27. Ibid.

28. On the semiofficial press see Nurit Schleifman, "A Russian Daily Newspaper and Its New Readership: *Severnaia Pchela* 1825–1840," *Cahiers du monde russe et soviétique,* XXVIIII (2), April-June 1987: 127–44; Charles A. Ruud, *Fighting Words: Imperial Censorship and the Russian Press, 1804–1906* (Toronto, 1982), 58–59, 64–65; N. L. Stepanov, " 'Severnaia Pchela' F. V. Bulgarina," in *Ocherki po istorii russkoi zhurnalistiki i kritiki* (Leningrad, 1950), 1:310–11.

29. M. Korf, *Voshestvie na prestol Imperatora Nikolaia Iogo* (St. Peterburg, 1857), 220.

30. *Imperatorskaia glavnaia kvartira; istoriia gosudarevoi svity; tsarstvovanie Imperatora Aleksandra II* (St. Petersburg, 1914), 9. Henceforth, IGK, ts. Al. II.

31. D. A. Rovinskii, *Podrobnyi slovar' russkikh gravirovannykh portretov* (St. Petersburg, 1886), 1:19–20; IGK, ts. Al. II, opp. 6.

32. *Severnaia Pchela*, September 7, 1831.

33. IGK, ts. Al. II, 43.

34. Ibid., 284.

35. Shil'der, *Imperator Nikolai Pervyi; ego zhizn' i tsarstvovanie* (St. Petersburg, 1903), 2:13.

36. S. S. Tatishchev, *Imperator Aleksandr II, ego zhizn' i tsarstvovanie* (St. Petersburg, 1903), 1:9–10; Maréchal de Marmont, Duc de Raguse, *Mémoires* (Paris, 1857), vol. 8, 118–19.

37. "Istoricheskoe opisanie Sviashchennogo Koronovanie i Miropomazaniia ikh Imperatorskikh Velichestv Gosudaria Imperatora Nikolaia Pavlovicha i Gosudaryni Imperatritsy Aleksandry Feodorovny," *Otechestvennye Zapiski*, 1827, 31:45–47. Henceforth, "Istoricheskoe opisanie."

38. *Imperatorskaia glavnaia kvartira; istoriia gosudarevoi svity; tsarstvovanie Imperatora Nikolaia I* (St. Petersburg, 1908), 219–20. Henceforth, IGK, ts. Nik. I; V. I. Zhmakin, "Koronatsii russkikh imperatorov i imperatrits, 1724–1856," *Russkaia Starina* (1883) vol. 38, 14. The rules designated Grand Duke Michael regent in the circumstance that there was no heir of age to ascend to the throne. PSZ, 537, August 22, 1826.

39. "Istoricheskoe opisanie," 31:196–99.

40. *Vues des cérémonies les plus intéressantes du couronnement de leurs majestés Impériales l'empereur Nicholas Ier et l'impératrice Alexandra à Moscou* (Paris, 1828), 5; IGK, ts. Nik. I, 222.

41. Marmont, 8:132–33; E. F. Komarovskii, *Zapiski* (St. Petersburg, 1914), 256–57.

42. "Dva pis'ma gr. D. N. Bludova k supruge ego," 1047; Shil'der, *Imperator Nikolai Pervyi*, 2:7.

43. Tatishchev, 1:62.

44. "Aleksandr II; Dnevnik, 1834 g." TsGAOR, 678-1-280, 1.

45. Ibid., 21.

46. *Severnaia Pchela*, April 26, 1834, 365–66; *Russkii Invalid*, April 27, 1834, 407–408.

47. I. A. Shliapkin, "Iz bumag odnogo iz prepodavatelei Aleksandra II," *Starina i novizna* (1917) 22:15.

48. My description is based on the account published in both *Severnaia Pchela*, April 26, 1834, 365–66; *Russkii Invalid*, April 27, 1834, 407–408; *Vysochaishe utverzhdennyi tseremonial prisiagi Gosudaria, Naslednika, Aleksandra Nikolaevicha* (n.p., n.d.); Tatishchev, 1:63–65; Grimm, 2:89–91.

49. Tatishchev, 1:63–64.

50. A. S. Pushkin, *Dnevnik Pushkina, 1833–1835* (Moscow-Petrograd, 1923), 10.

51. V. A. Zhukovskii, *Sochineniia* (St. Petersburg, 1902), 4:22–23.

52. *Russkii Invalid*, May 2, 1834, 424.

53. *Severnaia Pchela*, 172 (August 3, 1837): 685.

54. [A. N. Murav'ev], *Vospominaniia o poseshchenii sviatyni Moskovskoi Gosudarem Naslednikom* (St. Petersburg, 1838), 13.

55. *Russkii Invalid*, September 27, 1837, 960.

56. On the myth of "tsar and cossack," see Robert H. McNeal, *Tsar and Cossack, 1855–1914* (Oxford, 1987), 1–5.

57. *Russkii Invalid*, November 24, 1837, 1182–83; *Severnaia Pchela*, November 2, 1837, 989; Tatischev, 1:89; "Dnevnik B. Kn. Aleksandra Nikolaevicha vo vremia poezdki po Rossii, May 1–December 12, 1837," 95–96.

PART II

IMPERIAL IMAGINATION

DEFINITIONS OF EMPIRE carry with them notions of control—political, intellectual, and historiographic. Embodied in a museum, an ethnographic survey, or a narrative of conquest, the empire appears as a comprehensible whole and, at least provisionally, a political entity. The following essays emphasize the tentative, exploratory nature of imperial representation in Russia. The authors' accounts reveal two related aspects of "knowing" the empire in the nineteenth century: first, the diversity of languages, peoples, and folkways was a salient and praiseworthy feature of definitions of the empire, and, second, Russian scholars were reluctant to fit their empire into European ideas of hierarchy and civilization.

Kevin Thomas analyzes two proposals for a Russian National Museum in the first quarter of the nineteenth century. These ambitious attempts to unite and exalt myriad artifacts—books, monuments, maps, paintings, heroes, antiquities, clothes, weapons, utensils, buildings, languages, machines, animals, plants, icons—under the roof of a single state institution expressed the desire of scholars to display the empire in its extraordinary variety. Combined with prolific display was a devotion to the idea of historical progress: the Russian empire would appear in the museum to have inexorably assumed its manifold essence over time. The designers, Thomas emphasizes, were able to imagine a museum that could express both the empire's heterogeneity and its continuities.

The German-born scholars who proposed the Russian museum believed that through its display of cultural wealth, Russia would participate in international science; the Russian state, like other European countries, would take its place in the expanding knowledge of the world and its historical development. Although these initial proposals were not implemented, a quarter century later another approach to the envisioning of the empire met with greater success: this was the Russian Geographical Society, founded in 1845. Analyzed by Nathaniel

Knight, the struggles over the institutional model for the Geographical Society indicate that while scholars at this time remained attached to the celebration of diversity within the empire, they differed among themselves over the purpose of scientific exploration of the realm. The value of international science was in dispute, as many in the Russian elite insisted that the main purpose of geographic exploration was to reveal the empire to Russians rather than to world scholarship. The new emphasis on a Russian-oriented scientific inquiry led scholars farther down the path of descriptive and particularistic ethnography, as Knight shows, and encouraged representation of the empire as a unique assemblage of diverse peoples.

An assemblage is not a staircase. Distinctive qualities of mid-nineteenth-century Russian ethnography were its horizontal sweep across the diverse population of the empire and the absence of judgmental, hierarchical placement of peoples on the imperial map. In contrast to Western ethnography, Russian efforts in this period to distinguish each people (*narodnost'*) did not imply a hierarchy of "civilized" and "savage." Knight's observations on nineteenth-century Russian ethnographic culture remind us of the dangers of imposing Western conceptions on Russian thought.

4

Collecting the Fatherland

Early-Nineteenth-Century Proposals for a Russian National Museum

Kevin Tyner Thomas

·⸱⟨∞⟩⸱·

IN 1817, AN essay appeared in the weekly St. Petersburg journal *Syn Otechestva* (*Son of the Fatherland*) under the title "Predlozhenie ob uchrezhdenii russkogo national'nogo muzeia" ("Proposal for the Establishment of a Russian National Museum"). At once a justification of and a detailed plan for a massive public institution, it was drafted by a Prussian scholar, Friedrich von Adelung (1768–1843), who had worked in Russia since shortly before the turn of the century. He envisioned a government-funded, centralized repository of national artifacts, a space wherein "ardent sons of the Fatherland" could view with ease the Russian state. Such a national museum, Adelung explained to his readers, should contain libraries and specialized exhibition halls, including a "Russian Pantheon" of state heroes, an "Antiquities Hall," a "Collection of Russian Historical Monuments," a display of the empire's "Narodoznanie" (or ethnographic artifacts), a "Cabinet of Natural History," and a "Chamber of Machines and Models." Four years later the same journal published another museum proposal, one much indebted to Adelung's plan of 1817. It was entitled "Rossiiskii otechestvennyi muzei" ("Russian Museum of the Fatherland"), and its author was a bibliographer from Riga named Burckhard von Wichmann (1786–1822).[1]

Though they will be unfamiliar to most readers, these fascinating texts have a canonical character in the neglected field of Russian museum studies. We have a small handful of Soviet specialists to thank for rescuing Adelung's and Wichmann's projects from oblivion. The museum plans figure prominently in their histories of collecting in pre-reform Russia. For the most part, these histories draw the same conclusions from the proposals: they were two of the earliest attempts on the part of Russian society to seek from the autocracy necessary public institutions; Adelung's and Wichmann's respective articles were among the first efforts to embrace what were soon to be recognized as the truly rational forms of collecting and exhibition; and as such, the museum plans were key predecessors to subsequent developments in Russian museum organization. Ultimately, these Soviet accounts of collecting in the pre-reform era contend that the proposals serve as proof of Russia's significant contribution to the advancement of the museological sciences in nineteenth-century Europe.[2]

I share this literature's enthusiasm for the importance of these two often-overlooked essays, but I want to demonstrate that the implications of the texts deserve further attention. The predominantly Soviet scholarship I just spoke of takes its examinations of both the museum plans only as far as certain well-defined national and disciplinary lines allow. A Russo-centric gaze circumscribes the interpretive purview here. The projects of 1817 and 1821 are approached as local, Russian breakthroughs in museology, ones that put the country's scientific tradition in a more positive light. The collecting practices suggested by the proposals are narrowly explicated in terms of their outcome within the field of museum science. In short, these accounts are primarily interested in Adelung's and Wichmann's articles as evidence for a diachronic "tunnel history" of Russia's collections.[3]

Due in part to the rigid boundaries embedded within it, the existing literature does not contend with the range of concepts and strategies Adelung and Wichmann used when they turned to the museum as a way to create authentic and evocative representations of Russia and its past. This essay sets out to explore those concepts and strategies. It is part of a broader attempt to recapture the local logic and coherence of the period's beliefs about the collecting of artifacts of national and historical interest. I want to examine certain features of these texts as a way of opening up a wider discussion of how the era's elites perceived, classified, and made sense of their world.

> Museums, which contain everything, however slight, that is related to native/national Letters [*otechestvennye Slovesnosti*] and to works of national genius, offer to the inquisitive patriot the fullest possible survey of all that Nature and industry, Science and Art have produced in his fatherland.

Thus begins Wichmann's "Rossiiskii otechestvennyi muzei."[4] Adelung too starts off with a definition of sorts, though his is somewhat more modest. A national museum, he tells his readers, is "the fullest possible collection of all objects related to the History, to the condition [*sostoianie*], and to the works of a particular land and its inhabitants."[5] Adelung talks specifically about what he means by a *"natsional'nyi muzei"*: it is, he says, a new kind of institution which will allow the immeasurably vast and extraordinarily diverse Russian state to be viewed with ease. Wichmann, writing three years later, makes this specific sort of collection the common standard by which all museums are to be judged. Adelung goes on to cite but one example of an existing national collection: the Hungarian National Museum created in 1802.[6] Wichmann, on the other hand, contends that numerous examples of such museums already exist in the cities of neighboring states. The mere sight of the national collections in Budapest, Athens, Prague, Brünn, and Vienna, he claims, compels a Russian to ask himself why his own country lacks such a valuable monument, "one through which the State and the people could immortalize so majestically their existence and keep it alive for posterity."[7]

The differences in these two preliminary definitions hint at just how rapidly the national museum was becoming a natural fixture on the European cultural landscape.[8] But the proposals themselves appeared at a time when the propriety of the practices associated with such an institution was not universally accepted, least of all in Russia.[9] Across early-nineteenth-century Europe this type of collection was adopted in some cases, much discussed in others, but its final validation, both as a physical space and a mental construct, required considerable efforts. In other words, it was not yet obvious that a museum could and should represent the nation—or in Russia's case, a multinational state. Adelung's and Wichmann's projects permit us a glimpse of the sorts of intellectual labor that went into making the national museum a mode of apprehending the Russian Empire, past and present; in short, they point us toward some of the conventions by which this new kind of museological knowledge was produced. To bring these conventions into sharper relief, we must examine more closely not only what Adelung and Wichmann were proposing but what it was they were rejecting.

Both of their preliminary definitions for national museums contain appeals for completeness. Each author goes on to reiterate a deep commitment to exhaustive sets of artifacts. What they envision, however, is something more than a well-organized inventory of human knowledge about the realm of the tsar. Their conceptions of a national museum require the collecting of extensive materials, but they also demand that the identities of already collected objects be transformed. Adelung and Wichmann aim to convert every curiosity and every long-ignored or forgotten fragment into traces of the Russian fatherland, past and present. Their proposals suggest that the very concentration of these traces in comprehensive collections within the museum itself will, in turn, reveal a sought-for unity.[10] As we shall see, the attempt to create this representation of the fatherland required concomitant efforts to alter the very ways in which its constituent components—that is, potential artifacts—were collected and validated.

For his part, Adelung wishes to see four classes of objects which he groups under a series of headings: "Literature and Art"; "Monuments"; "Narodoznanie (Ethnography)"; and "Works of Nature and of Man."[11] Each class is then broken down into subdivisions. "All Literature and Art related to Russia" are to be contained in two distinct sections. The first is to be a centralized, systematically organized library of history (including chronologies, genealogies, and studies of numismatics), geography, statistics, and travel accounts (by Russians as well as foreigners). In addition, a portion of this national library will be set aside for a complete collection of all Russian literary works; serving as both library and museum, as a scholarly repository of sources, and as an exhibition, it will incarnate a "History of Russian Literature."[12] These various holdings are to be joined by two equally extensive collections: one of manuscripts and another composed of all the existing maps, plans, and drawings of Russia, its cities, its gardens, and its buildings.[13]

The second major subdivision of the proposed "Literature and Art" department is to contain a grand assemblage of "statues, busts, bas-reliefs, paintings, drawings, and engravings." It will occupy what Adelung calls the "first *Russian Pantheon* [*Russkii Panteon* (emphasis in the original)]"; its walls are to be ornamented with representations of "Russian Sovereigns, Military Leaders, State Officials, and other noteworthy sons of Russia" and with depictions of the major events of Russian history. Having been recontextualized within the confines of the Russian Pantheon, these once disparate artifacts shall be transformed into potent sources of both moral and artistic inspiration. Their singularity will give way to commonality. This space, Adelung pledges, shall become a "true temple of Russian History," one with a powerful capacity to engender love for the fatherland while at the same time making manifest, for the benefit of the Lover of Art and the young Russian artist alike, the progress of the country's fine arts.[14]

Another set of monuments is to be displayed in an adjacent "Antiquities Hall." Here Adelung envisions a comprehensive collection of the numerous Greek and Roman antiquities—coins, statues, tools, and so on—found within the Russian Empire, especially in the Crimea and along the shores of the Black Sea. These artifacts, testaments to Russia's participation in the events of antiquity,[15] are to be situated alongside other groupings: a numismatic cabinet containing all coins and medals minted in Russia; a "Collection of Russian Historical Monuments" including such items as Tatar and Mongol statuary; and a "Collection of Russian Arms" from the most ancient times to the present.[16]

Adelung's imagined ethnographic collection is, at least in part, to be understood in terms of the artifacts concentrated in the aforementioned Antiquities Hall. The ethnographic collection encompasses "all items related to the knowledge of the numerous peoples and generations inhabiting the vast Russian state."[17] "Peoples" here, however, clearly means non-Russians. Whereas the Antiquities Hall combines classical antiquities with Russian ones, the ethnographic collection, which is at once distinct from and yet linked to the other sections of the museum, offers a controlled spectacle of the empire's diversity: it is in the ethnographic exhibition, Adelung says, that "Russia" has the potential to amass a treasure of the most varied objects the likes of which cannot be rivaled by any other country on earth.[18] He proposes that four types of ethnographic materials be collected and exhibited: clothes—meaning all implements and materials used to decorate the body; weapons—spears, maces, swords— "which are not of Slavic origin"; and utensils—that is, instruments related to a people's way of life (in particular, Adelung wants to see models of different dwellings along with all of the tools used for farming and fishing).[19]

Records of all native languages are to be gathered here as well. Again, prospective riches abound. Over one hundred languages and dialects are spoken in the Russian state, Adelung reminds his readers. Such a cacophony of local tongues is anything but a threat. He is confident that by compiling dictionaries and grammars of every language in the empire—and by gathering these together in a Russian National Museum—the origins, histories, and affinities of those who inhabit the state will thereby be revealed.[20]

"Works of Nature and of Man," a compendium of ingenious objects of natural and human manufacture, comprise two final collections: a "Cabinet of Natural History" and a "Chamber of Machines and Models." In the former, the empire's fauna is to be represented with a complete exhibition of stuffed birds and animals. Bones and other fragments will portray those beings which have disappeared. These displays should join a complete collection of insects and another equally comprehensive one of minerals and gems. Examples of all of Russia's plants are also to be assembled in this space, and, as if to provide a segue to the collection which follows, those natural items which have practical uses for agriculture and industry will be placed in a special "Technological Cabinet."[21] This cabinet is, in turn, to abut the Russian National Museum's final collection, the Chamber of Machines and Models, a repository for what Adelung rather vaguely calls examples of all the best works of Russian "mechanical artists," whose products deserve to be committed to the memory of posterity.[22]

As for Wichmann's plan, our second author acknowledges Adelung's essay in a footnote in which he expresses the hope that the two proposals will not work at cross-purposes but rather function jointly so as to persuade others of the tremendous importance of a Russian National Museum.[23] His "Rossiiskii otechestvennyi muzei" then goes on to adopt every major category of artifacts put forward by Adelung. Wichmann continues the quest for completeness. He too first proposes a great central library, one which he hopes will "with the passage of a few years, not lack a single manuscript or book concerning our society."[24] This "society" is to have access to all sources of potential enrichment. Though it is not entirely clear, given his all-encompassing vision of its contents, what in fact would be allowed to exist outside the proposed national library, Wichmann also insists that the institution immediately obtain and make available to the public precise lists of the holdings of all other libraries, collections, and archives in Russia, be they owned by private individuals, the church, or the government.[25]

Whereas Adelung places maps, charts, and drawings of Russia, its cities, its gardens, and its buildings under the rubric of the national library, Wichmann positions them in a more distinct collection of their own, apparently to highlight their value. He treats them as mechanisms for visualizing the empire. Its progressive development and its vast, current diversity shall merge in this collection on a single, appreciable horizon. An exhibition of all depictions of Russia's public structures, native/national institutions, and factories, Wichmann holds, clearly shows that "In no other State has the Architecture in different periods undergone so many great changes (mostly from fire)."[26] He then posits a viewing subject of this collection and imagines the cumulative visual effect of concentrating in a single space these many ancient and recent cartographic and architectural materials: "How interesting it would be if a Russian was able to gaze upon this panorama!"[27]

Wichmann envisages a complete collection of all monuments within the borders of the Russian state. His list of candidate *pamiatniki* includes tombstones, inscriptions, pagan idols, statuary, and bas-reliefs. These, he says, should be arranged in a chronological order similar to that employed in Paris at the Musée des Monuments Français.[28] Their authenticity is not of paramount importance: Wichmann instructs that plaster casts and copies should be made when originals cannot be had. Much like Adelung, he claims that the gathering together and proper ordering of these real and imitation artifacts will give tangible form to the past; it will not so much explain history as simply evince the gradual progress of the arts in Russia. Individual inscriptions may indeed, as Wichmann points out, prove useful to students of Russian paleography, but the actual subject of the collection itself is not the isolated artifact: again, it is the supposedly self-evident relations between display pieces. Thus arranged, these monuments will provide a rich set of "reminders" [*napominaniia*] and examples for "Writers of History" and "Lovers of Art."

This collection, modeled after the French example, is in turn to be supplemented with an equally exhaustive set of Russian coats of arms, seals, and coins. Here too Wichmann allows for originals as well as reproductions. He says that those sons of the fatherland who are unwilling to part with certain pieces from their private numismatic collections, for example, shall be asked to donate imprints. What is crucial is that the order of succession of Russian coins and medals not be interrupted.

Wichmann makes an implicit distinction between the monuments of the Russians on the one hand, and the items of the empire's non-Russian "tribes" on the other. Again, diversity is to flourish within a closed, confined space. Like Adelung, he tenders a vast ethnographic collection. The exhibition should occupy a gallery

> in which must be preserved every sort of native/national dress, household implement, dish and good of the various tribes [*plemena*] who inhabit areas of our fatherland, and who are distinguished among themselves by their ancestries, customs, languages, and religions. In this same gallery must be preserved drawings depicting their physiognomies, dwellings, and temples as well as their ceremonies, festivals, and particular amusements.[29]

Wichmann's instructions for a natural history collection are even less specific than Adelung's. He proposes the formation of a complete "Natural Cabinet of the three Kingdoms of Nature," and once more emphasizes the transformative capacities of the collection itself. The mere accumulation of plant and animal specimens, soil samples, and minerals from every province in the empire will, he claims, release for the benefit of all countrymen nature's "magical powers."[30]

Adelung's "Russian Pantheon" also reappears in a modified form when Wichmann calls for an extensive portrait gallery of great Russian figures— "Sovereigns, heroes, Statesmen, Scholars, and other notable individuals from history."[31] The portraits are to be accompanied by all manuscripts, handwritten compositions, and letters related to the respective figures. "Admission to this temple of glory of the Russians," Wichmann boldly declares, "will not be based on ancestry or rank: it will include a depiction of any worthy citizen, in commemoration of the respect which is his due."[32] Then, as if to enhance its resemblance to a religious site, he adds that this glorious temple should be situated next to another gallery containing nothing but Russian icons arranged in chronological order.[33]

Wichmann's imaginary Russian national museum is made complete with a special hall which is to serve as a sort of polytechnical collection. It resembles Adelung's Chamber of Machines and Models but with an identity less bound up with a natural history cabinet. Here are to be exhibited the manufactured goods of the fatherland, namely products, crafts, and inventions. Most importantly, these items will display for all to see the skill and craftsmanship of native/national artisans. Wichmann again draws examples from neighboring states to drive home his point: the Frenchman surveys the products of his nation's arts and crafts; the Austrian strolls the halls of Vienna's Polytechnic Institute; both are captivated by the perfection of their countrymen's works; so too will a Russian feel no less pleasure in looking over the many fine products "which attest to the industriousness of his compatriots [*sootchichi*]."[34]

Adelung's and Wichmann's projects are, in a sense, diagrams of the ways in which Renaissance and early modern cabinets of curiosities, both private and princely, were retooled and redeployed in the early nineteenth century. Inspired by the examples of such rediscovered classical works as Pliny the Elder's *Natural History*, early Renaissance humanists embarked upon ambitious encyclopedic collecting programs. The museum, the classical site for the gathering of the muses, was resurrected as well, rapidly becoming—in part as a response to the massive influx of the materials emanating from the voyages of discovery of the late fifteenth and early sixteenth centuries—a favored repository for collected objects, a place where "curiosities" could be studied, discussed, and displayed.[35] Informed by an aesthetic which prized the exotic, the anomalous, and the concrete, these *Kunst- und Wunderkammern*, or cabinets of curiosities, juxtaposed and placed in close proximity multifarious kinds of objects—stuffed lizards, portraits, bones, antiquities, gems, books, lathe-turned miniatures, ethnographic artifacts culled from exotic locales—so as to reveal a marvelously stunning, coherent visual representation of the macrocosm's inexhaustible plenitude in microcosmic form.

The implications of such collections did not end at the wall of the collector's studio. The museum transcended its physical parameters: it came to serve as a broad conceptual system, a highly flexible epistemological structure through which collectors investigated and made sense of their world.[36] As cabinet and metaphor the museum was a transdisciplinary form of inquiry, a space wherein heterogeneous materials could be observed "without having to face or solve the problem of continuity."[37]

The cognitive status of these *Kunst- und Wunderkammern* did not go unchallenged. Galileo himself disparaged those "curious little men" who delighted in filling their studies with "things that have something strange about them . . . but are nothing but bric-a-brac."[38] Enlighteners such as D'Alembert derided polymathic hodgepodges.[39] In brief, by the mid-eighteenth century the once-profuse cabinets had collapsed under their own weight, increasingly incapable of arousing wonder, their owners now assailed as dilettantes.

As has been much remarked, especially in the wake of Foucault, the peculiar juxtaposition of objects in the *Kunst- und Wunderkammern* gave way to a comprehensive system of scientific tabulation. What did not fade, however, was the faith in the museum's capacity to confer coherence on large numbers of multifarious items. This faith dovetailed nicely with the Enlightenment's preoccupation with public instruction. In the second half of the eighteenth century, the focus of the museum was redirected: it came to serve as a site at which the treasures of private collectors and of the court could be transformed into sources of the public's enrichment.[40] At much the same time, collectors in Europe had begun to shift their gazes as well. In the collections of many antiquarians, for example, artifacts of classical antiquity and exotic curiosities lost their pride of place to objects closer at hand, fragments of "local antiquity," medieval curiosities of the surrounding region.[41] In this way, collecting, which had begun as a cosmopolitan practice *par excellence*, was overlaid with patriotic and nationalistic sentiments.

This process was not without tensions. Disenchantment with collections of exotic, multifarious curiosities came to a head at the very moment when Peter the Great was beginning to assemble his own such cabinets. The St. Petersburg *Kunstkammer*, founded in 1714 and opened in 1719, bore many of the contradictions of this crossover period. The museum certainly deserved its name. Peter's "wonder cabinet" came to contain, among other things, dried swordfish, Roman statuary, a live hermaphrodite, and anatomical exhibits fashioned out of children's skeletons. Yet the St. Petersburg *Kunstkammer* was also consciously fashioned as a site for the public education of Russia's noble elites. After Peter's death, the museum continued to house its vast assortment of bizarre objects collected from distant places, but it also emerged as the favored repository for all old and unusual artifacts found on the soil of the expanding Russian Empire.[42]

These sorts of contradictions were not isolated to the *Kunstkammer*. Yuri Slezkine's essay, "Naturalists Versus the Nation: Eighteenth-Century Russian Scholars Confront Ethnic Diversity," provides an excellent overview of how traditions of encyclopedism permeated the world of educated Russia in the eighteenth-century.[43] As he points out toward the end of the piece, the seemingly endless diversity generated by scholarly attempts to map, to chart, and to classify—in other words, to collect—the Russian empire ran up against the efforts of others (Mikhail Lomonosov is singled out as an early example) who felt compelled to provide the intellectual grounds for a more monolithic conception of Russian national identity. The greatest challenge, says Slezkine, "was to overcome ethnography by history . . . to conflate—once and for all—the various independent components of Russian nationality."[44]

The national museum idea was, in part, an attempt to dissolve—if not solve—this problem. Adelung and Wichmann argue that it possesses the capacity to display Russia's immense and unparalleled wealth of peoples. It can also stage for all to see—sons of the Russian fatherland as well as visitors from abroad—the empire's immemorial past, its historical development, and current greatness. By dislocating diverse objects from their original contexts and concentrating them in the museum, Adelung and Wichmann promise to create an emblem of the nation's riches while at the same time arresting the slippage of meaning which haunted Slezkine's ethnographers.

For the institution to work as a site for the dissemination of such knowledge, it clearly must be made accessible to at least a portion of the public. Adelung is quite specific in this regard. The museum, he instructs, must be open no less than "twice a week for the public, and permit on these days the entrance of all properly dressed persons." Also, at specially appointed times museum assistants are to accompany visitors through the halls and provide explanations about every object which lacks a sufficiently detailed description.[45]

What is perhaps less conspicuous are certain other related changes in convention. In their proposals, both Adelung and Wichmann emphasize that one of the principal virtues of a Russian National Museum would be its ability to protect artifacts of the fatherland from destruction. Adelung terms this a function "worthy of paramount attention." He argues that "thousands of curious objects" and "innumerable monuments of History and Art" are in the hands of private individuals who are often entirely ignorant of their actual value; here they languish, eminently susceptible to destruction by carelessness or by accident; if action is not taken, then irreplaceable traces of Russia and of its history will be lost forever.[46]

Adelung's lament was not new. In a letter written a little over a hundred years earlier, Nicholas Witsen, the Dutch author of a learned text on Siberia and burgomaster of Amsterdam who entertained Peter I on the tsar's first visit to Holland, discussed the Muscovite penchant for thoughtlessly melting down gold and silver artifacts extracted from burial mounds in Siberia. "The Russians do not love antiquities," he concluded.[47] Adelung knew well Witsen's work.[48] The former was in many respects an heir to a tradition of scholarly inquiry that the Dutch author had helped establish. Yet what separates Witsen from Adelung is the latter's assertion that artifacts must not only be loved and protected but that they can find their true meanings only when assembled under one roof. The clear implication of Adelung's proposal is that the lone enthusiast can no longer provide objects with their proper context.[49] Only a national museum possesses this power.

Wichmann takes this argument a step further. First he offers a sort of cursory history of educational institutions in Russia. The point of this passage is to stress the emergence of collective study in the Russian state: "the more individuals united their minds, the stronger became their actions."[50] By association, collecting must also be of a communal nature. He too then laments the destruction of historical materials, calling on the national museum to take the lead in efforts to prevent similar losses in the future. Individual collectors may mean well, but by acting independently they will only allow the history embedded in objects to drift away from the present. In a novel move, one which again shows the depth of his faith in the museum's capacities, Wichmann applies this argument to existing institutions as well: they too cannot do full justice to the items in their care. Private individuals are, therefore, not the only ones who should give up *pamiatniki*. He calls on the Imperial Public Library, the Hermitage, the Library of the Academy of Sciences, and all other native/national institutions to transfer with "diligent goodwill" everything that is required by this new establishment. He adds that since the Russian National Museum should undoubtedly be located in St. Petersburg, most of those institutions forced to relinquish part of their holdings will, being only a few doors away, have easy access to what was once theirs, but with the benefit of those objects finally being concentrated at a site in which their fullest meanings can be realized.[51]

Adelung's and Wichmann's visions of communal collecting hinge on making the national museum function as a temple in more than name.[52] After discussing the threat to Russian artifacts, Adelung speculates that every family in Russia has in its possession at least one potential monument of the fatherland.[53] Again, for these objects to acquire their true meaning, he contends, they must be given over to the care of the national museum. Toward the end of his proposal he suggests that the best way to obtain these items is by way of nationwide invitation. The smallest, seemingly most insignificant gifts will be duly noted. He implies that every true son of the Fatherland, upon realizing the loftiness of the goal at hand, will gladly donate all he can.[54] Wichmann's cursory history of collective study in Russia ends with his contention that while cooperation has increased and many personal centers of learning have sprung up, the country still lacks "the sort of institution in which Russians could bring offerings to the penates,[55] and toil only for the good of native/national science."[56] He also makes an example of himself. The first footnote in "Rossiiskii otechestvennyi muzei" lists his publications and adds that the author possesses a substantial collection of manuscripts and artifacts related to Russia, one which he will happily donate if a viable plan for a Russian National Museum is put into action.[57]

What Adelung and Wichmann call for are "sacrifices" to the new sciences of Russia. Both authors stipulate that the entrance to the national museum must be ornamented with a classical facade.[58] Carried over the threshold of this civic temple, a coat of arms, a fishing hook, a personal memoir, a tiger pelt—things suddenly recognized as fragile, disparate bits—enter into the collection

and thereby take their proper place as *pamiatniki*. To borrow from Krzysztof
Pomian's brilliant study of collecting, the objects function not unlike burial offerings. Extracted from the circuit of daily use and deposited in a single space,
they act as what Pomian calls "semiophores"—bearers of meaning, intermediaries between the visible secular world and a distant, absent, invisible realm.
This invisible world is at once spatially and temporally distant.[59] Adelung's and
Wichmann's museums are envisioned as communal sites for the mediation of
an "imagined community"—Russia—and of its immemorial past.[60]

It is no small irony that Adelung, the first person to articulate in print the
national museum's capacity for representing the Russian fatherland, was born
and trained in Germany.[61] Adelung has yet to find his biographer. Our knowledge of his career remains incomplete. It is clear, however, that at much the same
time that he was drafting his museum proposal Adelung was beginning to act
as a crucial figure in an international network of philologists, naturalists, antiquarians, and historians from all over Europe. The members of this network
were held together in part by their contributions to Johann Samuel Ersch and
Johann Gottfried Gruber's enormous nineteenth-century encyclopedia project,
Allgemeine Encyclopädie der Wissenschaften und Künste (which began to appear in
1818 and reached 167 volumes at the time of its discontinuance in 1850). Ersch's
letters to Adelung suggest that the latter sought to recruit Wichmann as a
German-speaking contributor to the *Encyclopädie*.[62]

Among other activities, Adelung also corresponded with linguists all over
the globe in an effort to bring to publication the final three volumes of that well-
known and bizarre polyglot word collection entitled *Mithridates*, the far-flung
endeavor initiated by his famous uncle, Johann Christian von Adelung, an eminent linguist and historian in his own right.[63]

Adelung's and Wichmann's projects were obviously designed to stimulate
Russian pride. Yet their simultaneous cosmopolitanism does indeed shed light
on the strange breed of "nationalism" that is being proffered in the proposals.
The writers do not see their projects as incompatible with ongoing attempts to
construct a universal history of mankind. Both call for teams of museum experts to travel to every city in Europe to search for materials related to Russia.[64]
Each hopes that such sojourns will have the additional benefit of opening up
fruitful dialogues with foreign bibliographers, archivists, antiquarians, and collectors. Wichmann proposes that the museum publish a journal so that scholars
at home and especially those abroad can be kept abreast of the institution's lat-
est activities.[65] If they seek to provide a framework in which diversity can be at
once displayed and neutralized, they seem little interested in buttressing claims
of ethnic superiority. The Russian National Museum is to take its rightful place
in a collection of other national collections.

Neither of these proposals was realized in the pre-reform era. Nor did they elicit much response. The court seems not to have given them serious consideration. Both plans solicit royal patronage. Adelung and Wichmann make it abundantly clear that only with the backing of the tsar will the national museum acquire necessary funding as well as the requisite powers to gather its materials.[66] They also present the institution as an emblem of the tsar's benevolence. Wichmann contends that it is only fitting that a Russian National Museum be called nothing less than the "Alexandrinum."[67] Yet it seems entirely plausible that Alexander himself did not perceive the institution as a proper representation of his power. He was not alone among his contemporary monarchs in failing to share fully the museum advocates' enthusiasm.[68] Here, then, we encounter yet another of the contradictions that marked the national museum idea in Russia at this curious juncture. The principal problem for Alexander appears to rest in the perceptible tension between the proposals' request for royal sponsorship and the way in which the projects themselves redistribute the meanings of the institution's objects. The building itself can be construed as a testament of Alexander's kindness and enlightenment, but the artifacts inside are, in a sense, decoupled from his person; they will cease to be direct representations of his glory and wisdom. Adelung and Wichmann, cosmopolitan scholars who had cast their lot with the elite of the Russian fatherland, ask the tsar to help them remake these objects as products of national genius.[69]

Notes

Comments by participants in the SSRC Workshop on Imperial Russian History are gratefully acknowledged. I would also like to thank Jane Burbank, Nina Caputo, Carlo Ginzburg, David Harden, Mitchell Hart, Hans Rogger, and Douglas Smith for having read and criticized versions of this essay.

1. Friedrich von Adelung, "Predlozhenie ob uchrezhdenii russkogo national'nogo muzeia," *Syn Otechestva* 37 (1817), 54–75. Burckhard von Wichmann, "Rossiiskii otechestvennyi muzei," *Syn Otechestva* 33 (1821), 289–310 (hereafter ROM). Both proposals were also circulated in pamphlet form, Adelung's in a Russian edition published in St. Petersburg in 1817 (hereafter PURNM), and Wichmann's in a German edition published in Riga in 1820.

2. For an early formulation of these conclusions, see G. L. Malitskii, "Osnovnye voprosy istorii muzeinogo dela v Rossii (do 1917 goda)," *Ocherednye zadachi perestroiki*

raboty kraevedcheskikh muzeev (Moscow, 1950), 166. The most extensive discussion of Adelung's and Wichmann's respective plans is found in A. M. Razgon, "Rossiiskii isto-richeskii muzei. Istoriia ego osnovaniia i deiatelnosti (1872–1917 gg.)," *Ocherki istorii muzeinogo dela v Rossii* 2 (1960), 224–99, esp. 226–28. The interesting recent essay by S. A. Kasparinskaia—"Muzei Rossii i vliianie gosudarstvennoi politiki na ikh razvitie (XVIII-nach. XX v.)," in *Muzei i vlast'*, ed. S. A. Kasparinskaia (Moscow, 1991), 8–95—again stresses the proposals' significance as evidence that "society" was beginning to take the initiative in museum affairs.

3. The phrase "tunnel history" is used by Roy Porter in his introduction to *Science, Culture, and Popular Belief in Renaissance Europe*, Stephen Pumfrey, Paolo L. Rossi, and Maurice Slawinski, eds. (Manchester, 1991), 2.

4. ROM, 289. A satisfactory translation of "otechestvennyi" is elusive. "Father-land" and "homeland" are awkward as adjectives. Though it too has connotations that are somewhat inappropriate, the doublet "native/national" seems closer to the mark.

5. PURNM, 1.

6. PURNM, 6.

7. ROM, 290–93.

8. On the spread of national and public collections in this period, see Germain Bazin, *The Museum Age*, trans. Jane van Nuis Cahill (New York, 1967), 169–239.

9. For a concise historical overview of the ambiguities which attended the emergence of the nineteenth-century national museums, see Krzysztof Pomian, "Musée, nation, musée national," *Le Debat*, no. 65 (May-August 1991), 166–75. Susan Crane's provocative study of the German context, "Collecting and Historical Consciousness: New Forms for Collective Memory in Early Nineteenth-Century Germany," Ph.D. diss., University of Chicago, 1992, focuses on the ways in which German collectors used museums as a means of propagating and institutionalizing a new collective "preservationist" agenda.

10. On the wider emergence of this sensibility in Europe, see Jaques Revel, "Forms of Expertise: Intellectuals and 'Popular' Culture in France (1650–1800)," in Steven Kaplan, ed., *Understanding Popular Culture* (The Hague, 1994), 255–73.

11. PURNM, 5.

12. PURNM, 7.

13. PURNM, 6–8.

14. PURNM, 9.

15. Adelung makes this claim near the beginning of his proposal. See PURNM, 2.

16. PURNM, 9–10

17. PURNM, 10–11.

18. PURNM, 11. Wichmann echoes the theme of diversity in his proposed ethnographic collection. The celebration of Russia's vastness and its bountiful diversity was a recurrent motif in the early nineteenth century. See Yuri Slezkine, *Arctic Mirrors: Russia and the Small Peoples of the North* (Ithaca, 1994), 73–92.

19. PURNM, 11.

20. PURNM, 11–12. On von Adelung's linguistic activities, see note 63 below.

21. PURNM, 13.

22. PURNM, 13.

23. ROM, 290.

24. ROM, 298.

25. ROM, 300.

26. ROM, 302.

27. ROM, 302.

28. ROM, 300.

29. ROM, 303.

30. ROM, 302–303.

31. ROM, 303–304.

32. ROM, 304.

33. ROM, 304.

34. ROM, 305.

35. The key literature on this subject is too vast to cite within the confines of this essay. Of course, the classic study is Julius von Schlosser, *Die Kunst- und Wunderkammern der Spätrenaissance* (Leipzig, 1908; and Braunschweig, 1978). Some of the most interesting examples of the more recent scholarship include Krzysztof Pomian, *Collectors and Curiosities. Paris, Venice 1500–1800* (Cambridge, 1990); Paula Findlen, "Museums, Collecting, and Scientific Culture in Early Modern Italy," Ph.D. diss., University of California, Berkeley, 1989; Lorraine Daston, "The Factual Sensibility," *Isis* 79 (1988), 452–70; and Carlo Ginzburg, "Montaigne, Cannibals, Grottoes," *History and Anthropology* 6, no. 2–3 (1993), 125–55.

36. See, especially, Paula Findlen, "The Museum: Its Classical Etymology and Renaissance Genealogy," *Journal of the History of Collections* 1, no. 1 (1989), 59–78.

37. Adlgisa Lugli, "Inquiry as Collection: The Athanasius Kircher Museum in Rome," *RES* 12 (1986), 116.

38. Quoted in Ginzburg, "Montaigne, Cannibals, and Grottoes," 140.

39. Barbara Maria Stafford, *Artful Science: Enlightenment Entertainment and the Eclipse of Visual Education* (Cambridge, Mass., 1994), 220.

40. Philip Fisher, "The Future's Past," *New Literary History* 6, no. 3 (Spring 1975), 589–91.

41. On this phenomenon, see the classic essay by Arnaldo Momigliano, "Ancient History and the Antiquarian," *Journal of the Warburg and Courtland Institutes* 13 (July-December, 1950), 285–315; and Francis Haskell, *History and Its Images: Art and the Interpretation of the Past* (New Haven, 1993).

42. See, for example, *Palaty Sanktpeterburgskoi imn. Akademii nauk, Biblioteki i Kunstkamery* (St. Petersburg, 1741); O. Beliaev, *Kabinet Petra Velikago* (St. Petersburg, 1800); P. Pekarskii, *Nauka i Literatura pri Petre Velikom*, vol. 1 (St. Petersburg, 1862); A. A. Spitsyn, "Sibirskaia kollektsiia kunstkameri," *Zapiski otdeleniia russkoi i slavianskoi arkheologii Russkogo arkheologicheskogo obshchestva* (St. Petersburg, 1906); V. V. Ginzburg, "Anatomicheskiia kollektsii F. Riuisha v sobraniiakh Petrovskoi Kunstkameri," *Sbornik muzeia antropologii i etnografii* 14 (1953), 263–305; T. V. Staniukovich, *Kunstkamera Peterburgskoi Akademii Nauk* (Moscow, 1953), and *Etnograficheskaia nauka i muzei* (Leningrad, 1978). O. A Neverov,

"Pamiatniki antichnovogo iskusstva v Rossii petrovskovogo vremeni," in *Kultura i iskus-stvo petrovskogo vremeni* (Leningrad, 1977), 37–55, and "His Majesty's 'Cabinet' and Peter I's *Kunstkammer*" in *The Origins of Museums* (Oxford, 1985); Helga Meyer-Harder, "Theatrum mundi: Die Petersburger Kunstkammer 1741," in Wolfgang Kessler, et al., eds., *Kulturbeziehungen in Mittel- und Osteuropa im 18. und 19. Jahrhundert* (Berlin, 1982), 27–40.

43. Yuri Slezkine, "Naturalists Versus the Nation: Eighteenth-Century Russian Scholars Confront Ethnic Diversity," *Representations* 47 (Summer 1994), 170–95.

44. Slezkine, "Naturalists Versus the Nation," 189.

45. PURNM, 19. For a more extensive treatment of the implications of public space in Russian society, see Douglas Smith's essay in this volume.

46. PURNM, 2–3.

47. The letter was reprinted in a Russian translation in an article by V. V. Radlov, "Sibirskie drevnosti," *Materialy po arkheologii Rossii* 15 (1894), 129. It appears in the Dutch original in J. F. Gebhard, *Het Leven van Mr. Nicholas Cornelisz Witsen (1647–1717)*, vol. 2 (Utrecht, 1882), 328–30.

48. The work for which Adelung is perhaps best remembered is his compilation of travelers' accounts of Muscovy, *Übersicht der Reisenden in Rußland bis 1700, deren Berichte bekannt sind* (St. Petersburg, 1846). Witsen figures prominently in this volume. That Adelung was aware of Witsen's work before the publication of his museum proposal is suggested by letters written to Adelung by Johann Vater in 1815; these discuss Witsen. See *Johann Severin Vater—Ein Wegbereiter der deutsch-slawischen Wechselseitigkeit (Zu Vaters slawisitischen Studien im Lichte seiner Briefe an Friedrich Adelung in Petersburg)* (Berlin, 1984) 114, 128. Unfortunately, these letters make no mention of Adelung's museum plan.

49. Crane makes a similar point about German collectors. See "Collecting and Historical Consciousness."

50. ROM, 292.

51. ROM, 308–309.

52. The image of the civic shrine was a common one in late-eighteenth- and early-nineteenth-century Russia, as it was in much of Europe. See James J. Sheehan, "From Princely Collections to Public Museums: Toward a History of the German Art Museum" in *Rediscovering History*, ed. Michael S. Roth (Stanford, 1994), 169–82. What is interesting to note here is the relationship between the metaphor and the actual functions of Adelung's and Wichmann's imagined institutions.

53. PURNM, 2.

54. PURNM, 14–15.

55. In Roman religion the penates were primarily household gods of the storeroom.

56. ROM, 292.

57. ROM, 290.

58. PURNM, 18; ROM, 301.

59. See "The Collection: Between the Visible and the Invisible," the first chapter of Pomian's *Collectors and Curiosities*, 7–44.

60. Pomian's theory of the collection fits well with Benedict Anderson's examina-

tions of those various mechanisms which made it possible to "think the nation." See his *Imagined Communities: Reflections on the Origin and Spread of Nationalism*, Revised Edition (London, 1991).

61. A smattering of biographical information on Adelung and Wichmann is contained in V. P. Kozlov, *Kolumby rossiiskikh drevnostei* (Moscow, 1981). On Wichmann, see also the brief entry in *Bol'shaia Entsiklopedia* vol. 5 (St. Petersburg, 1901), 162. On Adelung, see F. Köppen, "Fedor Pavlovich Adelung," *Russkii biografischeskii slovar'* vol. 1 (New York, 1962), 71–73; A. A. Formozov, *Stranitsy istorii russkoi arkheologii* (Moscow, 1986), 44; Eduard Winter, "Jenaer und Hallenser Briefe von J. S. Ersch an F. Adelung in St. Petersburg (1803–1819)," *Wissenschaftliche Zeitschrift der Friedrich-Schiller Universität Jena, Gesellschaft- und sprachwissenschaftliche Reihe*, Heft 7 (1957/58), 465–74; and the Introduction to *Johann Severin Vater*. For a piece that sheds new light on the community of scholars to which Adelung belonged in St. Petersburg, see A. V. Bekasova, "'Uchenye zaniatiia' russkogo aristokrata kak sposob samorealizatsii (na primere grafa N. P. Rumiantseva)," *Voprosy istorii estestvoznaniia i tekhniki* 1 (1995), 24–39.

62. See Winter, "Jenaer und Hallenser Briefe von J. S. Ersch an F. Adelung."

63. See *Johann Severin Vater*. Adelung's fascinating linguistic activities warrant a full study of their own.

64. PURNM, 13–14; ROM, 295.

65. ROM, 306.

66. PURNM, 14–15; ROM, 291, 294, 307–309.

67. ROM, 309. The implied reference to the great library of antiquity in Alexandria is surely not a coincidence.

68. On the similar reluctance of some German princes, see Crane, "Collecting and Historical Consciousness."

69. On the wider European implications of this shift, see Carol Duncan, "Art Museums and the Ritual of Citizenship," in *Exhibiting Cultures: The Poetics and Politics of Museum Display*, ed. Ivan Karp and Steven D. Levine (Washington, 1991), 94–95.

5

Science, Empire, and Nationality

Ethnography in the Russian Geographical Society, 1845–1855

Nathaniel Knight

———————————

A T A LAVISH St. Petersburg banquet in March 1845, the naturalist A. F. Middendorff, recently returned from a three-year expedition to Siberia and the Far East, regaled the assembled company of academicians and explorers with tales of the lands and peoples he had encountered in his travels. Among his audience was Admiral Fedor Petrovich Litke, tutor to the Grand Duke Constantin Nikolaevich and veteran of a long series of voyages of exploration. Inspired by Middendorff's tales, Litke along with his friends Ferdinand Wrangel and Karl von Baer resolved to implement a plan which they had been discussing for several years—the creation of a learned society specially devoted to the study of the lands, peoples, and resources of the Russian Empire. Encompassing the fields of geography, statistics, and ethnography, the Russian Geographical Society, the fruit of Litke's inspiration, was quickly approved by Nicholas I and in the autumn of 1845 was inaugurated into Russian academic life. With generous funding from the state, and the participation of Russia's most prominent scientists, the society quickly became a major force in Russian science and has continued to exist up to the present day.[1]

By its very nature the Geographical Society stood at an awkward juncture between the forces of science, empire, and nationality. As a semiofficial organization formally headed by the Grand Duke Constantin Nikolaevich, the Geographical Society was an intrinsic outgrowth of the apparatus of empire—a status which was accentuated in 1849 when Nicholas I granted the society the right to bear the title "Imperial."[2] But in becoming imperial, the Geographical Society did not cease to be Russian. At a time when the problem of national identity was at the forefront of intellectual life, the Geographical Society could not stand aloof from calls to identify itself not only with the imperial state but also with the Russian nation.

But while the object of study within the Geographical Society may have been Russia, the methods to be applied were those of international science, drawing on the insights of leading specialists from around the world. The establishment of the Geographical Society was itself, in part, a response to developments in the international scientific community, including the establishment of similar institutions throughout Europe and America in previous years.[3] In the eyes of its founders, the Geographical Society was to bring accurate information about the Russian Empire to the international community and in so doing facilitate Russia's contribution to the progress of world science.

Combining the forces of empire, nationality, and science within the confines of one institution created instability. Particularly in its early years, the Geographical Society was beset by a clash of contrasting conceptions regarding the relationship between these elements. Like a photographic catalyst, the Geographical Society made visible tensions latent in the nexus between state and science, between nation and empire. These tensions, as manifested in the activities of the Russian Geographical Society, are to be the topic of the present discussion.

Nowhere was the uneasy relationship between science, empire, and nationality more apparent than within the Geographical Society's Ethnographic Division. Unlike geography and statistics, ethnography, Russia's equivalent to ethnology or cultural anthropology, was a fundamentally new endeavor. The Ethnographic Division was the first scholarly institution in Russia explicitly devoted to the field, and the division's publication, *Ethnographic Anthology*, its first journal. Precisely because of the novelty of ethnography as an autonomous scholarly discipline, its practitioners were compelled to articulate their goals and methodology, revealing, in the process, differences in underlying conceptions. And as a science broadly devoted to "the study of various peoples living within the current boundaries of the empire,"[4] ethnography was particularly prone to the influence of the national and imperial context, resulting in a field that differed substantially from analogous disciplines in Western Europe and North America. For these reasons, after a discussion of the overall tensions within the Geographical Society in its early years, we will focus on ethnography, examining the process through which it developed its distinctive orientation.

Germans, Russians, and the Politics of Science

On October 7, 1845, at the inaugural meeting of the Geographical Society, Admiral Litke gave a speech in which he articulated his vision of the goals and challenges facing the new institution. First and foremost, Litke stressed that the task of the Geographical Society should be to study Russia:

> Our fatherland, which stretches in its longitude over more than half the circumference of the earth, is in itself a distinct part of the earth with its unique variations in climate, in geognosy, in flora and fauna, with numerous peoples and so forth. And I would add that this is a part of the earth which has been studied very little. These completely distinct conditions directly indicate that the main topic for the Russian Geographical Society should be the development of the geography of Russia.[5]

Litke's formulation, however, limiting the object of investigation to the Russian Empire and its immediate borderlands, left many questions unanswered. How exactly was Russia to be studied? What sort of investigations should be carried out? And to what end?

In considering the character of the new institution, the founders of the society were faced with two distinct models from within the realm of their direct experience suggesting a choice of potential orientations. As the dominant voice in Russian science, the Academy of Sciences provided a clear and forceful example of how a well-organized scientific organization should function. In his inaugural speech, Litke had, in fact, felt the need to explain why a Geographical Society was necessary outside the Academy of Sciences. While acknowledging its past achievements, Litke noted:

> the Academy has not had the opportunity to do enough for geography. More could have been done and this "more" is the task of the Russian Geographical Society. Therefore from a scholarly point of view the Geographical Society, while entirely independent, is something like an extension of the Academy for certain specific goals.[6]

In other words, while the Geographical Society promised a more detailed and specialized pursuit of its designated fields, Litke did not envision a fundamental difference in approach from that of the Academy of Sciences.

Beyond the Academy of Sciences, however, an alternative model for the Geographical Society existed in the various specialized departments and offices within the state bureaucracy working on matters related to geography, ethnography, and statistics. In his speech, Litke had specifically mentioned the Topographical Department of the General Staff and the Naval Ministry's Hydrological Department as potential partners with the Geographical Society.[7] However, an even stronger potential for collaboration existed with the various departments of the Ministry of Internal Affairs under the direction of L. A. Perovskii.

The Geographical Society was, in fact, under the formal jurisdiction of the

Ministry of Internal Affairs during its first years.[8] The connecting link between the two institutions was the field of statistics. Under Perovskii's leadership, the ministry had placed a strong emphasis on the collection of reliable information from all parts of the empire. Perovskii had allocated substantial additional resources to statistical work and had established a series of new bureaucratic organs drawing on the talents of Russia's leading statisticians.[9] Since the Geographical Society was to include statistics as a major component of its work, the founders, perhaps for personal as well as practical reasons, chose Perovskii over the Minister of Education, Count Sergei Uvarov, to sponsor the proposal for the new society and present it to the emperor.[10]

The choice between these two institutional models had significant ramifications for the future of the Geographical Society. The Academy of Sciences was intended to participate on an equal footing with similar institutions in the West in a universal scientific discourse. Insofar as the academy was designed to serve the empire, it was in an indirect manner: by supporting the work of world-class scientists through the academy, the autocracy was demonstrating its strength and prestige as a great power. It was precisely with the goal of making the academy a "showcase of Russia's contribution to modern scientific thought" that Count Uvarov induced some of the most renowned German scientists to pursue their scholarship in St. Petersburg as Russian academicians.[11] To make scholarly life more comfortable for these expatriates and to enhance its accessibility to a European audience, the academy published its journals and bulletins primarily in French and German. For Russians without a knowledge of these languages, the work of the academy remained largely out of reach.

The applicability of the model of the academy to the Geographical Society was far from self-evident. As an institution dedicated to the study of the Russian empire, the work of the society, one could reasonably assume, would be of particular interest to Russians themselves. The image of the Academy of Sciences—a colossus standing with its back to Russia and its face toward the West—was not only seen as inappropriate by some members of the Geographical Society, it was positively offensive.

On the other hand, for bureaucrats working in areas connected with geography, ethnography, and, particularly, statistics, the Geographical Society presented an enticing opportunity. While significant progress had been made in the 1830s and '40s, bureaucratic efforts to study the empire were often hindered by excessive secrecy, departmental rivalries, fragmentation, and a lack of authority to pursue broad topics. The Geographical Society represented the chance to transcend these obstacles, bringing the best minds from a variety of institutions together to work on problems of common interest. Thus while Litke may have seen the society as an extension of the Academy of Sciences, others envisioned it as an extension of the bureaucracy in which information could be assembled about the empire in a freer and more congenial atmosphere. For the group of young officials led by Nikolai and Dmitrii Miliutin, who have come to be known as the "enlightened bureaucrats," this promise of the Geographical Society was especially enticing. Fervently devoted to the cause of reform in general and the abolition of serfdom in particular, the enlightened bureaucrats were convinced that their goals could only be attained by gathering accurate and extensive information on the state of the empire. To see the Geographical Society, an ideal institution in which to pursue their aims, turn toward the quest for abstract scientific truth to be presented to a European audience in the style of the Academy of Sciences would have been a major disappointment, and the enlightened bureaucrats were prepared to go to great lengths to see that this did not occur.[12]

In response to these divergent visions, factions rapidly formed within the Geographical Society. The initial group of members dominated by Litke, Baer, and Wrangel had consisted largely of academicians of German origin, Naval and Army officers, most with non-Russian last names, and a smattering of high-ranking bureaucrats and independent scholars. As the founders of the society, members of this group were appointed to all responsible posts and secured a large majority within the society's governing council, creating the impression that the society was controlled by a German clique motivated by their own intellectual concerns rather than the needs of Russia.[13]

As the society opened its doors to a broader membership, its composition changed dramatically. In its first two years the society saw a powerful influx of new members who were younger, overwhelmingly Russian, and primarily connected with the bureaucracy, especially the Ministry of Internal Affairs.[14] It was not long before these new members coalesced into a strong opposition to the "German faction." By 1848 the "Russian faction" had gained effective control of the Statistical and Ethnographic Divisions, leaving the Germans in control of the Geographical Divisions and the society's governing bodies.[15] The stage was set for broader conflict.

Tensions between the two factions, which had steadily built up throughout 1846 and 1847, broke out into open conflict during 1848 in connection with plans to revise the society's charter. The original charter was valid only for a period of four years, after which time it was to be rewritten and submitted to the emperor for permanent approval.[16] The committee to revise the charter was to have half its members appointed by the governing council and the other half elected by the General Assembly. The result was a divided committee consisting of members of the German faction appointed by the council and a Russian group led by Nikolai Miliutin elected by the General Assembly.[17] In the first meetings, Miliutin put forward a series of proposals aimed at increasing the power of the rank-and-file membership. When these proposals were rejected, Miliutin and his comrades refused to attend further meetings.[18] The remaining members, led by Litke, took advantage of the situation to complete on their own a draft charter, which they submitted to the membership for comment in the summer of 1848. Comments on the proposed charter, which were sent in by many of the most active members of the Russian faction, reveal the broader issues at stake.[19]

Reaction to the proposed charter was overwhelmingly negative. Other than the specific issues of the internal governance of the society which Miliutin and his supporters had fought over in the committee, criticism tended to focus on two general issues: (1) the overall purpose of the Geographical Society and (2) the place of Russia within the world scientific community.

The most vehement protests from the membership were provoked by a seemingly innocuous addition to the preamble of the charter. The provisional charter had defined the mission of the society as: "the collection and distribution in Russia of geographical, ethnographic, and statistical information in general and about Russia in particular, along with the dissemination of reliable information about our fatherland in foreign countries." In the proposed charter a new goal had been added and given priority: "The development of earth sciences [*zemlevedenie*] in its main branches: geography, statistics, and ethnography."[20]

For opponents of the proposed charter, the new wording amounted to the elevation of pure science over the needs of Russia. It was as if, one member argued, the society had decided to change its name to the Geographical Society in St. Petersburg.[21] One of the most forceful and articulate critiques was written by V. V. Grigor'ev, a young orientalist serving in the Ministry of Internal Affairs. The society, he argued, arose out of a striving toward practical goals, and not for the satisfaction of abstract curiosity. Having proclaimed its objectives on many occasions, including in the inaugural speech given by Litke himself, the society had no right to change them. The enthusiastic response to the Geographical Society on the part of the state and educated society was largely due to this practical orientation. Grigor'ev used his own case as an example:

> I will speak for myself. I am not a geographer, nor an ethnographer, nor a statistician. . . . Geography in and of itself does not interest me nearly as much as archeology or linguistics. But in my soul I am a Russian and anything that can in any way be of benefit to Russia can not be foreign to me. The Society declared that it would labor for Russia, and I considered myself fortunate to join my feeble powers to the common mass. . . . If it had been said that the main goal of its establishment would be the advance-

ment of geography as a science, for the good of mankind in general and Western Europe in particular, I would never have even considered seeking the honor of becoming a member. The majority of members of the society are also not specialists in geography or statistics and, I venture to think, take part in the works of the society with the same patriotic motives as I.[22]

In rejecting an orientation toward pure science, Grigor'ev went so far as to deny in principle the need for Russian scientists to concern themselves at all with theoretical issues:

With regard to the theoretical development of geography, ethnography and statistics, there is no need to take this on ourselves. To do something before the time is ripe means only to spoil it. . . . Theory is the fruit of years of practical study and can be worked out successfully only in countries in which the field has been prepared by extensive practical labor. . . . Have we really accumulated such a vast reserve of empirical information that we can no longer manage with the particulars and feel a need to generalize, to build it all up into a unity?[23]

Grigor'ev's apprehensions, echoed by many of his colleagues, regarding the slant toward pure science and away from the needs of Russia, may seem exaggerated; however, some of the early activities and proposals within the Geographical Society may have provided genuine cause for alarm. In January 1846, for example, Litke had proposed a major expedition to study unusual volcanic activity on the Aleutian Islands—no doubt a worthy topic from a scientific perspective, but hardly a priority for "enlightened bureaucrats" seeking to marshal the resources of the Geographical Society in the cause of reform.[24] Likewise, at a time when the state of the peasantry in the Baltic provinces was a matter of keen interest on the part of the younger generation of bureaucrats, Andrei Sjögren's linguistic study of the Lieves, a tiny national minority in Lifland and Courland provinces, may have seemed a misdirected effort.[25] The purely academic tendency was personified by Baer, first head of the Ethnographic Division, who, despite his long residence in St. Petersburg, was never fully at ease with the Russian language and continued to publish his works almost exclusively in German or Latin.[26]

Critics of the proposed charter also objected to the notion that the Russian Geographical Society should issue publications in foreign languages in an attempt to attract the attention of foreign scholars. One of the most impassioned arguments in this regard was made by P. V. Golubkov. It was an issue on which Golubkov had a right to speak out if anyone did: he had recently donated 15,000 rubles to the Geographical Society to fund a translation of Karl Ritter's seminal work on world geography into Russian.[27] His contribution was motivated by a desire to enrich the level of scholarship in Russian by Russians. He was adamant that Russian could and should be a legitimate language of science, and argued that the Russian Geographical Society should make every effort not to emulate institutions such as the Academy of Sciences—"scholarly colonies whose works appear in Russia in foreign languages and therefore remain practically useless and unknown to the Russian public."[28] Agreeing to the principle of translating the Geographical Society's publications into foreign languages, it was felt, was the equivalent of saying that science has no value if it is carried out in Russian, that works must be published in French, German, or English in order to be a part of European intellectual life.[29] Critics of the proposed charter rejected this notion. It was up to the Western Europeans themselves, they argued, to follow scholarly literature in Russian and do their own translations—as Russians did with European literature. As Grigor'ev put it:

> I never understood why we Russians should take upon ourselves the enlightenment of Western Europe. What difference does it make whether they know about us or not. If we deserve it, Europe will find out about us without any effort on our part. If we are unworthy in their eyes, then there is no need to impose on them our acquaintance. The fear that without our special efforts, our works for the advancement of science will remain unknown abroad is entirely unfounded. There is not a single outstanding book in the field of geography which was not translated into French, German, or English soon after it appeared here.[30]

Golubkov concurred with Grigor'ev, noting that European scholars were generally much better informed about developments in Russia than was commonly assumed and that Russian science should be valued for its own merits rather than for its popularity among foreigners. In fact, he saw something of a hidden motivation in the practice of providing translations for foreign readers:

> In the desire to bring foreign languages into the publications of the Geographical Society, one can see not the necessity of communicating to foreigners accurate information about Russia, but rather a wish to make it easier for certain individuals who do not know the Russian language and do not wish to learn it to participate in the Society's activities.[31]

Golubkov did not say directly whom he had in mind, but Baer, for one, stands out as an obvious target.

Reaction to the proposed charter was one in a series of major blows to the position of the German faction. By the end of 1848 the Germans had lost their control over the council. When the new charter was adopted it reflected many of the criticisms voiced by Grigor'ev and his colleagues.[32] Only the personal intervention of Constantin Nikolaevich enabled Litke to prevent the adoption of several organizational points which he felt were "harmful in the present and dangerous to the future of the society."[33] Resentments created by Litke's maneuvering in turn helped lead to his defeat as leader of the Geographical Society in the elections of 1850. For the time being, the national model had won out over the pursuit of pure science.

In a sense, the dichotomy posed by the "Russian faction" between pure science and the needs of empire was a bluff. Neither Litke nor Baer would ever have disputed the need to apply the insights of science to practical tasks. The real dichotomy centered on the concept of science itself and stemmed more from the role of nationality than the needs of empire. For proponents of the academic approach, science transcended nationality. Science represented a universal discourse, carried on in the languages of Western Europe to be sure, open to all capable scholars and institutions regardless of nationality. The Russian faction rejected this notion, putting in its place a vision of science as a series of separate but interconnected national endeavors. Scholars in Western Europe, they pointed out, wrote in their national languages for their own countrymen. Why should Russians not do the same? Works of importance in foreign languages could be integrated into the national scientific discourse either through translations for the general reader, or through the work of specialists who would read these studies in the original in any event. Let the Europeans themselves discover Russian science, Grigor'ev and his colleagues argued. Better for Russians to concentrate on creating works that would be worthy of their attention.

Uncoupling national science from a universal discourse had significant implications for the development of individual disciplines. Freed from the domination of foreign models, individual fields could define their subject matter, goals and methodology in accordance with the specific context of the nation and the state. The field of ethnography provides an example of just such a process of autonomous development.

Two Visions of Russian Ethnography

At the time of the founding of the Geographical Society, Russian ethnography, as an independent discipline, was in its infancy. While descriptions of the peoples of the empire could be found in sources dating back to Kievan Rus', there had never been an institution such as the society's Ethnographic Division, specifically devoted to the pursuit of ethnography as a discrete and autonomous scholarly endeavor. Defining how exactly ethnography should be pursued was, therefore, a matter of some importance.

In its first year, the Geographical Society was presented with two clear and articulate visions of the object, goals, and methodology of ethnography, both read before the society's general assembly.[34] The authors, Karl von Baer, the eminent natural scientist and cofounder of the Geographical Society, and Nikolai Nadezhdin, editor of the *Journal of the Ministry of Internal Affairs* and former professor of aesthetics at Moscow University, were both motivated by a desire to formulate the parameters of ethnography as a scientific field. Their conceptions of the discipline, however, differed considerably both in terms of immediate tasks and underlying goals. In fact, Nadezhdin's presentation, delivered six months after Baer's, was one of the first blows in the conflict between German and Russian factions described above. Differences between the two conceptions rested largely on contrasting notions of the place of nationality in science.

In the most immediate sense the difference between Baer's and Nadezhdin's conceptions can be summed up in a distinction made in German science between *Volkskunde*—the study of one's own people—and *Völkerkunde*—the study of other nationalities. For Baer, ethnography was intrinsically a science of empire. When he referred to ethnography in Russia, the Russia he had in mind was a vast and largely unexplored territory populated by a multitude of diverse nationalities, some of whom were in danger of disappearing off the face of the earth. Baer did not seem to associate the state with any particular nationality. Instead he viewed it as the representative of general European enlightenment bringing "civilization" to the primitive peoples under its domain. Ethnography, Baer suggested, could help the state fulfill its civilizing mission in a humane and rationale manner. Guided by ethnographers, the state could adjust its intervention to coincide with the character and developmental level of its indigenous subjects, thus minimizing the often disasterous impact of civilization.[35] But eventually, Baer conceded, primitive ways would succumb to the inexorable march of progress and enlightenment. Ethnographers, therefore, should strive to collect and preserve cultural and material artifacts of less-developed populations for future generations to study and appreciate. Applied to the Russian empire, his discussion suggested a clear agenda: those peoples most threatened by the onset of progress should be studied immediately before their cultures were forever lost to humanity.[36]

If Baer's ethnography was a science of empire, Nadezhdin's was unquestionably one of nationality. From the outset he made it clear that his interest was in the Russian people rather than the peoples of Russia:

> According to the first line of our charter and the very name of our society, the main subject of our endeavors should be Russia. This patriotic concentration of our activity on our mighty fatherland, I venture to suppose, will continue to its natural, legitimate conclusion which, if I may be allowed

to summarize here, is as follows: within Russia, which in its present greatness is itself an entire enormous world, the main object of our attention
should be that which makes Russia Russian—i.e. the Russian person! I
have in mind the totality of distinctive features, facets, and nuances which
make possible a specific and unique mode of human existence, or, to put
it in more ordinary terms, the Russian nationality—in a nutshell, the ethnography of Russia proper.[37]

While not explicitly rejecting the study of other nationalities, Nadezhdin insisted that Russians should strive first and foremost to "know ourselves."
Rather than seeing ethnography as a tool of enlightened imperial administration, Nadezhdin regarded the field as an expression of national identity. But unlike the literary treatments of Russian *narodnost'* that had proliferated throughout the 1830s and 1840s, Nadezhdin's national ethnography was to be endowed
with the power and authority of science.[38] Nadezhdin distinguished "scientific"
ethnography from the work of amateurs by two fundamental features: the application of thorough and systematic methods in the collection of materials, and
the processing of these materials in the "purifying crucible of strict discerning
criticism." Only an institution with the stature and prestige of the Geographical Society, Nadezhdin felt, could meet the challenge of establishing the field of
ethnography in accordance with the demands of sciences.[39]

The differences between Baer and Nadezhdin over whether to give preference to the study of the Russian people reflect a deeper and more subtle dis-
agreement regarding the underlying goals of the discipline. For Baer the basic
question to be addressed by ethnography concerned the diversity of the human
race: what were the fundamental subdivisions of humanity and how were they
to be accounted for? At the heart of Baer's conception was a chain of being, a
hierarchical classification of races and peoples at the apex of which stood the
"caucasian race"—i.e. white Europeans. The task of ethnography, Baer felt, was
to explain this unequal diversity. If, as the Enlightenment philosophes believed,
human potential is fundamentally the same everywhere, why had most nations
and races not developed to the same level as the Europeans?[40]

Baer's response involved a precarious balance between environment and
race. He was, in general, a strong proponent of geographical determinism, so
much so that, in a later article, he argued that all of human history is predetermined by geography.[41] Nonetheless, Baer admitted that in certain instances the
influence of environment alone is not enough to explain differing levels of "civilization." Intellectual capacity, he concluded, must still be seen in relation to
morphological features, particularly the size and shape of the skull, although
he left open the possibility that these physical features themselves are the product of the influence of environment over many centuries.[42]

Baer's vision of ethnography, we can thus conclude, was essentially a hybrid of geography, addressing the problem of the interaction between humans and the environment, and comparative anatomy, aimed at classifying the subdivisions within the human race on the basis of measurable physical features. Conspicuously absent in this mix is the concept of the nation. For Baer, ethnography either focused on the inhabitants of discrete geographical regions subject to a common set of environmental conditions, or races delineated on the basis of physical characteristics.[43] While Baer refers throughout his work to various "peoples" and "tribes," the idea of the nation as an organic entity, imbued with a transcendental essence and playing a role preordained by fate in the world historical process, was not an element in Baer's intellectual makeup.

Nadezhdin, on the other hand, placed nationality at the very heart of his conception of ethnography. Like Baer, Nadezhdin saw a strong relationship between ethnography and geography. But where Baer envisioned the two fields as organically linked by the common problem of humans and the environment, Nadezhdin saw them as parallel endeavors connected by a similar descriptive and comparative methodology. The geographer, according to Nadezhdin, studies the specific features of the earth's surface in their native context in order to place them in their natural order—mountains are connected to ranges, tributaries to river basins—leading to an enhanced knowledge of the earth as a whole. Likewise, the ethnographer documents the diverse features of human existence in their native context—"where they are and as they are"—and then seeks to place these features into their natural ranks so that out of a seemingly chaotic mass of individual traits, a harmonious system of relationships emerges, constituting the totality of the human race.[44] The keystone of Nadezhdin's system, the fundamental unit out of which humanity is comprised, is nationality. "These natural ranks distinguishable in humanity," Nadezhdin wrote, "are precisely what are usually called nationalities [*narodnosti*]";

> and the corresponding subdivisions in the human race are nothing more than what are generally known as nations [*narody*]. Thus nations are the objects to be studied most closely, and the description of nationality is the content out of which is constructed ethnography. Its task: to connect the individual with the national, and through this to distinguish that which is common to all humanity.[45]

Thus Nadezhdin's differences with Baer go far beyond whether to give preference to the study of the Russian people. Regardless of the nationality under investigation, the goal remained the same—to study "the totality of all traits, external and internal, physical and spiritual, mental and moral out of which is composed the [national] physiognomy."[46]

Nadezhdin's and Baer's contrasting visions of ethnography reflect their divergent personal, intellectual, and national backgrounds. The son of a village priest from Riazan province, Nadezhdin spent his childhood in a peasant village where he absorbed an indelible sense of his own national identity.[47] Baer, in contrast, was an ethnic German born in Estonia, an imperial possession of the Russian Empire. National loyalty for Baer meant, above all, loyalty to the state and the monarch rather than personal identification with the nation.[48]

From an intellectual point of view, Nadezhdin and Baer reflect the influence of two distinct branches of German *naturphilosophie*. Baer, who completed his education and gained an international reputation as a scientist in Germany, worked in the tradition of the Göttingen School, which drew heavily on the epistemological teachings of Immanuel Kant. Emphasizing the inability of the human mind to comprehend the teleological processes of organic growth, the Göttingen scientists advocated a strictly empirical approach and rejected any attempt to rely on metaphysical explanations of the natural world.[49] The division of the human race into subbreeds or races was a major theoretical problem addressed by the Göttingen scientists, particularly Johann Friedrich Blumenbach. As a strict empiricist, however, Blumenbach could only permit a classification of species and races on the basis of concrete morphological features or the ability to interbreed. A system of classification drawing on something as intangible as "spirit" or "essence" had no place in the thought of Blumenbach or his follower Baer.[50]

Nadezhdin, who received a splendid classical education at the Moscow Theological Academy, was heavily influenced in his early years by the philosophy of Schelling, which in turn reflected the basic ideas of Herder. Schelling and his followers did not recognize an impenetrable boundary between the world of "things in themselves" and empirical knowledge. On the contrary, it was only through an act of "intellectual intuition" that the fundamental structure of the natural world became manifest.[51] It was precisely by means of such speculative leaps that the diversity of mankind was explained. In the tradition of Herder, mankind was seen to be divided into distinct nations, each one animated by a unique and immutable essence which revealed itself first and foremost in the creative expression of the common folk. The nation, therefore, was seen as an a priori category arising directly from the Absolute and consequently immune to the formative influences of external factors.

Nadezhdin's conception of *narodnost'* took shape in the 1830s under the influence of Schellingian philosophy. In 1836, however, his orientation shifted dramatically in connection with a deep personal crisis that arose in response to his decision to publish Petr Chaadaev's famous Philosophical Letter in his journal *Telescope*. In the scandal that ensued, Nadezhdin was viewed as the chief culprit, and was exiled for a year and a half to the remote northern town of Ust-Sysol'sk. Deeply shaken by his misfortune, Nadezhdin abandoned his previous fields of aesthetics and literary criticism along with the speculative philosophy that had shaped his early career and turned to the study of the history, geography, and ethnography of the Russian land based on strict principles of empirical scholarship.[52] But the concept of *narodnost'* on which his work continued to be based still reflected the philosophical world view in which it had originally taken shape. *Narodnost'* for Nadezhdin remained an immutable essence. Rather than deriving *narodnost'* from objective experience, *narodnost'* was to be accepted as an a priori principle. The task of ethnography, Nadezhdin felt, was to refine a pure essence of *narodnost'* from the raw ore of ethnographic data, removing elements introduced through contacts with other peoples which could obscure but never transform the fundamental spirit of the nation. Thus Nadezhdin's vision of ethnography represented a potent fusion of speculative and empirical thought in which the strivings of romantic nationalism were cloaked in the authoritative aura of science.

In Baer's and Nadezhdin's contrasting visions of ethnography we see signs of the same tensions that informed the larger conflict between the German and Russian factions. Baer's views are clearly directed toward a universal scientific discourse centered on theoretical problems concerning the whole of the human race. As such, his discussion falls well within the boundaries of Western European ethnology as it was developing at the time. His views reflect the fundamental dichotomy between civilized and savage, European and non-European, white-skinned and colored that lay at the heart of mid-nineteenth-century ethnology.[53] But Baer's program is at its weakest precisely in its failure to adapt the Western ethnological paradigm to the unique conditions of the Russian empire. Apart from a few specific references, there is nothing in Baer's discussion that would not have been applicable to the British or French empires. But while it may have been easy to maintain the dichotomy between civilization and savagery when juxtaposing British colonists with Australian Aborigines, it was far more difficult to determine who was the savage and who was not when comparing Russian peasants with their Tatar, Mordvin, or Chuvash neighbors. A far stronger sense of "otherness"—the cultural distance underlying all ethnographic research—existed independent of any racial or national differences in the dichotomy between Russian educated society and the enserfed masses. The fact that this dichotomy was seen to coincide with a sense of shared national identity made it tremendously attractive as an axis around which to orient a new, specifically Russian approach to ethnography which was articulated for the first time by Nadezhdin.

Nadezhdin's vision of ethnography as an independent science built on the concept of *narodnost'* embodies the notion of science as a national discourse. Notwithstanding the influence of German philosophy and the similar work of Slavic scholars, Nadezhdin's ethnography was a Russian science first and foremost, shaped more by the Russian striving toward distinctiveness (*samobytnost'*) than by aspirations to participate in a universal discourse. Perhaps for this reason, or perhaps despite it, Nadezhdin's conception has proved remarkably enduring. While waxing and waning in response to the relative strength of Western influences, the idea of ethnography as a science centered on nationality (or *ethnos*, as Nadezhdin's *narodnost'* has been rendered in its most recent incarnation) has been a persistent element in Russian ethnography, setting it apart from analogous disciplines in the West up to the present day.[54] The practical implications of Nadezhdin's conception were illustrated quite clearly in the activities of the ethnographic division to which we shall now turn our attention.

Ethnography in Practice

As the first two chairmen of the Ethnographic Division, Baer and Nadezhdin both strove to realize the research agendas implicit in their respective visions of ethnography. Baer's opportunity to implement his agenda was, to be sure, rather limited: by the end of 1847, a year before he resigned his post citing his inadequate knowledge of the Russian language, he had already lost effective control of the division.[55] But his activities in the two previous years nonetheless do reveal something about the nature of his thinking and the practical implications of his ethnographic vision.

As we have noted, Baer's first priority was the preservation of rare ethnographic data for future generations. It is not surprising, therefore, that he was a major supporter of the establishment of an ethnographic museum within the Geographical Society.[56] In addition, Baer sponsored an expedition, which he hoped would be the first in a long series devoted to peoples in immediate danger of cultural or even physical extinction.

In his speech before the Geographical Society, Baer had mentioned two peoples, the Lieves and the Krevings, inhabitants of the Baltic coast along the Gulf of Riga and Courland peninsula, which seemed to be on the verge of dying out. According to the most recent data, only seventeen speakers of the Lievan language were thought to remain.[57] In the summer of 1846, the Geographical Society, on Baer's initiative, sent out an expedition to study the Lieves and Krevings. The expedition consisted of the eminent Finnish linguist and academician Andrei Sjögren and a portrait painter by the name of Petzoldt.

Baer's apprehensions regarding the Lieves, Sjögren and Petzoldt discovered, were highly exaggerated. Rather than seventeen speakers of the language, Sjögren found more than 2,000 Lieves living in a series of fishing villages along the coast of the Courland peninsula.[58] The Krevings, on the other hand, turned out not to be a nationality at all—they were in fact Estonian islanders who had been brought to the mainland by landowners in the early eighteenth century to replenish the original population which had been decimated by plague.[59]

As a linguist, Sjögren was primarily interested in the Lievan language. His first task was to confirm its membership in the Finno-Ugric group. From that point he focused on its specific features and relation to other Finno-Ugric languages. He was also very concerned with historical issues—whether the Lieves were descendants of the people by the same name mentioned in historical sources from the middle ages. But Sjögren did not neglect broader ethnographic topics; he collected substantial information on national costume, dwellings, handicrafts, superstitions, holidays, and made vague attempts to describe the national character. Baer's primary interests, however, seemed to lie elsewhere. In his instructions for the expedition, while leaving most of the details up to Sjögren, he placed a special emphasis on physical features, requesting detailed physical descriptions and the collection of plaster casts of Lievan heads for purposes of craniology.[60] Sjögren was less forthcoming in this regard. The most he could say was that the Lieves were physically indistinguishable from their Latvian neighbors.[61]

The work of Sjögren's companion, the artist Petzoldt, on the other hand, could not but have pleased Baer. In the course of his travels, Petzoldt produced a fine series of drawings and watercolors showing the Lieves in native costume surrounded by objects essential to their daily life.[62] The participation of an artist was very characteristic of Baer's approach. In the tradition of the natural sciences, Baer was particularly concerned with the collection of artifacts—hence his interest in an ethnographic museum. While the expedition may not have brought back many actual artifacts, Petzoldt's drawings were an admirable substitute, having the advantage of depicting objects in their native context.

Sjögren's linguistic work was also a worthy fulfillment of Baer's preservationist agenda. The Lieves were not, it turned out, as close to extinction as originally feared. Even a century after Sjögren's expedition there was still a small, but significant population living along the Latvian coast.[63] But Sjögren's study, which he later continued with the support of the Academy of Sciences, was a major contribution to Finno-Ugric linguistics containing a wealth of information which would not have been accessible to later researchers.[64]

A national element, however, can also be detected in Sjögren's work. A native Finn of peasant background, Sjögren was part of a school of Finnish folklorists and linguists dedicated to recording and preserving the Finnish national heritage.[65] The various Finno-Ugric peoples within the Russian empire were a major concern of the Finnish ethnographers. Just as Nadezhdin and other Russian ethnographers saw the study of Slavic languages as an integral part of the ethnography of the Russian people, the Finns looked to their cousins in other parts of the empire for insight into their own national history and identity. Insofar as Sjögren's study fit into this broader agenda of Finnish ethnography, it reflected the potential of ethnography to act as vehicle for the expression of national identity.

Sjögren's expedition was the last opportunity Baer had to realize his vision of ethnography. A proposal he submitted in the following year to send Sjögren and Petzoldt on another expedition to study the non-Russian population of St. Petersburg Province was never acted upon.[66] By mid-1847, the "Russian faction" had gained a majority within the Ethnographic Division and was moving its activities toward the study of the Russian people and the vision of ethnography articulated by Nadezhdin.

The study of ethnic Russians required a methodology very different from expeditions to study small disappearing nationalities. To gather information on the Russian people in all its diversity, Nadezhdin and his colleagues chose to rely on a comprehensive questionnaire distributed through the provincial bureaucracy and completed by local correspondents.[67] Aside from the obvious logistical advantages to the use of a survey—covering such a vast territory through expeditions would have been next to impossible—local observers, it was felt, would provide superior data, making up for their lack of scholarly credentials by their detailed knowledge of local conditions.[68]

The reliance upon local correspondents had significant ramifications for the development of ethnography. In the most immediate sense, the use of a survey helped to engender a separation between the collection of materials and its scholarly analysis. As nonspecialists, local correspondents were not expected to direct their observations, as Sjögren had, toward particular interpretive or theoretical problems. On the contrary, the reports were valued as scientific data precisely by virtue of their descriptive orientation—the absence of any overtly subjective judgments and close adherence to the instructions provided. Reports arriving from the provinces were seen as raw materials, building blocks for a broader synthesis to be assembled by ethnographic scholars properly anointed into the mysteries of science. Thus, from the start, Nadezhdin's national ethnography assumed a bifurcated character. On one side stood the raw materials—detailed descriptions of language, customs, traditional crafts, and folklore judged on the basis of their photographic veracity. On the other side stood Nadezhdin's "purifying crucible of strict discerning criticism," the exact nature of which was still unclear. Naturally, the two sides were not evenly balanced, and out of this imbalance arose much of what was distinct about the Russian approach to ethnography.

The ethnographic survey, 7,000 copies of which were printed up and distributed in 1848, brought in a harvest of data far exceeding the most optimistic hopes of its authors.[69] By 1853, when a second version of the survey was sent out, over 2,000 responses had been received from throughout European Russia.[70] It was clear that the Ethnographic Division had tapped into a very rich source of information.

The vast majority of the correspondents remain practically anonymous; the most we can ascertain at times are names, geographical locations, and sometimes social background.[71] A survey of a representative sample, however, revealed the majority of responses to have come from parish priests, who, by virtue of their literacy and close proximity to the peasantry, were in a uniquely advantageous position to provide ethnographic data. Reports were also submitted by schoolteachers, government officials, landowners, seminarians, merchants, and even peasants.[72]

How can we explain this outpouring of ethnography from the provinces? One factor of enormous importance was the mystique surrounding the notion of science and the prestige of the Imperial Russian Geographical Society. A sense of local pride was another important factor: the notion that one's native region was of value to science and of interest to the Geographical Society was a powerful incentive for local correspondents to devote their time and energy to ethnography.[73] The ethnographic survey also did not require any particular skills or training beyond basic literacy and adequate powers of observation, making it a realistic project for enterprising correspondents. The Geographical Society took special measures to encourage this sense of pride: authors of the best reports were awarded the status of corresponding member, and others received certificates of gratitude or had their names printed in the society's journal.[74]

Having received such a cornucopia from the provinces, the Ethnographic Division was faced with the challenge of processing these materials—subjecting them to Nadezhdin's "purifying crucible" and turning them, in the process, from raw data into full-fledged ethnographic scholarship. The method of analysis Nadezhdin had proposed—a comparative examination of materials from throughout Russia in order to weed out the foreign influences and arrive at the true essence of *narodnost'*—proved distinctly unwieldy.[75] In part this was due to the sheer volume and diversity of the incoming data. The ethnographic survey had included six separate sections covering external appearance, language, domestic culture, social life, intellectual abilities and education, and folklore. Rather than analyzing the responses as a whole, it was decided to divide them up by subject matter conveying the appropriate materials to individual members of the Ethnographic Division who had volunteered to work on a particular topic.[76]

The extent to which their efforts bore fruit depended in part on the extent to which the demands of the survey corresponded with the ability of correspondents to produce adequate materials. Information on physical features, for example, did not attract any scholarly attention at all despite the fact that most reports had at least a brief discussion of the appearance of inhabitants. Without objective standards for the measurement of physical traits which could be consistently and systematically applied by correspondents, the information they provided was essentially anecdotal, making attempts at comparative analysis futile.[77]

Materials on language, "the main token and mark of nationality" according to Nadezhdin, were included in great abundance in the responses. But despite the care and diligence with which local correspondents compiled regional lexicons and described local dialects, their efforts failed to impress Izmail Ivanovich Sreznevskii, the prominent Slavic scholar and professor of St. Petersburg University who had volunteered to review these materials. Without the necessary training and experience, Sreznevskii concluded after reviewing the materials, efforts by amateurs to characterize local dialects will "never be completely satisfactory."[78] But despite Sreznevskii's negative judgment, materials from the ethnographic survey were readily absorbed into the preexisting literature of Slavic philology and dialectology. Philologists who had been debating the character and boundaries of various Russian dialects for at least twenty years had little difficulty seeing how the materials from the ethnographic survey could serve their purposes.[79]

Among the richest materials brought in by the ethnographic survey were samples of folklore recorded by local correspondents. This was one case in which the needs of the Ethnographic Division matched up well with the abilities of correspondents: recording folklore while preserving as much as possible the character of local speech was a task which local observers could fulfill with relative ease. There was also little question of how to handle these materials. First and foremost they needed to be published. The first and most famous publication of folklore to result from the ethnographic survey was Aleksandr Nikolaevich Afanas'ev's *Russian Folktales*, which remains to this day the most complete and authoritative collection of its kind.[80]

Integrating folklore into the framework of a scholarly discourse, however, remained a much more difficult task than simply collecting and publishing texts. Nadezhdin himself made a significant attempt at a scholarly analysis of folklore in his article "On Russian Myths and Sagas" presented to the Geographical Society in 1852.[81] Drawing on a variety of folklore genres, Nadezhdin strove in his article to reconstruct ancient Russian geographical conscious-ness—the sense of "where am I and what is around me?"—as preserved in oral tradition. Nadezhdin's speech was warmly received; however, none of his col-leagues followed his example and undertook similar studies. The study of Rus-sian folklore and mythology, a major element in the field of Russian ethnogra-phy as a whole, developed largely outside the boundaries of the Geographical Society.[82]

The remaining materials from the ethnographic survey fell into the broad category of *byt*—a concept covering all aspects of daily life from tools and household implements to customary law and rituals. Information on *byt* was particularly abundant in the responses to the survey. This, again, was an area in which local correspondents could provide acceptable materials with a mini-mum of guidance. For the Ethnographic Division, information on *byt* was par-ticularly significant in that it represented the core content of the field—the area least covered by existing disciplines.

The term *byt* itself reveals much about the nature of national ethnography. The concept of *byt*—the totality of material and cultural elements comprising a particular way of life—was unique to Russian ethnography. Unlike the notions of civilization, enlightenment, or culture that dominated the thinking of impe-rial ethnographers both in Russia and the West, *byt* was nonhierarchal and non-comparative: there are no levels or stages of *byt*. The very etymology of the word, derived from the verb "to be," betrays its essence: *byt* simply is.

But what is an ethnographer to do with *byt*? Integrating materials on daily life into a scholarly discourse proved a daunting task for members of the Eth-nographic Division. Konstantin Kavelin, the well-known historian who had re-cently resigned from Moscow University, had made an important step in this direction in his harsh critique of Aleksandr Tereshchenko's ethnographic com-pendium *Byt russkogo naroda* (The Way of Life of the Russian People) published in 1848.[83] Tereshchenko's book, Kavelin argued, contained much valuable fac-tual material, but suffered greatly from the author's arbitrary and unscientific methods of analysis. Using Tereshchenko's materials, Kavelin put forth some of his own ideas about how elements from peasant life could provide insight into historical and national processes.

The materials from the ethnographic survey provided Kavelin with the op-portunity to move beyond criticism and put the methods he had suggested in his critique of Tereshchenko into practice. It was a challenge which Kavelin, at least at the outset, accepted with pleasure. As a passionate opponent of serfdom who had found work in Petersburg in Nikolai Miliutin's Urban Section of the Ministry of Internal Affairs, Kavelin was particularly interested in the ways in which data on peasant life might provide insight regarding possible paths toward emancipation.[84] Kavelin's ultimate plan was to compile a systematic digest of the ethnographic reports arranged by topic in order to facilitate the comparative study of distinct cultural elements. He began the project with enthusiasm, writing out on hundreds of note cards excerpts from the manuscripts. But as more and more materials flooded in and the scope of the venture came to seem more and more daunting, Kavelin's project bogged down. In January 1853, after three years of work, Kavelin announced that he was giving up because "in a systematic digest the local flavor of the ethnographic material, which is so important for its study, is more or less lost."[85] Thus the first and most ambitious attempt to produce a comprehensive analysis of the ethnographic reports wound to a close, leaving no tangible results.

In the absence of a systematic digest, the next best alternative was simply to publish outstanding reports from the provinces verbatim. In 1853, the first volume appeared of the division's *Ethnographic Anthology*, containing a set of exemplary reports from local correspondents. The original plan had been to include in subsequent volumes Kavelin's digest and other analytical works. But when Kavelin's project stalled, the precedent set in the first volume was continued.[86] Reports from the provinces were published first in the society's regular journal and then as a collection in *Ethnographic Anthology*.

The effect of the society's failure to integrate its materials on *byt* into an analytical discourse was to reinforce the descriptive orientation of Russian ethnography as a whole. In *Ethnographic Anthology* Russian readers were presented with the first publication specifically devoted to the emerging discipline. What they found inside were descriptions of peasant life, generally well written and systematic, containing a plethora of fascinating details about local inhabitants. They did not find analysis, comparison, critical discussion of sources, or generalized theories—the traditional hallmarks of scholarship. Not surprisingly the impression emerged that this was ethnography and that there need not be a higher level of analysis. Throughout the 1850s and 1860s ethnography was broadly understood to mean the collection and compilation of materials on folklore and daily life of the common people.[87] Ethnography, in this sense, involved the production of autonomous representations of the *narod*. Standing on their own, these representations expressed the regional or national character of the populations described, but taken together they merged into a broad canvass representing and symbolizing the content of the empire as a whole.

Even when ethnographers turned their attention to the non-Slavic peoples of the empire, the *inorodtsy*, the basic paradigm of ethnography as the description of nationality remained in place. Despite the explicit orientation of the Ethnographic Division's survey toward ethnic Russians, a great deal of interest remained in the various peoples of the empire. The orientalist Pavel Savel'ev even drew up, in 1850, a special questionnaire on *inorodtsy* to be distributed alongside the original survey.[88] Savel'ev's program was never distributed, but in all likelihood it was integrated into a similar survey written by Nadezhdin and published by the Geographical Society in preparation for a proposed expedition to Kamchatka.[89] Nadezhdin had also begun, shortly before the onset of his fatal illness in 1853, a study of the Mordva and had completed a digest of references to them in the Russian chronicles and other historical documents.[90] After his death in 1856, Nadezhdin's materials on the Mordva were turned over to the writer and ethnographer Pavel Mel'nikov (Pecherskii), who used them for his own study which was published in the 1860s.[91]

The study of *inorodtsy* lent itself quite well to the descriptive orientation that had emerged in the work on ethnic Russians. For ethnographers studying the *inorodtsy*, basic factual information was the most pressing need. Studying indigenous peoples in outlying regions of the empire, many of whom remained practically unknown to scholars, presented a more coherent set of problems than studies of ethnic Russians: Who were these people? What did they look like? What language did they speak? What did they call themselves? Where did they live? What religion did they practice? What did they know about their past? Armed with these types of questions, ethnographers could feel a clearer sense of purpose and scholarly identity. At the same time, they could argue, with some justification, that what was most needed were plain accurate ethnographic facts uncolored by conceptual schemes and attempts at interpretation.

Although the Ethnographic Division as a whole accomplished relatively little in the study of *inorodtsy* during the 1850s, individual members did produce some substantial works. Local correspondents also submitted articles on indigenous peoples. The best of these works appeared in the society's journal throughout the 1850s and in a special volume of *Ethnographic Anthology* on *inorodtsy* published in 1858.

The works on non-Russian peoples published by the Geographical Society in the 1850s are notable for their descriptive style and the seemingly detached, nonjudgmental stance of the authors. Pavel Nebol'sin, an employee of the Ministry of Internal Affairs who engaged in ethnographic research while compiling statistical data on trade between Southern Russia and Central Asia, in an article on the Kalmyks, explained his differences with his eighteenth-century precursors as follows:

> Continually spending time with the Kalmyks and striving in all respects to share with them their ways and habits, with the goal of mastering as much as possible their manners and customs, I, perhaps, became so enamored with my subject that I became less strict than others with regard

to the deficiencies which are imputed to the Kalmyks and occupied myself with details to which others had not turned their attention.[92]

Throughout his long and thorough discussion covering such topics as the clan system, wedding rituals, nomadic migrations, dwellings, domestic implements, food, and hospitality, Nebol'sin does not attempt to place the Kalmyks in any kind of universal hierarchy of race or nation which would express and account for their "savagery." By and large, he seemed to accept the Kalmyks as they were and endeavored to learn as much as possible their way of life with a minimum of extraneous judgment.

Other works on the *inorodtsy* published by the Geographical Society, even those written by Orthodox clergymen describing aspects of religious life, tended to share Nebol'sin's descriptive orientation.[93] Whether or not this reflects cultural attitudes of Russians as a whole, it certainly is indicative of the priorities of the individuals who decided which works were worthy of publication. Nadezhdin, for one, was very explicit about the criteria which endowed ethnographic observations with scientific value. In his instructions for the Kamchatka expedition he recommended that ethnographers "state their impressions in the way in which they were received, not only without any adornment, but even without any analysis."[94] In another case, Nadezhdin singled out the work of a local correspondent on the grounds that he described peasant life "directly from nature, just as it is, without any elaboration and speculation."[95]

The position of these ethnographers with regard to *inorodtsy* becomes all the more striking when compared to their Western counterparts. We might consider, for example, the language used by a prominent American ethnologist also active in the 1850s, Henry Rowe Schoolcraft, to describe American Indians:

> Of all races on the face of the earth who were pushed from their original seats, and cast back into utter barbarism, they have, apparently, changed the least, and have preserved their physical and mental type with the fewest alterations. . . . As a race there never was one more impractical, more bent on a nameless principle of tribality, more averse to combinations for their own good, more deaf to the voice of instruction, more determined to pursue all the elements of their own destruction.[96]

The contrast between Schoolcraft and Russian scholars like Nebol'sin points out a fundamental difference in conceptions of science. Schoolcraft's attitudes were grounded in a broad vision of the universal history of humanity rooted in biblical orthodoxy. We see this in his degenerate view of human development— savagery as the result of a primordial fall from grace—and his perception of Indians as a single race rather than a collection of nations: what in another part of the world might pass for national consciousness is seen as a "nameless principle of tribality."

By focusing on nationality as the central object of investigation, Russian ethnographers avoided these global questions about the human race as a whole. It is certainly no accident, for example, that the driving force in the development of Western European ethnology and anthropology in the period prior to 1860, the debate between monogenists and polygenists over the unity of the human race, failed to evoke any significant response from Russian scholars, although there is no doubt that they were quite well informed as to the activities and interests of their Western colleagues.[97] When issues of racial distinctions were discussed, it was generally within the framework of comparative anatomy and later anthropology, which from the 1860s onward developed as a separate field devoted solely to the study of the physical features of mankind from the perspective of the natural sciences.[98] Thus, ethnography was left free to focus on the expression of nationality in the culture and *byt* of the common people. It was not until the influence of evolutionism began to be felt in the 1880s that the work of Russian ethnographers came to reflect a coherent overarching conception of the universal history of mankind.[99] By this time, however, the paradigm of ethnography as the description of nationality was deeply rooted in Russian science and would continue to be a persistent feature despite the efforts of academic ethnographers to instill a more theoretical approach.[100]

Conclusion

Thus far we have noted the distinctive features which characterized the field of ethnography in mid-nineteenth-century Russia: its focus on nationality, tendency toward descriptive narrative, and relatively tolerant attitude toward less developed peoples. How, then, can this orientation be explained? Addressing this issue brings us back to the problem of relationship between science, empire, and nationality.

As we have seen, the vision of science espoused by the men who dominated the Geographical Society after the defeat of the "German faction" was eminently practical, almost utilitarian. The "enlightened bureaucrats" were concerned with the application of scientific methods to produce useful information which would aid in governing the empire and preparing the groundwork for future reform. Abstract theoretical speculation on the nature of the human race was of little interest. Nebol'sin was a typical representative of this milieu, and his description of Kalmyk administration, social organization, and cultural mores abounds in the type of practical information an enlightened administrator might find of value.[101]

Above all, the enlightened bureaucrats were concerned with the abolition of serfdom, and here ethnographic description played a dual role. On the one hand, ethnographic descriptions of peasant juridical and social norms were valued for the direct insights they might provide into improved forms of local administration. On the other hand, representations of the Russian *narod* served as a tool in raising awareness of the need for reform. Accustomed to the nuances of Aesopian language, readers could easily be expected to juxtapose depictions of the peasantry as the bearer of Russia's most ancient national traditions with the reality of serfdom and draw the necessary conclusion.[102]

It would be inaccurate, however, to ascribe ethnography's distinctive features solely to utilitarian motives. Individuals such as Nadezhdin, Grigor'ev, and Sreznevskii, despite their close ties to the bureaucracy, were first and foremost scholars, and to account for the direction of their scholarship we must consider factors more deeply rooted in the nature of the Russian empire and Russian national consciousness.

Few would disagree that the fields of anthropology and ethnology in Western Europe were profoundly shaped by the context of colonial expansion and empire.[103] The pattern of Russian imperial expansion, however, brought a very different set of influences to the field of Russian ethnography. Russia's *inorodtsy* did not live across vast oceans in strange and formidable climates. They were the same peoples with whom Russians had coexisted in more or less close proximity for centuries. Their names appear in historical documents all the way back to the Kievan Primary Chronicle. Their relations with the Russian state often dated well back into the Muscovite period and, in some cases, had more in common with medieval feudalism than with nineteenth-century imperialism. Moreover, elites within the *inorodtsy* were readily absorbed into the Russian nobility; such notables as Karamzin, Cherkasskii, Kochubei, and Bagration readily betrayed their *inorodtsy* ancestors. Looking at relations between Russians and their non-Slavic neighbors, at least west of the Urals, a more meaningful parallel might be drawn to the internal integration of national minorities in Great Britain, France, and Spain, than with their colonial expansion. Viewed in this context, the debates between polygenists and monogenists were at best irrelevant to a discussion of relations between nationalities in the Russian empire.

Russia's own relations with the West may have been another factor acting against the acceptance of the Western ethnological paradigm. The "imperial" approach to ethnography was based on a strict and rigid hierarchy of nations and races with France, Germany, and Britain at the apex. For Russians caught in a painfully ambivalent relationship with Western European culture, such a "chain of being" may have been inherently distasteful. If Russia had not yet reached the same level of development as the West, this would have to be explained—a task which patriotically minded Russians such as Nadezhdin may not have relished, particularly if the explanation had to be couched in the racially and geographically deterministic rhetoric and methodology of Western ethnology. A far more attractive option was to build a science around the notion of *narodnost'*—the distinct features endowing every nation with its unique and unmistakable identity. In adopting this orientation, Russian ethnographers reflected a broader striving within educated society toward the ideal of *samobytnost'*—cultural expressions, including science, arising out of an organic unity with the spirit of the nation and directed toward fulfilling its needs. Thus while science may have played a role in shaping conceptions of empire and nation, empire and nationality undoubtedly played a role in shaping conceptions of science.

Notes

The author would like to thank Richard Wortman, Leopold Haimson, Mark Von Hagen, Alfred Rieber, David Koester, Yuri Slezkine, Laurie Manchester, and participants at the SSRC workshop "Visions, Institutions, and Experiences of Imperial Russia" for helpful suggestions and comments, and IREX, the Fulbright-Hays Dissertation Research program, ACTR, and the Harriman Institute for supporting the research which made this article possible.

1. On the founding of the Geographical Society see, A. I. Alekseev, *Fedor Petrovich Litke* (Moscow, 1970); and *Perepiska Karla Bera po problemam geografii. Publikatsiia perevod i primechaniia T. A. Lukinoi* (Leningrad 1970), 62–70. The standard works on the history of the Geographical Society are L. S. Berg, *Vsesoiuznoe geograficheskoe obshchestvo za sto let* (Moscow-Leningrad, 1946); P. P. Semenov, *Istoriia poluvekovoi deiatel'nosti Russkogo geograficheskogo obshchestva 1845–1895* (St. Petersburg, 1896), 3v; and *Dvadtsatipiatiletie Imperatorskogo Russkogo geograficheskogo obshchestva* (St Petersburg, 1872). For clarification of some persistent misconceptions and errors in the literature, see N. G. Sukhova, "Eshche raz o predistorii Russkogo geograficheskogo obshchestva," *Izvestiia Vsesoiuznogo geograficheskogo obshchestva*, 1990, t. 122, vyp. 5, 43–48.

2. On the granting of the title "Imperial," see ARGO (Arkhiv Russkogo geograficheskogo obshchestva, St. Petersburg), f. 1–1845, op. 1, no. 1, l. 99.

3. The first geographical society was founded in Paris in 1821. It was followed by the Berlin Geographical Society in 1828 and the Royal Geographical Society of London in 1830. Other geographical societies were founded in Florence (1824), Dresden (1831), Bombay (1836), Frankfurt (1837), Boston (1840), Rio de Janeiro (1839), and New York

(1850). See "Obozrenie geograficheskikh obshchestv," *Vestnik Imperatorskogo Russkogo geograficheskogo obshchestva* (henceforth to be referred to as *VIRGO*), t. 13, 1855, ot. 5, 8–14.

4. This definition of the object of ethnography is taken from the original proposal for the Geographical Society submitted to Nicholas I via L. A. Perovskii. See Berg, *Vsesoiuznoe*, 33. The author of this part of the proposal was almost certainly Karl von Baer, although Berg has other ideas on this account. For a discussion of Baer's role see N. N. Stepanov, "Russkoe geograficheskoe obshchestvo i etnografiia, 1845–1861," *Sovetskaia etnografiia*, no. 4, 1946, 188–89.

5. ARGO, f. 1–1845, op. 1, no. 1, l. 21. The text of Litke's speech is published in the *Zapiski Russkogo Geograficheskogo obshchestva*, t. 1, 1846, 29–32, and in Semenov, *Istoriia*, v. 3, 1896, prilozhenie 1, 1317–18.

6. ARGO, f. 1–1845, op. 1, no. 1, l. 21.

7. *Zapiski Russkogo geograficheskogo obshchestva*, kn. 1, 1845, 31–32.

8. The original notice of approval for the Geographical Society noted that the society was to be "under the jurisdiction of the Ministry of Internal Affairs which has authority over state statistics." See ARGO, f. 1–1845, op. 1, n. 1, l. 14. This status had no effect on the actual activities of the Geographical Society and was apparently eliminated when the society's permanent charter was approved in 1849.

9. See W. Bruce Lincoln, *In the Vanguard of Reform: Russia's Enlightened Bureaucrats, 1825–1861* (DeKalb, Ill., 1982), 109–25.

10. Litke was seemingly very satisfied with the choice of Perovskii to sponsor the proposal. Uvarov, he later wrote to Wrangel, would hardly have handled the matter so effectively. See Alekseev, *Litke*, 197.

11. Most notable among the scholars recruited by Uvarov in terms of the development of ethnography was Karl von Baer who settled in Russia in the mid-1830s. Alexander Middendorff, whose expedition to Siberia helped inspire the founding of the Geographical Society and who would serve briefly as the assistant chairman of the Ethnographic Division under Baer in 1846–47, was also recruited by Uvarov. Other scientists brought by Uvarov to Russia include the zoologist Johann Brandt, the chemists Hermann Heinrich Hesse and Moritz Jacobi, and the physicists, Heinrich Lenz and A. T. Kupffer. See Alexander Vucinich, *Science and Russian Culture, A History to 1860* (Stanford, 1960), 299–305. For more on Uvarov's efforts, see Cynthia H. Whittaker, *The Origins of Modern Russian Education: An Intellectual Biography of Count Sergei Uvarov, 1786–1855* (DeKalb, Ill., 1984).

12. On the enlightened bureaucrats and their participation in the Russian Geographical Society, see Lincoln, *In the Vanguard of Reform*, 91–101 and passim.

13. The composition of the society's council can be traced in *Dvadtsatipiatiletie IRGO*, 246 (chronological list of council members).

14. "Otchet Russkogo Geograficheskogo Obshchestva za 1846/47 god," *Zapiski RGO*, t. III, 1849, 16.

15. On the situation within the Statistical Division, see Berg, *Vsesoiuznoe*, 173–74.

16. Ibid., 36. Both Berg and Semenov claim that the provisional charter had been borrowed almost entirely from the Royal Geographical Society in London. However, a

closer examination calls this assertion into question. In fact, up until 1858, the Royal Geographical Society did not have a charter as such and was governed by a very simple set of bylaws. It is possible that the procedure through which the society's governing council was selected and replenished may have been borrowed from these bylaws. However, major aspects of the provisional charter, particularly regarding the society's various divisions, were completely unrelated to the Royal Geographical Society. See H. R. Mill, *The Record of the Royal Geographical Society, 1830–1930* (London, 1930). I am grateful to N. G. Sukhova for pointing out this discrepancy.

17. ARGO, f. 1–1845, op. 1, no. 1, l. 60; Semenov, *Istoriia*, 10.

18. "Otdel'noe mnenie D. A. i. N. A. Miliutinykh i V. S. Poroshina na proekt Ustava Obshchesva," app. 3, Semenov, *Istoriia*, v. III, 1320–21. The date of this memorandum is not listed in Semenov's book; however, we can infer from a later note by Nikolai Miliutin that it was written on May 19, 1848. See, ARGO, f. 1–1847, op. 1, no. 27, l. 186.

19. Comments to the proposed charter are assembled in ARGO, f. 1–1847, op. 1, no. 21. A digest of the comments compiled by Nadezhdin, Levshin, and Chevkin can be found on ll. 190–208.

20. RGIA, f. 853 (Grigor'ev), op. 1, no. 10. (Proekt novogo ustava Russkogo Geograficheskogo Obshchestva i zamechaniia k nemu.)

21. ARGO. 1–1847, op. 1, no. 21, ll. 137. This particular critique was submitted by P. S. Savel'ev.

22. RGIA, f. 853, op. 1, no. 10, l. 10. A manuscript of Grigor'ev's petition, cosigned by Konstantin Nevolin, can also be found in the archive of the Russian Geographical Society (f. 1–1847, op. 1, no. 21, l. 69) Excerpts have been published in N. I. Veselovskii, *Vasilii Vasil'evich Grigor'ev po ego pis'mam i trudam* (St Petersburg, 1887), 93–97.

23. Ibid.

24. "Osnovanie v S.-Peterburge Russkogo Geograficheskogo Obshchestva i zaniatiia ego s sentiabria 1845 po mai 1846," *Zapiski RGO*, t. 1, 1846, 41.

25. A. V. Golovnin, for example, produced a detailed study of the Latvian peasantry for the Ministry of Internal Affairs which he describes at length in his memoirs. See ORRNB (Otdel rukopisei rossiiskoi natsional'noi biblioteki), f. 208 (Golovnin), no. 1, ll, 68–86.

26. See the bibliography of Baer's works included in B. E. Raikov, *Karl Ber—ego zhizn' i trudy* (Moscow-Leningrad, 1961). Baer did publish occasional works in Russian after the mid-1840s, but these were simply translations of works he had written in German.

27. "Otchet Russkogo Geograficheskogo Obshchestva za 1848 g." *Zapiski RGO*, t. 4, 1849, 309.

28. ARGO, f. 1–1847, op. 1, no. 23, l. 160.

29. This point was made by Savel'ev in his memorandum. See ARGO, f. 1–1847, op. 1, no. 23, ll. 144–45.

30. RGIA, f. 853, op. 1, no. 10, l. 14. See also Veselovskii, *V. V. Grigor'ev*, 96.

31. ARGO, f. 1–1847, op. 1, no. 23, l. 165.

32. ARGO, f. 1–1847, op. 1, no. 23, l. 211. See also ARGO, f. 1–1848, op. 1, no. 8. (Zhurnal komissii dlia peresmotra vremennogo ustava RGO.)

33. ARGO, f. 1–1845, op. 1, no. 1, l. 95. Excerpts of Litke's memorandum are published in Semenov, *Istoriia*, t. 3, 1321–22.

34. K. M. Ber', "Ob etnograficheskikh issledovaniiakh voobshche i v Rossii v osobennosti," *Zapiski russkogo geograficheskogo obshchestva*, kn. 1, 94–115; N. I. Nadezhdin, "Ob etnograficheskom izuchenii narodnosti russkoi," *Zapiski russkogo geograficheskogo obshchestva*, kn. 2, 61–115. Baer's article was presented in March and Nadezhdin's in November 1846. Nadezhdin's article has recently been republished along with a short biographical sketch. See T. D. Solovei, "Nikolai Ivanovich Nadezhdin. U istokov otechestvennoi etnograficheskoi nauki," *Etnograficheskoe obozrenie*, no. 1, 1994, 103–106; and N. I. Nadezhdin, "Ob etnograficheskom izuchenii narodnosti russkoi," *Etnograficheskoe obozrenie*, no. 1, 1994, 107–117, and no. 2, 124–139.

35. Baer, "Ob etnograficheskikh issledovaniiakh," 86–88.

36. Baer wrote, for example, "the simple way of life corresponding to nature is more and more being driven out by Western enlightenment. Therefore, the need is all the more urgent to preserve for the future in accurate descriptions, the features of the popular way of life before it is too late." Ibid., 91.

37. Nadezhdin, "Ob etnograficheskom izuchenii," 61.

38. On ethnography and literature see A. N. Pypin, *Istoriia russkoi etnografii*, (St. Petersburg, 1890) v. 1, 390–424 and passim.

39. Nadezhdin, "Ob etnograficheskom izuchenii," 62–64.

40. Baer, "Ob etnograficheskikh issledovaniiakh," 80–81. Baer, to be sure, does not pose this question explicitly, but it is clear from his overall discussion that this is the fundamental conceptual problem to be addressed by ethnography.

41. Baer wrote in this regard: "When the earth's axis found its tilt, the waters parted from the dry land, and the mountain ranges rose up separating one country from another, the fate of the human race was already determined in advance. . . . All world history is nothing but the realization of this predetermined fate." K. M. Ber, "O vliianii vneshnei prirody na sotsial'nye otnosheniia otdel'nykh narodov i istoriiu cheloveka," in *Karmannaia kniga dlia liubitelei zemlevedeniia* (St. Petersburg, 1848), 232.

42. Baer, "Ob etnograficheskikh issledovaniiakh," 80–81.

43. For example, in his discussion of his travels with fishing artels in the Russian far north, his focus was not on the qualities that made the fishermen Russian, but rather the ways in which the harsh environment created a set of customs and values which were markedly different from those of ordinary Russians. See ibid., 113–15.

44. Nadezhdin, "Ob etnograficheskom izuchenii," 66–67.

45. Ibid., 67.

46. N. I. Nadezhdin, *Literaturnaia kritika; Estetika* (Moscow, 1972), 440–41.

47. The comprehensive biographical source for Nadezhdin's early years is N. K. Kozmin, *Nikolai Ivanovich Nadezhdin: Zhizn' i nauchno-literaturnaia deiatel'nost'* (St. Petersburg, 1912).

48. For a brief discussion of nationality as a factor in Baer's life and career, see Jane M. Oppenheimer, "Science and Nationality: The Case of Karl Ernst von Baer (1792–1876)," *Proceedings of the American Philosophical Society*, vol. 134, no. 2, 1990, 75–82. The

standard biography of Baer is B. E. Raikov, *Zhizn' i trudy K. M. Bera* (Moscow-Leningrad, 1961).

49. On the Göttingen School, see Timothy Lenoir, "The Göttingen School and the Development of Transcendental Naturphilosophie in the Romantic Era," *Studies in the History of Biology*, v. 5, 1981, 143–49.

50. On Blumenbach and his influence of Baer, see Timothy Lenoir, "Kant, Blumenbach and Vital Materialism in German Biology," *Isis*, v. 71, 1980, 77–108.

51. Lenoir, "The Göttingen School," 113.

52. The shift in Nadezhdin's orientation is most clearly illustrated by a series of historical articles which he published in 1837 in *Biblioteka dlia chteniia*. See "Ob istoricheskikh trudakh v Rossii." t. 20, otd. 3, 93–136; "Ob istoricheskoi istine i dostovernosti." t. 20, otd. 3, 137–74. "Opyt istoricheskoi geografii russkogo mira." t. 22, 27–79.

53. For a discussion of the overall development of ethnology in Western Europe, see George Stocking, *Victorian Anthropology* (New York, 1987), 47–77.

54. See Iu. V. Bromlei, *Etnos i etnografiia* (Moscow, 1973), 189.

55. Semenov, *Istoriia*, v. 1, 36.

56. In April 1848, Baer gave a long presentation to the General Assembly of the society, arguing in favor of the establishment of such a museum. See *Geograficheskie izvestiia*, vyp. 2, 1848, 35–40.

57. Baer, "Ob etnograficheskikh issledovaniiakh," 94. ARGO, f. 1–1846, op. 1, no. 4, ll. 7–9.

58. "Izvlechenie iz otcheta predstavlennogo russkomu geograficheskomu obshchestvu chlenom-sotrudnikom A. Shegrenom ob etnograficheskoi ekspeditsii v lifliandiiu i kurliandiiu." *Zapiski RGO*, 1847, t. II, 254–55.

59. Ibid., 259.

60. ARGO, f. 1–1846, op. 1, no. 4, ll. 31.

61. Shegren, "Izvlechenie," 255.

62. Several of Petzoldt's drawings are reproduced in Berg, *Vsesoiuznoe*. The originals are still preserved in the archive of the Geographical Society.

63. For information on the Lieves, see *Narody mira: etnograficheskie ocherki: Narody evropeiskoi chasti SSSR*. v. 2 (Moscow, 1964), 202–208.

64. Ibid., 208.

65. For biographical information on Sjögren, see *Russkii biograficheskii slovar'*, v. 15, 29–36. On the Finnish ethnographers, see "Stranstvyiushchie Finliandtsy i proizvodimye imi etnograficheskie issledovaniia," *Sankt-Peterburgskie vedomosti*, no. 154, 1848. For information on Mateas Kastren, the best known of the Finnish ethnographers, see Tokarev, *Istoriia russkoi etnografii*, 220–22.

66. ARGO, f. 1–1846, op. 1, no. 4, ll. 33.

67. For general information on the ethnographic survey, see M. G. Rabinovich, "Otvety na programmu Russkogo geograficheskogo obshchestva kak istochnik dlia izucheniia etnografii goroda," *Ocherki istorii russkoi etnografii, fol'kloristiki, i antropologii*, vyp. 5, 39. The actual text of the ethnographic survey has never been published. A final draft and galley proofs can be found in ARGO, f. 1–1846, op. 1, no. 4, ll. 60–73. A copy of

the final version as it was distributed can be found in the personal papers of Peter Keppen (ARGO, f. 2, op. 1, no. 215, ll. 14–20).

68. The text to the ethnographic survey noted that information was to be gathered "in the localities themselves by individuals who are well acquainted with the lifeways, language, character, and habits of those classes of the population in which national features are best preserved." ARGO, f. 2, op. 1, no. 25, l. 14. Not long before the survey was issued, a memorandum had been submitted by Aleksandr Ianovskii arguing specifically in favor of the use of local observers, particularly parish clergy. See ARGO, f. 1–1846, op. 1, no. 4, l. 45.

69. For an early review of the responses to the ethnographic survey expressing a sense of excitement and surprise, see K. D. Kavelin, "Nekotorye izvlecheniia iz sobiraemykh v IRGO etnograficheskikh materialov o Rossii, s zametkami ob ikh mnogostoronnei zanimatel'nosti i pol'ze dlia nauki," *Geograficheskie izvestiia*, vyp 3, 1850. Also published in Kavelin, *Sobranie sochinenii*, v. 4.

70. The correspondence regarding the distribution of the 1848 ethnographic survey was not preserved. However, similar correspondence for the second edition of the ethnographic survey can be found in ARGO, f. 1–1852, op. 1, no. 5 ("O napechatanii i rassylke etnograficheskoi programmy.") l. 22. The figure of 2,000 responses was published in *Etnograficheskii sbornik*, vyp. 1, (St Petersburg, 1853), vii.

71. This information can be found for most reports in D. K. Zelenin's *Opisanie uchenogo arkhiva Imperatorskogo russkogo geograficheskogo obshchestva* (St. Petersburg, 1915–17), 3. vols. Zelenin's information is far from complete, however. A fourth volume covering provinces from the letters S to Ia was never published.

72. The index was compiled by Aleksandr Ianovskii at Nadezhdin's request. Out of 305 manuscripts, 174 were from village priests. Schoolteachers and directors came in a distant second with thirty-eight responses, while government officials (*chinovniki*) contributed twenty manuscripts. Responses were also received from landowners (fifteen), corresponding members of the Geographical Society (ten), a doctor, seminarians (six), merchants and townspeople (eight), and peasants (seven). Twenty-five respondents did not reveal their identity. Semenov, *Istoriia*, 109–10. More detailed figures from Ianovskii's report can be found in *VIRGO*, t. 10, ot. 6, 1854, 17–18. The initiative to undertake the project was reported in *VIRGO*, t. 5, ot. 7, 1852, 48.

73. For an example of the pride felt by local correspondents, see the letters of Spiridon Mikhailov to A. I. Artem'ev, ORRNB, f. 37 (Artem'eva) no. 497. Excerpts have been published in S. M. Mikhailov, *Trudy po etnografii i istorii russkogo, chuvashskogo, i mariinskogo narodov* (Cheboksary, 1972), 232–40.

74. *VIRGO*, t. 2, ot. 1, 1851, 34.

75. See Nadezhdin, "Ob etnograficheskom izuchenii," 78–82.

76. "K. D. Kavelin v istorii osvobozhdenii krestian," *Russkaia starina*, v. 53, 438.

77. This point is made in Rabinovich, "Otvety," 38.

78. I. I. Sreznevskii, "Zamechaniia o materialakh dlia geografii russkogo iazyka," *VIRGO*, (1851), chap. 1, ot. 5, 16–19.

79. On Russian dialectology, see [N. I. Nadezhdin], "Plemia russkoe v obshchem

semeistve Slavian—po Shafariku," *Zhurnal Ministerstva vnutrennykh del,* chap. 1, 1843. Nadezhdin's system of Russian dialects is elaborated in full in an article which he wrote in German and published in *Jahrbücher der Litteratur,* v. 95 (Vienna, 1841). See also V. Dal', "Opyt oblastnogo velikorusskogo slovaria," *VIRGO,* t. 6, 1852, ot. 4, 1–72.

80. In his introduction to the first edition of his collection, Afanas'ev writes: "Other than stories which I myself recorded, the present work contains a rich supply of documents of this sort written down in various parts of the empire and sent to the Imperial Russian Geographical Society together with other ethnographic materials. . . . This magnificent collection contains much that is of the greatest interest. Many of the stories were written down superbly, preserving all the features of popular dialect. Others, while written in a language that is more literary than popular and not always grammatically correct, are free from any arbitrary or specially made up distortions." *Narodnye russkie skazki A. N. Afanas'eva v trekh tomakh* (Moscow, 1986) t. 3, 349. On the use of the Geographical Society collection for other folklore publications, see Berg, *Vsesoiuznoe,* 148, and M. K. Azadovskii, *Istoriia russkoi fol'kloristiki,* v. 2, 17.

81. N. I. Nadezhdin, "O russkikh narodnykh mifakh i sagakh," *Russkaia beseda,* 1857, t. 3, kn. 7, 1–19; t. 4, kn. 8, 19–63.

82. The study of Russian folklore was dominated in the 1850s and 1860s by the "mythological school" led by Fedor Buslaev, who, in turn, was heavily influenced by the teaching of Jacob Grimm. A reasonably good discussion of Buslaev and his colleagues can be found in A. I. Balandin, *Mifologicheskaia shkola i russkaia fol'kloristika: F. I. Buslaev* (Moscow, 1988). See also A. N. Pypin, *Istoriia russkoi etnografii,* v. 2 (St. Petersburg, 1891) 75–109.

83. K. D. Kavelin, "Byt russkogo naroda," *Sovremennik,* t. 11–1, 11–2, 12–2 (1848). The article was also reprinted in Kavelin's *Sobranie sochinenii,* v. 4 (St. Petersburg, 1900).

84. For Kavelin's views on ethnography and the abolition of serfdom, see "K. D. Kavelin v istorii osvobozhdenii krestian," *Russkaia starina,* v. 53, 438. See also "Zhizn' i deiatel'nost' K. D. Kavelina" in K. D. Kavelin, *Sobranie sochinenii,* v. 1, XXI.

85. *VIRGO,* t. 8, 1853, ot. 9, 22.

86. See minutes to the Ethnographic Division meeting of October 31, 1852, in *VIRGO,* t. 7, ot. 9, 20. For Kavelin's decision regarding the second volume of *Etnograficheskii sbornik,* see ARGO, f. 1–1850, op. 1, no. 23, l. 16.

87. For a good example of this view of ethnography, see Abbott Gleason's portrait of Pavel Ivanovich Iakushkin in *Young Russia* (New York, 1980).

88. "Otchet IRGO za 1851 g." *VIRGO,* t. 4, 1852, 75.

89. *Svod instruktsii dlia kamchatskoi ekspeditsii predprinimaemoi Imperatorskim Russkim geograficheskim obshchestvom* (St. Petersburg, 1852).

90. "Otchet IRGO za 1852 g." *VIRGO,* 1853, t. 7, ot. 1. 76; Semenov, *Istoriia,* v. 1, 111.

91. P. I. Mel'nikov (Andrei Pecherskii), *Ocherki Mordvy* (Saransk, 1981). The first part of Mel'nikov's study consists of a history of the Mordva, based on numerous excerpts from the Russian chronicles—precisely the materials that Nadezhdin had compiled on the Mordva. Moreover, Mel'nikov cites a Mordvin epic which had been collected in 1848

by the Bishop of Nizhnii Novgorod, Iakov (26). This is almost certainly derived from an article which Iakov had sent to the Geographical Society entitled "On the Mordva in Nizhnii Novgorod Province" which Nadezhdin had read to the General Assembly in February 1849. See *Geograficheskie izvestiia*, vyp. 1, 1849.

92. P. I. Nebol'sin, "Ocherki byta Kalmykov," *Biblioteka dlia chteniia*, t. 113–114, 1852, 25. A similar portrayal of nomadic tribes can be found in P. I. Nebol'sin, "Inorodtsy Astrakhanskoi gubernii," *VIRGO*, t. 2, 1851, ot. 5, 1–30. Nebol'sin's articles were published as a separate volume in 1854 entitled "Rasskazy proezhego."

93. See, for example, [Protoierei Vishnevskii] "O religii nekreshchennykh Cheremis Kazanskoi gubernii," *Etnograficheskii sbornik*, vyp. 4, 1858, 209–18. Originally published in *VIRGO*, t. 17, 1856, ot. 2.; and [Arkhimandrit Veniamin] "Samoedy Mezenskie," *Etnograficheskii sbornik*, vyp. 4, 1858, 19–82. Originally published in *VIRGO*, t. 14, 1855, ot. 2. Veniamin's article is particularly interesting in its description of missionary activities among the Samoedy in the 1820s.

94. *Svod instruktsii dlia kamchatskoi ekspeditsii*, 28.

95. *Geograficheskie izvestiia*, vyp. 1, ot. 1, 1849. The work in question was later published in *Etnograficheskii sbornik*, v. 2, under the title "Byt Belorusskikh krest'ian."

96. Henry Rowe Schoolcraft, *Historical and statistical information respecting the history, condition and prospects of the Indian tribes of the United States* (Philadelphia, 1851), vol. 1, 15–16.

97. On the debates between monogenists and polygenists see Stocking, *Victorian Anthropology*, 47–77. The journals of the Russian Geographical Society regularly reported on meetings of foreign scientific societies. For a report that touches directly on the issues of the unity of humanity, see the summary of a paper given at the London Asiatic Society "On the best methods of ethnological investigation for uncovering the history of the human race" in *VIRGO*, 1852, t. 5, ot. 5, 48–50. A review of Schoolcraft was published in *VIRGO*, t. 4, 1852.

98. For a good discussion of the distinction between anthropology and ethnography as it was understood both in Russia and in England, France, and Germany, see A. Bogdanov, "Materialy dlia antropologii kurgannogo perioda v Moskovskoi gubernii," *Izvestiia Obshchestva liubitelei estestvoznaniia*, t. 3, 1867, 2–6.

99. For an overview of evolutionism and Russian ethnography, see Tokarev, *Istoriia russkoi etnografii*, 354–61.

100. See, for example, D. N. Anuchin, "O zadachakh russkoi etnografii," *Etnograficheskoe obozrenie*, t. 1, 1889, 1–35: and N. M. Mogilianskii, "Predmet i zadachi etnografii," *Zhivaia starina*, 1916, 1–22.

101. The career of V. V. Grigor'ev, who served in Orenburg in the 1850s and was responsible for relations with the various peoples of Central Asia, provides a particularly vivid example of the complexities involved in attempts to integrate ethnographic knowledge into administrative practice. See N. N. Veseolvskii, *Vasilii Vasil'evich Grigor'ev po ego pis'mam i trudam: 1816–1881* (St. Petersburg, 1887), 110–225.

102. On the connection between ethnography and the abolition of serfdom, see

D. A. Korsakov, "Zhizn' i deiatel'nost' K. D. Kavelina" in K. D. Kavelin, *Sobranie sochinenii* (St. Petersburg, 1897) vol. 1, XXIII.

103. For discussions of this issue, see George W. Stocking, ed., *Colonial Situations: Essays on the Contextualization of Ethnographic Knowledge*, History of Anthropology, vol. 7 (Madison, Wis.: 1991).

PART III

PRACTICES OF EMPIRE

THIS SECTION PRESENTS four fresh conceptualizations of issues in the social history of the Russian empire. The subjects are varied, but each essay has a well-established analytical or narrative framing. We have intentionally combined topics relating to questions of "empire" with subjects examined on the source base of central "European" Russia. The empire, after all, included the center as well as the borderlands, and populations were ethnically diverse throughout the realm. The functioning of imperial Russia's institutions should be considered over the full extent of the country.

The essays by Thomas Barrett and Willard Sunderland shift from the elevated view offered in the previous section on imperial imagination to new angles of vision on the process of empire building itself. The established narratives of this topic detail, on the one hand, the march of progress and enlightenment into the borderlands through the agency of imperial institutions and ethnically Russian colonizers or, on the other, ruthless conquest and repression of indigenous peoples by military operations and Russifying rule.

Barrett's essay on the Caucasus, "Lines of Uncertainty," challenges these stories. In an examination of the frontier and the empire in process of formation, he sees neither the *"sblizhenie"* (coming together of peoples) of rosy Soviet accounts nor the starkly dichotomized conflicts evoked by the rhetoric of colonization and anti-colonial struggle. Instead, Barrett analyzes the Caucasus as an arena of shifting possibilities for individuals and communities. The "frontier" in its social dimension was less a border than a mingling of economies and social systems that encompassed smuggling, banditry, expanded marriage and family opportunities, spying, production for warfare and for expanding settlements. Barrett regards Russian narratives of heroism and captivity (framed in opposition to "Caucasian barbarity") as attempts to clarify and simplify loyalties in circumstances where the interests of individuals and groups could not be easily identified and disentangled.

Willard Sunderland also invites us to envision the multidimensional process of colonization as cultural interaction. The first thing to note is that many of the colonizers are not Russians at all but people of diverse ethnic backgrounds pursuing a common objective: better lands and a better life. This pragmatic meaning, which ordinary people give to their moves into the borderlands, differs greatly from elite constructions of this activity. Again contrary to the usual picture of Russians pushing aside less advanced peoples on the frontier, the process of interaction, as Sunderland describes it, often involved accommodation and practical arrangements for sharing resources and providing mutual assistance. The many ethnic groups mingled, if not blended, in a society of varied cultures that retained much of their integrity while adjusting to and adopting practices from one another. Occasionally, Russians either individually or in whole villages "went native," adopting the way of life of the dominant ethnic group in the region. Sunderland ends with an exploration of cases of ethnic stereotyping and the pragmatic use of these images by people in border areas.

While Sunderland's vision of the frontier attributes strong agency to peasants and emphasizes their ability to alter cultural and material practices, Steven L. Hoch's essay addresses the impact of institutions of exploitation on peasant lives. His foil is Robert Brenner's contribution to an often-cited debate that occurred in the pages of the journal *Past & Present* about twenty years ago. Brenner argued that the key to extracting the surplus product of peasant labor was the landlord's control of peasant movement. In Brenner's view, the peasant's lack of freedom was more important than the evolution of markets or larger demographic developments. Despite the attractiveness of this analysis to historians of the Russian serf economy, Hoch contends that it misrepresents relationships in Russia, which are built on very different principles of exploitation.

Hoch rejects analyses of the Russian peasant economy that are based on class and private-property concepts of Western thinking. He argues that in Russia landlords were able to exercise control only by working through patriarchal heads of peasant households who operated their own regime of subsistence agriculture designed to equalize burdens among productive units and diminish the risk of famine. The village economy rested on early marriage, high fertility, and periodic land redistribution that reallocated the resource base to those most in need of it and best prepared to use it. This arrangement yielded high per capita grain productivity and, accordingly, an adequate diet and good survival chances for the Russian peasant family. What it did not produce was a strong sense of private property in land and a legal system on the Western model to adjudicate disputes over ownership. This lack is often considered a failing of the Russian people. But why, Hoch implies, should an economic system that provided a high degree of survivability and a limit on the power of lords to extract a surplus be regarded as a failure? Our inclination to accept Western practices as universal standards of value prevent us from appreciating the success of Russian practices in meeting the populace's material needs.

Since the revolution of 1917, the history of the Russian church has languished. A few intrepid souls in Russia and abroad continued to study Russian religious philosophy, but little progress was made toward new conceptualizations of the church. Studies of the contemporary church were in many cases martyrologies, while historical treatments with a longer view followed the established prerevolutionary pattern of internal descriptions of institutional policy focusing on top church administrators. A fresh approach emerged in the late 1970s in Gregory L. Freeze's work on the social history of the parish clergy. Under the influence of the explosion of social history in the West, Freeze produced pathbreaking monographs on the parish clergy in imperial Russia. But these studies remained internal to the clerical estate—descriptions and evaluations of the development of this "caste" in interaction with state policy.

Freeze has now moved beyond his pioneering studies to a new conceptualization of religious history in Russia; his current work looks at how the church functioned in relation to the rest of society. His essay in this volume surveys the strengthening of the institutional structure of the church in the imperial period through bureaucratization, professionalization, and functional specialization. He gives particular attention to the church's new focus on its spiritual mission. The church set about standardizing popular orthodoxy by upgrading its churches and their sacral inventory, regularizing texts, music, and holy days throughout the country, and validating the veneration of official saints while extirpating the worship of unofficial saints. Much effort was given to the clear demarcation of the sacred and profane. The church sought to confine the sacred within church buildings and not allow it to pour out into the streets and mingle in the crowds; outdoor processions were a special problem in this regard, even though they were much loved by Russians and thought essential for combating certain evils. Similarly, church leaders endeavored to exclude the profane from the church: to keep out alcohol use, fights, parties, shrieking women, folk icons.

The Russian church in the imperial period has often been portrayed as a passive body having little impact on society. Freeze's studies demonstrate the weakness of this view. The church was delineating and actively enforcing a distinction between the sacred and profane. Although it was not able in most cases to force people to comply with its demands, it did compel them to decide what they believed and to assess whether or not it fit within the official definition of orthodoxy.

6

Lines of Uncertainty

The Frontiers of the Northern Caucasus

Thomas M. Barrett

————··◦◦◦◦··————

T HE CAUCASUS MAY be likened to a mighty fortress, marvelously strong by
 nature, artificially protected by military works, and defended by a numerous garrison." This oft-quoted line was written by General A. A. Veliaminov in
1828 in a memoir which advocated the use of powerful military force to subdue
the tribes of the north Caucasus. To take this fortress, a wise commander must
"lay his parallels; advance by gap and mine and so master the place." The extension of a fortified line farther and farther towards the mountains, using it as
a base for attacks, was essential to Veliaminov's strategy of conquest.[1]

"The line," as it was often simply called, began in the mid-eighteenth century as a defensive string of forts, Cossack villages, and observation towers.
There were even concealed outposts where Cossacks would hide at night; if they
heard the approach of threatening groups of tribesmen, they sent a signal to the
nearest tower or Cossack village. Then bells would be rung, shots fired, wood
bundled with resin-soaked tow set ablaze as a smoke signal, and Cossacks and
troops would rush to the break in the line.

The Caucasus military line versus the mountain "fortress": these are the
images, the lines of separation, usually evoked by Western and pre-Soviet historians of the north Caucasus and the Russian experience there, lines which
also included the Russian "borders" of the Terek and the Kuban and the lines
of contest with Persia and the Ottoman Empire. As the story goes, the Russian
state began pushing to the south with the conquest of Kazan' and Astrakhan
in the sixteenth century and forts were established in the north Caucasus soon
thereafter. Large-scale warfare began with Peter I's Persian campaign (1722) and
a series of wars with Persia and the Ottoman Empire on Caucasian lands ensued
throughout the eighteenth and nineteenth centuries. The military line crept

south into the north Caucasus, beginning with the Kizliar-Mozdok line (1769), and fortress after fortress advanced Russian forces further into the mountains. After the completion of the Caucasus military line in 1832, the Black Sea coastal line was raised to the west, cutting off the peoples of the Caucasus from the Black Sea and contact with Turkey. The native peoples resisted the Russian encroachment with guerilla warfare and major conflagrations, culminating in Shamil's holy war (1834–1859). When the Circassian resistance was finally defeated in 1864, the conquest of the north Caucasus was complete and the region became a pacified colony of the Russian Empire.

The Western historiography of that conquest has greatly advanced in this century, from John Baddeley's 1908 *The Russian Conquest of the Caucasus* to the recently published collection of articles, *The North Caucasus Barrier*, and Moshe Gammer's *Muslim Resistance to the Tsar: Shamil and the Conquest of Chechnia and Daghestan*—the first substantial attempts to portray the mountaineers' resistance to the Russian advance. But the history of Russia and the north Caucasus remains essentially military history: the lines are still drawn tightly, with only a shift in perspective from the Russian push to the Caucasian barrier.[2]

As I shall argue, the Russian advance through the north Caucasus was much more than a military conquest: it was also a frontier process involving the in- and out-migration of large numbers of people, the settlement and creation of new communities, and the abandonment of old ones. And, as on all frontiers, borders were crossed and allegiances shifted continually by Russians and Ukrainians, by mountain peoples, by Armenians and Georgians.[3] To understand the Russian annexation of the north Caucasus, we must look behind the military lines, to the movements of peoples, the settlements and communities, the transformation of the landscape, and the interactions of neighbors, not just in war but in everyday life.

Prerevolutionary Russian historiography focused on the military conquest of the region and discussed administration, resettlement policies, and the use of native peoples only as they facilitated Russian expansion.[4] Soviet historians studied the peoples of the north Caucasus for their own sake and developed national histories to represent many of the ethnic groups there. Here the tendency was either to downplay destruction by the Russian military or to portray it as fending off the real enemies of the Caucasus (Persia, the Ottoman Empire, the Crimean Khanate) or as a part of an oppressive, but ultimately progressive, tsarist "colonial politics" that brought the north Caucasus into the timetable of history.[5] Soviet studies of migration and ethnic mixing in the North Caucasus, of the development of the regional economy, of cities, and of Cossacks often make grandiose claims about the closeness and mutual influence of Russians and mountain peoples, but with no real examination of frontier life with all of its complexity, tensions, and violence. Only bits and pieces are extracted, that inevitably add up to "drawing together" (*sblizhenie*) and "the friendship of peoples" (*druzhba narodov*).[6]

If Soviet historians tended to define Russian frontiers as zones of *sblizhenie*, Western historians either have seen them as colonies or borders or have not seen them at all. Their few attempts to cast Russian history in terms of an expanding frontier have foundered on an overly metahistorical, Turnerian approach, more concerned with the spirit of the state than life at the edge, and backed up by little supporting research. All of Russian history is presented as frontier history, beginning with Kiev and ending with Siberia, with little distinction between the different periods of Russian migration and always omitting the Caucasus (and usually the lower and middle Volga). Or, the Russian frontier is simply equated with the American one: Kazan' becomes St. Louis, the conquest of Novgorod is likened to the acquisition of Ohio from Britain, and the conquest of Ukraine is Russia's Louisiana Purchase.[7] A few historians have been more restrained in their approach but still make a quick leap from Kazan' to Siberia, ignoring the fact that colonization moved south well before it moved east, and that the lower Volga was as non-Russian as Siberia until the late eighteenth century.[8] Similarly, major works on migration, colonization, and frontier society focus mostly on Siberia, or on the steppe frontier and the settlement of Ukraine and the Crimea. It is usually forgotten that these migrations were part of a larger and more diverse process (and that the steppe extends to the foothills of the Caucasus).[9]

Extremely valuable recent work has been done on the non-Russian edge of the expanding frontier and it is partly due to these studies that historians of Russia no longer flirt with Frederick Jackson Turner's notion of the frontier as an engine of progress.[10] But they too depict the transformation of Ukrainian, Crimean, Volga, and Siberian borderlands into Russian regions more as a political process than as a social one. Our understanding is limited mostly to conquest (war and administration), while the "constructive" aspects of Russian colonization (the creation of new social identities, ethnic relations, landscapes, regional economies, and material cultures) have yet to be explored. Or the social history focuses exclusively on the "losers" and their repression, resistance, extinction, and emigration.

The type of frontier history needed for the north Caucasus, and for other Russian frontiers as well, should draw upon developments in the historiography of the American frontier in the last twenty years. Turnerian type of frontier history has finally been abandoned, with its free white settlers moving west to "vacant" lands and gloriously creating American individualism and democracy in the process. In its place, historians are writing about a more complicated process, involving people of various colors and nations, environmental manipulation, cultural mixing, social stratification, and grand myth making.[11] Three trends in American frontier historiography are particularly promising for Russian historians, generally fitting under the rubrics of environmental history, social history, and ethnohistory. The purpose of this paper is not to explore any one of these in great depth, but to justify a frontier conceptualization for one borderland region of Russia and to sketch out what such a history might entail.

Environmental Manipulation and "Species Shifting"

Not only was the economic development of the American west often an assault on nature, destroying as well as creating, but it was a movement of alien organisms (crops, weeds, animals, microorganisms) into new ecosystems. Native attitudes toward land were supplanted by European notions of land as a commodity. Extensive, resource-intensive cultivation techniques became dominant over small-scale, more ecologically appropriate methods. As William Cronon, George Miles, and Jay Gitlin have written, "the familiar frontier tension between reproducing the old and embracing the new expressed itself in new settlement landscapes that increasingly resembled those of Europe and in new political economies better adapted to New World ecosystems."[12]

Environmental history is particularly important in understanding a frontier, where settlers try to construct new communities in unfamiliar ecological contexts. How settlers are transformed by and how they transform their landscapes are integral parts of their struggles and opportunities.[13] The environmental history of the north Caucasus is especially complex; there are few regions in the world with such extremes and diversity of nature, including the numerous microclimates of the mountains and foothills, the cycles of flooding and drought in the valleys, and the contrast of the mountains with the steppe—near desert along the Caspian Sea—and the swampy Terek lowlands. Here, the camel butts heads with the ox, the buffalo with the mountain goat.

In this diverse and unforgiving environment, in contrast to the American experience, colonists were more the recipients than the purveyors of disease. One of the reasons why the annexation of the Black Sea coast of the Caucasus was fraught with disaster was because it was a terrain that could not be mastered in short time, either by the plow or by Russian immune systems. The Russian settlement patterns that resulted in so many deaths were opposite from traditional, ecologically conscious patterns. Circassians settled in the piedmont and the mountains, avoiding the malarial swamps along the coast and the frequent fogs that were detrimental to orchard crops; Russian settlement, on the other hand, began at the coast and the low-lying rivers. Here, food had to be shipped in via the Black Sea or obtained through trade with Circassians. And in forts both along the Black Sea and in the Kuban region of the Black Sea Cossacks, the attrition rate was enormous as settlers and soldiers died in large numbers from the plague, malaria, typhus, scurvy, and cholera. G. I. Filipson, an officer serving on the Black Sea in the 1840s, likened Sukhumi to "a stone grave" where 16 percent of the lower ranks died from diseases annually (making the average life span there six years). This was also the typical death rate for each major resettlement to the Kuban, except for the 1848 resettlement of 2,000 families when 36 percent of the males died, mostly from cholera. Curiously, the spa industry of the north Caucasus got its start because of the high rate of sickness in the region: before it was Pushkin's favorite spa, Piatigorsk was Konstantinogorskaia fortress, where sick soldiers and Cossacks went in 1780 to bathe in hot springs under Kalmyk tents.[14]

In the rich steppe of the north Caucasus, Russians met with greater success in establishing an agricultural economy, settlement, and political control. But it took more than a century; even as late as 1833, famine in the Stavropol' province forced the government to lend three million rubles to state peasants for the purchase of grain and to allow some 40,000 peasants to return temporarily to the interior of Russia.[15] And Russian control was accomplished with a political economy that was radically different from the heartland, based as it was upon Cossacks, state peasants, and native peoples (not on serfs), and on a more diversified economy.

There were plans for the colonization of this steppe as early as 1764, and the first major land grants were made in the following decades. But most landowners sold or neglected their estates and those few who did settle did not engage in agriculture at first but rather used the land almost exclusively as pasture for cattle. One colossal failure was Prince A. A. Viazemskii. This favorite of Catherine II received more than 189,000 acres of the Caucasus steppe in 1783–1786, founded Chernyi Rynok as the center of his holdings, and resettled 1,000 serfs from the central provinces. His attempts at large-scale wheat cultivation were unsuccessful as were efforts to teach his peasants sea fishing and viticulture. He soon sold the estate to another noble, who in turn divided it and sold the bulk of it three years later. By the beginning of the nineteenth century, Chernyi Rynok was a miserable settlement of fifty peasant homes.[16]

Soviet historians emphasize a lack of capital as an essential factor in the failure of the manorial economy, but environmental factors were also important. Resettled peasants had difficulty adjusting to the new climate, diseases, and the new agricultural calendar; many became sick or died. The village of Pokoinoe, founded in 1766 on the Kuma River by peasants from southern provinces, was so named, according to one resident, because so many died from "swamp fever" (they became *pokoiniki*, deceased).[17] The Nogai Tatars called the village "bad place."

What occurred at the intersection of native and Russian agricultures? Russian officials tended to view foothill and mountain agriculture as primitive, but the light plow, terraced slopes, irrigation systems, sophisticated manuring, and regionally adapted grain varieties made for an ecologically appropriate and intensive agriculture that in many respects was superior to Russian extensive plowing. Agriculture was especially intensive in Dagestan where there was a well-developed irrigation system and a widespread use of fertilizers such as manure, ashes, silt, straw mixed with turf and dung, and even bird droppings. Soviet historians claim that native techniques and crops were greatly influential among the Russians and that Russian crops and techniques spread among the mountain people. But the more important flow of influence, at least until the mid-nineteenth century, seems to have come from the south. Kizliar would have never succeeded as a large and permanent settlement without Persian rice and millet, Derbent wheat, and, most importantly, the grape vines and irrigation canals indigenous to the region. Even in the north Caucasus steppe, where extensive agriculture dominated, the farmers relied upon Kuban wheat.[18]

How important was the ecological devastation that the Russian forces wrought in wearing down the resistance of the mountaineers? The wood felling made famous by the Tolstoy story "Rubka lesa" was significant not just in eliminating the woodland cover of hostile tribes, but in depriving them and others of scarce building and heating material. Baddeley points to Shamil's restrictions on tree cutting in Chechen lands as evidence of a defensive posture against the Russian ax. But Russians weren't the only ones to fell trees. Wood and wood products (lumber for building and cooperage, oxcarts and wheels, vineyard stakes and hoops) were major items of sale by Chechens and Kabardians to Russian settlers. Until 1840 the Chechens living closest to the Caucasus military line annually floated 500 to 800 rafts of lumber and firewood down the Sunzha and the Terek to Kizliar, and they carted there 5,000 to 6,000 oxcarts of vineyard stakes. The Russian demand for wood was so great—and the belt of accessible forested land between steppe and mountain so narrow—that it must have stimulated native overcutting in some areas.[19]

Wood felling, of course, also affected Russians. Geographer D. L. Ivanov wrote in 1886 of the great soil erosion in the Stavropol' region, a result of Russian settlement and deforestation. Settlements such as Dubovka (oak) and Berestovok (birch bark), named for their silva, were denuded of forests; many areas that had been rich in trees, shrubs, and wildlife were quickly transformed into bare slopes, gullies, gorges, and weeds. When founded in 1790, Kruglolesskoe (forest-encircled) had been surrounded by a thick forest. At the end of the nineteenth century only a "pitiful remnant" survived on the west side and the village was now known by locals simply as Krugloe (round). The story of Chernolesskoe (black forest), founded by Russian settlers in 1799, was typical:

> According to old-timers, the village was probably named "Chernolesskoe" because at the time of its founding there grew along the entire stretch of the Tomuzlov River large trees, exclusively of deciduous species. Wild pigs and goats were found in abundance in the forest; there were even deer and bears which had made their way from the forest of the Caucasus mountains. In our time, not even vestiges of this forest remain.[20]

It would be a mistake to ignore the importance of such natural bounty to the fledgling Russian settlements, which were often named for the riches of the land (Obil'noe, Blagodatnoe—abundant; Medvedskoe—bear; Orekhovskoe—nut; Grushevskoe—pear). The results of its overexploitation also need to be fully examined.

Even more significant than wood felling in wearing down the mountain peoples' resistance and in transforming the local economy was the denial or restriction of access to winter pasture and the salt lakes of the plains. Pasturing was often an extensive operation, with different tribes pooling labor and resources, and with cattle drives moving as far afield as 400 kilometers for winter pasture. Also, the mountain economy was restricted by a fragile ecology, one aspect of which was a dearth of usable land. But agriculture was necessary for almost all of the native peoples, if only to provide food for their cattle and horses. This was an economy that an occupying military could easily disrupt, except that Russian forts and settlers were also dependent upon it until the victory of the plow over the steppe.

Frontier Exchange

This term comes from Daniel H. Usner, Jr.'s *Indians, Settlers, & Slaves in a Frontier Exchange Economy: The Lower Mississippi Valley before 1783.* By it, he means the "networks of cross-cultural interaction through which native and colonial groups circulated goods and services," including "small-scale production, face-to-face marketing, and prosaic features of livelihood."[21] Such processes may appear insignificant from the vantage point of the center; for those at the frontier, they were the foundation of regional economy and shared culture. Frontier exchange is, of course, vital for the livelihood of settlers (and conquerors) on all frontiers and helps to structure native-colonist relationships and dependencies. Russian history and the history of the north Caucasus have focused on what frontier exchange evolved into, in Soviet terms "the drawing in of the North Caucasus into the all-Russian market," and not what it meant for regional society, economy, and culture.[22]

Local trade in the north Caucasus was conducted in forts, Cossack villages and trading posts, and in the mountains by itinerant Armenian merchants. This trade was extensive across the region and continued to grow, even when the war of conquest was at its peak in the 1840s and 1850s. Mountain people traded a wide range of goods, including livestock, grain, wood, arms, sheepskins, clothes, leather goods, and other handicrafts in exchange for salt, fish, caviar, cotton fabric, iron and lead products, and manufactured goods. The capture and ransom of prisoners was also a part of local trade.

Several aspects of frontier exchange need to be explored in order to understand the Russian experience in the north Caucasus. First, in the nineteenth century Russians attempted to create native dependencies on manufactured goods to lure tribes into submission through a taste for "the fruits of civilization." But if one looks closely at eighteenth- and nineteenth-century local trade, the question as to who was dependent on whom becomes more complicated. Russia never succeeded in creating in the north Caucasus a trading colony where locals would provide large amounts of raw materials such as furs and cotton for the enrichment of Russian merchants. At least as important in the frontier exchange were domestically manufactured clothing and weapons, saddles and other leather products, and what we would now call processed foods (dried fruit) and specialized horticultural products (nuts, madder, fresh fruit), items that require a higher level of skill to produce than raw materials that are produced en masse, such as Russian grain.

Lines of dependency could get quite confused on this distant frontier that in some ways was technically more sophisticated than the heartland. A curious fact of the Russian conquest of the Caucasus is that Cossacks were armed by silversmiths and metalworkers from the mountains. Cossack weaponry—sabre (*shashka*), dagger (*kinzhal*), and until the mid-nineteenth century the mountain rifle—was manufactured mostly in mountain villages and obtained through trade. This skewed the development of handicraft production north of the Caucasus military line; Russians and Cossacks did not engage in metal handicrafts at all, preferring to obtain metal goods either from the south or from the north. Native skilled laborers, such as blacksmiths and silversmiths, were also welcomed to ply their trade at Russian forts and villages; most of the artisans at Kizliar and Mozdok were from beyond the Terek.[23] And all of the Russian forts into the nineteenth century tried to widen their economic bases by attracting settlements of Armenians, Georgians, Chechens, Kabardians, and others involved in trade, agriculture, sericulture, and various handicrafts.

A second aspect of frontier exchange requiring further exploration is the attempt, largely unsuccessful, to regulate Russian-native trade through a quarantine line of trading posts and salt magazines. In this fertile ground for an underground economy, smugglers regularly breached the customs line and black-market relationships created bonds of conspiracy. The inspector of one trading post reported that the sale of salt, the main item of trade, had nearly stopped at seven quarantine posts after new Cossack forts had been established further in the interior of Kabarda in the 1820s; Cossacks would simply bring salt from other towns and trade or sell it to Kabardians and others at these non-quarantine settlements. A contemporary estimated that the value of contraband trade was more than twice that of the official trade with the mountain people and called smuggling a normal practice.[24] The growth of unregulated market and bazaar trade and the prevalence of Armenian merchants, versed in mountain languages and traveling to interior villages, also doomed Russian trading posts.

Third, we must know how native economies were affected by Russian demands. The trade in handicrafts and clothing such as *burkas*, *cherkeskas*, and *papakhas* seems to have strengthened the local economy since the number of goods produced for trade greatly expanded over time. But specialization had its advantages too: the commander of the Kizliar fortress, A. I. Akhverdov, reported in 1804 that the Kumyks of the village of Endirei became "well enriched" by purchasing captives from mountain people and then reselling them at a good profit to the inhabitants of Kizliar to work as indentured servants in the vineyards. Situated like a gate at the foot of the mountains, Endirei was well placed to take advantage of the lucrative trade. Not only does this anecdote show that the Russian fort town was "nativized" enough to use slaves from the mountains to develop viticulture, it also illustrates that the Russian presence reoriented parts of the native economy and created riches for those involved.[25]

Russians also participated in the native traditions of captivity. While the slave trade was heartily condemned by the Russians, outlawed in 1804 and eventually stopped, they had to submit to the mountain practice of hostage taking and prisoner ransom (probably a very significant source of income in the scarcity economies of the north Caucasus). Not only did the forts keep native hostages (*amanaty*) as a formal security guarantee against tribes with whom they had an agreement, but, in the event of the death of a hostage, they were instructed by the College of Foreign Affairs to seize replacements if a substitute was not provided. Raiding parties sent to capture hostages or retrieve prisoners or stolen livestock occasionally turned into plundering raids no different from the attacks on Russian settlements by the mountain peoples.[26]

The "Middle Ground" and Ethnic Frontiers

The treatment of Native Americans in the historiography of the American frontier has undergone a seismic shift in the last half-century: at first, they were hardly portrayed at all; then they became victims who were exploited, annihilated, and assimilated. For the last several decades, the practice of ethnohistory has led to a depiction of Indians as resisters, emphasizing conflict with whites and their preservation of islands of traditional culture. Miles has complained that, despite the flourishing of Native American history, the new studies remain marginal: "By depicting Indian and white cultures in antithetical terms, they make it virtually impossible to imagine an approach in which Indian history can be incorporated into the mainstream of American historiography."[27] Because so much basic work needs to be done on the history of non-Russians in the Russian Empire, studies of borderland peoples and national minorities are at risk of the same marginalization. Good frontier history will not only be important to the history of, say, the Caucasus or Karelia, but to the history of Russia as well.

It is essential to view the frontier during the early stages of Russian settlement not so much as a new Russia on the periphery but as a unique creation with cultural sharing on all sides. Before the Russian state and Russian settlers were predominant, accommodation between peoples necessarily existed. As Richard White has explained in his important study, *The Middle Ground: Indians, Empires, and Republics in the Great Lakes Region, 1650–1815,* "As commonly used, *acculturation* describes a process in which one group becomes more like another by borrowing discrete cultural traits. Acculturation proceeds under conditions in which a dominant group is largely able to dictate correct behavior to a subordinate group." What he proposes instead is an examination of "the middle ground," "the place in between: in between cultures, peoples, and in between empires and the nonstate world of the villages. . . . It is the area between the historical foreground of European invasion and occupation and the background of Indian defeat and retreat."[28] Aspects of White's middle ground include marriage, negotiation over violence, alliance maintained through rituals, and the social relations formed through trade.

A middle ground certainly existed between Russians and the native peoples of the north Caucasus in the seventeenth, eighteenth, and early nineteenth centuries, and at times it was vast. It was created primarily through intermarriage, frontier exchange, and traditions of mountain hospitality. The middle ground of the north Caucasus shaded into regions of acculturation where individuals crossed the ethnic frontier—often through desertion, flight, or captivity—and became nativized or Russified. Historiography has concentrated on what the middle ground became—how it contracted into military lines and lines of ethnic typecasting;[29] what I am most interested in, and what I will discuss in the remainder of this paper, are the lines of uncertainty that helped create fluid ethnic frontiers and a vast middle ground in the north Caucasus.

One prerequisite for a middle ground, the absence of a "dominant group . . . largely able to dictate correct behavior," was manifest in the north Caucasus through the eighteenth century. Even after 1864 Russians were not able to dictate behavior throughout most of the area, nor were they ethnically dominant except in a few enclaves. Forts were regularly contested, relocated, abandoned, and reestablished. For example, the first Russian fort built in 1567 at the mouth of the Sunzha was relocated four times after attacks, and then abandoned for good in 1653 when the garrison was transferred to Terskii Gorod. The latter was then moved and abandoned in 1722 for Sviatoi Krest, which was abandoned for Kizliar in 1735. Even after the establishment of the Kizliar-Azov line in 1778, the Russian presence could be fluid. Vladikavkaz was abandoned two years after its founding in 1784 because of the Mansur uprising and was reconstructed only in 1803. The shifting fortunes of Ekaterinograd, first founded in 1777 on the middle Terek at the foot of the mountains, is another example. With appropriate pomp, Ekaterinograd was transformed from a Cossack village into the capital of the Caucasus viceregency (*namestnichestvo*) in 1785. P. G. Potemkin, the vice-regent (and cousin of the more famous Potemkin) moved his residence there, constructed a luxurious palace, and erected a massive, classical-style triumphal arch with a huge cornice, four columns, and the inscription "the road to Georgia." Two years later the capital was transferred northwest to Georgievsk, then to Astrakhan in 1802, and Ekaterinograd reverted to a lonely Cossack village with a triumphal arch in the middle of a field.[30] The stated reason for the move was the remoteness of Ekaterinograd; the raids of Mansur along the line no doubt helped force the issue. The next fortress designated to be a north Caucasus capital, Stavropol', was more accessible to the rest of Russia and located safely in the steppe.

The uncertainty of the abandoned triumphal arch merits the same scrutiny as the aggressive cockiness of the Ermolov forts and camps of 1818–1819, Groznaia (menacing), Pregradnyi (barrier), Zlobnyi (malicious), Vnezapnaia (unexpected, as in a surprise attack), and Burnaia (violent). It is easy to overestimate the importance of a few Russian forts and settlements in the north Caucasus or elsewhere, especially during the eighteenth century. The entire Caucasus and the Caspian swarmed with bands of brigands until the end of the century. Russia conducted a sustained military offensive in the north Caucasus only after 1817; still, up to the 1860s, "peaceful" tribes shifted sides at will and travel remained dangerous not only in the mountains but in the foothills and steppe as well. On this, like all frontiers, friends and neighbors were often more important to one's livelihood and security than a barely existent state.

Combined with a vacillating military presence, Russians faced demographic uncertainty up to the nineteenth century: it was, in other words, far from being strictly a "Russian" frontier. Only at the end of the eighteenth century did Russians become a slight majority in the province, which did not include the unconquered mountain region beyond the Terek and Kuban rivers. Kizliar and Mozdok remained largely non-Russian even later; and in 1869 Russians and Ukrainians made up only 123,036 of the 469,278 residents of Terek *oblast'*.[31]

Russian settlement in the north Caucasus may be divided into three stages. From the 1560s up to 1721, free Cossack villages appeared along the eastern Terek and the first Russian forts were built in the same region; the Terek Cossacks were withdrawn from the authority of the Foreign Office (*Posol'skii prikaz*), put under the command of the War College, and transformed into servants of the state. Only in the second stage (1722–1775) did the Russian government begin resettling significant numbers of Cossacks and other service people. Several new forts were built along the Terek, including the first permanent one, Kizliar. During the third stage (1776–1860) the military line was completed and pushed further into the mountains; Cossacks were resettled all along the line, the Zaporozhian Cossacks were reconstituted as the Black Sea Cossacks and awarded lands in the Kuban region, and the resettlement and spontaneous migration of large numbers of peasants began. The Russian influx was simultaneous with a great reshuffling of native populations, including the immigration of Armenians and Georgians; a movement of Ossetians from the mountains to the foothills and plains; a migration of Nogais from the steppe across the Kuban River and to the Ural, Crimea, and Caspian steppes; and finally a massive out-migration of perhaps 700,000 Circassians in the 1850s and 1860s.[32]

As soon as a permanent Russian presence was established along the Terek, groups of native peasants and slaves settled there, often causing serious diplomatic complications. One of the first notorious captivity incidents involved Russian protection of native fugitives. In 1774, the botanist Samuel-Gotlieb Gmelin, on a research expedition in the Caspian region, was captured in Dagestan by the sovereign (*utsmi*) of Kaitag, Amir-Hamza. Some 200 of his subject families had fled years earlier to Russian protection, and he demanded either their return or a payment of 30,000 rubles in exchange for Gmelin.[33] Beginning in the 1740s Kabardians continually complained to the Russian government about the flight of their slaves to Russian settlements. The Russian foundation of the fort

of Mozdok in 1763, at the site of a Kabardian village, aggravated the situation
as hundreds of Kabardians escaped to Russian protection. A Kabardian delega-
tion was sent to St. Petersburg in 1764 to request that the fortress be destroyed,
that they be compensated for Christian fugitives, and that any other fugitive
subjects of theirs be returned; the requests were, of course, denied. At the time
there were more than 200 converted Kabardians in Mozdok. In 1767 some 10,000
peasants fled to the fortified area between the Terek and Malka rivers and
erected a bridge across the Terek for an escape route. Despite promises of Russian protection by the commander of Kizliar fortress, the peasants reached
an agreement with their lords concerning lower taxes and the right to flee to
other proprietors, and many returned. In 1771 after another Kabardian petition,
Catherine II agreed to return fugitive Kabardian slaves and to pay fifty rubles
for each Christian.[34] This decision was made because Russia did not want to
aggravate its relations with the Ottoman Empire (which considered Kabarda
feudal territory) and because it was thought that many converted Kabardians
had no real interest in Christianity.

Russia had also decided to turn its attention to the Ossetians, supposedly
"wayward Christians" who had become the objects of special missionary activities. The resettlement of Ossetians from the mountains to the valleys began
with the founding of Mozdok (1763) and Vladikavkaz (1784). In fact, Mozdok
was originally intended to be a fortified settlement—Osetinskaia fortress—to
which Ossetians, Georgians, Armenians, and other "people of Christian nations" would be invited to resettle, where they would have freedom to construct
churches and practice their faith and where Muslim residences would be prohibited. Mozdok was constructed instead but still with the intention of making it a magnet for Ossetian resettlement. Ossetian resettlement increased in the
1820s when Ermolov began removing Kabardians from the area of the Georgian
military highway and settling Ossetians there; by the 1840s there were some
21,000 Ossetians living in the Vladikavkaz plain.[35] Many enrolled in Cossack
service, especially in the Mozdok Cossack Brotherhood and the Mountain Cossack regiment.

In the eighteenth and nineteenth centuries, the Russian government ex-
pended even more effort luring Armenians to the north Caucasus. The first major land grant was awarded in 1710 to an Armenian from Karabakh, Safar
Vasil'ev, for the cultivation of mulberry gardens (for silkworms) in the Kizliar
region. In the eighteenth century, large numbers of Armenians from Turkey
and Persia resettled in the Terek River basin; others fled there from mountain,
Crimean, or Nogai captivity. During this period, Kizliar and Mozdok were
largely Armenian: in 1796, there were 2,800 Armenians and only 1,000 Russians
at Kizliar; in 1789, 55.6 percent of the population of Mozdok was Armenian and

Georgian. Nearly 3,500 more Armenians resettled in 1797 along the Caucasus military line from khanates in Dagestan and along the Caspian Sea. Armenians engaged in silk production and viticulture and were the backbone of regional trade in the north Caucasus. Another large group of Armenians moved in 1839 from across the Kuban to settle along the western part of the Cossack Line at Armavir, where the residents (even in 1859) spoke a Circassian dialect and resembled the mountain people.[36] Armenian in self-identity, Christian in faith, members of the Russian Empire, surrounded by Cossacks, and Circassian in speech, dress, cuisine, and custom—the Armavir Armenians demonstrate how complex this ethnic frontier could be.

The first, most numerous, and most widely dispersed "Russian" settlers in the north Caucasus were Cossacks. I should also tag "Cossack" with quotation marks because Cossackdom in the north Caucasus can hardly be reduced to a single ethnicity or a simple estate designation. One constant, however, is that by the eighteenth century, Cossacks of the north Caucasus were defined by the Russian state as its servants, obliged to provide military, courier, construction, or other service. This does not mean, of course, that they all did so—many rebelled against specific duties, formed gangs of marauders, or deserted to the mountains. How "Cossack," for example, was Iakov Alpatov of the Cossack village of Naur who twice fled for the mountains, converted to Islam, and formed a thieving band of Chechens and Cossacks in the 1850s that robbed farmsteads, stole cattle, and took captives, not only from Cossacks but also from Kalmyks and Nogais well into the steppe?[37]

The first Cossack communities that sprang up along the Terek in the sixteenth and seventeenth centuries were populated by a diverse mix of people on the run: migrating or fugitive Cossacks, Old Believers, slaves captured by Russian forces, and natives of the Caucasus fleeing slavery, punishment, or blood revenge. When the original Terek Cossack communities were formally enrolled in Russian service in 1721, they had already lived in the region for two centuries as independent settlers, pirates, and brigands. The Volga-Caspian-Terek route was well worn in both directions: as a path to settlement in the Caucasus; as a base of plunder, fishing, and trade; and as a conduit for uprisings in the heartland. Villages popped up and disappeared; their inhabitants were killed, taken captive, or joined other settlers. Terek Cossacks streamed north to participate in the major Cossack disturbances of the seventeenth and eighteenth centuries; refugees from the same washed back to the distant shores and thick woods. The most famous rebel in this period was probably the "False Peter" (Petrushka) who came from the Terek, sailed north to link up with Ivan Bolotnikov, and plundered up and down the Volga. Stenka Razin began his "outlaw" career as a pirate of the Caspian (and lower Volga) and used Chechen Island, off the coast where the Terek issues into the Caspian Sea, as one of his bases. Other Cossack pirates plagued the Caspian Sea in the eighteenth century: as late as 1737 the Persian consul in St. Petersburg complained of Russian pirates on the Caspian, some seventy boats in all, with a base on an island close to Baku. Pugachev was also active in the Terek; enrolled in the Terek-Semeinoe host in 1772, he agitated about the inadequacy of Cossack pay, was arrested at Mozdok, and escaped.[38]

But the Caucasus was not just the southernmost shore of the great Cossack sea, ebbing and flowing with raiders of the north. It was also where Cossacks went ashore and settled, married native women, fought with and against the groups from the mountains and the steppe, and merged with the local communities. Captain Johann-Gustav Gerber's snapshot description of the different peoples of the western bank of the Caspian Sea in 1728, even with its precise, bureaucratic delineations, shows how confused the line between Cossack and non-Cossack remained. There were Greben Cossacks, descendants of the original fugitive peasants, and Cossacks who lived off plunder (*vorovstvo*) and resided in the mountains of the north Caucasus. He says that they previously had suffered much from the raids of their neighbor "Tatars," who carried off their women and children (who most likely were of "Tatar"-Cossack mixed marriages), but now lived amicably with them. The Terek Cossacks, the garrison at the Terek fortress, were a combination of Don Cossacks and Terek Tatars who had converted to Christianity. The Terek Tatars were Islamic, spoke "Nogai," lived in tents ("like Nogais"), not only raised cattle but fished and sold salted and dried fish to the "Tatars" of the mountains. According to other sources, "Terek Tatars" was the designation for Cossacks and native peoples who fished around the mouth of the Terek; they were also known in the eighteenth century as the Terek Nogais. The Stavropol' Tatars spoke Russian, were Christians, and were Cossacks. The village of the Dagestanians and Kumyks of Andrei (Endirei) was established by "fugitive Russian people and Cossacks, who lived off of thieving" and united with "such Tatars who practiced similar trades."[39]

The composition of the Cossacks of the north Caucasus became increasingly complex as Russian interest in the region grew in the eighteenth and nineteenth centuries. With each new fort, groups of Don, Volga, Khoper, and Yaik Cossacks were resettled from interior provinces. Non-Russians, including Armenians, Georgians, and all of the peoples of the north Caucasus, were continually accepted into Cossack regiments. Chechens, Kabardians, Ossetians, and other native peoples either joined established Cossack units, or formed their own, such as the Gorsko-Mozdok regiment, the Mountain Cossack regiment, and the Kizliar irregular command. Most Muslims converted to Orthodoxy, but the Gorsko-Mozdok regiment had some Islamic members. As late as 1858, 10 percent of the Cossacks of the Caucasus military line were Islamic. Resettled state peasants, fugitive serfs, and retired soldiers also entered Cossack service in large numbers. In 1832–1833, more than thirty state-peasant settlements were simply redesignated as Cossack villages. When the Zaporozhian Cossack host was reformed as the Black Sea Cossacks and awarded the lands along the Kuban in 1792, thousands of non-Zaporozhians who had fought beside them in the Turkish War also moved there. One historian estimates that only 30 percent of the original Black Sea Cossacks were real Zaporozhians. Of the rest, 40 percent were volunteers who had served with them in the war, and 30 percent were Poles, Russians, Moldavians, and others who had moved to the new frontier with them.[40] During the next sixty years more than 80,000 Cossacks and peasants from Ukraine were transferred there, joined by thousands of non-Cossacks from Cossack *oblast*'s (*inogorodnye*) who illegally joined the migrating colonists.

There was also considerable Russian and Ukrainian peasant flight to the north Caucasus. Peasants joined resettlements of state peasants or Cossacks, or they founded settlements of their own, sometimes undetected for decades. According to folk tradition, many of the villages of the north Caucasus were initially hideouts for bands of fugitive serfs. Petrovskoe on the Kalaus River, for example, was supposedly founded by the fugitive serf, Petr Burlak, who settled in the dense forest there in the 1750s and joined with neighboring "Tatar" villages in banditry. Other fugitive serfs later joined Burlak, many with their families, and a Russian village came into being, deep in the woods. The Burlatskii Ravine on the right bank of the Buivola River sheltered fugitive peasants who supposedly settled there to escape military duty and their landlords, and to lead a life of robbing and plundering.[41]

Peasant flight to the north Caucasus increased in the 1820s, when state resettlement of state peasants and Cossacks gave rise to rumors of freedom from taxes and obligations in the south. Nicholas I made a special announcement in May 1826 that rumors of peasant and serf freedom in the Caucasus were false and that all who fled there would be punished with the full force of the law. This did not achieve its purpose, as thousands of peasants flowed into the north Caucasus for the next three decades; with the need to populate the region and develop the agricultural economy there, local authorities often overlooked the status of the new arrivals. Sometimes they were lured by more than rumors: the governor of Saratov reported in 1832 that fugitives were returning there and to the land of the Don Cossacks to recruit others; the same was reported in Voronezh and Ekaterinoslav. Occasionally, armed bands returned to claim their families and property. Black Sea Cossacks also sent agents to recruit fugitives to their labor-scarce region.[42]

In 1837 peasant flight was directed especially at the Anapa fortress region where it was claimed that fugitives would be sheltered and enrolled as Cossacks, and, in one variant, would receive tickets allowing them to return and redeem their families. Thousands went—some peasants even had false passports and overtly migrated there in troika-hitched carts. There were reports of bands of fugitives on the outskirts of Temriuk, living a *haidamak* existence, fishing and robbing, and "always going about armed like Zaporozhian Cossacks" with muskets, pistols, and pikes. Perhaps the dream of a bygone life of wild freedom lured some peasants; more important, no doubt, was the reception that fugitives received from the Cossacks who either enrolled them immediately or sheltered them on their farms or with their fishing crews, where they were greatly valued because of the scarcity of labor.[43]

The most important facet of north Caucasus society, besides the relative freedom of settlement, was probably the dearth of labor. The rarest type of settlement was that predominant in the rest of Russia: the serf-based manorial village. In 1857 less than 3 percent of the population of the north Caucasus (Stavropol' province and Terek and Kuban *oblast's*) was serf; except for sparsely settled Arkhangelsk and Siberia, it was the region of the empire with the lowest percentage of serfs.[44]

The labor shortage colored the social world of Cossacks and state peasants, who hired large numbers of laborers to work in their fields and gardens. In the summer months in the 1850s, Cossacks of the Caucasus military line hired some 4,000 farm workers; Black Sea Cossacks hired nearly 15,000. State peasants also employed thousands of workers annually, mostly to work on their farms. Some of these seasonal workers were peasants from the interior of Russia, others were natives. In the mid-nineteenth century, some 20–25,000 seasonal workers from the mountains lived in Kizliar from spring to autumn, so many that a special office for the assistance of "peaceful *gortsy* non-residents" was created in 1842. During the 1850s some 15,000 Nogais worked for landlords and Cossacks in the Kizliar *uezd*.[45] The number of natives in towns and Cossack villages grew even larger during bazaars and on market days.

The towns, indeed, were a major point of interethnic interaction. With natives from all corners streaming into north Caucasus cities for trade and seasonal work, and others living there permanently, these hubs of regional commerce took on a lively, ethnically diverse character. But not all Russian towns of the north Caucasus were equally variegated. The old fort towns such as Kizliar and Mozdok were the centers of local trade, ethnic diversity, and Russian-native interchange. Ekaterinodar, the Black Sea Cossack capital, remained almost exclusively Cossack, but during market and fair days thousands of people from beyond the Kuban would flood the town. Speaking of the Circassians in Ekaterinodar which he visited in 1843, Moritz Wagner wrote, "It is a strange thing to see these men, who had invaded the country a few days before, perhaps, plundering and killing, now moving peaceably among groups of Cossacks."[46] Stavropol', the fastest-growing town of the north Caucasus in the nineteenth century, was the administrative center and a Cossack/state-peasant town. Through the mid-century, Vladikavkaz remained a military town, with a periphery of Ossetian settlements.

On the fringes of the towns and Cossack villages of the Caucasus military line were various native settlements and villages of the so-called "peaceful" mountain peoples. These were tribes that had nominally pledged allegiance to the Russian Empire and had discontinued mounting raids on the Russian line. But, depending on the fluidity of the military presence, peaceful tribes could quickly switch sides and join invaders. There was continual interaction between these bordering settlements and the fort towns and Cossack villages of the line, but also a good deal of suspicion on both sides. V. A. Potto called the "peaceful Chechens" that lived between the Sunzha and Terek Rivers "the most wicked and dangerous" of all the neighboring settlements: "Peaceful villages served as a haunt for brigands of all the tribes of the Caucasus; bands are sheltered here before they make a raid on the Line; all criminals find a hearty welcome here, and nowhere are there so many Russian deserters." Wagner described the situation of the Circassian tribes on the left bank of the Kuban with more sympathy, recognizing the difficult situation these people faced: "Hemmed in between the Russians and their opponents, they do their utmost to remain neutral, pledge friendship to both parties, fight one day for the Russians and the next for their compatriots, and act as scouts and spies for both."[47] This band of uncertainty was perhaps the major frustration for the Russian state in the north Caucasus; commanders tried to simplify the situation through indiscriminate punitive raids.

At the outer edge of the band of uncertainty were Russians and others who had deserted. The number was probably never that great, but the fact that the ethnic frontier had always been so fluid created considerable concern among local officials about who was fighting with the mountain people. In the eighteenth century local commanders held the Terek Cossacks in suspicion because of their ethnic and cultural proximity to the mountain tribes. After Sviatoi Krest was founded in 1722, the army planned to relocate the Greben Cossacks (the earliest Cossacks of the Terek) there. But because of fears of their fleeing across the Kuban, they were left in place. Again in the 1770s, suspicions arose that the Grebentsy were colluding with the Nekrasov Cossacks, refugees from the Bulavin uprising who lived in the lower Kuban region, mounting raids on the Russian settlements with the Kabardians and siding with Turkey in the Russian-Turkish War of 1768–1774. In 1774 General Ivan De Medem ordered that they be called into service only with great caution.[48] Throughout the eighteenth century during periods of turbulence, forts occasionally prohibited interaction with natives from the interior for fear of collusion.

Desertion was a perpetual concern of Russia during the period of the most intense military activity in the north Caucasus after 1817. Periodic demands were made for different villages to return Russian deserters and in 1842 Nicholas I ordered local commanders to proffer salt as a bribe. In 1845 a proclamation was issued by Viceroy of the Caucasus, Prince Mikhail Vorontsov to the Russian deserters promising a full pardon for those who returned: "The Commander-in-chief hopes that deserters will hurry to take advantage of the monarchial pardon and mercy, and will not want to remain longer in destitution among the heterodox."[49]

But many decided to remain and, according to eyewitness reports, they lived a none-too-miserable life. A Cossack taken into captivity testified that there were some 300 Russian deserters at Shamil's village of Vedeno, looking after artillery, marrying Chechens, dressing in "Circassian coats," and living "sufficiently well." Captain A. I. Runovskii reported that there were many Russian deserters who converted to Islam, married mountain women, and created a happy family life. Many such women, he said, left their parents' homes to marry Russian deserters because they treated their women better than the mountain people did; the deserters also were under the special care of Shamil, who took strict measures to protect them from the petty oppression of their new neighbors. There were reportedly 400–600 Russian soldiers living with Shamil at Dargo. Rumors circulated that he lived in a European-style house built by Russian deserters, that he had a corps of 4,000 "of all nations" built upon an original corps of Russian and Polish deserters and that Shamil's predecessor, Hamza Bek, was constantly accompanied by Russian bodyguards. There were even stories that the writer Aleksandr Bestuzhev-Marlinskii, whose body was never recovered after he died in battle in 1837, was still alive and fighting alongside Shamil.[50] What is important is not so much the veracity of such rumors but their currency. That they could exist at all testifies to the great uncertainty on this ethnic frontier. Because of intermarriage, interactions, conversions, acculturations, and desertions it was often difficult to tell just who was who in the Caucasus. As Pushkin remarked after meeting a Persian court poet on the way from Kazbek to Tiflis, who turned out not to be a "bombastic Oriental" after all but a European-style gentleman, it was best not to judge a person in the Caucasus by his sheepskin cap and painted nails alone.[51]

There were many ways that Russia tried to resolve the uncertainty of the north Caucasus frontier. Strictly military solutions—such as General Aleksei Ermolov's practice of indiscriminately destroying mountain villages after attacks on the Russian line—have been well treated by historians. His special flying divisions with artillery went from village to village in Kabarda, for example, demanding submission, the cessation of raids, and resettlement. The random destruction of villages, the torching of gardens, stealing of cattle, clear-cutting of forests, and the forced resettlement of peoples seem desperate attempts to eliminate the uncertainty, to harden the lines between "us" and "them." And in large measure it worked, for the Ermolov system may be held responsible for the increasing viciousness of the war in the north Caucasus, and for Shamil's success in forging an alliance of disparate mountain peoples to fend off the Russians. But there were other techniques used to shore up allegiances and clarify identities, such as the creative ethnography applied to the kaleidoscope of peoples and the use of captivity narrative and myths of heroism. Capturing and ransoming prisoners, for example, were normal practices on both sides for centuries, but in the nineteenth century they became sensationalized, publicized as the dominant means of crossing the military line, and stereotyped as Caucasian acts of terror and torture but civilizing when perpetrated by Russians.

Myths of heroism were abundant also: I will conclude with one that illustrates how important such topics are to the history of the hardening of the frontier. One of the earliest heroic myths of the Russian frontier in the north Caucasus involves the battle at the Cossack village of Naur on 11 June 1774. According to the report by General De Medem, some 10,000 Kabardians attacked this village, newly established by resettled Volga Cossacks, and were repulsed by 800 villagers, including women who fought with scythes and poured hot water on the heads of the attackers. Most importantly, the raid occurred within a context of discontent, and abandoned and threatened allegiances. Among the Kabardian dead was found the body of Korgok Tatarkhanov, who three years earlier had received a charter in St. Petersburg, the rank of captain, and an annual salary of 150 rubles. Only days before the attack, Nekrasovtsy had been in the area appealing to the neighboring Greben Cossacks to abandon their allegiance to Russia. Pugachev had also been to Naur two years earlier, agitating among the new arrivals about the inadequacy of their pay; he had been appointed by Naur and two other Cossack villages to travel to St. Petersburg to protest their conditions.[52]

What had been a remarkable defense, but within a context of very uncertain alignments, over time became a tale of the essential "Russianness" of the Cossacks. N. F. Samarin visited Naur in 1862 and by then the story had been fully transformed: The number of Kabardians had been inflated (to 14,000) and the number of Cossacks diminished (200). Children participated, throwing rocks from the walls of the fort; women fought with scythes *and* sickles: one heroine cut off three Kabardian heads. They poured not only boiling water on the attackers but also that most Russian of foods, cabbage soup. According to Samarin, the siege was raised on 11 June—the day of the apostles Bartholomew and Barnabas—so the Cossacks built a church in their honor; the legend arose that those apostles, clad in white and riding white horses, suddenly appeared among the enemy camp and terrified them into retreat. Thus, 11 June became a holiday at Naur: Cossacks from the entire regiment would gather for parades, "war games," and outdoor merrymaking (*gulian'e*). The battle also entered the stock of popular expressions. When Cossacks from Naur met Kabardians, they would ask, "Hey friend, didn't you gulp cabbage soup at Naur?" This obviously had deep meaning for the Kabardians also, for many bloody fights resulted from the taunt.[53] Thus the battle of Naur became not only a Cossack tall tale but also was rooted in the everyday life of Naur Cossacks. While it is impossible to determine who was more important in the creation of the myth, the Cossacks or those who wrote about them, it is obvious that the Russification of the story simplified an event with multiple meanings and worked to the advantage of the Russian state.

This is the Russian frontier yet to be studied, one created by ethnic diversity, demographic mobility, shifting allegiances, cultural sharing, economic interdependencies, and an ecology that settlers were as tied to as the natives. It was not a frontier devoid of boundaries, for, of course, there were many— boundaries created by politics, war, violence, and geography and boundaries in everyday life, such as ethnic taunts. But in the end, it was much more complicated than Russians charging on white (or black) horses.

Notes

Originally published in *Slavic Review* 54, no. 3 (Fall 1995): 578–601.

1. F. von-Kliman, "Voina na vostochnom Kavkaze s 1824 po 1834 g. v sviazi s miuridizmom," *Kavkazskii sbornik*, 15 (1894): 524.

2. John F. Baddeley, *The Russian Conquest of the Caucasus* (London: Longmans, Green and Co., 1908); Marie Bennigsen Broxup, ed., *The North Caucasus Barrier* (New York: St. Martin's Press, 1992); Moshe Gammer, *Muslim Resistance to the Tsar: Shamil and the Conquest of Chechnia and Daghestan* (London and Portland: Frank Cass, 1994). See also W. E. D. Allen and Paul Muratoff, *Caucasian Battlefields* (Cambridge: Cambridge University Press, 1953). See also the following works on the image of the Caucasus in Russian literature

and society, a subject more of the center than the frontier: Uwe Halbach, "Die Bergvölker (*gorcy*) als Gegner und Opfer: Der Kaukasus in der Wahrnehmung Russlands," in *Kleine Völker in der Geschichte Osteuropas*, eds. Manfred Alexander, Frank Kämpfer, and Andreas Kappeler (Stuttgart: Franz Steiner Verlag, 1991), 52–65; Thomas M. Barrett, "The Remaking of the Lion of Dagestan: Shamil in Captivity," *Russian Review* 53 (July 1994), 353–66; Susan Layton, *Russian Literature and Empire: Conquest of the Caucasus from Pushkin to Tolstoy* (Cambridge: Cambridge University Press, 1994).

3. I use "mountain people" (*gortsy*) in the same loose sense that Russians of the time did, to designate the mountain- and foothill-dwelling peoples of the north Caucasus. This term encompassed a bewildering array of ethnicities, ranging from the Adyge in the west to the numerous peoples of Dagestan in the east. Whenever possible, I will use a more precise ethnic designation. Of course the peoples of the north Caucasus were also steppe nomads, such as the Nogais. Further, many Ukrainians in the north Caucasus were classified as Russians; I am forced to use "Russian" to mean primarily Russians and Ukrainians.

4. The leading military historian of Russia in the Caucasus was probably V. A. Potto. See his *Kavkazskaia voina v otdel'nykh ocherkakh, epizodakh, legendakh i biografiiakh*, 5 vols. (St. Petersburg: Tipografiia R. Golike, 1885–1891) and *Utverzhdenie russkogo vladychestva na Kavkaze*, 3 vols. (Tiflis: Tipografiia Ia.K. Libermana, 1901–1904).

5. For example, S. K. Bushuev, ed., *Istoriia Severo-Osetinskoi ASSR* (Moscow: Izdatel'stvo Akademii nauk SSSR, 1959); G. D. Daniialov, ed., *Istoriia Dagestana*, 5 vols. (Moscow: Nauka, 1967–1969); T. Kh. Kumykov, ed., *Istoriia Kabardino-Balkarskoi ASSR s drevneishikh vremen do nashikh dnei*, 2 vols. (Moscow: Nauka, 1967); N. A. Smirnov, *Politika Rossii na Kavkaze v XVI–XVII vv.* (Moscow: Izdatel'stvo sotsial'no-ekonomicheskoi literatury, 1958); N. S. Kiniapina, M. M. Bliev, and V. V. Degoev, *Kavkaz i Srednaia Aziia vo vneshnei politike Rossii. Vtoraia polovina XVIII-80e gody XIXv.* (Moscow: Izdatel'stvo Moskovskogo universiteta, 1984).

6. The best general Soviet histories are B. B. Piotrovskii, ed., *Istoriia narodov Severnogo Kavkaza s drevneishikh vremen do kontsa XVIII v.* (Moscow: Nauka, 1988); and A. L. Narochnitskii, ed., *Istoriia narodov Severnogo Kavkaza konets XVIIIv.-1917 g.* (Moscow: Nauka, 1988).

7. Joseph L. Wieczynski, *The Russian Frontier* (Charlottesville: University Press of Virginia, 1976); George V. Lantzeff and Richard A. Pierce, *Eastward to Empire: Exploration and Conquest on the Russian Open Frontier to 1750* (Montreal: McGill-Queen's University Press, 1973); Roger Dow, "Prostor: A Geopolitical Study of Russia and the United States," *Russian Review* 1, no. 1 (November 1941): 7–8. Even a recent article by Denis Shaw uses Turner's frontier. See Judith Pallot and Denis J. P. Shaw, *Landscape and Settlement in Romanov Russia, 1613–1917* (Oxford: Clarendon Press, 1990), 13–32.

8. Donald W. Treadgold, "Russian Expansion in the Light of Turner's Study of the American Frontier," *Agricultural History* 26, no. 4 (October 1952): 147–52; A. Lobanov-Rostovsky, "Russian Expansion in the Far East in the Light of the Turner Hypothesis," in *The Frontier in Perspective*, ed. Walker D. Wyman and Clifton B. Kroeber (Madison: Uni-

versity of Wisconsin Press, 1957), 79–94. Intensive settlement in the lower Volga did not begin until the 1780s. See V. M. Kabuzan, *Narody Rossii v XVIII veke, Chislennost' i etnicheskii sostav* (Moscow: Nauka, 1990), 90.

9. Donald W. Treadgold, *The Great Siberian Migration* (Princeton: Princeton University Press, 1957); Raymond Fisher, *The Russian Fur Trade, 1550–1700* (Berkeley: University of California Press, 1943); Terrence E. Armstrong, *Russian Settlement in the North* (Cambridge: Cambridge University Press, 1965); William H. McNeill, *Europe's Steppe Frontier, 1500–1800* (Chicago: University of Chicago Press, 1964); E. I. Druzhinina, *Severnoe prichernomor'e v 1775–1780 gg.* (Moscow: Izdatel'stvo Akademii nauk SSSR, 1959); N. D. Polons'ka-Vasylenko, "The Settlement of the Southern Ukraine (1750–1775)," *The Annals of the Ukrainian Academy of Arts and Sciences in the U.S.* 4–5 (Summer-Fall 1953). One of the few works on a non-Siberian frontier is Michael Khodarkovsky's *Where Two Worlds Met: The Russian State and the Kalmyk Nomads, 1600–1771* (Ithaca: Cornell University Press, 1992). While mostly interested in Kalmyk society and relations with the Russian state, Khodarkovsky briefly discusses (308–35) Russian colonization along the Volga and the resulting clashes with Kalmyks. Two other exceptions are Boris Nolde, *La Formation de l'Empire russe*, 2 vols. (Paris: Institut d'Etudes slaves, 1952–53) and Andreas Kappeler, *Russlands erste Nationalitäten. Das Zarenreich und die Völker der Mittleren Wolga vom 16. bis 19 Jahrhundert* (Cologne: Bohlau, 1982).

10. Alan Fisher, *The Crimean Tatars* (Stanford: Hoover Institution Press, 1978); Azade-Ayse Rorlich, *The Volga Tatars* (Stanford: Hoover Institution Press, 1986); Zenon H. Kohut, *Russian Centralism and Ukrainian Autonomy* (Cambridge: Harvard University Press for the Harvard Ukrainian Research Institute, 1988); James Forsyth, *A History of the Peoples of Siberia: Russia's North Asian Colony, 1581–1990* (Cambridge: Cambridge University Press, 1992).

11. For reviews of recent American frontier history, see William Cronon, George Miles, and Jay Gitlin, eds., *Under an Open Sky: Rethinking America's Western Past* (New York: W. W. Norton, 1992); Patricia Nelson Limerick, Clyde A. Milner II, and Charles E. Rankin, eds., *Trails: Towards a New Western History* (Lawrence: University of Kansas Press, 1991).

12. Cronon, Miles, and Gitlin, *Under an Open Sky*, 12. The authors use the term "species shifting" in this article.

13. It is no accident that many of the classics of environmental history deal with frontiers. See Alfred W. Crosby, *The Columbian Exchange* (Westport: Greenwood, 1972); and William Cronon, *Changes in the Land* (New York: Hill and Wang, 1983).

14. Iu. T. Pyshnova, "Historical-Geographic Aspects of the Development and Settlement of the Black Sea Coast of the Caucasus," *Soviet Geography* 15, no. 3 (March 1974): 156–63; G. I. Filipson, "Vospominaniia," *Russkii arkhiv* 22, 1 (1884): 204, 211; I. V. Bentkovskii, *Zaselenie Chernomorii s 1792 po 1825 god.* (Ekaterinodar: Tipografiia Kubanskago oblastnago pravleniia, 1880), 48, 69, 121; V. S. Bogoslavskii, *Piatigorskiia i s nimi smezhnyia mineral'nyia vody* (St. Petersburg: Tipografiia A. S. Suvorina, 1883), 7–8; A. V. Fadeev, *Rossiia i Kavkaz pervoi treti XIX v.* (Moscow: Izdatel'stvo Akademii nauk SSSR, 1960), 67. Like-

wise, the real killer in the early forts of the northeast Caucasus was rampant disease, not raiding mountaineers.

15. A. P. Pronshtein, ed., *Don i stepnoe Predkavkaz'e XVIII-pervaia polovina XIX v.* (Rostov-on-Don: Izdatel'stvo Rostovskogo universiteta, 1977), 60, 116.

16. Fadeev, *Rossiia i Kavkaz*, 35–41.

17. A. Tvalchrelidze, *Stavropol'skaia guberniia v statisticheskom, geograficheskom, istoricheskom i sel'sko-khoziaistvennom otnosheniiakh* (Stavropol': Tipografiia M. N. Koritskogo, 1897), 408.

18. Piotrovskii, *Istoriia narodov Severnogo Kavkaza*, 378–79; B. A. Kaloev, "Zemledelie u gorskikh narodov Severnogo Kavkaza," *Sovetskaia etnografiia* 3 (May-June 1973): 46. On the grain trade in Kizliar see N. P. Gritsenko, *Goroda Severovostochnogo Kavkaza i proizvoditel'nye sily kraia* (Rostov-on-Don: Izdatel'stvo Rostovskogo universiteta, 1984), 109; T. Kh. Kumykov and E. N. Kusheva, eds., *Kabardino-russkie otnosheniia v XVI–XVIII vv.: Dokumenty i materialy* (Moscow: Izdatel'stvo Akademii nauk SSSR, 1957), 2:215–18; Fadeev, *Rossiia i Kavkaz*, 63–65; *Akty sobrannye Kavkazskoi arkheograficheskoi komissii* (Tiflis: Tipografiia Kantseliarii glavnonachal'stvuiushchego grazhdanskoi chast'iu na Kavkaze, 1870), 4:37 [hereafter *AKAK*]. On Kuban wheat, I. V. Rovinskii, "Khoziaistvennoe opisanie Astrakhanskoi i Kavkazskoi gubernii," *Trudy Stavropol'skoi uchenoi arkhivnoi komissii* 2 (1910): sec. 4, 58–60; "Vzgliad na Kavkazskuiu liniiu," *Severnyi arkhiv* 2 (January 1822): 181.

19. T. Kh. Kumykov, *Vovlechenie Severnogo Kavkaza vo vserossiiskii rynok v XIX v.* (Nal'chik: Kabardino-Balkarskoe knizhnoe izdatel'stvo, 1962), 93–96; A. P. Berzhe, *Chechnia i chechentsy* (Tiflis: Kavkazskii otdel Imperatorskago russkago geograficheskago obshchestva, 1859), 89; Baddeley, *The Russian Conquest*, xxxvi.

20. D. L. Ivanov, "Vliianie russkoi kolonizatsii na prirodu Stavropol'skago kraia," *Izvestiia Imperatorskago russkago geograficheskago obshchestva* 22, no. 3 (1886): 225–54; Tvalchrelidze, *Stavropol'skaia guberniia*, 62, 204.

21. Daniel H. Usner, Jr., *Indians, Settlers, & Slaves in a Frontier Exchange Economy* (Chapel Hill: University of North Carolina Press for the Institute of Early American History and Culture, 1992), 6.

22. This is the title of Kumykov's book (see note 19) and a common frame of analysis for many Soviet historians of the Caucasus.

23. O. V. Marggraf, *Ocherk kustarnykh promyslov Severnogo Kavkaza s opisaniem tekhniki proizvodstva* (Moscow: Tipografiia S. V. Gur'ianova, 1882), xiv–xl; G. N. Prozritelev, "Kavkazskoe oruzhie," *Trudy Stavropol'skoi uchenoi arkhivnoi komissii* 7–9 (1915): sec. 10, 1–5; "Statisticheskiia izvestiia o Kavkazskoi oblasti i zemle voiska Chernomorskago," *Zhurnal Ministerstva vnutrennykh del* 3, no. 5 (1830): 124–27.

24. Kumykov, *Vovlechenie*, 34–35; S. M. Bronevskii, *Noveishie geograficheskie i istoricheskie izvestiia o Kavkaze* (Moscow: Tipografiia S. Selivanovskogo, 1823), 2:142–45.

25. Narochnitskii, *Istoriia narodov Severnogo Kavkaza*, 80; A. I. Akhverdov, "Opisanie Dagestana. 1804 g." in *Istoriia, geografiia i etnografiia Dagestana XVIII-XIX vv. Arkhivnye materialy*, eds. M. O. Kosven and Kh.-M. Khashaev (Moscow: Izdatel'stvo vostochnoi literatury, 1958), 213.

26. P. G. Butkov, *Materialy dlia novoi istorii Kavkaza s 1722 po 1803 god* (St. Petersburg: Tipografiia Imperatorskoi akademii nauk, 1869), 1:163. On raids: V. P. Lystsov, *Persidskii pokhod Petra I* (Moscow: Izdatel'stvo Moskovskogo universiteta, 1951), 98; "Materialy dlia statistiki Kizliarskago polka Terskago kazach'iago voiska," *Voennyi sbornik* 12 (December 1869): 213; F. I. Soimonov, *Opisanie Kaspiiskago moria* (St. Petersburg: Imperatorskaia akademiia nauk, 1763), 102; I. Popko, *Terskie kazaki so starodavnikh vremen* (St. Petersburg: Tipografiia Departamenta udelov, 1880), 253–54.

27. George Miles, "To Hear an Old Voice: Rediscovering Native Americans in American History," in *Under an Open Sky*, 55.

28. Richard White, *The Middle Ground: Indians, Empires, and Republics in the Great Lakes Region, 1650–1815* (Cambridge: Cambridge University Press, 1991), x.

29. The few historians who have been interested in those who crossed the ethnic frontier tend to use the notion of "co-optation." By failing to explore why choices were made, this approach continues to turn those who should be subjects into manipulated objects of history. Would we see, for example, Gogol' as a co-opted member of the elite from the Ukrainian frontier?

30. V. B. Vinogradov and T. S. Magomadova, "Gde stoiali sunzhenskie gorodki?" *Voprosy istorii* 7 (July 1972): 205; V. A. Potto, *Pamiatniki vremen utverzhdeniia Russkago vladychestva na Kavkaze* (Tiflis: Tipografiia Shtaba kavkazskogo voennogo okruga, 1906), 1:55–57.

31. Kabuzan, *Narody Rossii*, 227; N. I. Voronov, ed., *Sbornik statisticheskikh svedenii o Kavkaze* (Tiflis: Kavkazskii otdel Imperatorskago russkago geograficheskago obshchestva, 1869), sec. 2, p. B, 20–21.

32. Alan W. Fisher, "Emigration of Muslims from the Russian Empire in the Years after the Crimean War," *Jahrbücher für Geschichte Osteuropas* 35 (1987): 356–71.

33. *AKAK* (Tiflis, 1866), 1:87. Gmelin died in captivity.

34. *AKAK*, 1:81, 85; Piotrovskii, *Istoriia narodov Severnogo Kavkaza*, 395; Kumykov and Kusheva, *Kabardino-russkie otnosheniia*, 2:269–73; Butkov, *Materialy*, 1:317–19.

35. B. P. Berozov, *Pereselenie osetin s gor na ploskost' (XVIII-XX vv.)* (Ordzhonikidze: Ir, 1980), 56–59; B. A. Kaloev, *Osetiny*, 2nd ed. (Moscow: Nauka, 1971), 65.

36. *Armiano-russkie otnosheniia v pervoi treti XVIII veka, Sbornik dokumentov* (Erevan: Izdatel'stvo Akademii nauk Armianskoi SSR, 1964), 2:37–41; Piotrovskii, *Istoriia narodov Severnogo Kavkaza*, 374, 463; N. G. Volkova, "O rasselenii Armian na Severnom Kavkaze do nachala XX veka," *Istoriko-filologicheskii zhurnal* 3 (1966): 260; N. G. Volkova, *Etnicheskii sostav naseleniia Severnogo Kavkaza v XVIII-nachale XX v.* (Moscow: Nauka, 1974), 200–201.

37. N. Samarin, "Dorozhnyia zametki," *Severnaia pchela*, no. 133 (1862): 550–51; Tvalchrelidze, *Stavropol'skaia guberniia*, 277.

38. S. A. Kozlov, "Popolnenie vol'nykh kazach'ikh soobshchestva na Severnom Kavkaze v XVI-XVII vv.," *Sovetskaia etnografiia* 5 (1990): 47–56; V. B. Vinogradov and T. S. Magomedov, "O meste pervonachal'nogo rasseleniia grebenskikh kazakov," *Sovetskaia etnografiia* 3 (1972): 31–42; *Vosstanie I. Bolotnikova: Dokumenty i materialy* (Moscow: Sotsekgiz, 1959), 84, 109–10; *Krest'ianskaia voina pod predvoditel'stvom Stepana Razina: Sbornik dokumentov* (Moscow: Izdatel'stvo Akademii nauk SSSR, 1954), 1:120, 140–41; Butkov, *Materialy*,

1:168; V. V. Mavrodin, ed., *Krest'ianskaia voina v Rossii v 1773–1775 godakh: Vosstanie Pugacheva* (Leningrad: Izdatel'stvo Leningradskogo universiteta, 1966), 2:76–77.

39. I.-G. Gerber, "Opisanie stran i narodov vdol' zapadnogo berega kaspiiskogo moria. 1728 g.," in *Istoriia, geografiia i etnografiia Dagestana*, 60–63, 69. Gerber was a member of a commission sent to Dagestan to establish the Russian-Turkish border in the region.

40. D. I. Romanovskii, *Kavkaz i Kavkazskaia voina* (St. Petersburg: Tipografiia Tovarishchestva "Obshchestvennaia pol'za," 1860), app., iv; Pronshtein, *Don i stepnoe Predkavkaz'e*, 54–55; L. B. Zasedateleva, *Terskie kazaki* (Moscow: Izdatel'stvo Moskovskogo universiteta, 1974), 184–216; Bentkovskii, *Zaselenie Chernomorii*, 19–20.

41. Tvalchrelidze, *Stavropol'skaia guberniia*, 269, 399.

42. Narochnitskii, *Istoriia narodov Severnogo Kavkaza*, 59; A. V. Predtechenskii, ed., *Krest'ianskoe dvizhenie v Rossii v 1826–1849 gg. Sbornik dokumentov* (Moscow: Sotsekgiz, 1961), 223–25; N. Varadinov, *Istoriia Ministerstva vnutrennykh del* (St. Petersburg: Tipografiia Ministerstva vnutrennykh del, 1861), 3: bk. 2, 292; F. Shcherbina, "Beglye i krepostnye v Chernomorii," *Kievskaia starina* 16 (June 1883): 239, 244.

43. Predtechenskii, *Krest'ianskoe dvizhenie*, 331–32, 672; Shcherbina, "Beglye i krepostnye," 240–45. The minister of war was so alarmed by the movement south that he proposed the construction of a cordon, stretching from Astrakhan and Saratov to Ekaterinoslav, to keep serfs from escaping to the Caucasus.

44. V. M. Kabuzan, *Izmeneniia v razmeshchenii naseleniia Rossii v XVIII-pervoi polovine XIX v.* (Moscow: Nauka, 1971), 167–70.

45. A. F. Fadeev, *Ocherki ekonomicheskogo razvitiia stepnogo Predkavkaz'ia v doreformennyi period* (Moscow: Izdatel'stvo Akademiia nauk SSSR, 1957), 168–69, 188–91; Narochnitskii, *Istoriia narodov Severnogo Kavkaza*, 76.

46. Moritz Wagner, *Travels in Persia, Georgia, and Koordistan* (London: Hurst and Blackett, 1856), 1:127.

47. Potto, *Kavkazskaia voina*, 2: pt. 1, 86–87; Wagner, *Travels in Persia*, 1:129.

48. Butkov, *Materialy*, 1:79; *AKAK*, 1:84, 87–88.

49. *Dvizhenie gortsev severo-vostochnogo Kavkaza v 20–50 gg. XIX veka. Sbornik dokumentov* (Makhachkala: Dagknigoizdat, 1959), 356–57, 486.

50. *AKAK*, 12:1398; *Dvizhenie*, 471, 498; Baddeley, *The Russian Conquest*, 397; Friedrich Wagner, *Schamyl and Circassia*, trans. Kenneth R. H. Mackenzie (London: G. Routledge and Co., 1854), 88; Baron August von Haxthausen, *The Tribes of the Caucasus*, trans. J. E. Taylor (London: Chapman and Hall, 1855), 98. There were also rumors that Shamil himself was Bestuzhev-Marlinskii, that he had joined a mountaineer robber band, escaped to Persia, or was living in the mountains with five wives. See A. L. Zisserman, *Dvadtsat' piat' let na Kavkaze (1842–1867)* (St. Petersburg: Tipografiia A. S. Suvorina, 1879), 1:329; Lauren G. Leighton, *Alexander Bestuzhev-Marlinsky* (New York: Twane Publishers, 1975), 35.

51. Alexander Pushkin, *A Journey to Arzrum*, trans. Birgitta Ingermanson (Ann Arbor: Ardis, 1974), 30–31.

52. *AKAK*, 1:88; Mavrodin, *Krest'ianskaia voina*, 76.

53. Samarin, "Dorozhnyia zametki," 550; Potto, *Kavkazskaia voina*, 1:76–79; Potto, *Pamiatniki*, 1:19–20.

7

An Empire of Peasants

Empire-Building, Interethnic Interaction, and Ethnic Stereotyping in the Rural World of the Russian Empire, 1800–1850s

Willard Sunderland

————··◁∞▷··————

A S FAR AS patriotic Russian observers were concerned, the early nineteenth century was a promising time for the Russian empire. Industry and commerce were expanding, population was increasing, "enlightenment" was supposedly spreading across the land, and the empire itself, with territories stretching all the way from Curland to California, seemed far and away the largest state the world had ever seen.[1] While Russia was undeniably vast, however, even the most enthusiastic of Russian patriots had to admit that many of Russia's vast spaces (especially in the south and east) were thinly populated, only partially agricultural, and therefore (given the prejudices of the day) terribly short on either utility or civilization. What was needed to improve this situation (it was generally agreed) was to infuse the borderlands wherever possible with more people, more agriculture, and more settlement. The Russian state, of course, had long been partial to this idea and had taken sporadic measures to promote migration to the borderlands ever since the mid-sixteenth century, but in the first half of the 1800s, Russia's colonization machine (due in large part to the state's growing interest and involvement) began cranking with a new intensity. During this period, over three million rural settlers of all types and categories either moved voluntarily or were forced to relocate to the borderlands, mostly to the vast "empty" steppes of southern European Russia, where they built thousands of new villages and carved out millions of acres of new fields and pasture.[2] To Russian writers, all of this settling and colonizing suggested the unfolding of truly wondrous transformations. As one pair of ecstatic observers noted at the turn of the 1800s, "Where once there were uncrossable steppes, home only to wild beasts, we now see populous cities, flourishing with commerce. . . . Unpopulated places are being populated and colonies formed."[3]

The following essay offers what I hope are new perspectives on Russia's supposedly wondrous settlement history in the first half of the nineteenth century. My main focus here is on the multiethnic social worlds of settlement that unfolded in the imperial countryside during this period. Attention to this dimension of the empire's history is long overdue. Writing on the empire has generally been dominated by studies that stick closely to the themes of Russian conquest, Russian imperial control, and then ultimately the rejection of Russian rule and the struggle for national autonomy and liberation in the imperial borderlands. While this framework is undeniably important, the almost exclusive focus on political history has tended to obscure our appreciation of the empire as a richly complicated multiethnic and multiconfessional society. The net result is that we now know more about imperial policies and strategies than we do about the interactions and connections between different ethnic communities that lay at the very heart of the empire's social world. A fresh look at the multiethnic arena of settlement thus offers a chance to realign our perspectives and develop a clearer picture of the workings of the empire at the grassroots level. In what follows, I explore this grassroots level by looking at three interrelated issues. I begin with an analysis of Russian peasant attitudes towards colonization and empire-building, then move to a discussion of interethnic interaction in settlement locales, and conclude with an examination of the role ethnic stereotyping may have played in the rural byways of Russian-non-Russian relations. Much of the material presented here is drawn from research on the provinces of Tavrida (i.e., the Crimean peninsula and adjacent mainland territories), Orenburg, and Kazan', though my comments occasionally range into other parts of the empire as well.

Russian Peasant Mentalities and the Building of the Empire

In the first half of the 1800s, the grand narrative of Russian colonization was beginning to come together. Though the famous historian V. O. Kliuchevskii would not popularize the idea of colonization as the "basic fact" of Russian history until the end of the 1800s, work on creating a special place for colonization in the Russian national saga had already gotten under way a century or so earlier. Beginning in the late 1700s, squads of Russian explorers, travelers, poets, and historians began roaming physically and symbolically around the empire, uncovering national missions, stalwart pioneers, and promising landscapes that seemed to cry out for settlement. The defining feature of

colonization as far as Russian elites were concerned was positive transformation. Russian settlers in *Zabaikal'e*, for example, were applying "their passion for
agriculture" and quickly transforming drowsy valleys of Buriat yurts into "a
contented and prosperous colony;"[4] in the northern Caucasus, other peasants
were changing "deserts" into "beautiful and fertile country;"[5] and just about
everywhere else more settlers and more settlements were needed in order to
bring Russia's great potential to life.[6] Colonization was seen as a vital force
for progress and forward motion. As one historian put it, speaking of the great
changes wrought by settlement in the Russian south in the first half of the 1800s,
"the historian or observer will be astounded at the colossal successes that have
been achieved here in less than a half-century, feats unheard of in other parts
of Russia or even Europe . . . and surpassed perhaps only in America."[7]

But while it is relatively easy to uncover what Russian elites were thinking
about colonization, identifying what the colonists themselves (i.e. the peasants)
thought about it is much more difficult. Russian peasant society in the first half
of the nineteenth century was largely nonliterate and, as a result, settler men-
talité remains notoriously hard to describe. No one (as far as I know) has yet uncovered a Russian peasant settler from the early 1800s who recorded his or her
view of the world as amply as, say, Carlo Ginzburg's Friulian miller or Laurel
Thatcher Ulrich's New England midwife.[8] Peasant views of the settlement process tend to be trapped in tight, laconic, and often mediated sources, such as
proverbs, resettlement petitions, village histories recorded by priests and ethnographers, and a handful of settler letters that date only from the late nineteenth and early twentieth centuries. Parsing peasant ideas out of these sources
is daunting, to say the least. All the same, by using these sources cautiously, it
is possible to decipher something of what peasants were thinking when they
embarked on resettlement, especially in regards to why they were moving, what
they were looking for, and what they felt were the best ways to go about getting
what they wanted.[9]

It is important to note from the outset that mobility, while perhaps not a
defining characteristic of peasant society, certainly had an important place in
peasant social life. Peasants traveled to nearby villages to visit neighbors, to attend church, or to buy and trade at *volost'* fairs, and they occasionally covered
much greater distances, sometimes hundreds or thousands of versts, when they
set out on seasonal work (*otkhod*) or on religious pilgrimages. This movement,
as well as peasant contact with itinerant traders, troops on maneuver, *stranniki*,
gypsies, and other "wanderers," undoubtedly facilitated the spread of information and contributed to what peasants knew and thought about the world
beyond the village.[10] All the same, itinerant or temporary movement was one
thing; permanent resettlement was another. Despite the mythology of the "no-

madic" Russian peasant who supposedly relished being on the move, permanent relocation was not something the average peasant could afford to consider lightly.[11] Relocating over long distances often meant leaving behind relatives, ancestral graves, and everything that one was familiar with, then spending all (or almost all) of one's resources on the road, and ultimately turning one's fate over to new places, new officials, and new neighbors. As rural proverbs and traveling customs suggest, peasants tended to be well aware of the dangers, costs, and uncertainties of long-distance travel.[12]

Given the many obstacles and risks, what motivated state peasant settlers to take their chances on resettlement? In the early-to-mid 1800s, much as in earlier and later times, there were numerous "push" and "pull" factors that got peasants moving, including economic destitution stemming from local land shortages and poor harvests, tax and land incentives for resettling, and the desire to join kin or to escape the pressures of the old village commune. But, perhaps just as importantly, peasant settlers could be motivated by rumors and tales of abundant lands on the frontier (such as the legendary islands of *Belovod'e*), rumors that were then mixed, played, and replayed within what peasants learned of the state's official resettlement policy. Here, in fact, we see a curious symmetry between state policy and the peasant view of the world. To imperial statesmen, such as V. P. Kochubei and M. M. Speranskii, peasant resettlement seemed a perfect way to redistribute the empire's population more effectively and to solidify Russia's hold over its borderland provinces. To the peasants, however, the state's resettlement program, with its granting of land and various allowances and tax exemptions, was official confirmation of their own popular expectations of land and social justice on the frontier.[13] The official invitation to resettle was certainly not the factor that clinched the peasants' decision to move. Peasants had been moving to the borderlands independently for centuries without much concern for the state's strictures or endorsements. But state support for the process in the early nineteenth century must have added to peasant expectations and could well have been an issue in the disorderly scrambles for "better lands" that often occurred in the new areas of peasant settlement.

The search for "better lands" is key to understanding the peasant settlers' psychology. To take one example, in Orenburg province in the early 1800s, provincial officials frequently complained that incoming settlers would arrive on the lands that their representatives (*poverennye*) had selected and then promptly abandon them and set out to look for other sites. "The peasants," one official wrote, "often conclude that the land they have chosen is unsuitable and infertile (*neudobnaia i nevygodnaia*) and that new lands will be better." Such restless quests frequently resulted in parties of settlers "roaming" for years around the prov ince.[14] In some cases, peasants even roamed the whole empire looking for "better lands," such as Vasilii Rubanov's party from Voronezh province that originally moved to Orenburg and then abandoned their new homes because they were not "suitable" and petitioned to move again to the northern Caucasus;[15] or 710 *odnodvortsy* from Ukrainian provinces who moved in the other direction, first to the Caucasus and within a year petitioned to relocate again, this time to Siberia.[16] It is difficult to know exactly what peasants were hoping to find when they went looking for "better lands." Some parties may have been looking to rejoin relatives that they had been separated from on the road; others may have been responding to real deficiencies in the lands that their scouts had selected; and still others may have been taking advantage of the relative abundance of "open" land in a given area to secure the best village sites available.

The idea of "better lands," however, seems to suggest something more than just a concrete physical site with objectively "better" conditions. Rather, it seems to connote a kind of ideal place where settlers would be able to find a better life than the one that they had known in their former villages. The expectation of finding some kind of improvement in their new places was obviously part of the way peasant settlers looked at the settlement proposition. As a group of Kursk settlers wrote to the Orenburg governor in 1831, "we took joy in expecting plentitude and abundance on our allotted lands," only to find them hilly, rocky, and almost without woodlands.[17] "Better lands" to these and other settlers was probably not a specific site; instead it was a place (any place) that could offer better soils, larger fields, bigger harvests, better access to water and timber, and therefore greater prosperity and greater happiness. What was most important about this new place was simply that it was "better" in some meaningful way than that which the settlers had left behind. The ideal of settlement was thus vague, yet, at the same time, it was also evocative enough to motivate settlers to keep looking for it until they found it (or at least came close).

Thus, when peasant settlers kept looking for still "better lands," it is likely that they were driven by the same mixture of practical necessity and idealized expectation that seems to lie at the bottom of most settler initiatives in most other places. The seemingly chaotic to-and-fro movement of many settlers is, therefore, not surprising. As Paul Carter suggests in his critique of Australian exploration and settlement, colonization rarely unfolds as a predetermined "one-way road." Rather, every act of colonization is also an act of exploration in which individuals make choices (many of them quite serendipitous) about where to stop, where to turn, and whether to go left, right, north, south, east, or west. As a result, Carter argues, the whole settlement process is unavoidably marked with backtracking and zigzagging and generally looks nothing like the straightforward linear progression that is ultimately glossed over it retrospectively in settlement narratives, artistic portrayals, and history books.[18] The unfolding of Russian peasant colonization, when viewed from the peasants' perspective, appears to conform to this scenario. As peasant settlers moved, they also explored and made individual choices, within their own circumscribed circumstances, about what they wanted to find and where they wanted to go.

But once peasants found their "better lands" and established their new settlements, how did they then see their role in the imperial borderlands? Certainly peasant settlers were well aware that they were serving the interests of the state. Peasants frequently expressed this awareness in their petitions to the government, reiterating that they moved to their new homes with special privileges and the blessings of the tsar and "his excellencies" the ministers of finance or state domains.[19] They also tried to take advantage of their favored status, whenever they could, to bargain for better arrangements for themselves over other settlers, whom they accused of resettling illegally (i.e. without the permission of the government), and over different non-Russian groups (*inorodtsy*). In fact, the peasants' whole approach to settlement seems to reveal an astute understanding of the state's predicament in the borderlands. There was so much confusion in the settlement process and so much seemingly open land in areas like the New Russian provinces and Orenburg that peasants could easily sidestep official procedures and simply claim a stretch of land that appealed to them, even if it formally belonged to other owners. While this grab-it-now-and-work-out-the-details-later approach often provoked long and drawn-out land disputes, the strategy usually paid off. The state, by and large, did not evict settlers if they had already set up their villages and built "well-established housing" (*prochnye doma*) because the settlers were simply too important where they were and too costly to move. This general practice shows through clearly in the story of settlers from Tambov and Voronezh who moved illegally (*samovol'no*) onto Kalmyk lands in Orenburg province. Settlers who had not started farming and were still living in dugouts (*zemlianki*) or quartering in other peoples' homes were forced to leave while forty-one households with "well-established housing" were allowed to stay.[20] As this example suggests, if peasant squatters could build quickly, they stood a good chance of being able to exploit their importance to the state and turn it to their advantage.

But did this awareness of serving the state's interests lead peasants to identify with the state's larger imperial enterprise in the borderlands? Did it have any effect on how they related to their new "alien" neighbors? Before answering these questions, it is worth stressing that ethnicity was not a central marker in the Russian rural world of the early-to-mid-nineteenth century.[21] Furthermore, colonization itself was not an ethnic issue. Different ethnicities were colonizers (Chuvash, Mari, and Mordvin peasants in Orenburg province, for example); so too were members of different faiths (i.e. German Mennonites, Muslim Tatars, and Ukrainian Old Believers); and all of these groups, to a greater or lesser extent, were accorded privileges and incentives to resettle. All the same, Russian Orthodox settlers, moving legally to the borderlands and establishing themselves within new multiethnic environments, must have had an awareness of how their Orthodox Russian identity could work for them in their new situations.[22] Despite a certain sense of *dépaysement* for settlers, the social environment of settlement in places like, say, Orenburg or the mainland districts of Tavrida province was still very much Russian, dominated by Russian officials, the Russian language, and Russian institutions. Of course, this did not necessarily mean that Russian settlers were always favored by the system. State officials certainly made efforts to defend what they saw as the rights of supposedly "voiceless" peoples, such as seminomadic Bashkirs and Nogays, but in the hierarchy of ethnicities within the empire, Russian peasant settlers, as "backward" as they might have appeared in other contexts, were definitely seen to stand a cut above such "uncivilized" groups.

Though indirect, there is evidence to show that Russian peasants were well aware of the fact that their Russianness could be an advantage. A case involving Russian settlers and Nogays in Tavrida province suggests that settlers made full use of their knowledge of the language and Russian legal procedure when securing their cause over their "alien" adversaries.[23] Another in Orenburg reveals settlers drawing the sympathy of the Russian administration by complaining of a neighboring Tatar village's hostility toward "Russian people."[24] As these examples suggest, Russian ethnic awareness, while not central to the peasants' identity, was an element that could be activated and become a part of the way peasants defined their world, especially in instances when it served their interests vis-à-vis the state or other patrons.[25] In doing this, Russian peasants were certainly not alone. Throughout the rural world of the empire, numerous ethnoreligious and corporate communities had their own administrative structures that tended to provide a basis for social identities. Bashkirs in Orenburg province, for example, had their own canton administration (after 1798); Orenburg Cossacks had their own host (as of 1755); German settlers in New Russia were under the administration of the Guardianship Office in Odessa (beginning in 1800); while Nogays in Tavrida had their own special administration between 1805 and 1833. In their wranglings and bargainings with the Russian settlers around them, all of these groups used these administrations and their ethnoreligious affiliations to their advantage whenever they could.[26] The Russian peasant manipulation of Russian identity was, therefore, not exceptional and it did not always work, but its usefulness was something that Russian settlers were no doubt always aware of.

Despite the fact that Russian settlers appear to have been ready to use their Russianness when it suited their purposes, it is highly unlikely that the average settler-*muzhik* in the early 1800s ever thought of himself as an empire-builder serving the greater cause of Russian progress. It was the Russian state and educated society (*obshchestvo*) that envisioned the Russian settler as a tool for turning wastelands into breadbaskets, increasing the Slavic element in the borderlands, or offering a friendly helping hand to the empire's more "backward" peoples. But Russian peasant views do seem to have dovetailed in intriguing ways with the basic premise underlying the state's overall position on colonization. Just as the Russian state felt that it was the Russians' natural right to settle the empire, so too did the peasants. As the historian Svetlana Lur'e has suggested, Russian peasants tended to identify Russia not with Russian statehood (*gosudarstvennost'*) but rather with the people (*narod*) or with the peasant commune (*mir*). Hence, to the peasants, "any place inhabited by Russians by that very fact becomes Russia, regardless of whether or not [this place] is actually located within the territorial borders of the Russian state."[27] The Russian settler, in other words, could feel at home wherever he went (given certain environmental limitations, of course) and this ran parallel to the lofty idea, so trumpeted by Russian elites, that Russian colonization itself was a just and entirely natural process. In this sense then, Russian peasant settlers were consummate colonizers. Neither motivated by deep-seated prejudices nor by a sense of their own mission, the peasants (to their own way of thinking) were simply moving into and settling the "empty spaces" of their own country.

Worlds of Interaction

The Russian Empire, as eighteenth- and nineteenth-century writers were fond of observing, was home to an astounding array of peoples and cultures. The empire housed language groups from Finnic to Slavic to Turko-Mongolic; faiths from "shamanism" to Islam to Orthodoxy; and an alphabet soup of peoples at all stages of human development from the most benighted and primitive "children of nature" to the most sophisticated, urbane European gentlemen.[28] The great diversities of the empire were especially striking in the settlement worlds of the borderlands. In areas like mainland Tavrida and Orenburg alone, one found an eclectic range of social, ethnic, and confessional groups, including Cossacks, German colonists, non-Orthodox "sectarians," seminomadic Nogay and Bashkir herders, and Chuvash, Mari, Mordvin, Tatar, Ukrainian, and Russian peasants. Russian settlers in these heterogeneous landscapes obviously interacted with the other rural communities around them, and it was these worlds of interaction, more than any other factor, that defined the nature of the empire's social life at the grass roots. In this section, I dwell briefly on two aspects of these worlds of interaction: first, the importance of local concerns in determining the tone of interethnic relations in the countryside; and second, the extreme fluidity of cultural change and assimilation that characterized the settlement milieu. Neither of these issues has received adequate attention in contemporary scholarship.[29]

While there were certainly wide disparities in Russian settlement patterns in different parts of the empire at different times, it is safe to generalize that many Russian settlements in the borderlands were established in close proximity to non-Russian villages. The empire was literally dotted with thousands of rural localities like Molochnye Vody in Tavrida province where, as one observer noted, "ethnically different villages (*raznoplemennye poseleniia*) are located so close to one another that one travels but a few versts before encountering a new way of life and a new language."[30] Living in such proximity, in some cases even sharing the same village, Russian settlers and *inorodtsy* peasants had many venues for contact in daily life. They met at marketplaces, at village fairs, in taverns and churches (in the case of Orthodox *inorodtsy*), at joint events of mutual aid (*pomochi*), and in the fields. Russian peasants celebrated alongside Turkic and Finnic villagers at folk gatherings such as the Bashkir *dzhiny* (or *yïyïn*) and teams of Russian and non-Russian charlatans worked together to swindle their neighbors.[31] This kind of contact was neither remarkable nor particularly unique to the Russian Empire.[32] But what exactly were the issues that most influenced the tone of interethnic relations in the empire's settlement places? How did Russian peasants and their neighbors "get along"?

Given the basic needs of the peasant economy, it is no surprise to learn that interethnic relations in the countryside were profoundly influenced by intensely practical concerns such as access to land, water, timber, and other basic commodities. Different communities in different localities settled these issues in different ways. In areas with intense settlement, as I mentioned earlier, settlers often embroiled themselves in long, usually violent land disputes with other settler parties, private landlords, Cossacks, and *inorodtsy* communities. In Orenburg district (*uezd*), which saw a staggering number of settlers (mostly Russian state peasants) in the late 1820s and early 1830s, Bashkir landowners (*votchinniki*) constantly petitioned the government to protest that settlers were cutting down their woods or using their pastures. These disputes could drag on for years or decades, such as a nearly thirty-year case involving Bashkir peasants from the village of Taimasovo and two neighboring Russian settlements accused by the Bashkirs of knowingly building homes and a church on Bashkir property.[33] In some localities in Orenburg *uezd*, there was so much hostility that Bashkir villagers would descend on Russian settlements, stoning the peasants and threatening harsher reprisals if the settlers did not move out.[34] Yet in the very same district at the same time, other settler communities established amicable (or at least mutually beneficial) relations with neighboring Bashkir villages, swapping fields and pasturelands, negotiating rent payments, and joining together to hunt down local horse thieves. One group of settlers from Kursk even curried favor with local Bashkirs to ensure that they could pass safely through Bashkir settlements (*auly*) on the road to the nearest church.[35]

These local conflicts and accommodations were the single most important factor in establishing the nature of interethnic relations in the countryside. That is not to say that larger, overarching forces such as state policy or religious prejudice did not play a part. Religious attitudes, for example, certainly had an impact on how Orthodox and Muslim communities viewed each other and how and when they chose to fraternize. Likewise, government policies, which moved different groups in and out of a certain area and encouraged some contacts (Russian peasants with German colonists, for example) while discouraging others (Orthodox settlers with "sectarians") also contributed to the mix that shaped the nature of life in multiethnic localities. On a deeper level still, we can assume that popular ethnic stereotypes, as evidenced in peasant folktales and children's songs, had some impact on interethnic relations. As a rule, however, these supralocal structures, while influencing the boundaries of contact and exchange, did not operate as the sole or even dominant determinant of how people "got along." Local conditions of settlement, and the local arrangements between different groups, were much more important.

The eclectic area of Molochnye Vody in Tavrida's Melitopol' district offers a rich illustration of the tapestries of interethnic agreements that could be stitched together at the local level. Here Russian and Ukrainian Orthodox, Russian Dukhobors, Muslim Nogays, and German Mennonites, Lutherans, and Catholics lived side by side as distinct cultural communities that occasionally viewed each other with derision or suspicion but nonetheless managed to establish workable and tolerant social relations. This relationship was based on two key foundations: a commitment to practical arrangements over the use of local resources and the mutual recognition of the separateness of certain spheres of social life, such as marriage, worship, and custom. In this mixed social milieu, German Mennonites hired Nogay shepherds and Ukrainian fieldworkers; Russians and Germans leased Nogay farmland or swapped for it in mutually brokered land trades; Mennonites borrowed herbal medicines from Nogays while Nogays visited Mennonite doctors; German craftsmen helped to build homes for Russian "sectarians;" everyone traded with one another at local fairs; almost no one converted or intermarried across religious lines; and, on at least one occasion in 1854, Russians, Ukrainians, and a Nogay all drank and sang together at the name's-day celebration of a certain Efrosina Gedankova in the village of Elnizagach.[36] Of course, this generally workable world of social relations was not idyllic. Acts of crime, violence, and suspicion occurred between the different communities, and, on a deeper level, all groups certainly did not come out evenly in economic terms or in terms of the treatment they received from the Russian state.[37] All the same, what most characterized relations at Molochnye Vody in the early-to-mid-1800s was a practical approach to resolving local issues. Local concerns drove disparate groups together and established the parameters of conflict and accommodation.

Stripping down the empire to look at interethnic interactions at the local level, one also comes to see much more vividly the multidirectional movement of economic, social, and cultural borrowings. In the first half of the nineteenth century, however, Russian visions of the empire tended to ignore this view and emphasized instead the one-way Russian impact on native cultures. Though Russian writers and historians readily admitted that Russia's past contained a rich legacy of ethnic mixings and mergings, by the age of Muscovy and beyond, it was the Russian state and the Russian people who were supposed to influence the empire's subject populations and not the other way around. The march of the Russian state, and, by extension, of Russian religion, language, and custom (*byt*, *nravy*) into the borderlands was seen as an unstoppable parade of destiny and progress that would inevitably sweep all of the empire's lesser-developed peoples into its path.[38] In this grand parade, the Russian peasant (ironically enough) was cast as a veritable *Kulturträger* whose general adaptability (*uzhivost'*, *uzhivchivost'*), strong "spirit of nationality," and knack for colonization allowed him to move all over the empire and assimilate native peoples with ease.[39] But the very adaptability of Russian peasant culture meant that things could also work the other way around. Depending on circumstances of settlement and contact, Russian peasant communities commonly appropriated native elements and incorporated them into their own social and cultural systems. Regional peasant cultures in areas of dense interethnic mingling like the Middle Volga, the northern Caucasus, and Siberia attest to these syncretic realities.

On occasion, however, Russian peasants did not just borrow cultural motifs and practices from their native neighbors; they also partially or fully assimilated with surrounding *inorodtsy* peoples. In such instances, much to the dismay of patriotically minded Russian observers, the Russian peasant ceased being Russian altogether and instead slipped down the scale of "civilization" and turned into "the Other." Cases of this sort, though statistically rare, could be found all across the imperial borderlands, and they provide fascinating evidence of the cultural complexities of life in settlement areas. Examples from the first half of the nineteenth century are numerous: In the Crimea, for example, in the 1840s, an orphaned Russian peasant ran away from home as a boy, lived for fifteen years in Tatar villages, converted to Islam, took a Tatar name, and married a Tatar woman before finally being recognized by Russian peasants from his former home and arrested for "apostasy" (*otstuplenie ot pravoslaviia*);[40] on the Caspian steppe, Russian Cossacks supposedly borrowed a great deal from their nomadic neighbors;[41] in the far reaches of the Siberian north, hundreds of Russian peasants and townsmen looked like Yakuts and lived "à la Samoède;"[42] and in Kazan' province in the 1840s, at least one Russian village was uncovered where all the peasants spoke Chuvash, wore Chuvash dress, and were completely Chuvashized "in their manners, behavior, and facial appearance."[43]

Of course, these examples of Russian "nativization," while clearly upsetting to educated Russian sensibilities, were certainly not the norm. In the eclectic world of borderland settlement in the first half of the 1800s, wholesale assimilation, whether of Russians "going native" or of natives "going Russian," was rare. Some Russian settlers in some places clearly borrowed heavily from native cultures while native peoples, for their part, experienced varying levels of cultural Russification, as they (to different extents in different places) adopted the Russian language, took up agriculture (in the case of nomadic or hunter-gatherer societies), and/or converted to Orthodoxy (in the case of non-Christian groups). On the whole, however, Russian settlers and their non-Russian neighbors did not engage in efforts to assimilate one another. Though assimilation (i.e. Russification) was at various times the goal of the Russian state and the Orthodox church, for commoners in the countryside, the persistence of ethnoreligious difference was seen as entirely natural and, therefore, rarely questioned. As a Chuvash peasant in Kazan' once remarked to some frustrated Russian officials, it was only fitting that "the Chuvash should keep to the Chuvash faith [i.e. paganism], the Russians to the Russian, and Tatars to the Tatar" because they were all different peoples.[44] Russia's settlement worlds, in other words, reveal a great deal of cultural change moving in multiple directions but also, at the same time, a great deal of cultural persistence. Russian settlers and their non-Russian neighbors (to varying degrees, depending on the groups involved) saw each other as different, and they were generally more than content for things to stay that way.

Ethnic Typecasting and Peasant Responses

Examples of Russian common folk taking on the ways of Tatars, Yakuts, and Kazakhs suggest that historians of the empire should pay more attention to the multiple outcomes of social life in Russia's settlement worlds. In general, our scholarship has tended to miss these points because it approaches the history of the empire in strictly bipolar terms, either from the Russian perspective or from the point of view of individual ethnonational communities. In the first instance, the focus tends to be on policy and administration, usually as devised from the imperial center. In the second, it falls more on resistance and the struggle for national autonomy, usually among national elites or at least among politically conscious classes. Both approaches have important merits, but both also have a principal failing in that they tend to focus on one end or the other of the Russian/non-Russian intersection without paying enough attention to the intersection itself. The vast intersection of cultures, however, is vitally important for understanding the nature of the Russian Empire. As the historical anthropologist Greg Dening has remarked in reference to crosscultural contact in the Pacific, the arena of the crosscultural encounter (symbolized for Dening by the physical space of the beach) is where we can uncover "the misreadings of meanings, the transformation of meanings, the recognition of meanings" between disparate peoples and their views of the world.[45]

Of all the issues caught in the great intersection between Russians and native communities, the question of ethnic or ethnoreligious typecasting is perhaps the least explored. This lacuna is certainly understandable. Almost everything relating to ethnic stereotypes, including how and where they are produced, how they move between different cultural spheres, and how profoundly they influence judgment and behavior, is hard to pin down and, therefore, extremely difficult to measure, compare, and analyze. At the same time, however, the importance of ethnic stereotypes is clear. In its most obvious sense, ethnic stereotyping, the reduction of complex cultural qualities to a distilled "national character" or essence, is central to the way societies and individuals organize their visions of other people.[46] In the case of empires, much as in any polity, stereotyping is also (obviously) about power. When "imperial" peoples categorize and characterize subordinate ones, they invariably do so in ways that justify (or at least attempt to justify) the imperial relationship and reinforce the distinct status of the imperial group.[47] In the Russian imperial context in the early-to-mid-1800s, Russian stereotyping of the various peoples of the empire was ubiquitous. Wherever educated Russians looked, they found suspicious Poles, sober-minded Germans, tightfisted "yids" (*zhidy*), fierce "mountaineers" (*gortsy*), clever and calculating Armenians, lazy and submissive Moldavians, gentle Tunguses, half-savage Kazakhs, and coarse, malodorous Kalmyks.[48] None of these stereotypes were necessarily fixed or unidimensional. As scholars such as Yuri Slezkine and Susan Layton have shown, Russian representations of non-Russian peoples could be multifaceted, ambivalent, and prone to change over time, but they certainly always informed the way educated Russians and the Russian state dealt with subordinate national communities.[49]

Stereotypes, however, were not simply produced by Russian officials, writers, missionaries, and ethnographers and then deployed against native peoples. Inasmuch as stereotypes influenced official Russian policy, they were also part of what non-Russians had to respond to in their dealings with the Russian state. This then begs the question: were *inorodtsy* groups at all aware of the stereotypes that circulated about them in the official Russian world? Unfortunately, direct evidence to answer this question is nonexistent, but it is nonetheless plausible to assume that many native communities must have been at least somewhat informed of these stereotypes. As perennial subalterns or "underdogs" (to use Teodor Shanin's term), peasants, whether Russian, Mexican, or German, were generally very sensitive to the hierarchies and operations of power both inside and outside their village worlds.[50] Furthermore, as Daniel Field has shown in the Russian case, peasants appear to have been aware of official attitudes and perceptions, like the so-called "myth of the peasant," and could apparently manipulate (or at least try to manipulate) these beliefs when it served their interests.[51] Official perceptions, then, did not simply come crashing down on passive Russian peasants; these perceptions were reacted to, engaged with, and redeployed by the peasants themselves. In the section that follows, I explore one curious case that suggests that non-Russian peasants may well have engaged in similar maneuvers to manipulate and redeploy official ethnic stereotyping.

In 1846, Iakov Osipov, an Orthodox (*kreshchennyi*) Chuvash peasant from Kazan' province, was arrested and accused of threatening to kill the tsar.[52] In what looks like a classic case of village infighting, Osipov had been denounced by a disgruntled neighbor for allegedly stating that he would "cut down the tsar himself" if his fellow villagers put his name on the list for an upcoming recruitment. Following his arrest, Osipov initially denied the charge, claiming, somewhat disingenuously, that he had been misunderstood in Chuvash and had only professed the most loyal sentiments about the tsar. When the questioning heated up, however, Osipov quickly crumbled. He fell to his knees and admitted "in tears" that he had indeed threatened the tsar, though he insisted he had spoken "out of ignorance . . . without thinking and without the slightest intent." The official investigating the case, a certain *shtab ofitser* Denisov, immediately interpreted Osipov's behavior according to a stereotypical script. In his report to the Kazan' military governor, Denisov argued that Osipov deserved to be pardoned as there was no evidence that he had "subversive intentions" or even "the barest understanding" of the crime he had committed. Osipov's threat was "nothing more than the unpremeditated and thoughtless raving of an unbridled savage." This conclusion was all the more obvious given the feelings of "terrible fright [followed by] the most profound and sincere repentance [that the accused displayed] when he was explained the full seriousness of his crime." Some three weeks later, the governor received a letter from the Third Section pardoning Osipov and the case was closed.

Unfortunately, there is no way of knowing Osipov's thoughts during his interrogation. The events, as they appear in the Kazan' archive, are described in the investigator Denisov's words and inscribed with his implicit interpretations and meanings. In fact, Denisov's imprint as author of this text is so strong that one could argue that there is no way to study the "real" Osipov here, only an Osipov that Denisov "created" and "coded" as a stereotypical Chuvash. But as Ginzburg and James C. Scott have suggested, dominant texts, despite their obvious biases, can still be read to uncover a "hidden transcript" of resistance or at least a more subtle play of action and reaction than historians might at first assume. As Ginzburg writes in his reflections on the anthropological value of inquisitorial records, "we must learn to catch, behind the smooth surface of the [dominant] text, a subtle interplay of threats and fears, of attacks and withdrawals." In other words, the actions of the accused as they appear in "hostile" documents can still be uncovered and evaluated once we accept the fact that a truly mutual encounter has taken place.[53] Based on this kind of reading, it becomes possible to suggest that the defendant Osipov may well have been entirely aware of what he was doing. Certainly his actions, statements, and gestures all seem to demonstrate a remarkable grasp of how a lowly Chuvash peasant like himself "should" have acted in his situation.

Osipov's displays of befuddled innocence and emotionality, for example, fit perfectly with common Russian views of the Chuvash as amiable but dull-witted "children of nature." In early-nineteenth-century accounts, the Chuvash routinely appear as meek, humble, quiet, somewhat thickheaded, and incorrigibly superstitious "half-savages" who behave themselves more like children than grown adults.[54] This general "Chuvashian" image, while hardly flattering, was not entirely negative. Despite their dim minds and lack of culture, the Chuvash were recognized as basically loyal subjects, capable of acknowledging the virtues and achievements of Russian civilization, and hence deserving of a certain amount of assistance and sympathy.[55] This rendering of the Chuvash as gentle savages comes out wonderfully in an article by a provincial official (a Russianized Chuvash himself) who proudly shows off a statue of the great Russian poet G. R. Derzhavin to three benighted Chuvash villagers. The official describes the three Chuvash bumpkins as understandably impressed, even awestruck, by the statue, much like the barbarians of old who, despite their own "savagery (*dikost'*)," were still able to recognize the grandeur of Greek civilization.[56]

Thus, given the prevailing stereotypes of the day, a Russian interrogator in Kazan' in the 1840s might certainly have expected a Chuvash suspect hauled in on conspiracy charges to appear dumb, emotional, and, at the same time, more than just a little overwhelmed by the whole procedure of Russian "civilization" unfolding in the interrogation room. But did the Chuvash defendant Osipov know that he was expected to act "Chuvash" in this way? It is, of course, impossible to know whether he did or not, but there were clearly avenues for peasants like Osipov to come into contact with Russian stereotypes about the Chuvash in the countryside. Russian priests and missionaries, judging from their sermons and admonitions (*uveshchaniia*), expressed similar views about the Chuvash. So too did local officials in their reports. What is more, Russian peasants who lived in close contact with Chuvash communities appear to have shared some of the views circulating in the minds of the more educated members of Kazan' society, like the investigator Denisov. Russian peasants in Kazan' province certainly had derisive sayings about "stupid" or "unclean" Udmurt and Mari villagers and a few quips about the Chuvash suggest similar attitudes.[57]

Osipov's case has a familiar ring to it. Historians like Field and David Moon have shown that Russian peasants, too, would feign ignorance or claim to have misunderstood the law to escape punishment in similar situations.[58] Is Osipov's strategy just another example of subaltern dissimulation? In a sense, it is, but with an ethnic edge. In Osipov's case, in addition to his doing what any peasant in his predicament might do, one also senses a specific response to the Russian image of the Chuvash as a people who, unlike Russian peasants, are just too naive, too simple-hearted (*prostodushnyi*) to harbor "subversive intentions," let alone carry them out. This do-no-conscious-evil stereotype, which educated Russians associated with other non-Muslim "aliens" in Kazan' province, such as Maris, Mordvins, and Udmurts, seems to have been manipulated fairly frequently. The Kazan' archive contains numerous files in which different *inorodtsy* peasants are caught performing pagan rituals and sacrifices, and, in every instance, the peasants eventually admit to their "crime" and beg for forgiveness as ignorant, would-be Christians who have suffered from a regrettable lack of religious attention and instruction. In one case, Chuvash villagers from Cheboksary district confessed in their interrogations that they performed their sacrifice "out of ignorance" and claimed they "would have abandoned such practices long ago if their priest and deacons had taken prohibitive measures."[59] In another, Mari peasants went to the investigating official, fell to their knees, and "sincerely repented," explaining that they committed their sacrifice "out of ignorance and because [they were] still new to the Church, not because they wished to resist the law." In this instance, the official recommended pardoning most of the perpetrators, noting that the Mari were clearly a people "as ignorant as they are meek [*robkie*] and submissive to the state."[60] In Osipov's case, one sees a similar pattern. By first denying then confessing his crime and, finally, by appearing not even to understand the meaning of what he did, Osipov seems to cater to this same do-no-conscious-evil stereotype.

If this reading of the case is correct, Osipov was at least generally aware of the image of the Chuvash in the Russian world and was playing a role. His statements, referring to his own ignorance and thoughtlessness, as well as his sobbing and throwing himself on his knees before his interrogator, exploit the ambivalences in the prevailing Russian image of the Chuvash. Osipov, then, may well have been engaging in an act of what Mary Louise Pratt has intriguingly called "autoethnographic expression," that is a practice through which "colonized subjects . . . represent themselves in ways that engage with the colonizer's own terms" and thus establish images of themselves that are "in response to or in dialogue with . . . metropolitan representations."[61] I do not want to argue here that Osipov was a supremely conscious defendant skillfully picking his way through all of his judge's prejudices. It could well be that he had simply internalized a pattern of behavior that reflected the influence of dominant Russian stereotyping. It is significant to note, however, that, consciously or unconsciously, Osipov was able to find room for maneuvering and avoiding punishment within Russian ethnic discourse. In a sense, Osipov was fortunate that he was a Chuvash. He probably would not have found as much latitude in trying to curry the favor of a Russian interrogator if he had been a Tatar, a Pole, or a Jew, for example. But the awareness, which he appears to display, of how his community was perceived by Russian officialdom must have been important for all native groups, even for those who benefited from relatively more sympathy from the regime. Knowing how the Russians knew you was an essential part of the non-Russians' adaptation to social life in the Russian Empire.

Conclusion

The multiethnic rural world of the Russian Empire was home to a remarkably complex range of local environments where Russian settlers and different ethnoreligious communities lived side by side, interacting, communicating, cooperating, conflicting, occasionally influencing and even assimilating one another, and always maneuvering to secure the best possible position for themselves vis-à-vis the state and each other. If there was one constant feature to this diverse and fluid social landscape, it was undoubtedly the omnipresent fact of interaction itself: interaction between Russian settlers and the state during the resettlement process; between settlers and their neighbors in their multiethnic localities; and between native peoples and the state during the give-and-take over imperial prejudice and stereotyping. Taken together, all of this interaction produced a complicated but at the same time integral imperial world. Russian peasants and their various non-Russian neighbors were often quite different in ethnic, religious, and cultural terms, and they often regarded one another as profoundly alien, yet they were also tied fastly together in myriad ways in their local places. Studying the complex ties that bound the Russian Empire's disparate communities together adds immeasurably to our sense of the empire and the way that it "worked" at its most basic level. If the empire as a whole can be compared to a kind of skyscraper with the corporate boardrooms of high politics and high culture taking up the top stories, then the multiethnic social world of the countryside makes up the *rez-de-chaussée*, the imperial ground floor. To reach a fuller understanding of the empire, historians need to look more closely at this part of the building.[62]

Notes

Research for this article was made possible by grants from the International Research and Exchanges Board and the American Council of Teachers of Russian. My thanks also to David Ransel, David Moon, and especially Jane Burbank for their helpful comments on an earlier version of this piece.

1. This positive portrayal appears in E. F. Ziablovskii, *Zemleopisanie rossiiskoi imperii dlia vsekh sostoianii* (St. Petersburg, 1810), vol. 1, 3. For other patriotic references to Russia's supposedly unrivaled size, see Sergey Plescheef, *Survey of the Russian Empire, According to its Present and Newly Regulated State* (London, 1792), 3–4; N. S. Vsévolojsky, *Dictionnaire géographique-historique de l'empire de Russie* (Moscow, 1813), vol. 2, 164; M. P. Pogodin, "Pis'mo k gosudariu tsarevichu velikomu kniaziu Aleksandru Nikolaevichu v 1838 godu," in his *Istoriko-politicheskie pis'ma i zapiski vprodolzhenii Krymskoi voiny 1853–1856* (Moscow, 1874), 2; and A. Roslavskii, "Sravnenie Rossii v statisticheskom otnoshenii s drugimi pervoklassnymi evropeiskimi derzhavami," *Moskvitianin*, 1844, pt. 3, 232. Despite early-nineteenth-century Russian claims to the title of largest state in history, even at its greatest extent, the Russian/Soviet empire comes in only third behind the Mongol and British empires. See Rein Taagepera, "An Overview of the Growth of the Russian Empire," in Michael Rywkin, ed., *Russian Colonial Expansion to 1917* (London, 1988), 4.

2. For more on the scale and varying rates of settlement across the empire during the first half of the nineteenth century, see S. I. Bruk and V. M. Kabuzan, "Migratsiia naseleniia v Rossii v xviii-nachale xx veka (chislennost', struktura, geografiia)," *Istoriia SSSR*, 1984, no. 4, 41–59; Ia. E. Vodarskii, *Naselenie Rossii za 400 let (xvi-nachalo xx vv.)* (Mos-

cow, 1973), 93–100; and V. M. Kabuzan, *Izmeneniia v razmeshchenii naseleniia Rossii v xviii-pervoi polovine xix vv. (po materialam revizii)* (Moscow, 1971), 28 passim.

3. L. Maksimov and Shchekatov, eds., *Geograficheskii slovar' rossiiskogo gosudarstva, sochinennyi v nastoiashchem onogo vide* (Moscow, 1801), pt. 1, introduction. The order of the two sentences is reversed in the original.

4. A. I. Martos, *Pis'mo o vostochnoi Sibiri 1823–1824* (Moscow, 1827), 114.

5. P. S. Pallas, *Travels through the Southern Provinces of Russia in the Years 1793 and 1794* (2d. ed.; London, 1812), vol. 1, 316.

6. For a few remarks on the need for and possibilities of colonization in various parts of the empire, see S. Siestrzencewicz, *Histoire du royaume de la Chersonèse Taurique* (2d ed.; St. Petersburg, 1824), 432; Anatole de Démidoff, *Voyage dans la Russie méridionale et la Crimée par la Hongrie, la Valachie et la Moldavie* (Paris, 1854), 252–253; P. Nebol'sin, *Pokorenie Sibiri: istoricheskoe issledovanie* (St. Petersburg, 1849), 145; A. Pisemskii, "Putevye ocherki," *Morskoi sbornik*, 1857, vol. 27, no. 2, 238; and P. Zubov, *Kartina Kavkazskogo kraia, prinadlezhashchego Rossii i sopredel'nykh onomu zemel' v istoricheskom, statisticheskom, etnograficheskom, finansovom i torgovom otnosheniiakh* (St. Petersburg, 1834), vol. 1, 15–18.

7. A. Skal'kovskii, "Sravnitel'nyi vzgliad na Ochakovskuiu oblast' v 1790 i 1840 godakh," *Zapiski odesskogo obshchestva istorii i drevnostei*, 1844, vol. 1, 257.

8. Carlo Ginzburg, *The Cheese and the Worms: The Cosmos of a Sixteenth-Century Miller* (Baltimore, 1980); Laurel Thatcher Ulrich, *A Midwife's Tale: The Life of Martha Ballard Based on Her Diary* (New York, 1990).

9. My discussion here and throughout this paper centers on the empire's state peasant population, a broad category that could include homesteaders (*odnodvortsy*), non-Russian "aliens" (*inorodtsy*), and Cossacks. State peasants, who lived on state lands and were directly subject to the state's administration, enjoyed a different legal status than manorial serfs.

10. The range of peasant knowledge about issues such as geography, current events, and history was idiosyncratic but often quite broad. See M. M. Gromyko, "Kul'tura russkogo krest'ianstva xviii–xix kak predmet istoricheskogo issledovaniia," *Istoriia SSSR*, 1987, no. 3, 41, 45–51.

11. Observers from August von Haxthausen to Nikolai Gogol' to John Maynard have made much of the Russian peasantry's supposed propensity for movement, though rarely with the necessary qualifications. Maksim Gorkii's remark is perhaps the most famous: "The instinct of the nomad seems to survive in the Russian peasant. . . . There is always somewhere to go; the empty plain unrolls on every side and the distance calls seductively." Maxim Gorky, "On the Russian Peasantry," in R. E. F. Smith, ed., *The Russian Peasant 1920 and 1984* (London, 1977), 12.

12. Some telling proverbs include, "A poor halting place is better than a good road"; "When setting off, better make yourself five pairs of shoes (*lapti*)"; and "Praise distant places, but stay at home." See V. I. Dal', *Poslovitsy russkogo naroda* (St. Petersburg, 1879), vol. 1, 329–33, 400–405. To ward off dangers on long travels, peasants would often recite spells or have psalms transcribed and tied to their crosses. See the text of one of these spells in *Russkoe narodnoe chernoknizh'e* (Moscow, 1991), 79.

13. As David Moon has argued, folk images such as *Belovod'e* and self-serving "mis-interpretations" of official legislation seem to have fused in the peasant way of thinking, providing a ready-made justification for flight or resettlement. See his *Russian Peasants and Tsarist Legislation on the Eve of Reform: Interaction between Peasants and Officialdom, 1825–1855* (Basingstoke, England, 1992), 58–59. On *Belovod'e*, see K. V. Chistov, *Russkie narodnye sotsial'no-utopicheskie legendy xvii–xix vv.* (Moscow, 1967).

14. Tsentral'nyi gosudarstvennyi istoricheskii arkhiv respubliki Bashkortostana (TsGIA RB), f. I-2, op. 1, d. 1506, l. 56; Gosudarstvennyi arkhiv Orenburgskoi oblasti (GAOO), f. 6, op. 5, d. 10643, l. 1(b).

15. Rossiiskii gosudarstvennyi istoricheskii arkhiv (RGIA), f. 383, op. 30, d. 151, ll. 68–69, 71–73(b).

16. N. Petrovich, "Pereselenie gosudarstvennykh krest'ian v Sibir v nachale xix veka," *Arkhiv istorii truda v Rossii*, 1924, bk. 12, 114–16.

17. GAOO, f. 6, op. 5, d. 10419, l. 2(b).

18. Paul Carter, *The Road to Botany Bay: An Exploration of Landscape and History* (Chicago, 1987), 138–39 passim.

19. Most settler petitions begin with a formulaic introduction in which the peasants indicate that they resettled "with the permission" (*s dozvoleniem*) of their communes, the minister, the governor, and the provincial treasuries involved. For several examples, see RGIA f. 383, op. 1, d. 190, ll. 49–72(b).

20. RGIA, f. 383, op. 30, d. 927, ll. 74–76(b).

21. Defining the scope of ethnicity in the rural world in the imperial period is very difficult, but on the whole it's clear that markers such as religion and locality (*rodina, zemlia*) played a far more overt role in setting the boundaries of the peasants' identity and allegiances. On the nature of ethnicity and the power of ethnic and ethnoreligious boundaries, see Fredrik Barth, ed., *Ethnic Groups and Boundaries: The Social Organization of Culture Difference* (Boston, 1969).

22. This view is dismissed by a number of Russian historians who insist that the Russian people enjoyed little or no advantage in the borderlands and instead tended to bear the brunt of the empire's injustices, such as serfdom and military recruitment. For a sample of such views, see V. Kozlov, " 'Imperskaia' natsiia ili ushchemlennaia natsional'nost'?" *Moskva*, 1991, no. 1, 131–41; and N. Nikitin, "Suverennoe pravo . . . o 'korennykh' i 'nekorennykh' narodakh i 'obnovlenii' nashei federatsii," *Moskva*, 1991, no. 4, 106–23; no. 6, 122–44. See also N. I. Tsimbaev, "Rossiia i russkie (natsional'nyi vopros v rossiiskoi imperii)," *Vestnik moskovskogo universtiteta*, series 8, *Istoriia*, 1993, no. 5, 31. The question of the Russian *narod's* relative advantage or disadvantage within the empire is complex. For an informative and balanced assessment of the problem, see Andreas Kappeler, *La Russie: empire multiethnique* (Paris, 1994), 144, 277–78.

23. P. de Gouroff, *De la civilisation des tatars-nogais dans le midi de la Russie européenne* (Khar'kov, 1816), 45–46.

24. GAOO, f. 6, op. 7, d. 161, l. 13(b).

25. Indirect Russian settler statements about why they deserved special treatment from Russian authorities appear here and there in peasant petitions, but the most explicit

example I have found was recorded in a surveyor's conversation with a Russian settler on the Kazakh steppe in the 1890s. Despite the fact that this settler's party had resettled illegally onto Kazakh lands, the peasant was confident that the state would ultimately let his party stay its ground. "After all," the *muzhik* asked, "who are [the Kazakhs]? They are unbelievers (*nekhristi*) and nomads (*orda*) while we are the tsar's; our folk serve in the army, we pay taxes and duties (*tiagosti nesem*). It's simply impossible not to give us the land. Plus, we've built a church here. Are we to leave it behind for the Kazakhs?" See A. A. Kaufman, *Po novym mestam* (St. Petersburg, 1905), 233.

26. One example of this kind of "identity politics" can be found in a petition submitted to the minister of state domains in 1841 by four Nogay villages in Tavrida that were attempting to keep the state from reducing their land allotments. The Nogay argued that losing any amount of land would drastically affect their sheep flocks, which, in turn, would seriously undermine their Islamic way of life because sheep were essential for their feast-day sacrifices, for paying the services of their mullahs, for their dowries, and for their general diet: "We depend on our flocks for meat," the Nogay wrote, "which Russian state peasants can replace with salted pork fat (*salo*), but we cannot for eating [pork] is prohibited by our faith (*zakon*)." RGIA, f. 383, op. 1, d. 190, ll. 40–41.

27. S. Lur'e, "Rossiiskaia gosudarstvennost' i russkaia obshchina," *Znanie-sila*, 1992, no. 10, 9.

28. For the flavor of some eighteenth-century descriptions of the empire's peoples, see, for example, Johann Gottlieb Georgii, *Opisanie vsekh obitaiushchikh v rossiiskom gosudarstve narodov, ikh zhiteiskikh obriadov, obyknovenii, odezhd, zhilishch, uprazhnenii, zabav, veroispovedanii i drugikh dostopamiatnostei* (St. Petersburg, 1799) 2 vols.; and G. F. Müller, *Opisanie zhivushchikh v Kazanskoi gubernii iazycheskikh narodov iako to Cheremis, Chuvash i Votiakov* (St. Petersburg, 1791). For a fascinating analysis of the way eighteenth-century Russians conceptualized the diversities of the empire, see Yuri Slezkine, "Naturalists versus Nations: Eighteenth-Century Russian Scholars Confront Ethnic Diversity," *Representations*, 1994, no. 47, 170–95.

29. The rich multiethnic dimensions of life in the imperial countryside are still vastly underexplored. Though the field of Russian peasant studies in the West has expanded considerably in recent years, it is still almost exclusively focused on Russian (and sometimes Ukrainian) peasants in core areas and has barely looked at the issue of multiethnic contact in the imperial periphery. Soviet ethnographers and folklorists, on the other hand, have studied this arena much more closely but their work tends to focus narrowly on crosscultural influences in the areas of material and popular culture. Much Soviet work has also been marred by a thick ideological emphasis on the Russian peasants' supposedly progressive influence on non-Russian groups. For a terse confession on this score, see *Istoriia krest'ianstva Rossii s drevneishikh vremen do 1917 g.*, vol. 3, *Krest'ianstvo perioda pozdnego feodalizma (seredina xvii v.-1861 g.)* (Moscow, 1993), 555.

30. "Putevye zametki pri ob"ezde Dneprovskogo i Melitopol'skogo uezdov v 1835 godu," *Listki obshchestva sel'skogo khoziaistva iuzhnoi Rossii*, 1839, no. 5/6, 315.

31. GAOO, f. 6, op. 4, d. 9552, l. 9; Tsentral'nyi gosudarstvennyi arkhiv Kryma (TsGAK), f. 15, op. 1, d. 765, l. 14(b).

32. There is a vast literature on interethnic minglings along different world frontiers. For a handful of recent works, see Richard White, *The Middle Ground: Indians, Empires, and Republics in the Great Lakes Region, 1650–1815* (New York, 1991); Daniel H. Usner, Jr., *Indians, Settlers, and Slaves in a Frontier Exchange Economy: The Lower Mississippi Valley before 1783* (Chapel Hill, N.C., 1992); David J. Weber, *The Spanish Frontier in North America* (New Haven, Conn., 1992); in David J. Weber and Jane M. Rausch, eds., *Where Cultures Meet: Frontiers in Latin America* (Wilmington, Del., 1994); and the forum "The Formation of Ethnic Identities in Frontier Societies," *Journal of World History*, 1993, vol. 4, no. 2, 267–324.

33. GAOO, f. 11, op. 6, d. 19 and d. 20. According to the GAOO files, this dispute lasted for at least twenty-seven years, from 1840 to 1867.

34. GAOO, f. 6, op. 4, d. 9332, l. 278(b).

35. I. Nevskii, "Selo Pokrovka Orenburgskago uezda," *Orenburgskie eparkhial'nye vedomosti*, 1898, no. 3, 108.

36. Evidence of the socioeconomic and cultural complexities of life in Molochnye Vody can be found in both published and archival sources. See "Byt molochanskikh menonitskikh kolonii," *Zhurnal ministerstva gosudarstvennykh imushchestv* (ZhMGI), 1841, pt. 1, bk. 2, 561; Bauman, "Zamechaniia o khoziaistve narodov, zhivushchikh po severnym beregam Azovskogo moria v Tavricheskoi gubernii," ZhMGI, 1845, vol. 15, pt. 4, 49; Idem., "Opisanie kazennogo seleniia Tokmaka v Tavricheskoi gubernii," ZhMGI, 1848, vol. 26, pt. 4, 7; "Statisticheskie svedeniia o Melitopol'skom uezde za 1838 god," *Zhurnal ministerstva vnutrennykh del*, 1839, vol. 31, 315; Daniel Schlatter, *Bruchstücke aus einigen Reisen nach dem südlichen Russland in den Jahren 1822 bis 1828, mit besonderer Rücksicht auf die Nogai-Tataren am Asowschen Meere* (St. Gallen, Switz., 1830), 107–108; James Urry, *None but Saints: The Transformation of Mennonite Life in Russia, 1789–1889* (Winnipeg, 1989), 96; TsGAK, f. 81, op. 1, d. 306, ll. 1–2; TsGAK, f. 27, op. 1, d. 2362, ll. 1-1(b) (for land-swapping arrangements); TsGAK, f. 26, op. 4, d. 839 (on Germans building homes for Russian Molokan); and TsGAK, f. 26, op. 1, d. 20040 (for the name's-day party).

37. German colonists at Molochnye Vody, and especially the Mennonites, had large landholdings of over 60 *desiatina* of arable land per farmer and were generally more prosperous than their Slavic and Turkic neighbors. If German Mennonites were the winners in this settlement world, however, Nogays and Dukhobors were clearly the losers as both groups ended up being moved out of the area either by force or with the tacit approval of the authorities in the early 1840s and 1860 respectively. For the relative economic standing of the rural dwellers of Molochnye Vody, see N. Gersevanov, "Priblizitel'noe opisanie khoziaistva khoziaev-zemledel'tsev srednego sostoianiia v Tavricheskoi gubernii," ZhMGI, 1848, vol. 26, otd. 4, 50–56. On the removal of the Nogay, see A. A. Sergeev, "Ukhod tavricheskikh nogaitsev v Turtsiiu v 1860 godu," *Izvestiia tavricheskoi uchennoi arkhivnoi komissii*, 1913, vol. 49, 178–222.

38. For more on how Russian historians represented the expansion of the empire and the specialness of Russian nationality (*narodnost'*) in the early 1800s, see David B. Saunders, "Historians and Concepts of Nationality in Early Nineteenth-Century Russia," *Slavonic and East European Review*, 1982, vol. 60, no. 1, 44–62; and Seymour Becker, "Con-

tributions to a Nationalist Ideology: Histories of Russia in the First Half of the Nine-teenth Century," *Russian History/Histoire russe*, 1986, vol. 13, no. 4, 331–53.

39. For a few notes on this score, see A. de Haxthausen, *Études sur la situation in-térieure: la vie nationale et les institutions rurales de la Russie* (Hanover, 1847–1853) vol. 2, 191; N. Filippov, *Poezdka po beregam Azovskogo moria letom 1856 goda* (St. Petersburg, 1857), 113; I. Berezin, "Metropoliia i kolonii," *Otechestvennye zapiski*, 1858, vol. 118, no. 5, 114; and S. V. Eshevskii, "Russkaia kolonizatsiia severovostochnogo kraia," *Vestnik evropy*, 1866, vol. 1, 218 passim.

40. TsGAK, f. 15, op. 1, d. 878, ll. 4–13.

41. Catherine B. Clay, "Ethnography and Mission: Imperial Russia and Muslim Turkic Peoples on the Caspian Frontier in the 1850s," *The Turkish Studies Association Bul-letin*, 1994, vol. 18, no. 2, 36.

42. Ferdinand Wrangel, *Narrative of an Expedition to the Polar Sea in the Years 1820, 1821, 1822, and 1823* (New York, 1841; reprint: Fairfield, Wash., 1981), 31; M. Alexander Castren, *Reiseerinnerungen aus den Jahren 1838–1844* (St. Petersburg, 1853; reprint: Leipzig, 1969), 280; and Makarii, "Zametki o Iakutske i o iakutakh," *Vestnik imperatorskogo russkogo geograficheskogo obshchestva*, 1852, pt. 4, 89. For more on the phenomenon of "nativized" Russian settlers in northern Siberia, see my "Russians into Iakuts? 'Going Native' and Problems of Russian National Identity in the Siberian North, 1870s–1914," *Slavic Review*, 1996, vol. 55, no. 4, 806–25.

43. A. A. Fuks, *Zapiski Aleksandry Fuks o chuvashakh i cheremisakh Kazanskoi gubernii* (Kazan', 1840), 11.

44. *Tsentral'nyi gosudarstvennyi arkhiv respubliki Tatarstana* (TsGART), f. 1, op. 2, d. 372, l. 1(b).

45. Greg Dening, *Islands and Beaches: Discourse on a Silent Land; Marquesas, 1774–1880* (Honolulu, 1980), 6.

46. For various discussions of the problems of stereotyping, see A. Inkeles and D. J. Levinson, "National Character: The Study of Modal Personality and Socio-Cultural Sys-tems," in G. Lindzey and E. Aronson, eds., *The Handbook of Social Psychology* (2d. ed.; Reading, Mass., 1969), 418–506; Arthur G. Miller, ed., *In the Eye of the Beholder: Contempo-rary Issues in Stereotyping* (New York, 1982); Phyllis P. Chock, "The Irony of Stereotypes: Toward an Anthropology of Ethnicity," *Cultural Anthropology*, 1987, no. 2, 347–68; Christie Davies, *Ethnic Humor around the World: A Comparative Analysis* (Bloomington, Ind., 1990); Maryon McDonald, "The Construction of Difference: An Anthropological Approach to Stereotypes," in Sharon Macdonald, ed., *Inside European Identities: Ethnography in Western Europe* (Providence, R.I., 1993), 219–36; and Penelope J. Oakes, et al., eds., *Stereotyping and Social Reality* (Oxford, 1994).

47. J. A. Mangan, "Images for Confident Control: Stereotypes in Imperial Dis-course," in his edited volume, *The Imperial Curriculum: Racial Images and Education in the British Colonial Experience* (New York, 1993), 7.

48. For a few references of this sort, see John D. Klier, "*Zhid*: Biography of a Russian Epithet," *Slavonic and East European Review*, 1982, vol. 60, no. 1, 1–15; N. Danilevskii,

Kavkaz i ego gorskie zhiteli v nyneshnom polozhenii (2d ed.; Moscow, 1851), 3–4 passim; Ronald Grigor Suny, "Images of the Armenians in the Russian Empire," in his *Looking toward Ararat: Armenia in Modern History* (Bloomington, Ind., 1993), 38–39; Ia. Saburov, "Dvorianstvo i poseliane v Bessarabii (v 1826 godu)," *Teleskop*, 1831, pt. 1, no. 4, 482–83; F. Bal'dauf, "Poslanie k P. N. Ochkinu," in *Sibirskie stroki: russkie i sovetskie poety o Sibiri* (Moscow, 1984), 17; Alexis de Levshin, *Descriptions des hordes et des steppes des Kirghiz-Kazaks ou Kirghiz-Kaïssaks* (Paris, 1840), 309; and Iu. A. Gagemeister, *Statisticheskoe obozrenie Sibiri* (St. Petersburg, 1854) vol. 2, 19.

49. Susan Layton, *Russian Literature and Empire: Conquest of the Caucasus from Pushkin to Tolstoy* (New York, 1994); Yuri Slezkine, *Arctic Mirrors: Russia and the Small Peoples of the North* (Ithaca, N.Y., 1994).

50. Teodor Shanin, *Defining Peasants: Essays Concerning Rural Societies, Explanatory Economies, and Learning from Them in the Contemporary World* (Oxford, 1990), 43.

51. Daniel Field, *Rebels in the Name of the Tsar* (Boston, 1976), 214.

52. TsGART, f. 1, op. 2, d. 532. The quotations in the following summary of the case are drawn from the special investigator's report, ll. 1–14.

53. Carlo Ginzburg, *Clues, Myths, and the Historical Method* (Baltimore, Md., 1989), 161. For James C. Scott's discussion of "hidden transcripts," see his *Domination and the Arts of Resistance: Hidden Transcripts* (New Haven, Conn., 1990).

54. For a few descriptions of the Chuvash in this period, see "Izvestiia o chuvashakh, zhivushchikh v Kazanskoi, Simbirskoi, Orenburgskoi i drugikh guberniiakh," *Kazanskii vestnik*, 1829, chap. 25, nos. 4–6; "Etnograficheskoe opisanie Kazanskoi gubernii," ZhMVD, 1841, pt. 39, 390; N. Leont'ev, "Etnograficheskie zapiski o Kazanskoi gubernii," ZhMGI, 1844, vol. 11, pt. 4, 122; Pell', "Khoziaistvennye zametki o Kazanskoi i nekotorykh chastiakh Nizhegorodskoi, Penzenskoi, Simbirskoi i Viatskoi gubernii," ZhMGI, 1845, vol. 16, otd. 2, 128–29; and V. Sboev, *Chuvashi v bytovom, istoricheskom i religioznom otnosheniiakh* (2d. ed.; Moscow, 1865).

55. For more on the ambivalences found in Russian attitudes toward the Volga peoples and the pervasive use of ethnic clichés, see Andreas Kappeler, *Russlands erste Nationalitäten: Das Zarenreich und die Völker der Mittleren Wolga vom 16. bis 19. Jahrhundert* (Cologne, 1982), 482–88.

56. S. Mikhailov, "Kazanskie inorodtsy pered pamiatnikom Derzhavinu," *Kazanskie gubernskie vedomosti*, 1853, no. 35, neoffitsial'naia chast', 277–78.

57. A. Mozharovskii, "Ocherki zhizni krest'ianskikh detei Kazanskoi gubernii v ikh patekhakh, zabavakh i ostrotakh," *Kazanskie gubernskie vedomosti*, 1868, no. 37, 317; P. Vasiliev, "Narodnye prozvishcha, nasmeshki, prisloviia i primety inorodtsam Kazanskoi gubernii," *Kazanskie gubernskie vedomosti*, 1868, no. 38, 323. By far the most negative epithets ("dogs," "swindlers") were reserved for the Tatars.

58. See Field's *Rebels in the Name of the Tsar* and Moon's *Russian Peasants and Tsarist Legislation* cited earlier in this paper.

59. TsGART, f. 14, op. 10, d. 61, l. 1.

60. TsGART, f. 1, op. 1, d. 249, ll. 7(b)–8.

61. Mary Louise Pratt, *Imperial Eyes: Travel Writing and Transculturation* (New York, 1992), 7.

62. For another architectural analogy to the empire, see Yuri Slezkine's imaginative article, "The USSR as a Communal Apartment or How a Socialist State Promoted Ethnic Particularism," *Slavic Review*, 1994, vol. 53, no. 2, 414–52.

8

The Serf Economy, the Peasant Family, and the Social Order

Steven L. Hoch

———·◁∞▷·———

THE CRUCIAL PROBLEM in examining a rural society is to understand the parameters that determine the success or failure of a population to keep in balance with the economic space it inhabits.[1] How did serfdom in Russia affect this balance? Were agrarian class relations the determining factor, or was serfdom overlain over an ecology, demographic regime, or social order, a thin, translucent cover sufficient only to distort our view of the inner workings of Russian peasant society? How important for Russia was the political power structure governing the ownership of property in the process of accommodation between economic and demographic processes? How much were value systems affecting interpersonal relations within the family (or household) and the wider collectivity key to this process of accommodation? To what extent did serfdom determine the intensity of peasant labor?

Robert Brenner, in a controversial article in *Past and Present*, opened a major debate among European agrarian historians when he attacked "what he considered to be a form of demographic determinism in the interpretation of the development of the preindustrial European agrarian economies."[2] He rejected the idea that long-term development might be explained either by changing market conditions, especially the supply and demand for land and labor (the demographic model), or by growing market development (the commercialization model). To Brenner, "serfdom involved the landlord's ability to control his tenant's person, in particular his movements, so as to be able to determine the *level* of the rent in excess of custom or what might be dictated by the simple play of forces of supply and demand."[3]

In this very late addition to the Brenner debate, let me begin by asserting that in Russia peasant unfreedom, especially restrictions on peasant movements, and landlord rights to arbitrary exactions,[4] were of lesser significance than peasant self-exploitation (A. V. Chayanov), patriarchal familism (Steven L. Hoch), and the repartitional land commune.[5] That is to say, in the question of exchange entitlements, the privileged position given by Brenner (along with most Soviet scholars) to class relations ignores key components in a highly integrated agrarian social system in which many forms of expropriation existed. Rural social relations fit much less readily than those created by industrial capitalism into the categories of class analysis, and dynamics of the Russian peasant family farm is an excellent example.[6] Familism, peasant self-exploitation, and mechanisms of land redistribution (where the latter existed) imposed strict limits on the manorial economy and determined the nature of class-based expropriation. Specifically, the redistribution of wealth in a patriarchal, household-centered, peasant society involves not merely master and serf, but serf over serf (or "free" peasant over peasant). This greatly complicates the problem of class relations.

It is surprising how much of the discussion of serfdom east of the Elbe, and especially for Russia, is phrased in terms of the key issues for Western Europe, especially what constitutes freedom. But Brenner's definition of freedom (or unfreedom), one often employed by historians, is but one kind and fails to address the relative freedom from destitution and the lesser vulnerability to Malthusian crises that Russian peasants enjoyed. In fact, being tied to the land is a much underrated notion; in Russia, from the mid-seventeenth century being a peasant (with few exceptions) implied an entitlement to land, which is not a bad deal, if you are subsistence-oriented. And, as we shall see, this was perceived by the state as such a good idea that the emancipation legislation of 1861, the so-called liberation of the serfs, would carry this even one step further.

The familistic practices of Russian peasant society were vibrant enough in the late imperial period (1861–1917) to lead "to the destruction of [rural] capitalism." In order to meet consumption needs, peasants "paid more for the land than the capitalized rent in capitalist agriculture."[7] Under serfdom, familistic and communal structures—whether they predated, coincided with, or arose as a response to the imposition of restrictions on the peasantry—proved to be major obstacles to manorial control. Lords by no means had complete control over the servile peasantry, especially regarding the intensity of serf labor, the disposition of productive resources, and peasant consumption norms and levels.

Manorial farming throughout the pre-emancipation period was small-scale peasant production, even where the primary intent of the lord was commercial cereal production.[8] The absence of large-scale estate production, the peasants' entitlement to land, and the lack of an essentially feudal infrastructure (coupled with the obvious lack of free wage labor) gave a very distinctive nature to servile relations in Russia. There was no struggle over commons, no conflict over traditional tenurial rights. Under the conditions of peasant family farming, decisions on employment and how to dispose of the land were not concentrated in a few hands. Peasants worked with their own inventory (implements, draft animals, and knowledge), and lords' fields were hardly distinguishable from those of the peasants. A consolidated demesne was less common than intermingled fields. Thus, the manorial factor in rural economic development (as opposed to commercialization of the manorial economy) was not significant. In other words, lords had little power to effect change in the structure of agricultural production, and they expressed little interest in agriculture itself, in spite of state-sponsored efforts to do so. For the lord employing compulsory labor, the result was what might best be described as high transaction (managerial) costs—benefits which ultimately accrued to serf patriarchs. Landlords needed a large number of intermediaries to compel the remaining servile population to work. The widespread practice of quitrent (*obrok*)—family farms resorting to the market to obtain money rents—further attests to the relatively competitive nature of the peasant household as the unit of production. Presumably, if quitrent were uncompetitive, no lord would have had recourse to this form of expropriation. Simply put, restrictions on movement in Russia did not have the same consequences of dependency as elsewhere. The peasant family farm survived largely intact.

Peasant goals in Russia were less to establish freehold control over the land (France) than to establish distributive mechanisms which reduced risk in an uncertain environment and limited the group most vulnerable to crisis by providing more equal access to productive assets. Nor were lords primarily interested in consolidation, creating large farms, and leasing them to capitalist tenants (England). Both Russian peasant and intramanorial society were remarkably free of those land disputes which seem at the heart of so many Western European rural communities. Perhaps rural Russia had come up with a solution to a problem which had so plagued Western Europe, one phrased in terms of land access or use and not in terms of rights. West of the Elbe, it was primarily land rights and disputes that fostered the development of mechanisms to address conflict. Resistance to seigneurial action and intrusion served to enhance peasant class power and heightened the political consciousness of the rural inhabitant, attributes barely visible among the servile population in Russia.

In much of servile Russia what was unique was that the land was mobile, not the population. Instead of family members moving in and out of the household through wage labor, sharecropping, tenancy, apprenticeship, or service in an attempt to adjust to changes in household composition and status, it was the land that moved around. This is in concert with the often noted weak sense of

property in Russian peasant society. But rather than lamenting this development as inhibiting the rise of freedom, capitalism, and bourgeois values, it
might equally be used as evidence that a vast legal system to ensure control of
productive assets was not required.

The periodic redistribution of land among households according to some
unit of consumption or production (adult males, married couples, or eaters—in
the aggregate it does not matter, demographically speaking they are all the
same) was more than a radical risk-reduction technique in a system of open
field cultivation. The egalitarian distribution of the key productive asset—the
balance of labor and land implied by the repartitional land commune—was the
optimal use of productive resources and necessarily maximized output irre-
spective of the structure of compulsion. Egalitarianism enlarged the total pie,
while leaving unaffected the conflict over the class distribution of goods. In addition, constant adjustment of a peasant family farm's access to land lessened
the pressure for migratory movements. Thus, one might reasonably argue, the
repartitional land commune facilitated fixing the peasant population in place,
a key goal of landlords in Eastern Europe, and especially in Russia with its low
population densities and the premium it placed on labor.

But the repartitional land commune came with high costs for lords. It was
even more resistant to rationalization and improvement than the simple open
field. With long-term capital improvements (manuring or drainage) unlikely to
accrue to the sufficient benefit of the peasant investor, the short-term intensity
of labor (proper and timely plowing, sowing, reseeding, weeding, harvesting)
became an even more significant factor in determining output than elsewhere.
This turned out to be a substantial constraint on the lord's ability to command
the fruits of servile labor. Equally, the movement of land, not people, created
greater familial stability—both structurally and in terms of membership. This
prevented Russian lords from taking much advantage of cyclical household
dynamics for arbitrary exaction (entry fines, exit fines) common in much of
the West.

Describing rural Russia as familistic implies not merely a peasant family
economy (Chayanov), but more importantly a social structure through which
authority was maintained, power distributed, and reward and punishment dis-
pensed. A patriarchal society at its foundation entails nothing more than the
movement of wealth and power away from the young and toward the old. With
the patriarchal structure which predominated in rural Russia, the household
(family) was more than anything else the unit of exploitation used not only
by the lord as a member of the political elite, but by serf patriarchs as well. A
patriarch sought to better his status not by claiming a disproportionate share
of wealth or productive resources in the village, not by competing with other

households, but by exploiting more efficiently the members of his own household. Status was defined by placement within the household, the ability to control economic and fertility decisions, and the power to maintain advantage over other household members.[9]

A high-pressure demographic regime upheld this familistic society. Peasant marriage in Russia was generally not dependent upon access to a relatively fixed number of units of physical capital, such as a farmstead. Population densities throughout European Russia were low. In any case, for peasants living in repartitional land communes (the vast majority), no such obstacle would have existed. Increasing evidence suggests there was remarkably little intrusion of the lord in serf marriage.[10] Thus, age at marriage and proportions married were more closely linked to the dynamics of the family farm than serfdom. Households were large. Three generations and multiple conjugal pairs lived under one roof and ate out of a common pot. An unusually high premium was placed on the reproduction of children not primarily to ensure elders adequate economic support in later years, but to provide them with a labor supply to exploit throughout their tenure as head of household. In turn, early and universal marriage and high fertility levels disabled the Malthusian preventive check (reduced fertility or a greater incidence of celibacy). With fertility being the primary determinant of the age structure of a population, the resultant high dependency ratios (the number of persons under 15 and 60 and over to the number 15 to 59) put yet another substantial constraint on the ability of the lord to extract wealth. Overall, therefore, the peasant family farm is best regarded as being the primary determinant of the rural economy, modified, to a greater or lesser extent, by serfdom.

The practice of land redistribution and the egalitarian distribution of wealth that resulted limited the accumulation of reserves and provided a substantial disincentive for capital investment. Coupled with the demographic patterns and social structures described above, they would, it seem, enhance the possibilities for increased poverty by creating a society highly vulnerable to economically positive checks (sudden sharp increases in mortality due to food shortages) and likely in the long term to overreproduce itself in relation to available resources.[11] But the evidence for rural increased poverty in Russia, in spite of all that has been alleged to the contrary, is quite weak. First, Russia had the largest output of cereals per capita in all of Europe, and contemporaries repeatedly complained of the constant overproduction of cereals.[12] Second, Russian cereal prices as measured by B. N. Mironov were chronically low when compared to Western Europe, even in spite of their rapid increase in the eighteenth and nineteenth centuries. It was only early Soviet scholarship which challenged this widely held view, when P. I. Popov argued Russia did not produce enough grain to feed the population. Subsequent historians of all persuasions have been ready to accept this dismal portrayal of Russian peasant society for reasons all too apparent. Both "Western and Marxist literatures explain that the Russian revolution was caused, in no small part, by the agrarian crises that plagued Russian agriculture."[13] But, in fact, pre-reform Russian agriculture was remarkably productive by European standards. Its productivity may have been low per unit of land—but too often we are fixed on this measure. Per capita output and availability were high; markets were distant and inaccessible. The late Jerome Blum, a leading scholar on the Russian peasantry, felt that these high levels of production were "needed to meet the deficiencies of bad years, and were carefully stored away for that purpose," a view shared by Kahan.[14] Subsequent assessments of Russian peasant diet have been even more favorable. To R. E. F. Smith and David Christian, "the dietary regime of nineteenth-century Russia was remarkably well-balanced. . . . It is the sort of diet to which some modern nutritionists are inclined to look with renewed respect." This broader statement confirms my earlier conclusions regarding the dietary regime of the serfs of Petrovskoe.[15]

The image of Russia suffering famine once in three years is surely incorrect, based as it is upon simplistic methodologies and inadequate sources.[16] Elsewhere in Europe even in the years of the worst national crises rarely were more than one-third of all parishes affected.[17] Work I am presently undertaking, which makes use of recently available Russian parish registers, suggests that in the eighteenth and nineteenth century an individual parish was likely to experience mortality levels 50 percent above the norm only once in eleven years. Of these crises, the majority appear wholly independent of harvest or grain price fluctuations. A doubling of mortality was an event visited on any parish only once or twice a century and more likely to be linked to those epidemic diseases where the nutritional state of the population was not a significant factor. As evidence, most mortality crises came in the late summer, suggesting that diseases spread by contaminated food and water rather than food shortage played the major role. Thus, subsistence crises were not only much less frequent than we have been led to believe, but were less severe.

Of much greater importance, it needs to be borne in mind that the Russian path to economic entitlement was structural, not institutional; social, not statist; and more peasant than manorial. Neither the state nor the manor invested much effort in survival mechanisms to respond to economic distress. For those who were left out, emergency grain reserves, almshouses, hospitals, dispensaries, and the like could rarely be found. Neither did the parish church play any significant role in poor relief. The basic response of Russian peasant society was to control access to productive resources. Institutional forms of assistance were not used. Though lords did distribute grain in times of dearth, the social order as embodied in the large, patriarchal family farm and the repartitional land commune rendered society structurally less vulnerable to subsistence crises.

All this did not impart to rural Russian society a strong sense of peasant community or class solidarity. Rather quite the opposite. Manorial intervention into Russian peasant society went through the intermediary of the patriarch, not the commune, in the vital day-to-day aspects of labor management and supervision. From the lords' perspective, patriarchy broke serf society into manageable units of control. To patriarchs, that is, the heads of peasant households, the fact that serfdom did not encroach upon their familial prerogatives and even enhanced their authority made them more amenable to collusion. Together they functioned in a "low maintenance" social system that by its fundamental structure advanced and protected their mutual interests. Each patriarch used familial structures to ensure he had a labor supply to exploit. Simply put, relations between serf patriarchs and lords were collusive, hedonistic, and cooptative. In Russia, cooperative exploitation was the result.

This image stands in sharp contrast to the prevailing view of a "traditionally antagonistic relationship" between lord and peasant.[18] It also helps to explain relative absence of peasant disturbances throughout the servile period.[19] Though Russian peasants may have evinced greater communal solidarity than American Negro slaves, as Kolchin argues, surely a better comparison would be with Western Europe, where peasant cooperation and self-government were generally more highly developed. Again, we have a very distorted picture here, largely the result of generations of Soviet scholars working on the so-called peasant movement. In this view, virtually any expression of unrest was assumed to be evidence of class conflict. But rarely was a distinction made between anti-autocratic protest and resistance to servitude. The ethnic dimensions or nonclass dimensions of many popular uprisings (so evident today) were simply discounted.[20] In the end, historians really ought to admit, with over 110,000 manors, twenty million serfs, and over 200 years of serfdom, we really have not found much.

The peasant social order not only survived serfdom, it outlived the state as well. Understanding the Russian autocracy as a strong/weak state helps explain the peasants' ability to resist manorial intrusion and prevent the restructuring of agrarian society. The autocracy may have monopolized political processes as understood in the traditional sense, but its ability to effect change, that is, the actual amount of power at its disposal, was small. The role of the state in the rural social and economic order was almost negligible. Throughout the servile period the state was forced to use landlords as its agents for the extraction of taxes, recruits, and government labor obligations. By the middle of the eighteenth century, the state no longer even sought to intrude in the regulation of lord/serf relations. The terms of servitude were negotiated between the two principal parties, and the state barely perceived itself as having independent interest or a separate role. At no point did the state ever seek to regulate the size of quitrent in order to ensure the viability of the peasant economy to pay state obligations. The manifesto of April 5, 1797, limiting labor obligations (*barshchina*) to three days per week, was, in fact, not a law but a suggestion and was taken seriously in only a few places.[21] Lords could have recourse to the state to control extreme deviance, but they lacked the force of the state behind them to compel a specific level of expropriation. In the vast world of servile relations (dues, obligations, commons rights, peasant inheritance rights, and forms of punishment) the state had little or no sense of what serfdom ought to be.

Indeed, I would argue that it was only in the middle of the nineteenth century that the autocracy decided to refashion rural society with state interests in mind, governed in part by a sense of what peasants should pay. The nobility were removed as agents of authority, and the autocracy regulated the terms of the peasants' financial and labor obligations. It attached the peasants to the land even more firmly than serfdom had done to ensure them a way of life, which it hoped would improve. The state divided power between itself and the peasantry, believing it had removed the nobility as a political authority in the countryside.

The serfdom that developed in Russia was particular and local, the function of a vast array of negotiations between lords and peasants. Serfdom was not a system, but a widely varying set of practices. There appears little uniformity among serf estates in the obligations owed masters. Within the same *uezd* (the smallest administrative unit) per capita quitrent could vary by factors of twenty or more.[22] Much less is known about labor obligations, but what we do know from actual manorial records reveals that the situation was substantially more variable and complex than is suggested by the widely accepted notion of three-day barshchina. We need to consider if such a wide spread is more likely explained by flexibility and negotiability than unbridled manorial power.

Studies on postemancipation levels of labor intensity have revealed that peasant "farm families possess considerable stocks of unutilized time. Accordingly, labor intensity rates, not being fully utilized, can fluctuate one way or another."[23] In Tver', in the early twentieth century, in only two months of the year, June and July, did the average working day exceed eight hours (9.3 and 9.1 hours respectively) and in eight months of the year averaged less than 6.5 hours. Research on peasants from Tambov, Iaroslavl', and Moscow provinces reached similar conclusions. "*In the [peasant] labor farm, rates of labor intensity are considerably lower than if labor were fully utilized.*"[24] Therefore, there is no necessary reason to assume that increases in the level of expropriation (under serfdom or capitalism), especially by elites interested primarily in income, necessitated fundamental structural changes in the peasant family mode of production.

Russian peasants were not merely premodern and precapitalist, they were prefeudal. This is what distinguished the second serfdom. Peasants lived a viable moral economy that proved resistant to feudal and capitalist attempts at restructuring its modes of production. Resistance was not political, in the usual sense of institutional and legal, and rarely communal. The fundamental moral principle was not fair prices or fair exaction, but fair access. Familism is a dependency which does not readily relate to traditional notions of freedom. At times, it was a dependency of great emotional and economic benefit; at times, a tyranny far worse than any class-based expropriation or repression.

If the implicit assumption in historical analysis is to be development, especially capitalist development, then rural Russian society will not measure up under any circumstances. But to favor interpretations of capitalist development is to ignore the vibrancy of the peasant family farm and the significance of the practice of land redistribution. The peasant family farm controlled the intensity of its labor and its allocation of labor resources. Periodic redistributions of land kept the key productive asset in balance with a family's labor capability. These familistic policies and land-use practices coupled with the observed demographic regime constricted class-based expropriation. It cannot be denied that the rise of serfdom meant the extraction of substantial wealth from the peasantry by the nobility. But it was not "the structure of class relations, of class power" that determined "the manner and degree to which particular demographic and commercial changes" affected "the distribution of income and economic growth."[25] Neither was it a neo-Malthusian homeostatic mechanism that was the motive force in Russian rural development—a population expanding beyond the means of subsistence and brought in check by war, famine, and disease. Brenner is clearly right that it does not all come down to population densities, the supply and demand for land and labor.

Russia did not follow the path of France (complete property rights and underdevelopment) or England (the obverse), nor Prussia or America for that matter. Russia took the path of class collusion, weak village solidarity, structural constraints on access to productive forms of wealth, and, most importantly, the peasant family farm. This did not lead to capitalist development, but neither did this lead to the development of underdevelopment. Russian history cannot be conceptualized in terms of the debate on the transition from feudalism to capitalism. Nor did Russian peasant society, resilient as it was to the imposition of external exploitative constraints, preclude agrarian development. In those parts of Chayanov's book few historians read are detailed "the family farm as a component of the national economy and its possible forms of development."[26] Vertical cooperative concentration, as Chayanov hoped, never came about. But, regardless of what came, the most thoughtful observers of Russian rural society—those members of the Organization and Production School—firmly believed something very different could have occurred. In the end, peasant self-exploitation, familism, and land redistribution practices fashioned the conditions of rural society until the early 1930s. The social order did indeed matter.

Notes

1. Roger Schofield, "Family Structure, Demographic Behavior, and Economic Growth," in *Famine, Disease, and the Social Order in Early Modern Society* (Cambridge, Mass., 1989), 279.

2. R. H. Hilton, "Introduction," in *The Brenner Debate: Agrarian Class Structure and Economic Development in Pre-Industrial Europe* (Cambridge, Mass., 1985), 1–2.

3. Robert Brenner, "Agrarian Class Structure and Economic Development in Pre-Industrial Europe," in *The Brenner Debate*, 26. Originally published in *Past and Present* in 1976.

4. Brenner's definition of unfreedom. Brenner, "Agrarian Class Structure," 26.

5. A. V. Chayanov, *The Theory of Peasant Economy*; and Steven L. Hoch, *Serfdom and Social Control in Russia, Petrovskoe, a Village in Tambov* (Chicago, 1986).

6. Robert G. Moeller, "Introduction," *Peasants and Lords in Modern Germany* (Boston, 1986), 5.

7. A. V. Chayanov, "On the Theory of Non-Capitalist Economic Systems," in his *The Theory of Peasant Economy* (Madison, Wis., 1986), 28. Originally published in 1924.

8. Michael Confino, *Systèmes agraires et progrès agricole: L'assolement triennal en Russie aux XVIIIe–XIXe siècles* (Paris, 1969).

9. Hoch, *Serfdom and Social Control*, 128.

10. John Bushnell, "Did Serf Owners Control Serf Marriage? Orlov Serfs and their Neighbors, 1773–1861," *Slavic Review* (Fall, 1993) 52:419–45; Hoch, *Serfdom and Social Control*, 91–132.

11. R. H. Hilton, "A Crisis of Feudalism," in *The Brenner Debate*, 123.

12. Jerome Blum, *Lord and Peasant in Russia from the Ninth to the Nineteenth Century* (Princeton, 1961), 332–33. In contrast, Paul R. Gregory, *Russian National Income* (Cambridge, Mass., 1982), 154, estimates per capita grain output in Russia in 1861, at the very end of serfdom, to be 79 percent of the level in France, 70 percent of the level in Germany, and 95 percent of the level in Austria-Hungary. It should be noted that Russia at this time, unlike Germany or France, exported relatively small amounts of grain. In addition, official published figures for Russia and subsequent attempts to correct them remain in all

likelihood underestimations of actual levels, especially for the period before 1885. See Hoch, *Serfdom and Social Control*, 30–36. Finally, Gregory's actual figure for Russia of 0.561 metric tons of per capita grain output, even after allowing for seed and feed, would still support a favorable cereal-based dietary regime.

13. Paul R. Gregory, *Before Command: An Economic History of Russia from Emancipation to the First Five-Year Plan* (Princeton, 1994), 36.

14. Blum, *Lord and Peasant*, 333; Arcadius Kahan, "The Tsar 'Hunger' in the Land of the Tsars," in *Russian Economic History: The Nineteenth Century* (Chicago, 1989), 116.

15. R. E. F. Smith and David Christian, *Bread and Salt: A Social and Economic History of Food and Drink in Russia* (Cambridge, 1984), 287; and my "Serf Diet in Nineteenth Century Russia," *Agricultural History* (April, 1982), 391–414.

16. See, in particular, Kahan, "The Tsar 'Hunger'," in *Russian Economic History*, 138.

17. John Walter and Roger Schofield, "Famine, Disease and Crisis Mortality in Early Modern Society," in *Famine, Disease, and the Social Order*, 59.

18. Brenner, "Agrarian Class Structure," 51.

19. Peter Kolchin, *Unfree Labor: American Slavery and Russian Serfdom* (Cambridge, Mass., 1987), 241–301.

20. Marc Raeff, "Pugachev's Rebellion," in *Preconditions of Revolution in Early Modern Europe*, Robert Forster and Jack Greene, eds., (Baltimore, 1970), 161–202.

21. Blum, *Lord and Peasant*, 445.

22. A. Ia. Degtiarev, S. G. Kashchenko, and D. I. Raskin, *Novgorodskaia derevnia v reforme 1861 goda: Opyt izucheniia s ispol'zovaniem EVM* (Leningrad, 1989), 147–98; and S. G. Kashchenko, *Reforma 19 fevraliia 1861 goda v Sankt-Peterburgskoi gubernii* (Leningrad, 1990), 159–94.

23. Chayanov, *The Theory of Peasant Economy*, 75–76.

24. Chayanov, *The Theory of Peasant Economy*, 75–76. Italics in the original.

25. Brenner, "Agrarian Class Structure," 11.

26. Chayanov, *The Theory of Peasant Economy*, 224–69.

9

Institutionalizing Piety

The Church and Popular Religion, 1750–1850

Gregory L. Freeze

————···◆◆◆···————

A LTHOUGH INSTITUTIONS HAVE long been a preferred subject of research in
Russian historiography, that scholarship has focused primarily on an institution and its servitors, not on its larger meaning in Russian society and culture.[1] That historiography may tell a great deal about a particular institution, about bureaucrats and their memoranda, but precious little about an institution's impact through the implementation and reception of policies. In particular, scholars have failed to consider the development of the Russian Orthodox Church (status, structure, and organizational culture) and its interaction with society. It is important not only to know how an organization grew and whom it employed, but how it interacted with the population in its charge, and how that interaction reverberated back on the institution itself.

Not surprisingly, the antiquated literature on the Russian Orthodox Church has done little to illuminate its impact on society and state.[2] Although recent research has begun to fill the gap on institutional history (organizational development, episcopate, parish clergy, seminary and educational system, and relationship to the secular state),[3] it has done little to explore the social and cultural impact of the Church on the daily lives of ordinary believers. Above all, it is vitally important to consider how "institutionalization" (transformation of the medieval Church into a centralized, rationalized, and professionalized organization) affected popular religion, which had hitherto been left to its own devices. Many contemporaries, especially parish clergy, looked askance at the Church's institutional development and believed that this "bureaucratization" (most visibly in the status and role of the bishop) had a devastating impact on the Church and its relationship to the laity.[4] That view, highly charged by the conflict between the white and black clergy, was more accusation than argument; empirical research is still lacking to determine how the Church's institutional development impacted religious belief and behavior. Did the institutional Church effectively counteract, or counterproductively accelerate, or indeed have any impact on the processes of religious change? In particular, how did the specific pattern of institutionalization in the Russian Church affect religious life at the parish level?

This essay draws upon a broad variety of printed and archival sources to make a preliminary survey of this complex, unexplored terrain.[5] It will first examine the meaning of institutionalization in the Russian Orthodox Church: its impulses, dynamics, and limitations. It will suggest that the specific pattern of institutionalization in the Church—the radical changes in its structure, status, and functional role—created a separate ecclesiastical realm called the *dukhovnoe vedomstvo* ("spiritual domain") in official jargon. From the 1740s, as this organization expanded and specialized, it undertook a concerted attempt to reshape religious life at the parish level.[6] That campaign was multifaceted; it included positive efforts to catechize, preach, and teach the fundamentals for a more self-conscious cognitive Orthodoxy.[7] But there was also a salient negative dimension: a determination to purge the unorthodox and unseemly, to contain the sacred within the walls of the parish church, to erect a boundary to separate the "spiritual domain" from the profane. This campaign, which in effect aimed to "institutionalize" piety, represented the first systematic attempt to regulate popular Orthodoxy. This essay proposes to consider how the assault by "virtuoso" Orthodoxy affected its "demotic" undergirding, and how that confrontation in turn impacted the Church itself.

Institutionalization and the Church

At first glance, it might seem bizarre to suggest that so ancient and prominent an element of medieval Russia might even admit to "institutionalization." In fact, however, the Muscovite Church—like the state—lacked essential components of a modern institution; its rudimentary organization displayed the same backwardness, the same particularism that was so characteristic of state administration in pre-Petrine Russia.[8] As a formal macro-institution, the Church was a juridical imaginary; in strict organizational terms, the pre-Petrine Church was an aggregate of several immense, de facto autochthonous dioceses, each a realm unto itself, with scores of monasteries and thousands of parishes, all littered across the broken Russian terrain. Although establishment of the patriarchate in 1589 in theory might seem to herald a "centralization of the Russian Church" (like that of the state), this, in fact, did not ensue. Instead, the patriarch reigned over his vast "patriarchal region" (*patriarshaia oblast'*, a super-diocese), exercising only nominal supervision over the other bishops and diocesan administrations.

And within both the patriarchal region and the dioceses, the hierarchs and their staffs simply lacked the means to exercise close control over religious life in the parish. They did not, in particular, even have local agents to represent their interests and impose their will. Rather, the primary link between bishop and parish was the "priestly elder" (*popovskii starosta*), an office only established in the sixteenth century and limited to ensuring the delivery of parish dues (*dannye den'gi*).[9] That fiscal function of course explains why the Church, like monocratic authorities in the civil sphere, allowed the "democratic" election of elders by their peers: such elections were of course designed not to express collective will, but to impose collective responsibility (*krugovaia poruka*). As a result, the election was a kind of surety, entailing the obligation to make restitution if the elder for any reason failed to deliver the assessments.[10]

Although bishops were hardly indifferent to the religious needs and foibles of their flock, before the mid-eighteenth century they did not make a significant, institutionalized attempt to reconfigure religious life at the grassroots. Had they sought to do so, they would have been foiled by the lack of administrative instruments and religious parish clergy to execute their will.[11] In addition, most bishops lacked the sheer time and opportunity to reform popular piety, especially in dioceses where the episcopate and monasteries owned a large number of populated estates with church peasants. Although the cultural and educational profile of bishops changed substantially under Peter the Great and in following decades,[12] before mid-century most bishops took only sporadic interest in combating popular superstition, deviance, and heterodox religious practices. They did not file regular reports to the Holy Synod in St. Petersburg and, like their forebears in Muscovy, were preoccupied with managing the immense church properties in their charge.

That benign neglect of parish religious life began to wane in the 1740s, as Church authorities in St. Petersburg began to restructure Church administration and to redefine its function and role. In many respects, this represented a resumption of the Petrine reforms, which had prescribed much but had changed little, especially at lower levels. This second Petrine revolution aimed to construct a separate, efficient ecclesiastical domain; the goal, as in Peter's reforms, was not to make the Church a "department of the state," but an efficient organization capable of overseeing and regulating religious life.[13] The Church thus underwent a new phase of institutionalization that, seeking to extend centralized ecclesiastical control over dioceses and especially parishes, consisted of four main processes: (1) synodalization; (2) professionalization; (3) specialization; and (4) bureaucratization.

"Synodalization" meant an entirely new level of ecclesiastical centralization, as the Synod changed from a remote authority (with nominal, episodic supervisory functions) into an active overseer of diocesan administration across the empire. Whereas the patriarchate *volens-nolens* had to concentrate on managing the vast patriarchal region directly under his jurisdiction, his successor—the collegial Synod—became an organ seeking to provide centralized, integrated governance for the Church. Although that status had been formally adumbrated in the Ecclesiastical Regulation of 1721, the Synod did not in fact assume this role until mid-century.[14] Henceforth, an ever-more-exacting Synod came not only to dictate empire-wide policies but also to provide close supervision over diocesan administration. By the 1770s the Synod formally institutionalized this oversight, mandating approval for diocesan resolutions, requiring annual reports and data, and dealing harshly with obdurate prelates who flouted its orders or ignored its authority. It now had both the means and the will to oversee diocesan administration and thus ensure standard empire-wide policy.

"Professionalization" refers to the significant improvement in clerical education and training, which now became the principal factor in shaping the careers of bishops and priests alike. Prior to the 1760s, seminaries remained minuscule in size, poor in quality, and vulnerable to frequent closings; thereafter, however, for the clergy they meant a significant, steady rise in their formal education and training, which, indeed, now became the primary factor in recruitment and career advancement, not only for bishops but also for parish clergy. Despite Peter's imperious injunctions, seminaries remained minuscule in size and subject to frequent closings before the 1760s; thereafter, however, they acquired stability, more complex curriculum, and above all ever-growing enrollments. As a result, by 1800 some formal education became a prerequisite for appointment as priest; a half-century later only candidates with a full ten-year course of training had any chance of becoming a priest.[15] Formal education of course had a still greater impact on the episcopal élite;[16] although some bishops were still recruited on the basis of "spiritual charisma," the most successful and influential were those who could fit into the enlightened world of St. Petersburg.[17] The new episcopate also internalized many attitudes of the Aufklärung[18] and modeled their own behavior after the "enlightened" rule in the secular domain.[19]

"Functional specialization" resulted from fundamental changes in the status and role of the Russian Orthodox Church in the course of the eighteenth century. Peter the Great not only circumscribed ecclesiastical authority in many secular matters (e.g., by assigning all civil offenses to state courts), but also specifically affirmed ecclesiastical authority in "spiritual matters." Hence, in the strictest literal sense, the Church became a "spiritual domain" (*dukhovnoe vedomstvo*); its array of powers had been narrowed, but absolutized within that "spiritual" sphere. The secularization of Church estates provided a further, still more powerful impulse to redefining the institutional role and identity of the Church. Initiated by Peter the Great and consummated (after many zigzags) in 1764, the confiscation of populated estates left the Church impoverished, yet better able to focus on its purely spiritual duties.[20] In that sense, secularization accomplished what Catherine the Great (even if hypocritically) had promised: it freed the bishops to concentrate on their spiritual mission. The reorientation was already apparent in ecclesiastical documents (preliminary memoranda by diocesan bishops) and the Synod's "instruction" (*nakaz*) for its deputy to the Legislative Commission in 1767. Although these documents addressed a broad range of issues, three-quarters of the text was devoted to problems of popular religious life.[21]

"Bureaucratization," which (in the nonpejorative Weberian sense) brought a rationalization of administrative structures and practices, simply mirrored parallel developments in the state. Despite the negative connotations of this term (especially among Church historians and publicists deeply influenced by Slavophile antibureaucratic sentiments),[22] bureaucratization significantly enhanced the control that Church authorities could exercise over religious life in the parish. For a variety of reasons (including state fiat and institutional isomorphism),[23] the Church gradually adopted the methods and norms of state administration, from paperwork to the routines of office work. These changes gave the Church a more elaborate, rationalized structure, with the functional specialization and the modus operandi of a modern organization. Diocesan administration lost its erstwhile patriarchal ambience; a consistorial board, armed with a regiment of clerks and a regular budget, assisted the bishop in exercising close supervision over monasteries and churches in its domain.

Most significant still, the bishops labored to extend their power from the diocesan capital to the parish. One essential step was to create a new lower-echelon office, that of the *blagochinnyi* ("superintendent"). In effect, the bishops replaced the elective clerical "elder" with the superintendent appointed from above; the latter was to concentrate specifically on upholding orthodoxy and good order (*blagochinie*, hence the title *blagochinnyi*) in the ten to fifteen parishes under his wardship.[24] Moreover, by the late eighteenth century, the bishop usurped the right to select and remove priests (previously a prerogative of the parish), significantly enhancing his power over parochial clergy and, indirectly, the parish itself. Finally, by the early nineteenth century, the Church mandated the election of a lay "church elder" (*tserkovnyi starosta*) in order to tighten diocesan control over parish funds.[25]

To be sure, one must not exaggerate the import of the above processes and changes, especially at the parish level. Administrative flat and episcopal wish did not automatically, or easily, become translated into reality. Thus the qualitative improvement in administration had its limitations, especially on the periphery, but even in central Russia, where it still suffered from significant deficiencies in structure, funding, personnel, and the like. More important still, the configuration of the "ecclesiastical domain" imposed serious limitations on the Church's authority over lay believers. The laity, in effect, belonged to the "secular domain" of the state, which alone was to prosecute and punish for civil offenses and, indeed, virtually anything that transpired outside the premises of the parish church. Hence the Church's power gradually contracted from parish community to parish church; although the Church still claimed authority in certain instances (for example, public penance), even in these spheres its role steadily declined, especially in the nineteenth century.[26] Thus the critical issue was whether, and how, the Church—armed with new ambitions and administrative tools—would seek to reconfigure popular piety.

Standardizing Orthodoxy

Russian Orthodoxy was Russian Heterodoxy—an aggregate of local Orthodoxies, each with its own cults, rituals, and customs. Religion, like other dimensions of life, was intensely particularistic, with kaleidoscopic variations from one parish to the next, not to mention broad regional differences. Each parish had its own traditions (icon processions, special services, favored saints, and the like), icons of particular reverence (sometimes with miracle-working properties), and unique forms of religious observance. Even the liturgy itself varied from parish to parish, as local clergy arbitrarily omitted "superfluous" sections of the full monastic service to reduce it to manageable proportions. From the mid-nineteenth century, as parish clergy began to compile "historical-statistical descriptions" of their parishes and professional ethnographers began to map out this complex world of popular religious behavior, the result was a mind-boggling kaleidoscope of what was ostensibly a common faith and common ritual.

This diversity was profoundly inimical to Church elites. As bearers of virtuoso Orthodoxy, they were disposed to equate irregularity with deviance or, at best, to assume the presence of some abject form of ignorance and superstition. Just as secular elites sought to establish empire-wide norms in law, administration, and social organization, ranking prelates endeavored to impose the same "imperial norm" on Orthodox religious life. While that regulatory ethos was hardly new, it was only from mid-century that bishops had greater opportunity and better instruments to superimpose central norms on local religion. This attitude informed the "instructions" to the superintendents and the everyday preoccupation of diocesan administration as it sought to purify popular piety and religious practice.

Given the configuration of the "spiritual domain" and the spatial and social parameters of its authority, the Church naturally had its greatest success in matters that pertained directly to the parish church and its material contents. The building itself was entirely under the control of ecclesiastical authorities (even in remote Siberia)[27] since the construction of new churches, or even the renovation of established ones, required the prior consent of diocesan authorities. The Church also took vigorous measures to ensure that the parish church was properly maintained and outfitted—on pain of closing the church and reassigning parishioners to another parish.[28] In the late eighteenth century, bishops systematized such control by enjoining their new corps of superintendents to inspect parish churches on a regular basis and to report any that were not properly maintained and cleaned.[29]

Similarly, Church authorities came to exercise closer control over the material possessions of parish churches—altars, icons, vestments, and the like. For instance, to enhance the aesthetics and dignity of churches, prelates demanded that parishes, even rural ones, replace the traditional pewter with silver vessels.[30] Despite the exorbitant costs, especially for poor parishes, most eventually complied; by the late eighteenth century, for example, only 4 percent of the parishes in Vladimir had failed to acquire silver utensils.[31] The bishops displayed a similar concern about icons in the parish church and were particularly distrustful of "ancient icons"—i.e., any that antedated the schism and might therefore include "schismatic" representations (for example, the two-fingered crossing).[32] Apart from mandating regular inspections and reports from the ecclesiastical superintendent, in the early nineteenth century the Church routinized its control by requiring each parish to compile an annual parish record, the *klirovye vedomosti*.[33] These reports included not only the service records of the local clergy, but also a systematic inventory of parish property and material possessions.

To ensure good order in the parish, Church authorities sought to control not only parish property, but also to regulate the religious rites performed there. Above all, that included a vigorous attempt to regulate and standardize religious services. At the most rudimentary level, the Church took measures to ensure parish observance of major holidays (secular as well as feast days), not merely by publishing a schedule of mandatory services, but also meting out draconian punishment to priests who failed to comply. It also prescribed a fixed time for church services, not only to ensure a standard order, but also to countermand capricious demands by peremptory noble landowners. As a result, any deviations for services (including matins) required prior authorization from the bishop.[34] The Church also took special measures to strengthen piety and observance in urban parishes. In particular, it began to require that city priests perform liturgies on a daily basis, not merely on Sundays and major holidays. For the sake of order and precedence, it also promulgated schedules to regulate bell-ringing in cities and, thereby, avoid the cacophony of competing and overeager bell-ringers.

In the same vein, the Church sought to ensure that each parish had all the requisite panoply of proper liturgical books. Amazingly enough, a century after the outbreak of the schism, the Church was dismayed to discover that many parishes not only had "ancient" icons but were also using old liturgical books, including some that antedated the Nikonian reforms. Although the Church had expressed concern about the old liturgical books earlier,[35] only in 1772 did it launch a systematic program to supply parishes with freshly printed volumes. The campaign ensued after the Synod ordered a full inventory of printed materials in each parish and was horrified to learn that "in many dioceses not only rural but also city churches" had old texts or even lacked some essential texts altogether.[36] Altogether, according to data for twenty-seven dioceses, parishes needed to receive a total of 85,138 volumes. Needs varied widely, from just several hundred in some dioceses to 15,033 in Kiev diocese; the situation in Suzdal diocese, which reported a need for nearly 4,000 volumes, was more typical.[37] The Synod thereupon ordered its typography in Moscow to print and distribute the required volumes.[38]

But when the Church endeavored to regulate religious services, not just buildings and books, it encountered far more significant difficulties and, especially, popular resistance. For a variety of reasons, the prelates therefore ignored the ubiquitous practice of unauthorized "abridgments" in the parish performance of the liturgy.[39] And when the bishops *did* dare encroach on religious practice, they encountered resilient opposition from below. That was perhaps most apparent in their attempts to standardize liturgical music so as to emulate the style prevalent in élite circles of St. Petersburg, which were profoundly influenced by Western (specifically Italian) models. Although the Synod first published a book of music texts (*obikhod*) in 1722, many parishes in fact continued to use manuscript texts as their guide. Not until 1797, at the behest of Paul I, did the Synod direct the parish to observe standardized printed texts and embark on a campaign that, over the next decades, aimed to make the new music standard in parish churches.[40] Significantly, however, the new liturgical music provoked resistance from parishioners, who disliked the new "Western" music and preferred the traditional—and heterogeneous—forms. To explain and persuade laity of the merits of the changes, in 1816 the Synod published a book-let, *Historical Reflection on Ancient Christian Liturgical Singing*.[41] Metropolitan Nikanor of St. Petersburg emphasized the strength of popular opposition and demanded that a Synod decree of 1846—forbidding the introduction of unau-thorized church music—be strictly enforced.[42] The issue generated growing con-troversy in high church circles in the mid-nineteenth century, when the director of the court choir, A. F. L'vov, attempted to mandate use of his own texts, which purported to revive ancient choral music, but actually modernized it. The result was a vigorous protest against the "innovation" and, especially, parishioners' displeasure with the unpleasant sound of the new music.[43]

It proved still more difficult to tamper with matters involving popular rev-erence, especially icons. Apart from "ugly" icons that offended the sensibili-ties of Church authorities,[44] the chief problem was "miracle-working" (*chudot-vornye*) icons. While such miraculous claims were not problematic in the case of icons that had been officially recognized as such, the Church was highly skeptical about reports of new icons with claims to such properties. The stan-dard procedure was to order a full investigation (for the explicit purpose of com-bating "superstition") and to punish anyone (above all, parish clergy) found guilty of deliberate fraud.[45] A case involving an icon at the Monastery of St. Boris and St. Gleb (Pereslavl' diocese) was typical. After receiving reports of mi-raculous cures by an icon, the bishop ordered a full-scale investigation; because the claims of prior illness were not substantiated, and because the monastery was found to reap huge revenues from hopeful pilgrims, the bishop ordered that the icon be confiscated and placed in storage at the diocesan cathedral.[46] Even without demonstrable fraud, bishops were inclined to expropriate the "miracle-working" icons in order to avert more rumors and outburst of popular super-stition.[47] For example, in a typical case from Iaroslavl' in 1823, a serf woman had dreamed of an icon (currently in storage at the parish church); after clergy ac-ceded to popular requests and put the icon on public display, it was immediately credited with performing miraculous healings. Such reports soon attracted such throngs of people ("of every rank") that diocesan authorities decided to confiscate the icon.[48] Similarly, after receiving reports of two "weeping" icons in Kishinev in 1822, the local bishop ordered an investigation to determine pos-sible fraud. Although he found no evidence of deliberate deception (the mois-ture had apparently dripped onto the icons by accident), the Synod directed that he confiscate the icon to discourage popular rumors and stories of new miracles.[49]

However well intentioned, the seizure of parish icons—predictably—met with determined resistance from below. In some measure, parishioners had sim-ple economic motives: it was no easy matter for poor parishes to replace icons deemed unaesthetic by diocesan experts.[50] But the most resilient resistance concerned ancient and, especially, miracle-working icons that the parishioners deemed to be a vital link to the divine, and hence their main hope for intercession and aid. Although most hierarchs acted with due circumspection, anxious to avoid any direct confrontation with obstreperous parishioners, they frequently encountered tenacious resistance. Thus, in one case in Pereslavl' diocese, where the bishop had confiscated an "ugly" icon in 1759, parishioners not only resisted but for years continued to file suits demanding its return.[51] More remarkable still was another case from Vladimir diocese. After diocesan authorities "arrested" a miracle-working icon in 1785, angry parishioners fired an endless salvo of petitions demanding its restitution; in 1919, amidst revolution and civil war, that same parish was still badgering the patriarch and central Church authorities to return the icon.[52] Sometimes, indeed, this grassroots opposition prevailed, especially if the parish included an influential nobleman with the right connections in St. Petersburg.[53]

Some believers resorted to violence, not mere petitions, to defend that which they deemed to be sacred. In 1785, the bishop of Vladimir ordered the local superintendent to seize an icon in Viazniki that was reputed to have miraculous qualities. The hapless cleric, however, met a firestorm of parish fury:

> In accordance with the order of Your Grace, we [the superintendent and another priest] went to the church on 2 May and, after unsealing the church, handed the icon to the local priests [to carry out]. However, as soon as we exited from the church with the icon, a huge throng of peasants from that parish surrounded the icon, refused to let us take it any farther, and took it away from us by force. Under the circumstances, the priests were forced to return the icon to the church, put it in its former place, and (in accordance with your order) to reseal the church.[54]

In some instances, popular resistance resulted in actual disorders that could only be suppressed with force.[55] Such violent confrontations doubtless had a sobering effect on parish clergy, effectively deterring them from overhasty denunciations of parish "superstition." As the bishop of Voronezh explained, the clergy's nonfeasance was largely due to their "fear of popular disorders."[56]

Tensions also exploded when the Church attempted to assert control over "unofficial" saints, i.e., figures of local veneration but as yet lacking canonical recognition by the Church. Whereas the Synod routinely recognized reports of miracles through the intercession of "official" (formally canonized) saints, it reacted quite differently to similar reports involving the plethora of "local saints," who were deeply revered by local populace (in a parish or diocese), but not officially recognized by the Russian Orthodox Church. Invariably, the Church exhibited considerable skepticism toward "saints" and miracles that had purportedly transpired through their intercession; such skepticism was all the more intense if there were grounds to believe that the clergy were exploiting the relics for personal gain. From the perspective of Church authorities, the principal concern was to avoid bestowing legitimacy on such objects of popular veneration, especially through special services conducted by local clergy. In particular, the Church acted to investigate any special services held to honor the local venerables. That was especially true when such services (for instance, a requiem in honor of locally revered persona) had uncertain origins and used local liturgical texts for special services in their honor. For example, when the Moscow Synodal Chancellery learned in 1745 that one monastery held special rites to commemorate a local saint, it immediately launched a full-scale investigation. When diocesan authorities were unable to explain the origin of the service (and could only identify the reputed author of the service text as a "certain Grigorii the Meek of Suzdal"), the Moscow chancellery ordered a learned archimandrite to review the text carefully and verify its orthodoxy.[57]

Apart from reviewing formal services conducted in the parish church itself, the Church found that it could do little to control what or whom the parishioners chose to venerate. Indeed, it even had difficulty assembling systematic information about local saints and miracle-working icons. Thus, when the Synod directed bishops in 1744 to compile systematic information on local saints and their miraculous relics,[58] diocesan authorities had little information on the matter. The bishop of Pereslavl', for example, knew of only three such relics;[59] the bishop of Vladimir had information on only one such site—the grave of Koz'ma Iakhrinskii, which was popularly venerated and the object of a special requiem every October 14, but never the source of "any kind of phenomena or healing from illness and ailments."[60] Information usually bubbled to the surface accidentally—as, for example, happened in Pereslavl' in 1766, when one church was found to have relics (pieces of cloth, allegedly from the mantle of various saints) that were the focus of special services by local clergy.[61] The remains of a local saint was reported to have similar powers; only long afterwards did the consistory learn of special requiems held to invoke divine intercession at her gravesite, which "continues to enjoy great reverence among the people" right into the twentieth century.[62]

The tension between Church and parishioner surfaced whenever the laity requested formal rites of canonization—and hence official legitimation—for local saints. Without exception, Church authorities proceeded with extreme caution that often bordered on outright skepticism. Not without cause: the presence of miraculous relics was a sure guarantee of a steady stream of pilgrims and therefore revenues. Furthermore, canonization was a complex process; above all, it required proof of "miracles" (usually cures) that demonstrated the saint's power to intercede between God and man. It also, customarily, entailed a belief in the incorruptibility of the remains.[63] Altogether, the Church canonized four men between 1751 and 1861, but in each case only after a protracted and intensive investigation of the purported miracles.[64] The Synod's abiding skepticism was amply demonstrated in the case of St. Tikhon (Sokolov) of Zadonsk. Even when the petition emanated from a nobleman (who proposed in 1798 to exhume Tikhon's body, presumably to verify rumors that his earthly remains were intact), the Synod summarily refused.[65] Nonetheless, Tikhon continued to be the source of numerous miracles, especially after his coffin was opened in the mid-1840s (during a general renovation of the cathedral containing his crypt) and his body proved to be intact and his clothing fully preserved.[66] The local office of the Third Section duly reported to St. Petersburg that Tikhon's remains were the focus of "a powerful religious movement" in the region.[67] Nevertheless, Church officials in St. Petersburg remained skeptical; when Archbishop Antonii of Voronezh (responding to local pressure) reiterated a proposal in 1846 to canonize Tikhon, the Synod—with the emperor's approval—flatly refused.[68] Another fifteen years would have to pass before Tikhon was finally given the rites of canonization—not accidentally, in 1861, amidst the tumult of serf emancipation, when political intent could hardly have been more transparent.

Most such applications, at least until the early twentieth century,[69] were rejected. A typical example is afforded in a case from Tver' diocese in 1838, when the local and influential prelate—Archbishop Grigorii (Postnikov)—received reports that the remains of two venerables, Sergii and Marfa, were purportedly discovered beneath a church in a local monastery. That rumor sufficed to unleash a stream of pilgrims to the monastery: "People of various social stations began to gather at the monastery in large numbers, with the apparent expectation that the remains of the monk Sergei and the nun Marfa would be exhumed for inspection on their nameday." It required vigorous, aggressive action by the bishop to disperse the laity and avert rumors and petitions to secure the canonization of the pair.[70]

Secluding the Sacred

The tension between official and popular Orthodoxy was still more intense when the Church attempted to "confine the sacred"—temporally and spatially—within the ecclesiastical domain. In part, its goal was to shield the sacred from profanation or misappropriation by the superstitious and Old Believers. But seclusion also conformed to the contours of the ecclesiastical domain, the sphere of competence where Church power was unequivocal. By containing the sacred within that sphere, the Church could safeguard the holy and assert its own authority, untrammeled and unmediated.

But secluding, even more than standardizing, brought the Church into direct conflict with pious laity. It was, after all, one thing to regulate church services, subjects clearly within the competence of the Church; it was quite another to control the sacred outside the perimeter of ecclesiastical space. Inevitably, any attempt by the Church to usurp the sacred would antagonize if not alienate pious believers; secluding was tantamount to desacralizing the secular space outside, to removing the sacred (with all its powers of aid, succor, and intercession) from the temporal domain. It meant not only a "de-churching" (*Entkirchlichung*) of secular society, but also denied the laity direct access to the power of the sacred. It was a policy certain to offend lay sensibilities.

Nevertheless, parallel with efforts to segregate the clergy itself from the worldly,[71] the Church sought to confine the sacred—and to exclude the profane—within the spiritual domain. One method was to confine the sacraments to ecclesiastical territory by requiring that such rites be performed *only* in the parish church. This sentiment partly underlay the Church's antipathy toward élite chapels (*domovye tserkvi*) in aristocratic residences as well as votive churches and chapels scattered across the landscape: all these were virtually immune to outside control and subject to the whims of the laity. Instead, the Church demanded that the sacraments (and things sacred) be confined within the perimeter of a church or monastery. In the most rudimentary sense, this policy applied to sacred objects (for example, the Elements used in Communion)[72] and the sacraments themselves. Marriage, for example, was to be held only in the parish church and during specified hours; the aim was not only to satisfy canon law but to avoid any illegal marriages (because of such factors as age and kinship).[73] A similar policy applied to baptism. Although it sometimes made exceptions (for example, in the case of feeble infants in the depths of winter), it generally mandated that the christening be performed in a parish church, not at home.

Church authorities sought not only to keep the sacred inside the parish church, but to keep the profane out. This applied, in the first instance, to the parishioners themselves, who were strictly forbidden to enter the altar and indeed urged to keep at a respectful distance from the iconostasis itself. In part the Church was simply enforcing canon, especially the rule forbidding laity to traverse the iconostasis and enter the altar; the rule was especially categorical for women.[74] The Church also forbade any secular use of the parish church. As the hub of community life in earlier times, it had quite naturally filled a number of functions, even serving as a community bank, but from the mid-eighteenth century bishops sought to eliminate that secular role. For example, one bishop received disturbing reports that "parishioners in the churches of Pereslavl' and [the surrounding district], when marriages are performed in those churches, bring to the church from home (as an indecent habit of commoners) spirits and beer, which, upon the conclusion of services, they drink in these holy churches." Castigating priests who fail "to prevent parishioners from such disgraceful conduct," the prelate categorically forbade such celebrations in the future.[75] In general, overtly exuberant celebrations tended to generate major disorders and immoral conduct, and the Church enjoined priests to dissuade parishioners from indulging in such festivities.[76] Ecclesiastical authorities also forbade even more genteel activities; in 1853, for example, the Synod banned concerts of secular music inside churches.[77]

Moreover, the Church sought to exclude profane behavior during services and to require that parishioners behave with proper decorum during services. Such policies had antecedents in pre-Petrine exhortations,[78] but institutionalization enhanced the Church's power to expose and combat lay misconduct during church services.[79] It was of course no simple matter to control lay conduct inside the parish church, especially in the case of those with a higher social rank. Some laymen vigorously resisted; when, for example, a priest in Moscow tried to silence a noisy parishioner, the latter caused even more commotion and accused the priest of starting a brawl.[80] Popular resistance impelled the bishop of Vladimir to complain in 1779 that priests were loath to punish rowdy parishioners out of "fear that, for so doing, they will suffer not only oppression and insults from all these parishioners, but even physical beatings."[81] Nevertheless, Church authorities adamantly insisted that parish priests strictly enforce these rules on conduct, even in the face of obstreperous and influential parishioners.[82]

The Church was particularly vigorous in prosecuting and punishing those who caused a disruption in the Holy Liturgy. That policy of course had ample precedent in the medieval Russia; the *Sobornoe Ulozhenie* of 1649 even prescribed capital punishment for such crimes.[83] Although the Church did not mete out so drastic a penalty, it did subject violators (especially clergy) to vigorous prosecution for causing a disruption (or, worse still, interruption) in the performance of a sacrament, above all, the divine liturgy. Although cases involving hapless clergy were most frequently reported (to obtain Synodal approval for a decision to defrock the offender),[84] the Church also took action against laymen, even prominent ones, accused of disruption. Reports of such "incidents" *(proisshest-viia)* became automatic after 1818 at the behest of Alexander I; although the order was triggered by cases of clerical misconduct, the ensuing reports included instances of lay disruption as well.[85] The latter, however, were liable to secular courts and, for all practical purposes, not directly accountable to ecclesiastical courts. In a typical case from 1831, the bishop of Minsk recounted how, in the midst of a divine liturgy, "a Cossack lieutenant *(sotnik)* Dem'ian Vibishchev, standing near the iconostasis, seized the book of the New Testament and struck it across the head of the nobleman Vasilii Shpakovskii, which caused a commotion in the church and brought the service to a halt." In such cases, the Church could make representations to secular authorities, but had to leave final disposition of the case to the latter.[86]

Given the residual power of parishioners and the limitations on ecclesiastical authority over the laity, it was exceedingly difficult for the Church to maintain sanctity and to prevent or punish laity for disrupting services. Significantly, the obligatory reports on "incidents" routinely declare that in an entire diocese everything "is in good order" and devoid of scandals and misconduct. Such reports reveal much more about ecclesiastical power than the actual state of affairs. Similarly, ecclesiastical archives contain relatively few files on the notorious tradition of *klikushestvo*, the outbursts of hysterical "shrieking" by women in a fit of religious ecstasy. Ever since the Ecclesiastical Regulation of 1721, the Church had been expressly enjoined to combat the phenomenon; the instructions to clerical elders in the 1740s, for example, despite its focus on financial matters, included an order to be vigilant for shriekers and to report them immediately.[87] While some "shriekers" were occasionally prosecuted,[88] such cases were extraordinarily rare; files about them appear but rarely in the vast archives of the Synod and diocesan consistories. Not that the phenomenon itself was rare; for example, the private notes of the well-informed traveler, August von Haxthausen, reported in 1844 that shriekers had "infected entire villages" in Voronezh diocese.[89] Evidently, the parish clergy—fearful of retribution by angry parishioners—turned a blind eye and simply declined to report the offenders.

Nor were Church authorities very successful in isolating the church from the pernicious influence of the ubiquitous tavern *(kabak)*. The latter, as bishops constantly complained, represented a major problem: the tavern competed with the church for the parishioners' attention and resources, and it also emitted a din of drunken shouts and cursing that interfered with the liturgy in nearby churches. In 1817, Archbishop Evgenii (Bolkhovitinov) of Pskov gave this graphic description of the problems caused by local taverns:

> they sometimes lead to the theft of church property by drunks, and quite often they give rise to disgusting shouts, dancing, quarreling, fighting, and sometimes even murders. As a result, especially on Sundays and holidays, there is (apart from the spiritual harm) considerable disruption in the performance of church services.[90]

Similarly, in 1851 Archbishop Gavriil (Rozanov) of Tver' complained about one tavern in the diocesan capital that was situated a mere 50 meters from a parish church; not only were rubbish and broken glass constantly cast into the church-yard, but during services on Sundays and holidays "one constantly hears a clamor, shouting, singing, bickering, and cursing of the drunken peasants who gather around the tavern."[91] The Synod first began to complain about such prob-lems in the 1740s, when it compiled massive data to show that the problem was pandemic, afflicting thousands of churches. Thereafter it made repeated at-tempts to have such taverns relocated and to require that they remain closed until the conclusion of church services.

Its efforts, however, met with little sympathy on the part of state authorities, who were plainly more fearful of endangering an important source of state revenues than causing disruptions in church services.[92] As a result, the Church was only able to prevail when it could demonstrate unequivocal legal grounds (e.g., cases where the tavern had been constructed in violation of its license).[93] The one point when the Church enjoyed more substantial success came in the reign of Alexander I, whose government—in the wake of the Napoleonic Wars— showed a heightened degree of religious sensibility and proved more accommo-dating on this issue.[94] Emboldened by the more favorable response, the Church was subsequently able to force 59 percent of the most grievous offending taverns (1,390 of 2,363) to relocate.[95] At the same time, the state also approved a Synod proposal to ban the sale and consumption of spirits until church services had been concluded.[96] In subsequent years, however, the state returned to a staunch defense of its own fiscal interests and resisted such attempts by the Church to inhibit the operations of tavern owners.[97]

The Church was still less successful in combating sacrilegious behavior on Sundays and religious holidays. Perhaps the most interesting case involved Bishop Tikhon (Sokolov) of Voronezh (the future St. Tikhon Zadonskii), who made a concerted effort in the 1760s to ban the "carnival" preceding Lent. He castigated parishioners for drunkenness on major holidays and ordered clergy to exhort their flock to avoid such "disgraceful and immoral" behavior during carnival, especially its last four days. He claimed that the peasantry, because of their "crude mentality," regarded carnival—not Lent—as the chief holiday sea-son and impatiently awaited the onset of secular festivities, which they then observed in an unchristian, immoral fashion. Speaking as "a son of the father-land" and in the name of "utility and salvation of sons of the fatherland, my brothers," Tikhon proposed an outright ban on carnival. However, the Synod, conscious that secular conduct lay outside ecclesiastical competence, not only refused to confirm Tikhon's proposal but even reproved him for intemperance, declaring that the Church must teach through example and precept, not edict.[98]

Nor was the Church able to repulse another major challenge: economic activities (especially fairs and bazaars) and work on Sundays and religious holidays. Despite long-standing decrees to observe the Sabbath,[99] most rural markets in fact were held precisely on these days, when the laity (especially peasants) were free to travel and engage in trade. Bishops were primarily concerned that such commerce diverted parishioners from church services, and some added the warning that it also led to much drunkenness, merrymaking, and sin.[100] Such complaints began to surface in the 1740s,[101] and by the 1770s Church authorities were attempting to persuade the government to restrict commercial activities on Sundays and holidays.[102] The menace, and episcopal concern, steadily mounted in the early nineteenth century. In 1835, for example, Bishop Arsenii Moskvin (later the influential metropolitan of Kiev) lodged a vehement denunciation of the marketplace and its pernicious effect on popular piety:

> On the occasion of the establishment of bazaars on Sundays in the cities and villages, both the parishioners and people from surrounding settlements are enticed away from church services (for various reasons). This naturally results in a marked cooling toward the faith (together with a decrease in church revenues), the ruination of morality, deviance into various sects, or at the very least disorderly conduct in churches by those who come in a state of inebriation (since on these days the taverns are usually open before and during the liturgy).[103]

A few years later, Bishop Vladimir (Alavdin) of Kostroma warned that the problem had steadily worsened and cast blame on the local squires: "If these fairs arose in Kostroma only twenty years ago, and did so spontaneously (without any decree from authorities), then it is just the serf-owning squires who support these [fairs] in order to gain more profit on workdays." His plea, like those in coming decades, fell on deaf ears: the local governor refused to prohibit the fairs for fear of harming trade in the province.[104]

In sum, Church authorities made a vigorous attempt to demarcate "sacred space"—to keep the holy inside, the profane outside church territory. The "spiritual domain" had not only a distinct juridical status, but also its own space and time: sacraments, icons, and all things spiritual belonged exclusively to that sacred sphere. Even within this sphere, however, the Church encountered serious difficulties, not only because of the secular state (which acted in its own interests), but also because of pious laity. The latter refused to recognize such boundaries and clerical claims to hold a monopoly on the sacred; the believers had their need to possess and control those sacred objects that could bring miracles of divine intercession and assistance.

The Sacred in Secular Space

If the Church had difficulty regulating religious life inside the parish church, it faced a far greater challenge from the sacred outside those boundaries—that is, the holy objects or holy persons outside its spatial jurisdiction. The attempt to contain the sacred within the ecclesiastical domain inevitably brought the Church into direct confrontation with pious laity, who were loath to recognize the Church's monopoly over the sacred. Above all, popular Orthodoxy emphasized the fundamental immanence of the divine, not merely inside the walls of the sanctuary or monastery, but all across the temporal landscape as well. Therein lay the awesome puissance of the divine, its capacity to perform miracles and to intercede through a timely rainfall, miraculous hearings, and the like. Moreover, parishioners could invoke the mantra of tradition: the Church had long recognized the need to sacralize the landscape through special rites, icon processions, and other invocations of divine intercession.[105]

In the case of some material objects of popular veneration, such as the miraculous appearance of "springs" with special curative powers, the Church had no compunction about taking aggressive measures. In 1748, for example, diocesan authorities in Suzdal responded promptly to reports that parishioners had discovered such a spring, whereupon they immediately erected a post with icons and induced clergy to intone special services.[106] Such natural miracles included substantial material gifts, as parishioners donated clothes, canvas, wool, flax, eggs, wax, money, and other valuables as a sacrifice. To avert fraud and deter superstition, both secular and Church authorities cooperated closely in doing whatever appeared necessary to combat such phenomena. A report from Minsk in 1843 affords one highly instructive case. Rumors about a tree that seemed to resemble an icon ignited a massive influx of believers (from "various social ranks") in search of a miraculous cure. To deter pilgrimages to an unauthorized religious site, diocesan authorities induced state officials to have the tree cut down. Even that drastic step had scant event: "The people are not dissuaded, but rather come in huge throngs from fifty or more versts to the stump that remained from the felled tree, not only on Sundays and holidays, but also on weekdays."[107]

As for the campaign against transporting the sacred into the temporal, the bishops could hardly dare to be so imperious and had to exercise considerably more caution. It, therefore, still authorized traditional rites to solicit divine mercy, but preferred that they be performed inside the church—for example, as a special prayer service against natural calamities like drought or epidemics.[108] But in the eighteenth century it showed a strong and growing aversion to such rites, above all, the traditional icon process that served to bless the landscape and its inhabitants. Like their peers in Western Europe,[109] Russian bishops feared that such processions would expose the holy to profanation and sundry scandals. As the bishop of Pereslavl' complained in 1767, the clergy leading such processions "permit the commoners to sing needlessly artificial and seductive songs in an indecent manner and to indulge in other popular superstitions, [which is] contrary to the law and [evokes] ridicule among the non-Orthodox." He also berated the clergy for avarice, asserting that they conducted such processions only to collect donations for their own material benefit.[110] And once the procession left ecclesiastical territory to roam through the parish, city, rural districts, or even an entire diocese,[111] the Church had no authority or means to ensure orderly conduct and the security of holy objects.

As a result, the eighteenth-century Church made a concerted effort to restrict and regulate such processions. Although it had made sporadic attempts to do so earlier,[112] it launched a systematic campaign only in the mid-eighteenth century. At first, ecclesiastical authorities simply took special measures to ensure good order—for example, directing that soldiers be present to avoid "any disruptions,"[113] or directing the clerical elder to ensure that "there be no disorders and disruptions in this spiritual ceremony."[114] The Synod issued a decree in 1767 requiring that icon processions in Moscow have the explicit authorization of the Synod and local prelate, and that spontaneous processions, organized at the caprice of local priests or parishioners, no longer be tolerated.[115]

The turning point came after the tumultuous events surrounding the bubonic plague of 1771 in Moscow, when crazed throngs—enraged by the Church's decision to seize a popular icon—ran amuck and murdered the local archbishop.[116] This affair redoubled the bishops' distrust of lay piety, especially if left uncontrolled in the public sphere. In the wake of the Moscow riots, the Synod ordered a full-scale inquiry into icon processions and, to its dismay, found an apparent proliferation of "unauthorized icon processions in addition to those rooted in tradition and permitted by superior authorities."[117] For the next several decades, the Church tolerated some major "ancient" processions (such as the famous trek from Bogoliubovo Monastery to the diocesan capital of Vladimir, a distance of some 10.5 versts), but systematically spurned lay requests to allow new ones. In typical cases from Riazan' diocese in 1814 (requesting permission to hold a procession to commemorate the salvation of Riazan' from Napoleonic forces two years earlier) and Kazan' in 1833 (to reestablish an earlier procession), the Synod rejected such petitions outright.[118]

These attempts to discourage icon processions provoked unyielding opposition from the laity, who stubbornly continued to arrange processions on their own authority. Such obduracy was even true in the city of Moscow; as the diocesan consistory complained in 1773, parish clergy—in flagrant contravention of orders from above—continued to hold processions with crosses and even icons, which were exposed to filth and inclement weather. Implicitly acknowledging the power and will of the parish, the consistory tactfully ruled that the processions might take only crosses (not icons) and reminded participating clergy to refrain from consuming alcoholic beverages themselves.[119]

Another major concern of Church authorities was the phenomenon of miracle-working icons *outside* churches and monasteries. One problem was "weeping" icons, which mysteriously began to shed tears and immediately became the focus of popular veneration and miracles.[120] More common and problematic were the "newly manifest icons" (*novoiavlennye ikony*), the miracle-working icons that magically appeared on the landscape and began performing healings. Since such icons were outside the Church's "sacred space," they were automatically a source of abiding suspicion that popular superstition, or clerical fraud, were involved. And not without cause: hierarchs often had good reason for such skepticism.[121] As a result, from the 1740s the Church waged an unrelenting struggle against "newly manifest icons" and any cleric who abetted popular veneration of them.[122] Such cases ordinarily led to a formal investigation, interrogation of witnesses, and punishment of clergy found to have collaborated in legitimizing such miracles.[123] For the clergy, failure to denounce and dissuade was a crime of nonfeasance; a priest in Vladimir, for example, was fined and imprisoned for one month in a monastery for failing to report and preach against a newly manifest icon.[124]

The cardinal features of "virtuoso Orthodoxy" were clearly evident in a case from Kherson diocese in 1829. On 13 March, the consistory received reports that tears had miraculously appeared on an icon in the home of a serf. The consistory immediately ordered that, "to ensure that there be no superstition because of [the people's] simplicity, or because some kind of fraud might be involved here," its agents and civil authorities were to make a careful investigation of the circumstances. It further directed that the icon itself be confiscated and admonished local clergy not to legitimize popular faith in the icon. Although the investigation revealed nothing amiss, and although the serf's master petitioned to have the icon returned, the bishop put the icon in permanent storage at the diocesan cathedral in order to avert any danger of "popular superstition."[125]

Despite resolute measures, especially to punish clergy for complicity or nonfeasance, the "miracle-working icons" continued to sprout with disconcerting regularity and to exert a powerful hold on believers. A report from Metropolitan Serafim (Glagolevskii) of St. Petersburg in 1837, about an incident in Iamburg District, is instructive. As usual, the initiative rested with a layman, who had seen a vision in his dreams that led him to find a "newly manifest icon." Despite these suspicious circumstances, he persuaded the local priest to conduct a special prayer service in veneration of the icon. Rumors about the icon, reinforced by the priest's apparent approval, sufficed to attract huge throngs of believers. The metropolitan promptly had the icon confiscated (although, for fear of popular resistance, this was done "without any publicity") and ordered a full investigation of the priest who had performed the prayer service.[126] In 1848, the bishop of Saratov reported about a similar "miraculously appearing" icon, which also attracted crowds of people from a broad range of social groups throughout the region—striking testimony to the enormous power and resonance of sacred icons in secular places. Authorities seized the icon and investigated its discoverer (a female parishioner), who purportedly concocted the case to solicit "donations"; she was eventually convicted of fraud and given a lashing as punishment.[127] That same year, after a young female visionary in Perm' diocese found another such icon (followed by the usual torrent of rumors and miraculous cures), the bishop sternly admonished local clergy not to comply with lay requests for special services to honor the icon.[128] Despite the strict prosecution of clergy and even laity, believers continued to find "newly manifest icons"—a powerful sign of divine immanence and intercession for believers but a cause of intense concern and skepticism for the clergy.

There was also a dark side to popular piety: "magic" and "sorcery." Here too the bishops had limited authority: although they could deal summarily with the clergy (who were fully subordinate to the spiritual domain),[129] they could do little with laity. In the mid-eighteenth century, they still had some vestige of their former power,[130] but that authority declined sharply in the ensuing decades. As a result, prosecution and punishment thus lay with civil authorities, not the Church. This became particularly evident after the establishment of the "conscience court" (*sovestnyi sud*) in 1785; henceforth it was only on special occasions that the guilty appeared before ecclesiastical authorities and suffered some form of monastic incarceration as a form of public penance.[131] Unless such incidents directly affected the parish church, they were simply outside the jurisdiction of ecclesiastical courts.

Similarly, there was little that the Church could do with respect to "lay spiritual figures"—classically, in the form of "fools-in-Christ" (*iurodivye*). Popular orthodoxy had a long tradition of veneration for the fools-in-Christ, who were known and revered for their renunciation of the world, their fusion of the insane and inane. Secular and ecclesiastical authorities, however, took a dim view of such figures, both because they were blamed for disrupting church services and because they appeared to represent nothing more than indolence and fraud.[132] Nevertheless, like the "shriekers," such lay figures rarely appear in Synodal or diocesan records. Although some bishops required the clergy to sign an oath to combat "superstition" in any form, including both "miracle-working icons" and fools-in-Christ, these directives had no discernible effect.[133]

Accommodating Popular Piety

Significantly, by the early nineteenth century the Church began to show signs of a new attitude toward popular piety. In contrast to the "enlightened" prelates in the second half of the eighteenth century, their successors in the nineteenth proved increasingly receptive to displays of unofficial, "demotic" Orthodoxy. Although they still railed against the laity's staggering ignorance and still sought to make the faithful understand as well as believe, the hierarchs showed a greater willingness to countenance and coopt popular Orthodoxy. In part, no doubt, the shift was a recognition of reality: the Church could not regulate popular Orthodoxy, especially its manifestations outside the church-yard. Indeed, from the outset, bishops were dismayed and often frightened by the fierceness of popular resistance to their attempts to purify the flock. That was apparent, for example, in the case of Porfirii (Kraiskii), who, immediately after becoming bishop of Suzdal in 1748, launched a vigorous campaign to ex-tirpate superstition and deviance. Within three years, however, Porfirii balefully conceded defeat and pleaded for permission to retire to a monastery: "It must now be conceded that [all my efforts] did not have the slightest effect, that the pastoral exhortation and spiritual correction has not had the least success: the power of Satan continues to dominate daily life, with virtually the same force."[134] Over the coming decades, in the face of violent opposition and endless petitions, even willful prelates were tempted to take the line of least resistance. In 1848, for example, Metropolitan Filaret (Drozdov) of Moscow decided not to confiscate a weeping icon "so as not to further inflame popular feelings and not to arouse hostile judgments."[135]

More important, by the early nineteenth century ranking prelates came to question whether they even *should* tamper with popular piety. In part, this shift in sentiment reflected the more conservative religious atmosphere of the post-Napoleonic era, when elites believed that—whatever its shortcomings—piety was a fundamental pillar of stability and a bulwark against the scourge of revo-lution. To this was added a powerful, special concern in Russia: incontrovertible evidence of an explosion in the number of Old Believers and sectarians. Al-though the data are notoriously unreliable and incomplete, they nonetheless provided alarming evidence of a sharp increase in religious dissent.[136] Faced with this monumental threat, Church leaders not only adopted special measures to combat dissent,[137] but also inclined increasingly to coopt, not combat, popular Orthodoxy.

An early indication of the shift came in the case involving a popular saint in Vologda, Prokopii Ust'ianskii. After his death in 1627, Prokopii soon became the object of local veneration and the source of miracles, especially after exhumations (in 1696 and 1739) purportedly showed that his remains were uncorrupted. Although the Synod repeatedly spurned petitions for an official canonization, in 1818 the local bishop renewed the effort and, with the emperor's permission, exhumed Prokopii's remains once more to verify their incorruptibility. Although the examination in fact revealed some signs of decomposition,[138] the fact that the body did not emit foul odors affirmed a traditional sign of saintliness. More important, the bishop noted that four thousand believers had signed a petition to the emperor requesting canonization, and he further emphasized that both the Orthodox Church and the faithful had, "from ancient times, accepted, respected, and revered shrines of our fatherland." To secure the emperor's support, the prelate slyly noted that "this will serve as new and convincing proof of Divine Favor for the happy reign of His Imperial Majesty." Most interesting of all, the bishop stressed that canonization would be useful in combating the schism, which of late had shown new signs of strength: "When these remains are everywhere proclaimed to be holy, when a number of people assemble to bow down before them, then these daily examples of piety will be emulated, and contact with knowledgeable people (by exerting their influence) will doubtlessly return them to the bosom of the Holy Church."[139]

The treatment accorded lay holy figures also reflected a cautious, but significant shift in Church policy. Even so stalwart a figure as Metropolitan Filaret (Drozdov) of Moscow, who was generally skeptical of reports about miracles and opposed their publication in the press, came to exhibit greater sympathy for popularly venerated figures. In 1836, for example, Filaret filed a report about popular veneration for a "holy fool and pilgrim" Evsevii, a layman who had resided in Moscow since 1815 and had died while at Strastnyi Monastery. Huge crowds attended his final rites:

> During the funeral services for him on 31 May and during the transport of his body to Simonov Monastery for interment, the gathering of people was again extremely large and accompanied by special reverence for the memory of the deceased. The reason for this, it must be said, is the view that beneath the external strangeness of his behavior was a life pleasing to God and the gift of prophecy. He was known for his lack of avarice and malice.[140]

That same year, Bishop Nikodim (Bystritskii) of Orel reported that the death of a seventy-five-year-old female anchorite, Melaniia Panfilova, had triggered an enormous reaction among the local population:

> Both during her burial and afterwards, the flow of people was enormous, with transparent zeal for the deceased. This zeal has magnified over time; many ill people came to Melaniia's grave and held requiem services. Some were allegedly cured. On 20 July, on the fortieth day after her death, amidst a multitudinous gathering of people, the mayor of Elets (Kholodovin) arrived and interrogated those who had been cured.

The bishop himself launched his own investigation and, from the abbess at the monastery where she died, learned that the anchorite had lived for fifty years in the convent, but had never taken monastic vows; when she died in poverty and total seclusion, she became a central focus of veneration among the local populace.[141]

Even the Holy Synod, which generally took a far more cautious attitude toward such matters,[142] showed some signs of accommodation. For example, the case of a "holy pilgrim Simon" came before the Synod in 1837, and it too involved the mass flocking of believers to a gravesite. It was rumored that candles burned there nightly; popular fervor escalated when a "self-manifesting icon" miraculously appeared and local clergy obligingly performed a liturgy to celebrate the event. Although the Synod hastened to have the miraculous icon confiscated and stored under seal at the diocesan cathedral, it acceded to popular veneration for Simon by authorizing the clergy to conduct a requiem (with the admonition not to exploit the faithful for material gain).[143]

At the same time, the Church made a vigorous effort to reaffirm the miraculous powers of icons officially recognized as miracle-working. In 1836, for example, Metropolitan Filaret of Moscow reported that a peasant woman, suffering from "possession by demons," was miraculously cured by the icon of the Kazan' Mother-of-God in Simonov Monastery.[144] More interesting was the Church's reaction to the attempt by state censors to suppress publication of news about such wondrous events. One telling clash occurred in 1853, when *Moskovskie vedomosti* carried reports about a miracle that occurred a decade earlier at the Ordyn' Monastery in Smolensk diocese. According to the published account, amidst prayer services for rain, 475 barges inexplicably stopped on a nearby river, within sight of the monastery—evidently a miracle and sign of divine power.[145] When a state censor took exception to the report, the Synod testily responded that the people all believed in the veracity of the event and had expressed their gratitude through generous gifts to the monastery. To question the event now, it added, "could offend Christian feelings," as if the government itself had doubts about the miracle.[146]

The Church took a similar view with respect to reports about miracles credited to the intercession of *officially recognized* miraculous icons and saints' relics. Apart from routinely filing reports about such events,[147] in the 1830s the Church even began to disseminate official accounts of them. In 1833, for example, it received reports about a young female peasant from Tobol'sk, who had journeyed across the empire to pray before a national shrine—the miracle-working icon of Mother-of-God in Pochaev Monastery in Volhynia diocese (the icon being named after a manifestation of the Virgin Mary there in 1340). According to the local prelate, the woman showed "obvious signs of the ailment of being possessed by evil spirits," for her fits of screaming and self-flagellation sharply increased "in the presence of the miracle-working icon or the relics of God's saints." After attending several prayer services before the uncorrupted remains of Iov (a revered former abbot of the monastery), however, she was suddenly healed—like many others before and after her.[148] Even the Synod, normally circumspect in such matters, hastened to have the report published in the journal of the St. Petersburg Academy, *Khristianskoe chtenie*.[149]

Perhaps most revealing of all, the Church showed a new tolerance for public icon processions. Ironically, the turning point was the fearsome cholera epidemic of 1831: pestilence, which had triggered a stricter policy earlier, now drove the Church toward a more accommodating policy.[150] To be sure, at times it still exercised caution; the same year, the Synod rejected a petition from Olonets diocese, ignoring the bishop's attempt to justify the procession by invoking the specter of "schism."[151] Nonetheless, in general the Synod itself approved and even sponsored well-organized, seemly public processions and ceremonies. Thus, amidst the famine of 1841, for example, the Synod ordered special services after Easter "beseeching grace for those who till the soil" and ordered village priests "to hold icon processions into the fields."[152] The shift also found reflection in ecclesiastical literature; a small brochure by a student at the élite Moscow Academy, for example, staunchly upheld icon processions on both canonical grounds and their practical usefulness in stimulating lay piety.[153] In 1848, the Synod again invoked public services to combat a new cholera epidemic.[154] Afterwards, the Synod suddenly began to receive an avalanche of petitions to hold annual processions to commemorate the miracle of divine intercession that had saved their community from pestilence in 1848. In most cases, the supplicants first obtained the approval of the local bishop and governor, who attested to the strength of popular will and the sufficiency of police measures to ensure good order during the processions.[155]

Although such concessions were fraught with risk and ambiguity, they reflected a growing sense of the need to coopt popular Orthodoxy, to bring the worldly—and believers—into the Church rather than to drive them away. This also corresponded to a fundamental shift in theology, one based on a new Christology and emphasizing the need for the Church and Orthodoxy to reshape rather than exclude the this-worldly.[156]

Conclusion

This essay has explored the attempt by the Russian Orthodox Church, armed with a more elaborate and efficient apparatus, to assert control and to regulate popular Orthodoxy. In the first instance, it demonstrates how "institutionalization" conformed closely to the parameters of the "spiritual domain" (*dukhovnoe vedomstvo*); it affected primarily the church and clergy, but to a far lesser degree the laity, who were outside the perimeter of the ecclesiastical sphere. The Church had its greatest influence within the space and time demarcated as "spiritual" and hence within its purview. Hence it could exercise maximum control over its own sphere; even here, however, its authority over the laity was narrowly circumscribed, even for transgressions within sacred space and time. And of course it had far less influence over religious life in the secular world outside its domain. In that sense, the peculiarity of Russian institutionalization was not that institutions failed to develop, but that they failed to penetrate the infrastructure and that they tended to vertical pillars, with specific populations and powers.

Second, the reformation from above met with powerful, intractable resistance from below—sometimes in the form of violent disorders (to prevent the confiscation of miraculous icons), but usually through evasion, dissimulation, and disinformation. It is tempting to suggest that, even if institutionalization did not foster dechristianization (by questioning miracles and encouraging a *popular* consciousness of the gap between the sacred and profane), it did promote dissent. The vertical pillar of the ecclesiastical domain, a small cylindrical shaft from the Synod to the parish church, left the parishioners on the outside. This pattern of institutionalization, in essence, constituted an inadvertent kind of "de-churching" of popular religion, which the official Church could neither reconfigure nor suppress. It is surely no accident that precisely this period of institutionalization also coincides with an explosive growth in Unorthodoxy— Old Belief and sectarianism; confessionalization (which defined, in quotidian religious observance, what was Orthodoxy and what was not) generated not only community but also dissent, as individuals became cognizant of what they did, or did not, believe. It was in the face of parish resistance and religious dissent that the Church was ultimately driven to change course and attempt to coopt popular piety.

Notes

1. That kind of research was long dominant in Russian historiography, partly because of the pervasive influence of the state school (*gosudarstvennaia shkola*), partly because institutions systematically preserved their records, thereby greatly facilitating research. Inspired by the myth of autocracy and right-wing Hegelianism, the state school made the history of the Russian state tantamount to the history of Russia; hence it was only natural to focus on state institutions. But even historians wont to deny the power of the state have been driven toward institutional history by the force of archival exigency: formal institutions bequeathed rich legacies of paper, making them easier targets of research. That was especially true in the pre-perestroika era, when access and research conditions—especially for foreign scholars—were severely restricted. Institutional history has remained the focus of much important scholarship, but in a modified and modernized form (for example, the prosopographical studies of those who served in these institutions, as in the pioneering work on the bureaucracy by P. A. Zaionchkovskii and Walter Pintner).

2. Compared to the voluminous modern scholarship on secular institutions, research on the Church is abysmal; even the old-fashioned institutional approach is in a primeval state of development. To be sure, prerevolutionary historians compiled numerous "institutional studies"—e.g., the T. V. Barsov series on the Synod, F. V. Blagovidov's work on the chief procurator and parish schools, P. V. Znamenskii's and B. V. Titlinov's monographs on seminaries, and countless antiquarian chronicles of individual dioceses, seminaries, missions, and parishes. For an inclusive bibliography, see Igor Smolitsch, *Geschichte der russischen Kirche*, 2 vols. (Leiden and Berlin, 1964–91).

3. Significantly, research virtually ceased for decades after 1917; only in recent years have Western and, more recently, Russian historians resumed research, although primarily within the parameters of the traditional focus on organizations and servitors.

4. For a classic denunciation of such "bureaucratization," see I. S. Belliustin, *Description of the Clergy in Rural Russia*, ed. G. L. Freeze (Ithaca, N.Y., 1985).

5. Apart from a complex of printed sources (diocesan gazettes, sermons, official publications, and private documents of clergy and believers), this essay is based primarily on archival sources. The principal Church archives include several central collections, chiefly those in Rossiiskii gosudarstvennyi istoricheskii arkhiv (hereafter RGIA) and Rossiiskii gosudarstvennyi arkhiv drevnikh aktov (hereafter RGADA). These have been supplemented by diocesan-level materials from provincial archives in St. Petersburg

(Leningradskii gosudarstvennyi oblastnoi arkhiv [hereafter LGOA]), Moscow (Rossiiskii gosudarstvennyi istoricheskii arkhiv g. Moskvy [hereafter RGIAgM]), Vladimir (Gosudarstvennyi arkhiv Vladimirskoi oblasti [GA Vladimirskoi obl.]), Kursk (Gosudarstvennyi arkhiv Kurskoi oblasti [hereafter GA Kurskoi obl.]), Kiev (Tsentral'nyi gosudarstvennyi istoricheskii arkhiv Ukrainy [TsGIAU]), Tver' (Gosudarstvennyi arkhiv Tverskoi oblasti [hereafter GA Tverskoi obl.]), and Odessa (Gosudarstvennyi arkhiv Odesskoi oblasti [hereafter GA Odesskoi obl.]). Archival notation follows the standard Russian practice: fond (f.), opis' (op.), god (g.), otdelenie (otd.), stol (st.), delo (d.), dela (dd.), list (l.), listy (ll.), oborot (ob.)

6. For the sake of clarity, "Church" refers to the total institution, "church" to a concrete parish.

7. See Gregory L. Freeze, "The Rechristianization of Russia: The Church and Popular Religion, 1750–1850," *Studia Slavica Finlandensia*, 7 (Helsinki, 1990): 101–36.

8. For pre-Petrine church administration see I. M. Pokrovskii, *Russkie eparkhii v XVI–XIX vv., ikh otkrytie, sostav i predely*, 2 vols. (Kazan', 1897–1913); I. Perov, *Eparkhial'nye uchrezhdeniia v russkoi tserkvi v XVI i XVII vv.* (Riazan, 1862); I. I. Shimko, *Patriarshii kazennyi prikaz* (Moscow, 1894).

9. Significantly, the election certificates of elders expressly stated that they were chosen "for the collection of the fixed assessed dues" (RGADA, f. 235 [Kollegiia ekonomii], op. 2, d. 6436, l. 5; op. 4, g. 1703, d. 187, d. 87, ll. 1–2). For details see Perov, *Eparkhial'nye uchrezhdeniia*, 106–10; V. Samuilov, "Desiatil'niki i popovskie starosty," *Tserkovnye vedomosti*, 1900, no. 35: 1393–96.

10. For the elder's duties, see the "Instruction" from Patriarch Adrian in 1697 in *Polnoe sobranie zakonov Rossiiskoi Imperii, 1-aia seriia* [hereafter PSZ(1)], 45 vols. (St. Petersburg, 1830), 3:1612. With good reason, the bishop of Suzdal complained in 1751 that subordinate officials simply confine themselves "to the collection of money from [priests] and pay no attention to their behavior and the sanctity of the church." *Opisanie dokumentov i del, khraniashchikhsia v arkhive Sviateishego Sinoda* (hereafter ODDS), 31 vols. (St. Petersburg, 1869–1916), 4:515.

11. The unreliability of the parish clergy derived primarily from their lack of formal education and from their economic dependence on parishioners. For typical data on the abysmal educational standards of priests in Vladimir and Pereslavl' dioceses, see V. Travchetov, "Delo o bogoprotivnom sne," *Trudy Vladimirskoi uchennoi arkhivnoi komissii*, 18 vols. (Vladimir, 1899–1918), 2:72, and Malitskii, *Istoriia pereslavskoi eparkhii*, 1:290. For the problem of material dependence (which persisted to the end of the *ancien régime*), see G. L. Freeze, *Russian Levites: The Parish Clergy in the Eighteenth Century* (Cambridge, Mass., 1977) and idem, *The Parish Clergy in Nineteenth-Century Russia: Crisis, Reform, Counter-Reform* (Princeton, 1983).

12. Thus Peter initiated the systematic recruitment of Ukrainian prelates, who could claim a superior education at the Kiev Academy and had sometimes even studied in Europe. See K. V. Kharlampovich, *Malorossiiskoe vliianie na velikorusskuiu tserkovnuiu zhizn'* (Kazan, 1914); A. Blazejowskyj, "Ukrainian and Bielorussian Students in Pontifical Collegio de Prop. Fide (1627–1846)," *Analectia Ordinis S. Basilii*, Magni sectio, II, vol. 9,

fasc. 1904 (Rome, 1974), 202–22; Erich Bryner, *Der geistliche Stand in Rußland. Sozial-geschichtliche Untersuchungen zu Episkopat und Gemeindegeistlichkeit der russischen Ortho-doxen Kirche im 18. Jahrhundert* (Göttingen, 1982), 29.

13. For the argument that the Church became more *like* the state, but not part of it, see G. L. Freeze, "Handmaiden of the State? The Orthodox Church in Imperial Russia Reconsidered," *Journal of Ecclesiastical History*, 36 (1985): 82–102.

14. Symbolically, in the 1740s the Synod abolished the "Synodal Region" (*sino-dal'naia oblast'*, the sequel to the former patriarchal region) that had encumbered the Synod—like the patriarch—with the onus of directly managing a vast realm several times the size of most dioceses.

15. See the data in Freeze, *Parish Clergy*, chap. 4.

16. Igor Smolitsch, *Geschichte der russischen Kirche*, 2 vols. (The Hague, Wiesbaden, 1964–1990), 1:389–427; Bryner, *Der geistliche Stand*, 66–81.

17. The primary models were Metropolitan Platon (Levshin) of Moscow and Met-ropolitan Gavriil (Petrov) of St. Petersburg. See K. A. Papmehl, *Metropolitan Platon of Mos-cow (Petr Levshin, 1737–1812): The Enlightened Prelate, Scholar and Educator* (Newtonville, Mass., 1983); B. V. Titlinov, *Gavriil Petrov, mitropolit novgorodskii i sankt-peterburgskii (1730–1801 gg.) Ego zhizn' i deiatel'nost'v sviazi s tserkovnymi delami togo vremeni* (Petrograd, 1916).

18. The Catherinean episcopate combined a mixture of Byzantine and Western learning, which they imbibed during their studies in the Russian seminaries and acade-mies. Western authors, especially in philosophy, exerted a substantial influence; the most prominent was F. C. Baumeister, whose *Elementa philosophiae recentioris usibus juventutis scholasticae recentioris* (Leipzig, 1755) was subsequently translated into Russian. For a list of textbooks at the Moscow Ecclesiastical Academy in 1789, see RGIA, f. 796, op. 70, g. 1789, d. 291, l. 1–1 ob. Three years later the work of Immanuel Kant was added to the list (ibid., f. 796, op. 73, g. 1792, d. 329, ll. 1–2).

19. P. Pototskii, *Zaboty russkikh pastyrei tserkvi o razvitii prosveshcheniia i propoved-nichestva sredi belogo dukhovenstva v epokhu imp. Ekateriny II-oi* (Kazan, 1909); R. L. Nichols, "Orthodoxy and Russia's Enlightenment, 1767–1825," in *Russian Orthodoxy under the Old Régime*, ed. R. L. Nichols and T. G. Stavrou (Minneapolis, 1978), 67–89.

20. On the secularization of church property, see I. A. Bulygin, *Monastyrskie krest'iane Rossii v period pervoi chetverti XVIII v.* (Moscow, 1977); M. I. Gorchakov, *O zemel'nykh vladeniiakh vserossiiskikh mitropolitov, patriarkhov i Sv. Sinoda, 988–1738gg.* (St. Petersburg, 1871); A. A. Zav'ialov, *Vopros o tserkovnykh imeniiakh pri imp. Ekaterine II* (St. Petersburg, 1900); A. I. Komissarenko, "Votchinnoe khoziaistvo dukhovenstva i sekuliari-zatsionnaia reforma v Rossii 20–60 gg. XVIII v." (doktorskaia diss., Moscow, 1984). To be sure, not all clergy welcomed the change; see, for example, the vociferous and famous opposition by Arsenii Matseevich, as recounted in M. S. Popov, *Arsenii Matseevich i ego delo* (St. Petersburg, 1912).

21. RGIA, f. 796, op. 47, g. 1766, d. 394; Titlinov, *Gavriil Petrov*, 159–89; G. L. Freeze, "State and Society in Catherinean Russia: The Synodal Instruction to the Legislative Commission of 1767–1768, in *"Aus der anmuthigen Gelehrsamkeit." Tübinger Studien zum 18. Jahrhundert*, ed. Eberhard Müller (Tübingen, 1988), 155–68.

22. Typical are the writings of A. A. Papkov, who attributed most of the Church's ills to its "bureaucratization." See, for instance, his *Upadok pravoslavnogo prikhoda, XVIII–XIX vv.* (Moscow, 1899).

23. P. DiMaggio and W. Powell, "The Iron Cage Revisited: Institutional Isomorphism and Collective Rationality in Organizational Fields," *American Sociological Review*, 48 (1983): 147–60.

24. The standard instruction came from Metropolitan Platon (Levshin) of Moscow: *Instruktsiia blagochinnym iereiam ili protoiereiam* (Moscow, 1775).

25. Culminating several decades of development, in 1808 the Church formally mandated and defined the office in the "Instructions to Church Elders" in 1808; see *PSZ(1)*, 30: 23027 (17 May 1808).

26. See G. L. Freeze, "Public Penance in Imperial Russia: A Prosopography of Sinners," in *Seeking God: The Recovery of Religious Identity in Orthodox Russia, Ukraine, and Georgia*, ed. S. K. Batalden (DeKalb, 1993), 53–82.

27. See N. D. Zol'nikova, "Deloproizvodstvennye materialy o tserkovnom stroitel'stve kak istochnik po istorii prikhodskoi obshchiny Sibiri (nachalo XVIII v.—konets 60-kh godov XVIII v.)," *Rukopisnaia traditsiia XVIII–XIX vv. na vostoke Rossii* (Novosibirsk, 1983), 102–16.

28. See, for instance, the instructions of 1746 for the clerical elder in Balakhna district (RGADA, f. 1183, op. 1, g. 1746, d. 407, ll. 7 ob., 8 ob.) and a Synodal resolution of 1753 (in RGIA, f. 796, op. 34, g. 1753, d. 494, l. 6–6 ob.).

29. For general exhortations to maintain and improve church buildings, see the 1772 resolution of the Synod *(Polnoe sobranie postanovlenii i rasporiazhenii po vedomstvu pravoslavnogo ispovedaniia. Tsarstvovanie Ekateriny Alekseevny* [hereafter *PSPREA*], 3 vols. [St. Petersburg, 1910–15], 1: 644), the 1797 decree by the bishop of Astrakhan (I. Savvinskii, *Istoricheskaia spravka ob Astrakhanskoi eparkhii za 300 let eia sushchestvovaniia, 1602–1902* [Astrakhan, 1903], 203), and the 1843 sermon by the bishop of Khar'kov (Innokentii [Borisov], *Slova, besedy i rechi k pastve Khar'kovskoi eparkhii*, 2 vols. [Khar'kov, 1847], 2:135–36).

30. For the campaign by the bishop of Vladimir in the 1760s, see [N. Malitskii], "Oloviannye sosudy v tserkvakh vladimirskoi eparkhii," *Vladimirskie eparkhial'nye vedomosti*, 1906, no. 46: 718–21.

31. N. Malitskii, *Istoriia pereslavskoi eparkhii, 1744–1788*, 2 vols. (Vladimir, 1912–17), 1:302–303.

32. For the Church's attempt to eliminate "ugly" as well as unorthodox icons, see K. Ia. Zdravomyslov, "K voprosu o nadzore Sv. Sinoda za ikonopisanie v XVIII v." in RGIA, f. 834, op. 4, d. 614; N. V. Pokrovskii, "K voprosu o merakh k uluchsheniiu russkogo ikonopisaniia," *Tserkovnyi vestnik*, 1901; N. V. Pokrovskii, *Ocherki pamiatnikov khristianskogo iskusstva i ikonografii*, 3 ed. (St. Petersburg, 1910).

33. For exemplars of *klirovye vedomosti* in Kursk, Tver', and Kiev dioceses, see GA Kurskoi Oblasti, f. 20, op. 2, d. 10; GA Tverskoi oblasti, f. 160, op. 1, d. 16298; TsGIAU, f. 127, op. 1009, d. 275.

34. See, for example, a request in 1804 to hold an early liturgy in a Moscow parish

(because the parishioners' duties made a later service impossible) in RGIAgM, f. 203, op. 29, d. 310.

35. In the 1740s instructions to clerical elders included the duty to verify that parishes had only the "newly corrected and printed" liturgical books, i.e., those adopted in the wake of the Nikonian reforms of the seventeenth century. Thus the instruction to clerical elders in 1746 in Balakhna District demanded that all service books be "newly corrected and printed." RGADA, f. 1183, op. 1, g. 1746, d. 407, ll. 7–8. See also the 1743 instructions for clerical elders by Metropolitan Arsenii (Matseevich) of Rostov, "Instruktsiia popovskim starostam ot 1743 g.," *Iaroslavskie eparkhial'nye vedomosti*, 1883, no. 18: 141–42.

36. RGIA, f. 796, op. 53, g. 1772, d. 203, l. 1 (Synod resolution of 25 May 1772).

37. Ibid., ll. 658 ob.–659.

38. Ibid., ll. 682–683 ob. (Synod resolution of 21 December 1776). Apart from catechisms (8,535 copies), the list of missing volumes includes a wide variety of liturgical books—such as the *Minei mesiachnye, Tserkovnye ustavy*, and *Trebniki*.

39. Revealingly, for all the regulatory passion (even the architecture of rural churches), ecclesiastical authorities failed to standardize the performance of the liturgy in parish churches. The chief problem was not deviance but the customary abridgment of the liturgy: rather than perform the full liturgy that lasted hours (as monasteries did), parish clergy routinely omitted various segments so as not to overburden themselves and their flock. Although ubiquitous and tolerated, the abridgment was not regulated by a standard instruction as to what might, or might not, be omitted. As a result, the excisions were arbitrary, making the liturgy different from one parish to the next. Nevertheless, the Church did no more than to issue, but not enforce demands that priests perform the full service. In essence, the Church did not wish to abolish excisions (which were a practical necessity), but did not dare to legitimize the practice, in all likelihood fearing Old Believer agitation that this was yet further proof that the "Nikonian Church" had broken with true Orthodoxy.

40. *Polnoe sobranie postanovlenii i rasporiazhenii po vedomstvu pravoslavnogo ispovedaniia. Tsarstvovanie Pavla Petrovicha* [hereafter *PSPRPP*], no. 99 (3 June 1797). In 1816 Alexander I specifically directed uniform usage of the texts by the director of the court choir, Bortnianskii (RGIA, f. 797, op. 2, d. 5319). But the Synod later tried to preserve traditional singing in monastic services; in 1830, for example, the Synod directed that Solovetskii monastery dismantle its choir and attempts to introduce harmonic music and, instead, restore traditional forms (*Polnoe sobranie postanovlenii i rasporiazhenii po vedomstvu pravoslavnogo ispovedaniia. Tsarstvovanie Nikolaia Petrovicha* [hereafter *PSPRNP*], no. 332 [14 November 1830]).

41. *Istoricheskoe rassuzhdenie voobshche o drevnem khristianskom bogosluzhebnom penii* (St. Petersburg, 1816). See GA Vladimirskoi oblasti, f. 556, op. 108, d. 108.

42. RGIA, f. 796, op. 131, g. 1850, d. 875, ll. 1–5.

43. RGIA, f. 796, op. 129, g. 1848, d. 1191; op. 131, g. 1850, dd. 875 and 1990. On the conflict between L'vov and Metropolitan Filaret (Drozdov) of Moscow, see RGIA, f. 796, op. 131, g. 1850, d. 1990, ll. 1–104 (including Filaret's lacerating critique of L'vov).

44. The Church attempted, with scant success, to establish control over the production of icons. As the bishop of Suzdal, after decades of diocesan efforts, complained in 1797: "Many state peasants and seigniorial serfs who appear in Suzdal are selling holy icons that they themselves have painted incorrectly" (GA Vladimirskoi oblasti, f. 560, op. 1, d. 1127 [report of 10 March 1797]). See also A. A. Bobrov, "O nadzore za prodavaemymi ikonami," *Trudy Vladimirskoi uchenoi arkhivnoi komissii*, 2 (1900), app., 64; N. Malitskii, *Iz proshlogo Vladimirskoi eparkhii*, 3 vols. (Vladimir, 1904–11), 2:145–47; S. Karpov, "Evgenii Bolkhovitinov, kak mitropolit Kievskii," *Trudy Kievskoi dukhovnoi akademii*, 1914, no. 3: 369; GA Odesskoi oblasti, f. 37, op. 1, d. 1784, ll. 1–4.

45. Harsh punishment was meted out to clergy suspected of fabricating or even accommodating purported fraud (presumably out of mercenary motives). In 1765, for example, authorities defrocked a priest found guilty of supporting rumors about a newly discovered "miracle-working" icon in his parish. See N. A. Skvortsov, *Materialy po Moskve i Moskovskoi eparkhii*, 2 vols. (Moscow, 1911–14), 1:56–57.

46. Malitskii, *Iz proshlogo Vladimirskoi eparkhii*, 1:74–81.

47. See, for example, the case from Kaluga reported to the Synod in 1835 (RGIA, f. 796, op. 116, g. 1835, d. 899).

48. RGIA, f. 796, op. 104, g. 1823, d. 662, ll. 1–15.

49. RGIA, f. 796, op. 103, g. 1822, d. 880. It issued an analogous directive in 1853 "to stop the unfounded rumors" about another "weeping" icon; see RGIA, f. 796, op. 134, g. 1853, d. 1438, l. 2 (26 August 1853). When local prelates proved less skeptical of such rumors, the Synod acted peremptorily to demand proper, prompt measures to excoriate rumors about unverified miracles. For example, in 1850, the archbishop of Chernigov reported that a young girl had allegedly been cured by an icon at Vvedenskii Monastery. Although the incident was confirmed by a formal investigation and other miracles followed, the Synod directed the prelate to keep his investigations secret and to avoid spreading rumors about the icon. See RGIA, f. 796, op. 131, g. 1850, d. 301.

50. As the bishop of Kazan candidly wrote in 1760, the number of "unseemly" icons was so immense that the parish churches were simply unable to comply. See the memorandum from Bishop Gavriil in RGIA, f. 796, op. 140, g. 1759, ll. 122–122 ob.

51. RGIA, f. 796, op. 53, g. 1772, d. 83, ll. 1–2 (Bishop Gennadii to the Synod, 15 February 1772).

52. See the details and references in G. L. Freeze, "Counter-reformation in Russian Orthodoxy: Popular Response to Religious Innovation, 1922–1925," *Slavic Review*, 54 (1994): 330–31n.

53. For example, in a case from 1793, a noble landowner induced the chief procurator of the Synod to arrange for the return of a much-venerated icon that local authorities had confiscated. See RGIA, f. 796, op. 75, g. 1794, d. 301, ll. 1–9.

54. N. Malitskii, "Smolenskaia ikona Bozhiei materi po vladimirskom kafedral'nom sobore," *Vladimirskie eparkhial'nye vedomosti*, 1907, no. 37: 578.

55. For example, see the case from Vologda in 1842, where a peasant claimed to possess relics from St. Nicholas and induced fellow parishioners to come to his defense; ultimately, authorities had to use force to subdue the recalcitrant believers, who were then

subjected to corporal punishment for their insubordination. See RGIA, f. 796, op. 123, g. 1842, d. 1203, ll. 1–19.

56. RGIA, f. 796, op. 61, g. 1780, d. 370, ll. 1–3.

57. It specifically ordered the archimandrite "to examine whether there is anything contrary to the Church or inclined toward the Old Belief." As it turned out, the service itself was innocuous. According to Archimandrite Gavriil, the text did have six "minor errors" on individual words, but contained nothing contrary to the Church or specifically disposed to support the Old Belief. See RGADA, f. 1183, op. 1, g. 1746, d. 157, l. 14 (report of 12 December 1746).

58. *Polnoe sobranie postanovlenii i rasporiazhenii po vedomstvu pravoslavnogo ispovedaniia. Tsarstvovanie Elizavety Petrovny* [hereafter *PSPREP*], 4 vols. (St. Petersburg, 1899–1911), 2:788.

59. See N. Malitskii, "Vedomost' o moshchakh," *Vladimirskie eparkhial'nye vedomosti*, 1907, no. 25: 403–11.

60. RGADA, f. 1183, op. 1, g. 1746, d. 157, ll. 1–2 (reply of 27 March 1746 to a query from the Moscow Synodal Chancellery).

61. Malitskii, *Istoriia pereslavskoi eparkhii*, 2:189–91.

62. Malitskii, *Iz proshlogo iz vladimirskoi eparkhii*, 2:26.

63. See E. E. Golubinskii, *Istoriia kanonizatsii sviatykh v russkoi tserkvi* (Moscow, 1903).

64. Interestingly, such investigations were themselves not free from falsification, as was evident in the case of St. Dmitrii Rostovskii. To be sure, the formal reports—lengthy and detailed—fully confirmed the reports of miracles (see "Chudesa ot moshchei sviatitelia Dimitriia Rostovskogo i po molitve k nemu," *Iaroslavskie eparkhial'nye vedomosti*, 1872, nos. 23–28, 33–34). But in 1765, just a few years after the canonization, in the wake of the defrocking and banishment of Metropolitan Arsenii (Matseevich) of Rostov, a local archimandrite confessed that he falsified reports about both the miracles and the uncorrupted remains of St. Dmitrii. A new examination of the remains indeed confirmed that his body had decomposed and impelled the Holy Synod to order an investigation of recent miracles (21 March 1765). A list of such miracles (from 1756 to 1782) included 198 separate cases, where believers were cured of demonic possession (forty-two cases), insanity (fifteen), "enervation" *(rasslablenie)*, and the like. See RGIA, f. 796, op. 205 ("secret section"), d. 49.

65. RGIA, f. 796, op. 79, g. 1798, d. 505.

66. RGIA, f. 797, op. 87, d. 152, ll. 1–4 (report of 26 August 1846) and 19–54 (description of "miraculous signs").

67. "Istoriko-statisticheskoe opisanie pervoklassnogo Zadonskogo Bogoroditskogo monastyria," *Voronezhskie eparkhial'nye vedomosti*, 1870, nos. 18–19, 21–22.

68. RGIA, f. 797, op. 87, d. 152.

69. See G. L. Freeze, "Subversive Piety: Religion and the Political Crisis in Late Imperial Russia," *Journal of Modern History*, 68 (1996): 308–50.

70. RGIA, f. 796, op. 119, g. 1838, d. 699.

71. From the mid-eighteenth century, the Church exhibited a growing desire to isolate the clergy from secular culture and society and to require that its servitors embody

the values and norms of the spiritual domain. This seclusion, it was hoped, would protect the clergy from corrupting influences, chiefly those emanating from the uneducated folk. For example, the Moscow consistory, after receiving reports of clergy mingling at popular gatherings, ordered that they avoid places "where the rabble *(chern')* commit every kind of indecent act" (RGIAgM, f. 203, op. 94, d. 260, l. 2–2 ob. [decree of 22 May 1773]). For further examples, see Rozanov, *Istoriia moskovskogo eparkhial'nogo upravleniia*, 2/2:351–52; "Nastavlenie iereiam Gervasiia, episkopa Pereiaslavskogo i Borisopol'skogo," *Rukovodstvo dlia sel'skikh pastyrei*, 1860, no. 20: 25–42; S. Karpov, "Evgenii Bolkhovitinov, kak mitropolit Kievskii," *Trudy Kievskoi dukhovnoi akademii*, 1914, no. 1: 103–4; "Zhizn' pastyria v mire," *Khristianskoe chtenie*, 1844, chast' 3: 443–44.

72. For example, see the 1763 decree by Tikhon (Sokolov) Zadonskii, forbidding clergy to store the Holy Elements in their homes rather than the church, in T. Oleinikov, "Sv. Tikhon v Voronezhe," *Voronezhskaia starina*, 14 (1915–16), 25–28.

73. See, for example, the Synodal decree of 12 August 1769 in RGIA, f. 796, op. 50, g. 1769, d. 307, l. 1–1 ob.

74. In 1761 the Metropolitan Arsenii (Mogilianskii) of Kiev complained that nuns were entering the altar to do the cleaning. To ensure that they touch no sacred objects, he ruled that only sacristans (unordained males serving in convent churches) perform this task and that only ordained clergy (priests and deacons) clean holy objects in the altar. See the text of the decree in I. Iankovskii, "Russkie ierarkhi XVIII i nachala XIX st.," *Poltavskie eparkhial'nye vedomosti*, 1883, no. 7: 310.

75. Malitskii, *Istoriia pereslavskoi eparkhii*, 1:121.

76. See, for example, the decree of the Kiev consistory (24 December 1764), admonishing priests to thwart such celebrations and to punish errant laity, in Iankovskii, "Russkie ierarkhi," *Poltavskie eparkhial'nye vedomosti*, 1883, no. 7: 314–15.

77. RGIA, f. 796, op. 134, g. 1853, d. 972.

78. For example, a seventeenth-century sermon by Simeon Polotskii admonished laity to stand quietly and reverently during the long liturgy. See Malitskii, "Denezhnye shtrafy," *Vladimirskie eparkhial'nye vedomosti*, 1904: no. 22: 642–44.

79. Indeed, at the behest of Peter the Great, the Church established a system of fines to punish those who dared to misbehave during services. That decree, like so many in his reign, was blithely ignored (see, for example, *ODDS*, 1:117, for reports from 1724 showing that no funds at all had been collected for violating the ban). In subsequent decades, however, the Synod took more energetic action to implement this order (see, for example, the decrees of 1742 and 1747 cited in Malitskii, *Istoriia pereslavskoi eparkhii*, 1:117). Local bishops also took more energetic actions to implement such directives; typical were the measures taken in Suzdal diocese to implement a Synodal decree of 1742 prescribing fines for those who converse during services (GA Vladimirskoi oblasti, f. 560, op. 1, d. 14). And some authorities took initiative on their own; see, for example, the 1746 instruction to clerical elders in Balakhna district (RGADA, f. 1183, op. 1, d. 407, l. 9), a 1743 decree by Metropolitan Arsenii (Matseevich) of Rostov ("Rasporiazheniia Arseniia Matseevicha po upravleniiu Rostovsko-iaroslavkoiu pastvoiu," *Iaroslavskie eparkhial'nye vedomosti*, 1868, no. 30: 256), and a decree by Metropolitan Timofei (Shcherbitskii) of Moscow in the 1750s

(N. P. Rozanov, "Preosv. Timofei Shcherbitskii," *Moskovskie eparkhial'nye vedomosti*, 1869, no. 27: 8). Some prelates took more forceful action. In 1765, for example, Bishop Pavel of Vladimir directed diocesan clergy to install, near the entrance to the church, boxes to collect fines "so that those entering would see them and refrain from conversing in church." If, however, "anyone has the temerity to speak in church, collect the requisite fine (i.e., one ruble per person)—regardless of their rank and status." See N. Malitskii, "Episkop vladimirskii Pavel," *Vladimirskie eparkhial'nye vedomosti*, 1910, no. 32: 580.

80. RGIAgM, f. 203, op. 17, d. 6.

81. N. F. Malitskii, "Rasporiazheniia ep. Ieronimiia kasaiushchiesia otpravleniia bogosluzheniia vo Vladimirskoi eparkhii," *Vladimirskie eparkhial'nye vedomosti*, 1907, no. 4:54.

82. For example, see the exhortations in Tikhon (Sokolov), *Nastavlenie khristianskoe* (St. Petersburg, 1783), folios 12–13; *Rukovodstvo detiam kak stoiat' pri otpravlenii bozhestvennoi liturgii i molit'sia vo vremia onoi* (St. Petersburg, 1833); Innokentii (Borisov), *Slova, besedy i rechi k pastve khar'kovskoi*, 2 vols. (Khar'kov, 1847–48), 2:33; *PSZ(1)*, 28:21,544 (8 December 1804) and 33:26,122 (5 February 1816); *Polnoe sobranie zakonov Rossiiskoi Imperii. Vtoroe sobranie* [hereafter *PSZ(2)*], 55 vols. (St. Petersburg, 1830–84), 15:13,853 (11 October 1840); RGIA, f. 796, op. 85, g. 1804, d. 680; op. 113, g. 1832, d. 251; op. 121, g. 1840, d. 1291; f. 797, op. 10, d. 26,607; *PSPRNP*, 438 (30 June 1832); "O blagochinii v tserkvakh," *Russkaia starina*, 108 (1901): 458.

83. See *Sobornoe ulozhenie* (Leningrad, 1987), 19, which orders capital punishment, "without any mercy," for those who cause an interruption in the performance of the liturgy.

84. Typical cases involved inebriated priests and sacristans who either failed to perform the rite or became embroiled in quarrels and fistfights with other clergy or laymen. For typical cases, see the files from Arkhangel'sk (1797), Tver' (1819), Vladimir (1819 and 1821), Vologda (1820 and 1823), and Chernigov (1836) in RGIA, f. 796, op. 78, g. 1797, d. 271; op. 100, g. 1819, d. 396; op. 101, g. 1820, d. 1039 and op. 104, g. 1823, d. 417; op. 100, g. 1819, d. 771 and op. 102, g. 1821, d. 17; op. 117, g. 1836, d. 1274.

85. RGIA, f. 797, op. 2, d. 6390. Originally, the emperor proposed to publish full reports of scandalous clerical misconduct, but was eventually persuaded to rely on vigorous punishment of offenders: as the Synod argued, such reports would only erode popular respect for the clergy and provide fuel for criticism by schismatics. In a decree of 13 July 1821 (ibid., l. 8–8 ob.), Alexander directed the Church to keep such scandals secret.

86. RGIA, f. 796, op. 112, g. 1831, d. 1067.

87. RGADA, f. 1183, op. 1, g. 1746, d. 407, l. 9 ob.

88. For one of the relatively few instances, see a 1741 case later published in I. Golyshev, "Dopros klikusham Akuline Afanas'evoi i Agaf'e Filatovoi klikkavshim v tserkvi Vladimirskoi Bogoroditsy slob. Mstery 1741g.," *Vladimirskie gubernskie vedomosti*, 1871, no. 46: 1.

89. E. Hizen, "August Freiherr von Haxthausen: Russische Kirche. Gesammelte Notizen aus Rußland," *Japanese Slavic and East European Studies*, 7 (1986): 102.

90. The report includes a list of eighty-eight parishes where taverns were located

within 100 meters of the church. RGIA, f. 796, op. 99, g. 1818, d. 1151, ll. 1–6; f. 797, op. 2, d. 8559, ll. 1–3 ob.

91. RGIA, f. 796, op. 132, g. 1851, d. 290, l. 1–1 ob.

92. See, for example, the exchanges in *PSPREP*, 1:444, 494; *ODDS*, 23:435 (with prolix data on the proximity of taverns to churches); *PSZ(1)*, 19:13,847; *PSPREA*, 2:786.

93. For example, in 1776 the Moscow diocesan consistory finally succeeded in forcing a tavern to relocate because of such violations (RGIAgM, f. 203, op. 29, d. 1501).

94. But with due caution: when the Synod raised the tavern issue, state authorities rejected summary action, but did express a willingness to consider measures so long as these did not disrupt income from the liquor trade. See the memorandum of the Senate and journal of the Council of Ministers, both from December 1818, in RGIA, f. 796, op. 99, g. 1818, d. 1151, l. 24–24 ob.; f. 797, op. 2, d. 8559, ll. 14–16 ob.

95. These figures, compiled by the Synod, overstate the actual rate of success. That is evident, for example, from the case of Vladimir diocese, where the bishop originally demanded the relocation of 190 taverns. He ultimately was persuaded to pare the list down to ninety-five taverns; only then did he succeed in having more than half (fifty-one) relocated. See RGIA, f. 797, op. 2, d. 8566, ll. 1–200 and *ODDS*, 23:435. A similar process unfolded in other dioceses; see, for instance, the file on Riazan' diocese in RGIA, f. 797, op. 2, d. 8573. In the end, nineteen dioceses reported the relocation of more than half of the offending taverns; eight other dioceses secured far less, sometimes only a fraction, of the requested closings. RGIA, f. 796, op. 79, g. 1818, d. 1151, ll. 185–354.

96. RGIA, f. 796, op. 99, g. 1818, d. 1151, l. 378 (Synodal decree of 7 November 1820); f. 797, op. 2, d. 9863, ll. 1–3 ob.

97. For a typical complaint about the continuing harm of taverns, and unsuccessful attempts to force their relocation, see the 1824 petition from a church elder and parishioners in Vladimir (RGIA, f. 797, op. 2, d. 8602, ll. 1–2 ob.). For cases with similar complaints and the failure to achieve results, see the files from Podolia in 1850 and Tver' in 1851 (RGIA, f. 796, op. 131, g. 1850, d. 1644 and op. 132, g. 1851, d. 290). Even the law on "dry hours" met with much evasion and had to be reaffirmed in 1839 (RGIA, f. 796, op. 120, g. 1839, d. 1183).

98. See Tikhon's decrees of 24 April and 16 June 1765 in T. D. Popov, "Sv. Tikhon, kak nravouchitel'," *Voronezhskaia starina*, 11(1912): 128. Tikhon was obviously embarrassed by the severe reproof: to keep the matter secret, he chose to reply in his own hand rather than use (as was customary) the services of a consistory clerk (RGIA, f. 796, op. 54, g. 1773, d. 157, ll. 1–3 ob., 7). See also N. N. Pokrovskii, "Dokumenty XVIII v. ob otnoshenii Sinoda k narodnym kalendarnym obriadam," *Sovetskaia etnografiia*, 1981, no. 5: 101–108.

99. For seventeenth-century laws specifically prohibiting work and trade on Sundays and holidays, see *Akty istoricheskie*, 5 vols. (St. Petersburg, 1841), 4:6; *PSZ(1)*, 1:453; A. V. Popov, *Sud i nakazanie za prestupleniia protiv very i nravstvennosti po russkomu pravu* (Kazan', 1904), 99–100.

100. See, for example, the sermon of Metropolitan Amvrosii (Podobedov) of St. Petersburg in his *Sobranie pouchitel'nykh slov*, 3 vols. (Moscow, 1810), 3:110–11.

101. An early complaint came from the archbishop of Nizhnii Novgorod in 1743, but did not elicit specific action from the Synod *(ODDS, 23:156)*.

102. *PSPREA*, 1:640; *PSZ(1)*, 19:13864a.

103. The Synod—aware that the government was unwilling to adopt any measures that might undermine such commercial networks—simply ignored Arsenii's memorandum. See RGIA, f. 796, op. 116, g. 1835, d. 1014.

104. RGIA, f. 796, op. 123, g. 1842, d. 542, ll. 1–3, 8–9, 12–17 ob.

105. For the history of religious rites against drought, see V. Prilutskii, *Chastnoe bogosluzhenie v russkoi tserkvi v XVII i pervoi polovine XVIII v.* (Kiev, 1912), 325–28; for descriptions of icon processions concerning rain (to start, or halt, precipitation), see the documents from the mid-eighteenth century in N. A. Skvortsov, *Materialy po Moskve i moskovskoi eparkhii v XVIII v.*, 2 vols. (Moscow, 1911–14), 2:642–60.

106. RGIA, f. 796, op. 32, g. 1751, d. 3, ll. 19 ob.–20.

107. RGIA, f. 796, op. 124, g. 1843, d. 1142.

108. For examples, see *Polnoe sobranie postanovlenii i rasporiazhenii po vedomstvu pravoslavnogo ispovedaniia* [hereafter *PSPR*], 10 vols. (St. Petersburg, 1869–1916), 8:2721, 2811; Skvortsov, *Materialy*, 2:642–60; RGIA, f. 796, op. 121, g. 1840, d. 714; *Izvlecheniia iz otcheta po vedomstvu dukhovnykh del pravoslavnogo ispovedaniia* [hereafter *(IVO [Year])*] (St. Petersburg, 1837–63, *IVO(1841)*, 38 and *IVO(1848)*, 27.

109. For examples of the antipathy that Western elites felt for popular piety and public rituals, see the accounts of campaigns against processions in Germany: G. Korff, "Zwischen Sinnlichkeit und Kirchlichkeit: Notizen zum Wandel populärer Frömmigkeit im 18. und 19. Jahrhundert," *Kultur zwischen Bürgertum und Volk*, ed. Jutta Held (Berlin, 1983), 136–48; Christof Dipper, "Volksreligiosität und Obrigkeit im 18. Jahrhundert," in *Volksreligiosität in der modernen Sozialgeschichte*, ed. Wolfgang Schieder (Göttingen, 1986), 73–96; Wolfgang Schieder, "Religion in der Sozialgeschichte," in *Sozialgeschichte Deutschland: Entwicklungen und Perspektiven im internationalen Zusammenhang* (Göttingen, 1987), 9–31.

110. To eradicate such scandals, Bishop Sil'vestr (Lebedinskii) directed that only the parish clergy should participate in the processions, that they carry only the cross (not icons), that they not leave the territory of their own parish, and that they avoid any superstitious acts to accommodate the "common people." See N. P. Malitskii, "Iz proshlogo Vladimirskoi eparkhii," *Vladimirskie eparkhial'nye upravleniia*, 2/1: 158–59.

111. Moscow, for instance, had several citywide processions each year: on the first week of Easter, 26 August (day of the icon of the Vladimir Mother-of-God), 22 October (day of the icon of the Kazan Mother-of-God), and the Thursday after Pentecost. See Rozanov, *Istoriia moskovskogo eparkhial'nogo upravleniia*, 2/1:158–59.

112. The processions were already a source of concern in the seventeenth century (see, for example, the decree of 29 June 1688 on maintaining "good order" in icon processions in *PSZ[1]*, 1:430 and Popov, *Sud i nakazanie*, 101–2), but a systematic campaign did not come until the reign of Peter the Great. The Synod first took measures in 1722 by banning processions to perform rites in private homes or to collect donations for the parish church (see *PSZ[1]*, 5:3910; *PSPR*, 2:419, 476; *ODDS*, 2/1:244). Two years later, heeding

a directive from the emperor, the Synod specifically prohibited ("except for the holiday of Christmas") parish processions to private residences without a special invitation (*ODDS*, 4:393; *PSPR*, 4:1344). Both because the parish clergy had a strong material interest in such processions and because many parishioners desired them, this order was observed in the breach and formally abrogated in 1744. As the Synod explained, the decree had enraged many believers, especially those who were too ill to journey to churches. It, therefore, authorized house-to-house processions, but issued specific instructions to ensure decency and order (*PSPREP*, 2:583).

113. RGADA, f. 1183, op. 1, g. 1747, d. 353, ll. 1–16.

114. The elder did his duty by denouncing one deacon who had "committed many disorders" and shouted obscenities. Although the deacon denied the accusation, other testimony pointed firmly toward his guilt. The consistory, therefore, ordered that he be given a "merciless punishment with a lash" and, in the event of recurrences, be summarily defrocked and expelled from the clerical estate (RGIAgM, f. 203, op. 154, d. 10).

115. *PSPREA*, 1:356.

116. Rozanov, *Istoriia moskovskogo eparkhial'nogo upravleniia*, 2/2:77–82, 88–92; *PSPREA*, 1:639.

117. RGIA, f. 796, op. 52, g. 1771, d. 439, l. 1–1 ob.

118. RGIA, f. 796, op. 95, g. 1814, d. 407; op. 114, g. 1833, d. 515.

119. Rozanov, *Istoriia moskovskogo eparkhial'nogo upravleniia*, 3/1:138–40.

120. For example, in 1819, diocesan authorities in Kherson reported a "weeping icon" that had begun to attract huge crowds and won still greater attention through multiple miracles (the cures concerned eight cases of epilepsy, two cases of paralysis, and two other unspecified ailments). GA Odesskoi oblasti, f. 37, op. 1, d. 87, ll. 1–287.

121. In some cases, the clergy were indeed the perpetrators. For example, in a case from Suzdal in 1748, a priest had encouraged parishioners to place a post at a mysterious spring, to mount icons nearby, and to make pilgrimages with money, clothes, and other material gifts (RGIA, f. 796, op. 32, g. 1751, d. 3, ll. 19 ob.–20). More often, however, it was lay zealots or charlatans who were the main culprits. Thus, in 1770, an elderly woman in Moscow diocese took a "miracle-working" icon to the homes of wealthy believers and induced a local priest to celebrate religious services for the icon (RGIAgM, f. 203, op. 29, g. 1640, l. 18).

122. Such campaigns emanated from the 1740s, even before the establishment of superintendents; see, for example, the demand by Metropolitan Arsenii (Matseevich) of Rostov that the diocesan clergy sign an oath to report any "false miracles" ("Rasporia-zheniia," *Iaroslavskie eparkhial'nye vedomosti*, 1868, no. 30: 237). See also the 1746 instruction in RGADA, f. 1183, op. 1, g. 1746, d. 207, l. 9 ob.

123. For a 1749 case in Suzdal diocese, see GA Vladimirskoi oblasti, f. 560, op. 1, d. 44.

124. RGIA, f. 796, op. 131, g. 1850, d. 1150, ll. 1–7.

125. GA Odesskoi oblasti, f. 37, op. 1, d. 947.

126. RGIA, f. 796, op. 118, g. 1837, d. 1046, ll. 1–2.

127. RGIA, f. 796, op. 129, g. 1848, d. 1462, ll. 1–9.

128. RGIA, f. 796, op. 129, g. 1848, d. 1499, ll. 1–4.

129. For the case of a priest's son, who was apprehended and prosecuted for transmitting a "heretical magic notebook," see RGADA, f. 1183, op. 1, g. 1760, d. 39.

130. Thus one peasant from Pereslavl' diocese, found guilty of invoking "various absurd chants and incantations," was given one hundred blows with the whip at a consistory, and then incarcerated in a monastery, "where he is to be used in appropriate labor for three years, to make fifty prostrations per day, and to remain constantly under strict supervision so that he not enter into covert or overt conversation with anyone." Malitskii, *Istoriia pereslavskoi eparkhii*, 1:136–37. In some cases, the degree of guilt was unclear, for the accusations of sorcery were added as an aggravating element. For example, when merchants in Viazniki complained about the misfeasance of a local official, they also accused him of possessing "magic letters" and of "summoning dark forces." RGIA, f. 796, op. 36, g. 1755, d. 168, ll. 1–2.

131. For an 1831 case in Tavrida diocese, see RGIA, f. 796, op. 112, g. 1831, d. 1052, ll. 34–36.

132. See, for example, the decrees of 1722 (*PSPR*, 2:477) and 1732 (ibid., 7:2600), as well as the discussion in I. Kovalevskii, *Iurodstvo o Khriste i Khrista radi: iurodivye vostochnoi i russkoi tserkvi*, 2d ed. (Moscow, 1900), 154–57.

133. For an example of such a decree from the bishop of Suzdal in 1775, see GA Vladimirskoi oblasti, f. 560, op. 1, d. 491.

134. RGIA, f. 796, op. 35, g. 1754, d. 528, ll. 1–3 ob.

135. RGIA, f. 796, op. 129, g. 1848, d. 877, l. 2.

136. According to official (and doubtlessly incomplete) data for 1764, the empire had only 42,972 registered Old Believers, chiefly in Nizhnii Novgorod, Arkhangel'sk, and Moscow gubernii (RGIA, f. 796, op. 45, g. 1764, d. 105, ll. 45–47). Newer data, compiled by the state in the first half of the nineteenth century, showed a quantum leap in the number of dissenters: their ranks doubled by 1801 (84,150) and tripled again by 1825 (273,289). See RGIA, f. 796, op. 139, g. 1858, d. 548, ll. 4–5. To be sure, the general increase in population made the percentage increase smaller, but the absolute numbers—and sixfold increase in six decades—could not fail to leave a strong impression on Church and state officials. Data from individual dioceses were still more alarming; authorities in Orenburg, for example, reported that in the decade after 1843 the ranks of Old Believers had swelled from 18,355 to 46,655 (N. Cherniavskii, *Orenburgskaia eparkhiia v ee proshlom i nastoiashchem*, 1 [Orenburg, 1900]: 403–4). And government estimates ran still higher. The governor of Kostroma, for example, claimed that his province alone was home to 105,000 Old Believers—a figure five times that of the Church's (20,434). See RGIA, f. 796, op. 134, g. 1853, d. 78, l. 154.

137. See, for example, the materials on the "secret committee on the Old Belief" in Moscow diocese in RGADA, f. 1183, op. 11, dd. 4–7, 11.

138. The gruesome report of the investigation revealed that, while not free of corruption, much of Prokopii's remains had been preserved: "Half of the ear [was missing], but the left was almost intact; in the exterior part of the nose [the cartilage] is lacking; there is a well in the right eye towards the nose; the lower lip is missing. . . . " RGIA, f. 796, op. 82, g. 1801, d. 832.

139. Despite those arguments and reports of more miracles at Prokopii's sepulcher, the cautious Synod denied the petition because it "does not contain such confirmed evidence and discoveries that would be substantial and sufficient" to reverse its decision of 1801. It also ordered the bishop, "in accordance with his pastoral duty, by means of seemly and sensible measures, to try to diminish the efforts and intentions of petitions for a national canonization" (RGIA, f. 796, op. 82, g. 1801, d. 832, ll. 17–45).

140. RGIA, f. 796, op. 117, g. 1836, d. 822, l. 1–1 ob. (Filaret's report of 2 June 1836).

141. RGIA, f. 796, op. 117, g. 1836, d. 1178, ll. 1–9 ob. (Nikodim's report of 15 August 1736).

142. In the foregoing case from Orel, for example, the Synod took exception to the bishop's apparent sympathy and reprimanded him for making a "public" investigation, since that only served to increase interest in the case (RGIA, f. 796, op. 117, g. 1836, d. 1178, ll. 13–14). Similarly, in response to Filaret's response, the Synod merely "took cognizance" of the report (d. 822, l. 2).

143. RGIA, f. 796, op. 118, g. 1837, d. 750, ll. 1–27.

144. RGIA, f. 796, op. 117, g. 1836, d. 851, ll. 1–2. For a similar report from Innokentii (Veniaminov) of Kamchatka, about the miraculous cure of a woman after communion, see ibid., op. 127, g. 1846, d. 1427, ll. 1–2.

145. "Ordynskaia pustyn'," *Moskovskie vedomosti*, 1853, no. 47.

146. RGIA, f. 797, op. 23, otd. 1, st. 2, d. 223, ll. 4–5 ob.

147. For example, see the files on miraculous cures of a crippled peasant in 1817, a crippled daughter of a merchant in 1822, and a deaf mute in 1833 in RGIA, f. 796, op. 98, g. 1817, d. 778; op. 103, g. 1822, d. 760; op. 114, g. 1833, d. 247. Analogous cases involving saints' relics are found in reports about Pochaev Lavra in Volhynia diocese and the crypt of St. Feodosii Uglitskii in Chernigov (ibid., op. 114, g. 1833, d. 542; op. 117, g. 1836, d. 878; op. 150, g. 1849, d. 186).

148. RGIA, f. 796, op. 114, g. 1833, d. 862, ll. 1–2 ob.

149. RGIA, f. 796, op. 114, g. 1833, d. 862, l. 23.

150. For example, see the Synodal decision authorizing Orel to hold a procession to commemorate its "salvation" from the cholera epidemic of 1831 (RGIA, f. 796, op. 114, g. 1833, d. 1159).

151. RGIA, f. 796, op. 114, g. 1833, d. 383, ll. 1–8.

152. *IVO(1841)*, 28.

153. I. Anichkov-Platonov, *Rassuzhdenie o krestnykh khodakh Pravoslavnoi tserkvi* (Moscow, 1842).

154. *IVO(1848)*, 27.

155. For an example of a successful application, see the case from Kherson diocese in GA Odesskoi oblasti, f. 37, op. 1, d. 1774.

156. See G. L. Freeze, "A Social Mission for Russian Orthodoxy: The Kazan Requiem of 1861," in *Imperial Russia, 1700–1917: State, Society, Opposition*, ed. Marshall Shatz and Ezra Mendelsohn (DeKalb, Ill., 1988), 115–35; idem, "Die Läisierung des Archimandriten Feodor (Bucharev) und ihre kirchenpolitischen Hintergründe. Theologie und Politik in Rußland der Mitte des 19. Jahrhunderts," *Kirche im Osten*, 28 (1985): 26–52.

PART IV

INDIVIDUALS AND PUBLICS

ALTHOUGH "society" has been a descriptive category for historical study of Russia for more than a century, meaning has been rendered to this term more by its dichotomous other, the "state," than by investigation of its possible social and symbolic composition. All three essays in this section scrutinize Russian society by shifting attention away from political struggle in the conventional sense and toward the specificities of interactions, values, and logics at different periods and in different arenas of social life. A merchant's diary, polemical publications, and newspapers offer opportunities for uncovering the concerns that animated people in the empire, drew them into relationships with each other, and defined their notions of public life.

David Ransel's sketch based on an eighteenth-century merchant's diary reveals both the individuality and the social embeddedness of his protagonist, Ivan Alekseevich Tolchenov. Microhistories not only have the capacity to bare the ordering minutia of daily life, but they can also disclose the human connections that constitute the fabric of social existence. For Tolchenov, a grain merchant from Dmitrov, both business and pleasure depended on contacts with people from different status groups. Tolchenov's trade meant knowing and dealing with sellers and buyers of grain, but his diary also records frequent interactions with princes, ordinary noble landlords, military men, state officials, clergy, merchants of all ranks, enterprises, serfs, people from the provinces and large cities, as well as his own immediate and extended family.

Although Tolchenov's multiple cross-class relations suggest a more interconnected society than conventional images of Russian merchants invoke, Ransel's account also makes clear his protagonist's ambition to rise above merchant status. Through lavish entertainments of social superiors, the embellishment of the local church, the construction of a splendid home with an orangery, and the purchase of education for his sons, Tolchenov strove for a more secure

253

and more refined life and, in the process, drove his family into debt and downward mobility. Ransel's account returns us to the primacy of the family as a
social unit, for in both good times and in bad, Tolchenov took action in what
he perceived to be the best interests of his family. His diary displays the tensions
between clan stewardship and individual aspiration as well as offering a rare
glimpse into the affective bond between a parent and his young children.

Douglas Smith looks at the same era in which Tolchenov lived and explores
the thought of people, who, though they undoubtedly visited the same theaters
and museums as Tolchenov, had a much different stance toward the cultural life
of Russia. Smith's subject is the polemics that swirled around Freemasonry.
If Tolchenov's social relations centered on personal contacts ritualized through
hospitality, Smith's educated public met itself in print and in civic clubs. Writers
on the controversial topics of the day appealed to the presumed reason of an
emerging "public opinion" (*publika*). Smith traces the emergence of this public
over the course of the century, mapping a transition from a ceremonial notion
of "public acts" performed by rulers and notables to the self-awareness of a literate and sociable public, with its own institutions—the theater, the press,
clubs, and Masonic lodges.

Smith's essay relocates the controversies over Masonry in the context of
civic, rather than state, concerns. The main issue was Masonic secrecy, a practice
that threatened the new culture of public discussion. The controversy over Freemasonry was a constituting discourse of the Russian public, as writers argued
in print over the significance of secret societies devoted to a commonly held
goal—the cultivation of individual virtue in the cause of social well-being.
Smith points out that the late-eighteenth-century public was by no means open
to all subjects of the empire. As in Western Europe, the formation of a Russian
public required outsiders: less privileged people, usually defined by dress, were
not admitted to its formal or informal institutions. But the controversy over
Freemasonry, in particular the criticism of Masons' claim to moral superiority
and exclusivity, captures an extroversive moment in the history of social self-
definition in Russia.

The debate over suicide in the Russian press of the 1860s to 1880s, described
by Irina Paperno, found the Russian public in an altogether different mood. The
public of the reform period had grown numerically and, like the press that
served it, was highly differentiated. Paperno suggests, however, that there was
a possibility for widely disseminated reporting and for widely shared interpretations of what were deemed to be issues of public concern. The profuse attention to suicide reveals the public's fascination with the idea of its own fragmentation, disorder, and decay.

Paperno focuses on the types of knowledge journalists and scholars brought to the representation of suicide. Publicists combined the evidence of statistical studies with organic notions of society to produce a powerful rhetorical potion that transformed individual acts of self-destruction into collective pathology. Suicide was seen to have social (not individual) causes and thus to reflect the ills or the illness of the social body. This emphasis on collective causality only enhanced the public's fascination with specific narratives of physical annihilation, and the press obligingly served up many a bloody story of those shot, ground up, and drowned. What Paperno emphasizes is the way that these violent, final acts of self-assertion were appropriated as cultural signs. The thought of the times was profoundly metaphorical, and the suicide "epidemic" revealed the public's readiness to absorb the individual into a collective social organism, to conflate the physical and the symbolic, and to integrate scientific knowledge into a pessimistic social imaginary.

10

An Eighteenth-Century Russian Merchant Family in Prosperity and Decline

David L. Ransel

A FEW YEARS AGO, Michael Confino challenged historians to study Russia as an integrated social body and not as a collection of isolated groups.[1] Yet to analyze the interactions between people of different social positions and to integrate what scholars until now have seen as Russia's socially specific cultures is no easy task. Archival sources are organized and preserved by institution and social position. The interactions we observe, when they go beyond a single ministry, party, or estate, are usually two-sided. We examine petitions from subordinates to superiors, or we look at court cases that pit a person of one social estate against a person of another. These limited and usually conflictual documents tell us less about what held Russian society together than about points of stress and possible rupture.

A second barrier to the study of Russia as a common culture is the powerful and continuing influence of our liberal and Soviet predecessors. Both these schools reduced Russian history to a struggle between state and society and in the process emptied these two concepts of much of their complexity and overlap.

Microhistory offers a way over the barriers posed by the structure of preserved knowledge and dichotomous conceptual schemata. The rich texture of a close-up view of an event or life gives new vitality and complexity to concepts like state and society. At the same time, such an account removes the burden of making claims about the statistical significance or representativeness of our narratives. We do not ask of *Montaillou*, *The Return of Martin Guerre*, *The Cheese and the Worms*, or *The Midwife's Tale* that they justify some standard of representativeness.[2] We simply delight in and learn from the detailed interactions of the many different people who populate these narratives. Their intimate descriptions of life (and the analyses in which skillful historians present them) are powerful enough to convince us of their significance.

Microhistory offers more than just a reduction of scale, more than well-written local history. The Italian scholars who developed this approach in the 1970s and 1980s took their inspiration, interestingly enough, from a Russian source: Tolstoy's theory of history in *War and Peace*. The Italians were reacting against the traditional grand narratives and also against the new "serial" methods associated with quantification and the Annales school.[3] Both of these stances shared the functionalist practice of taking a series of observations and imposing on them a constructed order or regularity. By experimenting with observations on a radically reduced scale, Italian practitioners of microhistory discovered that the interpretations built on the macrohistorical and serial methods obscured, or sometimes remained altogether blind to, relationships that were essential to an understanding of the social order. To take one example, what historians working on the macro level thought to be a modern "depersonalized" market in land turned out on closer inspection to be a land exchange in which prices were set by kinship bonds. One of the key problems in microhistory is, accordingly, the degree of fit between macro and micro observations. The photography critic and historical theorist Siegfried Kracauer, using an analogy from film, adopted a highly pessimistic stance on this question, contending that no necessary correlation existed, but most practitioners of microhistory understand the relationship between a wide angle of vision and a tightly focused observation to be problematic rather than ultimately incommensurable.[4] The main point about microhistory is that, instead of closing off the generative potential of the evidence by clamping it into a given design, the method explores the latitude actors enjoy for making choices contrary to the normative reality or hegemonic discourse of their time and can, therefore, reveal what is unseen in observations at a macro level.

The manuscript diary of the Russian merchant Ivan Alekseevich Tolchenov likewise permits us to penetrate the smooth surface of the normative reality of the life of this social estate.[5] Tolchenov's daily journal, one of only a handful of merchant diaries for eighteenth-century Russia, is just as terse as most other diaries of commoners from this time. Even so, it offers an extraordinary view of the patterns of Russian life. For a period of forty-three years, the author penned his brief entries, recording the rituals and rhythms of daily life, structures of the days and seasons, the quality of agricultural output and the conditions of its transport, family events and social contacts with an array of people from lords to laborers, and much more. The content of personal and business relations are seldom revealed; that is, conversations or even topics of conversations are not reported. Accordingly, much of the story can be understood only when supplemented by research in other sources. Nevertheless, a picture emerges that is altogether different from the static, stereotypical understanding we now have of merchant community and family life as exclusively traditional, patriarchal, and self-enclosed.[6]

Research for this initial sketch is too preliminary to allow application of the type of microhistorical analysis discussed earlier, which requires mastery of context; the story that follows is intended merely to give a flavor of the diary evidence in advance of a planned full-length study of the life of this merchant family.

One of the diary's strengths is its record of cross-class communication. We see a merchant in frequent contact with people of four social spheres: his merchant colleagues, the local nobility, the clergy at all ranks save for the very highest (excluding metropolitans, for example), and state officials. This merchant family even owned serfs, who were members of its large household. The family lived in close, daily contact with people from every social level. Hints of this rich interactive social picture appear in what follows, but for this initial sketch I will confine my observations to family relations. With these limits in mind, let us turn to the life of Ivan Alekseevich Tolchenov, a merchant from Dmitrov, a town sixty kilometers north of Moscow.

Locale and Family Background

Dmitrov, whose founding dates to the eleventh century, is by Russian standards an ancient city. It played a role in early Russian princely politics and twice suffered destruction by the Mongol-Tatar invaders of the thirteenth century. By the late fifteenth and sixteenth centuries, life in Dmitrov had improved, as the city shared in the renewed prosperity of the trading towns to the north of Moscow. It was in this period that two of Dmitrov's most impressive cultural monuments were built: the Boris and Gleb monastery and the Annunciation cathedral, both of which figured importantly in the life of Tolchenov and his family. The end of the sixteenth century saw economic decline in Dmitrov. Trade routes to the north shifted toward the Iaroslavl-Vologda direction, and Dmitrov's commerce and population shrank. The Time of Troubles caused further losses of trade and population so that by the middle of the seventeenth century after conditions had improved somewhat, the city counted only 242 homes (*dvory*, i.e., homes with their adjacent outbuildings and lands) and a population of 1,300, according to M. N. Tikhomirov. Thereafter, investments by the tsarist court in local meadows and fish ponds helped to build the economy of Dmitrov until by 1705 the population reached 2,000.[7]

The building of St. Petersburg contributed importantly to renewed prosperity for Dmitrov in the eighteenth century. Peter I recruited artisans and traders from the city for work in the burgeoning new capital. The redirection of trade routes to the north and northwest likewise boosted Dmitrov's commerce.[8] Its trade, which until this time had been primarily in market gardening and small manufacturing sales locally and south to Moscow, broadened to include a varied and growing proto-industrial base. When the historian Gerhard Friedrich Müller visited Dmitrov in 1779, he found it a lively commercial and artisanal center with a number of small manufactories in the surrounding countryside. A work from 1787 reports a population in the city of 3,000, plus four cloth manu-factories, three galloon makers,[9] six malt houses, eight tanneries, and five tallow works. The nearby countryside boasted nine cloth factories, two sailcloth shops, one hundred galloon makers, four brick works, twelve tanneries, and several other manufactories. Included in these was a china factory founded in 1766 by an Englishman whose wares, according to Müller, were comparable to the best in foreign countries.[10]

The greatest source of wealth for the commercial leaders of Dmitrov was their grain trade to St. Petersburg. In the late eighteenth century, Dmitrov mer-chants were among the largest purveyors of grain to the northern capital, a trade based on purchases to the east and south along the Volga and its tributar-ies, supplemented by local purchases from large landlords like the Golitsyns and Saltykovs. A portion of the purchased grain was then stored and ground in the Dmitrov area before being moved by barge and overland to St. Petersburg for sale. Müller in 1779 noted Dmitrov merchants bought 30,000 sacks (or about 5,000 tons) of grain annually and ground over 162 tons of rye and barley in five mills that dotted the region.[11] It was principally this grain trade that furnished the wealth of the Tolchenov family.

I should have said one branch of the Tolchenov family, for there were several dating from the seventeenth century. The progenitor of Ivan Alekseevich's branch, Boris Tolchenov, was born about 1658 and produced six sons who sur-vived into the eighteenth century and left progeny of their own. The line lead-ing to the diarist went through Il'ia Borisovich, grandfather of the diarist. It was this grandfather and his sons (including the father of the diarist) who drew their wealth from the grain trade. Il'ia Borisovich amassed considerable capital, enough to rise to the first guild, but he also produced five surviving sons among whom his capital had to be divided. The result was that none of the sons could, on the basis of their father's bequest, muster resources sufficient to register higher than the second merchant guild. The deeply rooted practice of partible inheritance in Russia was a key element in the high rates of vertical mobility among Russian propertied families whether of the merchant class or the nobil-ity.[12] Such chance occurrences as the sex and number of surviving children made a large difference in the opportunities for the next generation, as we see in this line of Tolchenovs.

Other practices could, however, counteract some of the effects of partible inheritance. One of these, the "adoption" of an in-marrying son-in-law (or *priëmysh*) in families with no son, worked to the advantage of the diarist's father, who was able to marry into the family of the wealthy first-guild merchant Fedor Kirilovich Makarov. The archives contain two "amicable protocols" (*poliubovnye zapisi*) concerning this arrangement. The first, dated 1750 and evidently a portion of the marriage contract, declared the new son-in-law Aleksei Il'ich and his wife the owners of all of Makarov's movable and immovable property, even while he was still alive. The second "protocol," drawn up in 1763, took back some of what the earlier one granted. This time Aleksei Il'ich was given permanent ownership of two properties in Dmitrov, plus a number of shop stalls and spaces for others, a tannery, and a brewery. He retained the family capital, but now, instead of it being designated as his property, it was merely under his supervision. "Aleksei may keep this capital forever for commercial dealings," Makarov instructed, "but each year he must give an account of the profit made on my capital, apart from his own, and put that profit to uses that I shall determine."[13]

This change was occasioned by another family event and a troubling one at that, for it threatened the stability of the Makarov-Tolchenov alliance. We learn the details from the diarist, when he reports on the death in 1763 of his maternal grandmother, the wife of Makarov. "On July 22 at the setting of the sun, my grandmother Marfa Matveevna died and on the 28th was buried in the west end of the nave of the Vvedenskaia church then under construction. In this same year, on September 22, my grandfather Fedor Kirilovich married a second time, taking Fedosiia Mikhailovna, the daughter of the priest Mikhail Artemonovich of Pokrov village in Kashin district, and he did this secretly without telling either my parents or other relatives. This inflicted terrible pain, especially on my mother, but it did not irreparably destroy accord in the family."[14] Within two months of the death of his wife, this fifty-two-year-old grandfather had brought home a twenty-eight-year-old wife,[15] a stepmother younger than her stepchildren (who already had children of their own). The new family contract was evidently intended to provide in some fashion for this new member of the family and her possible progeny. Two years later, Fedosiia Mikhailovna gave birth to a son, Andrei, who in his adult years was a frequent companion of the diarist, his step-nephew. Makarov died in 1771, and the bulk of his capital seems to have remained under the supervision of Aleksei Il'ich Tolchenov. It is clear from later references, however, that a sizable portion of this legacy remained legally separate, designated as the "Makarov capital," and eventually had to be transferred to Andrei Fedorovich at his majority. It was at that time, the year 1788, when the diarist Ivan Alekseevich Tolchenov could least afford it, that he had to turn over to his step-uncle this trust of 11,000 rubles, a small fortune.

The diarist's father, Aleksei Il'ich, was an energetic and successful business-man and a person of considerable stature among the local elite. Not only was he the richest merchant in Dmitrov,[16] he was elected by his peers to represent them at the Catherinian Legislative Commission of 1767–68. The Russian histo-rian N. I. Pavlenko, though he admires Aleksei Il'ich's enterprising spirit, ac-cuses him of not giving attention to the tannery, brewery, and shopping stalls he inherited from his father-in-law.[17] But is this fair? Aleksandr Aksenov, a spe-cialist on the merchants of this era, could find no evidence of the tannery being in Aleksei Il'ich's control in the 1760s and believes that he turned the tannery and brewery over to a nephew of Fedor Makarov who had been placed under Makarov's protection; this nephew, I. A. Makarov, later accumulated a substan-tial capital from such enterprises and moved to Moscow to become inscribed as a "distinguished citizen" (*imenityi grazhdanin*), a status requiring a 50,000 ruble capital. Or, possibly, Aleksei Il'ich sold off the tannery and brewery (and no doubt leased the shopping stalls at a good profit, as was customary) in order to concentrate on the lucrative grain trade.[18] He also drew his less wealthy brothers (though all enjoyed second-guild status with declared capital of at least 5,000 rubles) into this business as agents and managers of mills, thus strength-ening both the firm and the extended family.

The diary of his son offers many examples of Aleksei Il'ich's tireless activity on behalf of his firm, listing the frequent rounds he made of his mills and daily engagement with affairs. He was quick to seize an opportunity for profit, as can be seen from his response to the news in late September 1774 of famine threat-ening regions of the Middle Volga and Ukraine. "Having learned of the sharp rise in prices in the southeast and Ukrainian areas due to the small harvest, father sent me [north] on September 30 together with [his agent] Afanasii Popov to Sosninsk wharf for the purchase of rye flour. On the Volkhov River and in Ladoga large numbers of grain barges were at a standstill because of low water, and some merchants were selling cheap due to low prices." However, the news traveled faster than Tolchenov. When he and Popov arrived at the northern Volga wharves, they found that "all the merchants, having heard about the price rises to the south, were wary of selling cheap."[19] Even a trip farther north to Ladoga with his uncle Dmitrii Il'ich failed to yield the right price. Although this venture did not pan out, the action was typical of the spirit that made Aleksei Il'ich's enterprises prosper.

The one arena in which Aleksei Il'ich did not enjoy success was the pro-duction of a large enough progeny to guarantee his family line. A large number of sons, as noted earlier, could divide a family fortune into parts too small to allow any single heir significant economic and political influence. But a failure to produce heirs could have even more unfavorable consequences for the family. Aleksei Il'ich and his wife Fedos'ia Fedorovna, despite a normal fertility record, brought only one of their nine children beyond the first months of life. The single surviving child, the diarist Ivan Alekseevich, added to the entry on his father's death in 1779 the melancholy inventory of his parents' reproductive efforts:

1. My sister, Avdot'ia Alekseevna, was born on February 9, 1752 and died on September 2 of the same year.

2. I, Ivan Alekseev, whose day of birth has already been noted [October 15, 1754].

3. A sister was stillborn on August 11, 1757.

4. My brother, Fedor Alekseevich, was born on May 11, 1760, and died on May 31 of the same year.

5. My brother, Aleksandr Alekseevich, was born on August 17, 1762, and died on the 31st of the same month and year.

6. My brother, Mikhaila Alekseevich, was born on May 15, 1764, and died on June 7 of the same year.

7–8. Twin brothers, Fedor and Aleksei Alekseevichi, were born on January 24, 1766, and died on the same day.

9. My sister, Anna Alekseevna, was born on December 1, 1767, and died to the deep regret of my parents on the same day without having been baptized.[20]

Ivan continued this entry with the sad note that "from this day forward my mother began to be ill, which eventually turned into the consumption that ended her days." His mother's death occurred in 1768 while she was staying with her husband in St. Petersburg during the continuation of the Legislative Commission. She was buried, as was appropriate for the wife of a prominent merchant, in the cemetery of the St. Alexander Nevskii Monastery. The archbishop of St. Petersburg presided.[21]

Youth and Prosperity[22]

At age 20, Ivan was already married and actively engaged in the family business. We find him in the spring of 1774 in the rounds of almost continual travel that marked his youth.

1774. March 6. In the morning left for Moscow. 10th returned home. 15th at 2:30 again left for Moscow with my wife, overnighting in Sukharevo. 16th at 7 in the morning we arrived safely. 25th heard mass at the Annunciation Cathedral. 27th at 3 in the afternoon left for the Shirin mill, overnighting in the village of Rastovtse. 28th had dinner in Gorodok and arrived at the mill in the evening. 30th in the morning started home. 31st at 9 in the morning arrived safely. April 8 at 8:08 in the morning[23] left for the Tvertsa River and the village of Troitskoe for the loading into barges of the grain that had been stored there over the winter. . . . 14th we loaded the third and final barge. 15th just before evening we launched the barges and overnighted opposite the village of Golubovo; I slept on the barges. 16th in the morning uncle Ivan Il'ich and I rode to Tver', where we began the purchase of empty barges at the price of 30–40 rubles. 17th we continued our barge purchases. 18th, having finished this and hired drivers to take them to Rybnaia sloboda, at 11 in the evening we started for home.

At this point, Ivan had been traveling and working in the family firm for seven years. Boys in merchant families started their careers young. Ivan's first trip to load barges on the Tvertsa River took place in 1768 when he was only 13 years old. He was then under the supervision of a family agent Afanasii Popov, who was detailed to teach him the business, and he and Ivan moved north with the summer barge traffic through canals, rivers, and lakes toward St. Petersburg.[24] As it happened, this maiden voyage was interrupted by news of his mother's death, which reached him in Novgorod and was accompanied by instructions from his father to hurry to the capital overland. From that year onward, young Ivan was constantly on the move on behalf of the firm. In the winter, he rode east and south to supervise the purchase of grain in Orel, Promzino gorodishche (on the Sura River, Penza guberniia), Lyskovo on the upper Volga, and other far-flung trading towns, while through the summer he transported the grain north from the family's mills and storage points to St. Petersburg for sale. Until the death of his father in 1779, Ivan spent nearly 200 days a year on the road. These travels were his "universities," in which he learned much, especially in his visits to the two capital cities, where he was impressed with the style of living, the churches, museums, and theaters. Here, no doubt, he acquired the ambitions and tastes that would figure prominently in his later adult life.

Marriage occurred early in this family, a characteristic of wealthy merchant families. Those with fewer resources were not in a position to contract useful alliances and tended to delay.[25] Ivan's father, Aleksei Il'ich, made his own financially advantageous marriage when he was only eighteen years old. In turn, he arranged a favorable match for Ivan soon after the boy's nineteenth birthday.

In this case, the bride was found among the Moscow merchant class. For this branch of the Tolchenov family, Moscow was the principal marriage market. All of Ivan's uncles had married women from Moscow merchant families, and the second marriage of Ivan's father also was to a Moscow merchant woman.[26] It was not unusual for merchants to seek out-of-town brides, and they may have preferred this strategy as a way of expanding the family's network of mutual aid and enterprise. But the class endogamy typical of this branch of the Tolchenov family was by no means a social imperative. Men from other branches of the same family found their brides among "lesser town dwellers" (*meshchane*), daughters of priests, and even landless monastery peasants.[27]

Ivan's marriage was to Anna Alekseevna Osorgina. He expressed the decision to marry in a way that suggests the marriage was arranged by the parents, as was customary, and did not result from earlier encounters with his betrothed that may have implied mutual affection.[28] "On January 6 [1773] with the approbation and inducement of my father, I decided to marry. On the 9th, we rode to Moscow on that matter. The 14th[29] I viewed the young woman, the daughter of the merchant Aleksei Ivanovich Osorgin in Kozhevniki, who was destined by heavenly fate to be my spouse. The 17th the agreement [between the father of the bride and father of the groom] was negotiated. The 20th we went back for a time to Dmitrov. The 22nd we returned to Moscow. The 24th was the final compact [*zagovor*]."[30] Three days later the marriage took place. Unfortunately, the diarist writes nothing about the terms of the agreement that the fathers spent three days hammering out. This alliance, which added to the several other close Moscow in-law relations that Ivan enjoyed by virtue of his uncles' marriages, gave him a large familial network in the city, whose members he visited during his frequent stays there in subsequent years. Later, his wife's brother served as a major business partner to whom Ivan entrusted the management of a Moscow manufactory enterprise.

While marriage was a pivotal bond, another important relationship in the Russian family system, one often analyzed in connection with early Russian princely politics, was that of senior uncle. Power and wealth in Russian families of the modern era flowed downward from father to son (usually the eldest son), but considerable authority resided with uncles, and especially with the most senior of them, which was no doubt evidence of the continuing importance into modern times of clan bonds in providing personal and group security in a highly unstable social and economic environment. We see this relationship at work in the Tolchenov family.

In the excerpt quoted at the start of this section, we encountered Ivan's senior uncle, Ivan Il'ich, as the young man's companion in barge purchases in Tver'. But this is not where he usually turned up. Their most frequent contacts were as visitors in one another's homes in Dmitrov. The number of their contacts increased measurably after the sudden death of Ivan's father in 1779 at the age of forty-seven. Aleksei Il'ich died from a series of strokes suffered while on the road home from Trinity Monastery in Sergiev Posad, from which he had only a few hours before departed in evident good health. This unexpected blow evoked eloquent expressions of grief and woe from Ivan, quite out of character with his usual lapidary diary entries. And no wonder. In addition to leaving him shocked and saddened, the death transferred to him at age 25 full responsibility for managing the robust and far-flung trade his father had built up. In the days following the death and for years afterward, we find him in frequent consultation with uncle Ivan Il'ich. The content of their discussions does not appear in the diary, but the regularity of visits with this senior uncle on days before departure and within a day of return from Ivan's business travels suggests that the senior uncle was functioning as a stand-in for the father and elder adviser for the clan. The merchant family seems to have preserved this characteristic feature of early Russian family dynamics.

Ivan's new position as head of the family firm also had advantages. As the sole surviving son, all the wealth and power of the family now became his possession. Instead of spending half the year on the road, he settled down in Dmitrov and used this wealth and power to indulge his aspirations for a different kind of life. In part, of course, his new position required a different kind of life and more time at home, as he was expected to play a role in the administration of local merchant corporate bodies, including service on the municipal court (Magistrat) and other governing institutions. It is clear, nevertheless, that Ivan very much wished to cut a figure in local society. In this, he was following in his father's footsteps, but he did so on a lavish scale.

His father had been active in assisting the parish church, the Vvedenskaia church. Ivan continued this involvement but did not confine it to completing the metal covering for the previously wooden cupola that his father had promised to furnish.[31] He soon after committed himself to the purchase of a seven-tiered copper chandelier weighing nearly 600 pounds, and then to the building of a huge belltower for the same church, the latter effort occupying several years and demanding large outlays during the 1780s. After finishing these projects, he undertook the construction of a chapel in the Il'inskaia church in another part of town (evidently the family's earlier parish church before their home was transferred to the parish served by the Vvedenskaia church).[32]

These conspicuous displays of piety and largesse were part of a broader effort to create an impressive style of life, which included entertaining prominent local noble families, state officials, and clergymen, including among the last the abbot and other superiors of the Boris and Gleb Monastery at the edge of town.

Boris and Gleb monastery in Dmitrov, where the Tolchenovs often
attended church and where they are buried. Photo by David L. Ransel.

At the height of his influence and wealth, Ivan was spending much of his social
and business time with two princely families in the vicinity: the I. F. Golitsyns,
at whose estate he often attended Sunday mass and then stayed for dinner and
the rest of the day, and the I. P. Obolenskiis, with whom he exchanged visits at
least once a week.[33] Court dignitaries, military commanders, government ministers, or high churchmen who were on official visits to the city, or sometimes
merely passing through on the way to some other place, would be welcomed
and entertained by Ivan Tolchenov. In some cases, he could boast (and gladly
did) that the dignitary in question stayed at his house overnight. Such hospitality was expected of the town's wealthiest merchant, and Ivan's father had
also provided what was appropriate to his station. But in Ivan's case, it became
less the fulfillment of an obligation than a desired object in its own right. It flattered his vanity to rub shoulders with privileged people, and his hospitality
seemed to be part of a conscious effort to lift himself into the ranks of the nobility. A number of merchants in the eighteenth century had beaten the heavy
odds against such an ambition—the Stroganovs and Demidovs most prominently—and these examples may have inspired Ivan to believe that his wealth,
charitable works, and connections could accomplish the same for him.[34] The

Tolchenov townhouse in Dmitrov. Photo by David L. Ransel.

very fact of his keeping a diary, an unusual practice for merchants in the eighteenth century, suggests such an aspiration.

Other evidence likewise points in this direction. Consider his construction of a beautiful masonry home, the first in Dmitrov, done in the style of noble townhouses of the era. This mansion is still standing today and looks much as it must have then, a three-story structure dominating streets lined almost exclusively with one-story log houses. Even more telling is Ivan's most remarkable passion, the construction and outfitting of an orangery. His desire for this exotic display of luxury was evidently longstanding, for he launched the project within two months of the death of his father. In early December 1779 on a trip to Moscow, Ivan acquired the plans for the building of his orangery, and obtained them, interestingly enough, from the gardener of the ennobled merchant family, the Demidovs. At a time when few nobles could boast an orangery, Ivan decided to build one on a grand scale, roughly fifty yards long. He threw himself into the project with gusto, making dozens of trips to Moscow in the early 1780s to examine other orangeries, to solicit advice on their management, and to purchase exotic plants (on one trip buying seventy fruit trees).[35]

How much all this cost Ivan is not known. He did record that in just two years he spent 7,000 rubles on his house alone, and this outlay was far from the full cost. When we recall that his father's declared capital as the wealthiest merchant in Dmitrov was 35,000 rubles and that his closest competitor claimed only 10,000, we have some notion of what Ivan's conspicuous consumption meant in terms of its drain on his treasury.[36] In addition, his taste for a life beyond his means led him into gambling, and losses there likewise set him back. Yet his commerce in these years was prospering, and if it did not do well enough to offset his expenses, its success gave him confidence that he could freely indulge his fancies and ambition.

Children and Education

Although the diary frequently mentions members of Ivan's immediate family, it does not contain much information about the quality of family relationships. Ivan reveals very little, for example, regarding his contacts with or thoughts about his wife, even though they were close companions and spent an increasing amount of time together as the years went by. This silence is significant, if not surprising. Even Russian nobles did not acquire a language for talking about their spouses (apart from poetry) until Turgenev and Dostoevskii arrived to create it.[37] Somewhat more information is conveyed about Ivan's relationship to his surviving children. I begin this section with diary entries during the month preceding the death of his daughter, again to give a flavor of the diary as a whole but also to contrast these terse remarks with more reflective ones that he later made when summing up the events in question.

> October 1787 . . . 14th spent the whole day at home, and in the evening uncle Mikhail Il'ich was at my place. 15th heard mass at the cathedral and the rest of the time I spent at home feeling miserable over the illness of my children Leniushka and Katen'ka. 16th did not go anywhere. 17th I heard vigils and mass at Vvedenskaia church, and in the evening uncle Mikhail Il'ich visited us. 18th spent the whole day at home. 19th vigils and early mass I heard at Vvedenskaia church; the district police captain [*ispravnik*], public prosecutor, and [collegiate assessor] Gruzdev spent the evening with me. . . . 26th I heard mass as Vvedenskaia church; spent the day at home and in the evening until midnight was at the Magistrat building attending meeting of the city council. . . . 31st heard vigils and mass at Vvedenskaia church; Iushkov, the police chief, and Gruzdev spent the evening at my place.
> November. 1st did not go anywhere. 2nd spent the day at home and the

evening at the home of the police chief. 3rd was at home the entire day; we lost hope for my daughter Katen'ka's survival. 4th at 7:28 this morning she passed away to my deepest regret for she had been a joy; after dinner we rode to the monastery to speak with the abbot about permission to bury her there; uncles Ivan Il'ich and Mikhail Il'ich and their families spent the evening at my home. 5th in the morning we took the body of our deceased daughter to the monastery and after mass the funeral service was performed by the abbot together with the brothers and the local parish clergy, and then she was interred. All the clergy who participated in the funeral then dined at our house together with uncle Ivan Il'ich and Fedor Loshkin and their families.

The reproductive record of Ivan and his wife Anna improved on that of Ivan's own parents (it could scarcely have been worse). Yet, as was the case in much of Russia until the twentieth century, more than half their children died within their first days or months of life. This family, in fact, suffered above average losses, having lost 12 of their 16 children before the age of one.[38] If a child died within a few days of its birth, Ivan made little of the event in the diary, except to record that the proper formalities had been observed. For example, the diarist's son Vasilii was born January 1, 1782. A couple of days later, Ivan left for a business trip to Moscow, arriving back home with some in-laws for the baptism on the 9th. Three days later, among other business, he notes that Vasilii was seized by a severe illness and colic pains. The entry for the following day reads: "I served my appointed hours on the municipal court and then returned home. At seven in the evening my son Vasilii passed away."[39] This event did not even warrant mention in his summing up of the important happenings of that year, which included such other things as the success he and his men enjoyed in catching fish or the movement through town of a hussar regiment.[40]

However, if a child survived for a time, Ivan became attached to it, in the case of his daughter Katen'ka apparently deeply so. Hints of this emerge in the brief diary entries above, but we see it far more convincingly in the summing up of the events of the year in question.

October 1787 was a particularly difficult time for the family because two children suddenly fell severely ill, first eight-year-old Aleksei (Leniushka) and then a day later one-year-old Ekaterina (Katen'ka). The illness, which presented as a fever and rash accompanied by severe sore throat, may have begun as scarlet fever or other streptococcal infection (though at first the family's doctor suspected it might be smallpox), and moved rapidly to a pneumonia in the boy. He felt such weakness and pressure in his chest that by the third day he asked his father to allow him to say confession and receive the last sacraments. Soon after doing so and also receiving some medical treatment, the boy began to feel some relief. By the end of a week, he and Katen'ka were both much improved, "for which," Ivan writes, "my wife and I were inexpressibly happy."[41]

But while Leniushka had fully recovered a few days later, Katen'ka, though back to her usual play and learning to walk when held by the hand, continued to show disturbing symptoms. She refused solid food, the rash came and went, a fever lingered. Then on October 27 she took a turn for the worse. "On the 31st she was so weak that she could not sit up using her arms for support, and her chest was so congested that she lost her voice and could only with great difficulty swallow water or milk. Now my wife and I succumbed to all the sadness that only a parental heart can know when being deprived of such a lovely child." In the next days, Katen'ka weakened further, exhibiting a larger and darker rash and increasingly severe symptoms of the pneumonia that finally claimed her life on the morning of November 4. Her father describes in loving detail the white calico, gold ribbon, and silk stockings and slippers in which she was buried as well as many other details of the funeral, including the role played by Katen'ka's favorite horses in pulling the coach bearing her coffin. And then he adds: "So, by the power of God and in punishment for my sins was I deprived of this extraordinarily lovable child. Right from her birth she was completely healthy and well-behaved, and as she grew she was always sprightly and happy, and her games and play were in advance of her years, just as her intelligence was well ahead of her age, for she understood everything right away and even went beyond what you would expect. For example, seeing that a door in a room was not closed or that . . . jars of kvas were not covered, she noticed all that herself and was not content until the things had been put right. She loved horses and cows, and her favorite thing to do was to visit our sorrel horses and to feed them oats, pet them and kiss them. She loved fruits very much, and she developed quite a taste for them when she was but a half year old, and when she was only eight months old she was already picking cherries from the tree. Her face resembled mine exactly and she was so very sweet, and she had two teeth, one of which at her death remained not quite fully grown out. She had not yet begun to walk on her own but could make a circle around the chairs without support—and to me she was exceptionally affectionate."[42]

For children who survive, education becomes an issue. By all accounts, formal schooling was a rarity among Russian merchants of the eighteenth century, despite the efforts of Catherine II to make it available. Her first education adviser, Ivan Betskoi, designed a commerce school for sons of merchants, and the ennobled merchant Prokofii Demidov contributed funds for its construction in Moscow in 1772. Contrary to hopes, very few merchants proved willing to send their sons to the school (some complained of its proximity to the Imperial

Foundling Home and the low status this implied), and the student body came principally from the petty officialdom.[43] For the Tolchenov family, however, education was an important value, one they willingly invested in. Ivan was too young to be able to attend Betskoi's commerce school in Moscow, and his education was traditional. He began learning how to read at age five, apparently mostly on his own. "Although I studied at home without the supervision of a real teacher and was almost an autodidact, in less than a year I began to read with ease all kinds of publications. I then learned how to write, but I must confess that for want of a teacher I did not master good penmanship. I also studied arithmetic through the three rules under the supervision of my father."[44] Unfortunately, it is not clear which of his family members—mother, father, or some other—played the primary role in stimulating Ivan's interest in study, or if the impulse came from some other source. Later at age fourteen in 1768 during his father's residence in St. Petersburg for the Legislative Commission, Ivan did some formal study of geography under the tutelage of a monk from the local seminary.[45] It is evident that Ivan enjoyed books and high culture; each successive decade of his life he recorded a growing interest in museums, theater, and world affairs, an attraction to Europeanized Russian culture that he combined easily with an abiding and deeply rooted commitment to Orthodox practice and spirituality.

The next generation received formal schooling. Ivan's first son, Peter, had to serve the same kind of early apprenticeship in business that Ivan had, moving up and down river with the rhythms of the grain trade. But Peter did so after having completed an expensive education at a private school in Moscow. The cost of instruction and upkeep for a year is listed in the diary; it amounted to 800 rubles, a sum beyond the means of all but the wealthiest nobles and merchants of the age.[46] The value placed on education by this family continued into the following generation as well. In 1805 we find Ivan's grandson, Vladimir Petrovich, at age ten studying in St. Petersburg at the Demidov commercial school, which had been moved from Moscow to the northern capital in the reign of Emperor Paul.[47]

The Family's Decline

Looking back from a distance of ten years, Ivan reflects in this excerpt on the beginning of his financial ruin in the mid-1780s.

> In general, although all three years in a row, i.e. 1784, 1785, and 1786, my commercial dealings were very favorable, I was unable to make any substantive increase in my capital. To be perfectly honest, I cannot at-

tribute this to anything other than my poor management, for I did not give a thought to saving money and did not restrain myself from unnecessary expenditures, thinking that "of my abundance there could be no end," as the psalmist writes. Therefore I spent money, denying myself nothing that I desired. I paid little attention to my commercial affairs and everywhere handled them through agents and perhaps improperly. Not only was I lazy, but I also undertook the building of a house beyond my means and pursued other unnecessary projects and acquaintances merely for the enjoyment of them; and it should be said that I could not [find time] to go to St. Petersburg but instead allowed [my agent] Tiut'kin to make a mess of my affairs there, and I scarcely ever went to my mills [to check on] the grinding of grain and when I did so I did not stay long, and the grinding took place with poor supervision and was not done as it should have been, the result being that a lot more flour was lost than was the case in the past. In a word, these prosperous years were wasted due to my inattention, and later I did not have such an opportunity.[48]

By 1788 Ivan was borrowing heavily to keep up his trade. In the year in question, he made excellent profits of nearly 12,000 rubles, close to his best ever. But these were more than offset by expenses that included 1,000 rubles for work on his residence, 500 for the belltower work and other payments to the church, 470 for repairs on his orangery, 800 for the education of his son, 1,300 for interest on loans, and over 6,000 in household expenses and gambling debts, plus a whopping 11,000 he had to turn over to his step-uncle in this year in fulfillment of the family contract in regard to the "Makarov capital."[49] The following year 1789 profits and expenses were both down considerably, but again expenses outran profits, this time by about 2,000 rubles.

This downward spiral continued in subsequent years and was accelerated by a peculiarly destructive trap into which Ivan fell in an effort to maintain his standing with creditors. His only hope of reestablishing his capital resources was to make big profits in the grain trade. To do this he had to borrow cash to purchase large consignments of grain each winter and to lease mills and barges for processing and transporting the grain, flour, and their by-products to market. In order to borrow adequate funds, he had to continue his lavish style of life so that his creditors would not lose faith in his ability to meet his growing financial obligations. But the lavish living was rapidly eroding this ability. Reflecting on his continued losses in 1792, he confessed that "I hardly had the strength any longer to avert [financial ruin]. But in order to conceal my miserable position and not lose entirely the confidence of others, I did not change my way of living and continued to hope for a fortunate turn of events."[50] Two years later we find him fighting off depression and engaging in avoidance behavior and denial, but by the end of the year finally conceding defeat. In this year, 1794, he was forced to abandon the grain trade for good, no longer able to command the requisite credit. His expenses again far exceeded his income, and they included prominently 3,000 rubles for the marriage of his eldest son Peter.[51] This was an investment well worth making, however, since it helped keep Peter afloat while his father was sinking. The father of Peter's bride also was able to play a role soon after in sheltering Tolchenov family assets from creditors.

The previous year Ivan had begun making some moves to protect himself and his family while he still had the confidence of the community, and his creditors had not yet learned about his lamentable balance sheet. The timber house he had occupied before building his splendid townhouse had been moved and restored at a new location. This now vulnerable asset Ivan sold to his step-uncle. About the same time, he passed up a chance to lease a grain mill and instead shifted his enterprise to another business and a new venue, Moscow, where his current creditors were less likely to be a problem and where his many relatives no doubt provided assistance in obtaining credit. Interestingly, he entered a business close to one of his vices: he leased a factory for making playing cards, and he turned over supervision of the factory to his wife's brother, Ivan Alekseevich Osorgin. The factory actually turned a decent profit of 788 rubles in his first year with it, and so Ivan was able to build a small rescue operation for himself in Moscow from this time on.[52]

Back in Dmitrov, however, Ivan could see the end of his business and social position fast approaching, even if for a time he managed to conceal from others his desperate situation. While still in good standing, he made another shady move to protect his most valuable asset from confiscation. He "sold" his magnificent home to his son's recently acquired father-in-law, a Moscow merchant. This fictive sale evidently involved merely the transfer of a deed of purchase to Peter's father-in-law, the hope being that the home could eventually go to Peter and his family rather than be lost entirely. Ivan continued to live in the house.

This ruse served for only a short time. In the following year, 1796, Ivan's creditors finally discovered his insolvency and his trick of "selling" his home. They came after him with a vengeance. To avoid them and the humiliation of exposure, Ivan sneaked away from home and hid out for the first half of the year at a grain mill still in his possession. For the remainder of the year he moved back to his house secretly and stayed hidden there. These efforts at concealment were merely delaying tactics to give himself time to sell off his assets, this time for real money and in a way that would help his children survive the crash with enough resources to maintain a position in the merchant estate, if not any longer in its higher ranks. Ivan sold off his house for 15,000 rubles and used the trees in his orangery as a means of paying off debts to a few persons whose trust he hoped to retain. His four-person serf family was sold to none other than the famous Count Aleksei Grigor'evich Orlov, hero of the Battle of Chesme.[53]

While relatives could be helpful in a crisis, they could also cause grief, as happened in the case of Ivan's brother-in-law, to whom he had entrusted management of the playing card factory in Moscow. In the same year that Ivan was selling off his properties and winding up his affairs in Dmitrov, this brother-in-law squandered most of the money and product of the playing card factory. He had to be given the boot and Ivan's son Peter was brought in to run the enterprise. But it seemed too risky for Peter to have his fortunes so closely tied to his father's, and Peter's new father-in-law asked that Peter be legally separated from his own family and placed under the protection of the father-in-law.[54] This stratagem proved effective in protecting Peter, and it was evidently also invoked in the case of his brothers. Peter was inscribed in the Moscow merchant estate. Ivan divested himself of virtually all his assets in Dmitrov and descended from the position of the wealthiest merchant in the city to the *meshchanstvo*, a status so "shameful," in his words, that he moved permanently to Moscow, where he lived in relatively modest circumstances managing the card factory and a retail outlet for playing cards until we lose sight of him in 1812 at the time of Napoleon's invasion and occupation of the city. Ivan distributed the financial assets from his sell-off to his younger sons (Aleksei, Pavel, and Iakov), allowing them to hold positions in the third guild of the Dmitrov merchant society. Even Peter's two sons, Ivan's first grandsons, were given enough to hold second guild membership in Dmitrov briefly. After two years, however, they followed their grandfather into the meshchanstvo.

Conclusions

The family had to destroy itself, or at least disassemble its parts, in order to save what it could. And this security, bought at the expense of the family's creditors, was made possible by the lack in Russia of adequate legal provision for bankruptcy. Merchants at the Legislative Commission of Catherine II had complained of just this lack and all the problems it caused for credit operations in the country, but the matter had not been put right yet in the 1790s.[55] Still, none of the relatives connected with the family's trade managed to do anything more than delay the family's and their own decline. Ivan's uncles (Ivan, Mikhail, and Dmitrii), who had played supporting roles in the family grain trade and were second-guild merchants in Dmitrov, lost ground after the collapse of Ivan Alekseevich's business and the family breakup. The two older uncles had to give up commerce and in 1805 enter the meshchanstvo; only the youngest, Dmitrii, succeeded in staying in the Dmitrov merchant class, though at its lowest rank, the third guild.[56] Likewise, Ivan's step-uncle, to whom the diarist had to turn over 11,000 rubles on his majority, was evidently tied to the family enterprise, and his fortunes seemed to be affected by the collapse. Though inscribed in the third guild of Dmitrov, in 1804 he and his son followed the diarist's descent into the meshchanstvo.[57]

There can be no question that personal and accidental factors had much to do with the success of merchant families. The abilities and choices of the head of a family made a difference, and Ivan Tolchenov bore a great responsibility for the failure of his family firm and the ruin he brought to himself and his relatives. But it is equally true that broader currents in technology, commercial climate, government policy, and international affairs affected the fate of this and other merchant families. The rise and fall of commercial families within two or three generations is a common story. Eighteenth-century Russia witnessed an especially rapid turnover, judging from evidence available on three main commercial centers. To take just Moscow, of 328 first-guild merchant families in 1748 only twenty-six maintained their position through the last two decades of the century. Of 235 first-guild merchants about twenty years later (1767), only ten managed to keep that rank to the end of the century.[58] At the end of the century, first-guild families amounted to 137, only twenty-one of which were still in that rank fifteen years later in 1815. In addition to those who stayed in rank, twelve more had risen to the nobility, it is true, but the remaining 76 percent had descended from the top rank, a majority falling out of the merchant class altogether.[59] Among these was the diarist's relative I. A. Makarov, the nephew of his father-in-law who, it will be recalled, made big money in tanneries and moved into the Moscow merchant class as a "distinguished citizen." By 1811, he had dropped to the second guild, and seven years later following his death, his son had to leave the merchant estate for the meshchanstvo.[60]

The larger forces working against a provincial merchant like Ivan Tolchenov were two. The first was the emergence of a Russian national market with a strong hub in Moscow, which drew more and more commercial operations toward itself. Leading merchant families in the district cities gravitated toward Moscow so that by the end of the century nearly 40 percent of the first-guild Moscow merchants were families who had recently moved there from other towns.[61] The Tolchenovs, too, were moving in that direction. The older generations married almost exclusively women of Moscow merchant families, and the diarist was able to establish his first son Peter in that city, if not on the solid footing that he had hoped. This larger movement drained capital from the district towns and, in turn, the trade, which required those capital resources. By century's end, district towns no longer had any first-guild merchants and even second-guild merchants were becoming scarce.

The second matter was one that had hobbled the merchant estate through-out Russian history, competition from the nobility and peasants. This became especially acute in the second half of the eighteenth century when the government removed protections from the merchants and opened enterprise to everyone. Nobles ran manorial manufactories using serf labor and benefiting from special tax exemptions and easy loans advanced by government banks. Ordinary peasants dominated the small trade at periodic markets, while a number of wealthy peasants (including serfs) established large manufacturing operations. These peasant industrialists did not have to perform the civic duties and pay the high taxes levied on merchants. The Continental Blockade imposed by Napoleon and, finally, his invasion and destruction of Moscow also contributed to the ruin of some merchant families.

Given the heavy odds against success as a merchant, Ivan Tolchenov's aspiration to join the nobility was not surprising. As we have seen, Ivan was a gambler. The gamble of self-fashioning, of somehow turning himself into a noble through his education and that of his son, his interest in theater and art, his charitable endeavors, his entertainments of princes and other dignitaries, his townhouse and orangery was not simply a fantasy. These activities flattered his vanity, but they also may have been the only reasonable path to security for his family in the long run. Nobles occupied a stable legal position that could not change with their capital holdings. They also had privileges and resources that gave them an advantage in business. How could one compete in the growing manufacturing sector without access to land and cheap labor, not to mention special subsidies, which nobles (and even serf industrialists) enjoyed? Moreover, the political climate was not entirely unfavorable to this aspiration at the time Ivan first began to entertain it. A substantial number of merchant families had moved into the nobility in the first half of the eighteenth century, and even as late as 1775 the new law on provincial governance provided openings for merchants to obtain rank, "wear the sword," and share in other privileges of the nobility. However, just ten years later, the Charter of Towns and related statutes withdrew some of these opportunities and sharpened the division between the top merchants and the nobility.[62] It was about this time, too, that Ivan's excessive expenditures in pursuit of an impressive style of life were beginning to catch up with him. A simultaneous turn in the legal environment and in his personal fortunes conspired to end Ivan's chances of rising into the nobility.

It is worth pointing out in this connection that the movement into the nobility of the wealthiest and most successful merchants during the preceding two centuries, while serving the personal interests of those families, was harmful to the merchant estate as a whole and probably also to Russian commercial development.[63] The rise of these families drained capital, leadership, and a sense of solidarity from this social group and left it all the weaker in the face of competition from above and below.

Finally, linked to the anxiety of being a merchant is another, deeper concern that comes out in the diary: the importance of honor, reputation, personal respect. This concern was expressed in many of the merchant instructions to Catherine's Legislative Commission and was obviously of great importance to Ivan. It is difficult to separate what is instrumental from what is personal in this. Russia had laws and courts but not legality in a modern sense; that is, personal relations were far more important than legal norms. And, consequently, reputation and the personal relations built on it were crucial to obtaining credit, protection, justice, right of expression, or any other public or private good.[64] Ivan's need to keep face by continuing to cut a figure in Dmitrov society even after his financial slide was instrumental to the extent that it allowed him time and credit to reorganize his plans and save what he could for his children and grandchildren. But it also served a personal need to maintain his sense of belonging to a social sphere that in reality was beyond him. Until his ruin was complete, he continued his contacts with the local nobility and high clergy, and he liked to think of some of them as his "friends," as he recalled in later years when he noted their passing with brief obituary comments in his diary. But once his money was gone, the visits from nobles and other dignitaries decreased, and Ivan (by then living in Moscow) was most often in the company of commercial people.

Notes

1. Michael Confino, "Issues and Nonissues in Russian Social History and Historiography," *Occasional Paper*, Kennan Institute for Advanced Russian Studies, no. 165.

2. These are recent defining works in cultural history: Emmanuel Le Roy Ladurie, *Montaillou: The Promised Land of Error* (Braziller, 1978); Natalie Zemon Davis, *The Return of Martin Guerre* (Harvard, 1983); Carlo Ginzburg, *The Cheese and the Worms: The Cosmos of a Sixteenth-Century Miller* (Penguin Books, 1982); Laurel Thatcher Ulrich, *A Midwife's Tale: The Life of Martha Ballard, Based on Her Diary, 1785–1812* (Vintage Books, 1991).

3. A brief background to the development of this approach in Italy can be found in the introduction by Edward Muir, "Observing Trifles," to the book *Microhistory & the Lost Peoples of Europe*, ed. Edward Muir and Guido Ruggiero, trans. Eren Branch (Baltimore, 1991). See also Giovanni Levi, "On Microhistory," in *New Perspectives on Historical*

Writing, ed. Peter Burke (University Park, Penn., 1991), 93–113; and Carlo Ginzburg, "Microhistory: Two or Three Things that I Know about It," *Critical Inquiry,* 20 (Autumn, 1993), 10–35.

4. For Siegfried Kracauer's view, see his posthumously published, *History: The Last Things before the Last,* especially chap. 5 (New York, 1969). For a recent detailed explication of Kracauer's ideas about history, Dagmar Barnouw, *Critical Realism: History, Photography, and the Work of Siegfried Kracauer* (Baltimore, 1994).

5. *Zhurnal ili zapiska zhizni i prikliuchenii Ivana Alekseevicha Tolchenova,* Rukopisnyi otdel Biblioteki Akademii Nauk, shifr 34.8.15. kn. 1–3 (I have filmed and transcribed this manuscript copy from the St. Petersburg archive of the Russian Academy of Sciences).

6. A stereotype repeated in the most recent Western book on Russian urban life: Daniel R. Brower, *The Russian City between Tradition and Modernity, 1850–1900* (Berkeley, 1990), chap. 1.

7. N. S. Vsévolojsky, *Dictionnaire géographique-historique de l'empire de Russie* (Moscow, 1813), 163–64. *Dmitrovskii krai: Istoriia, priroda, chelovek . . . Rasskazy, ocherki, vospominaniia* (Dmitrov, 1993), 24–29. M. N. Tikhomirov, *Rossiiskoe gosudarstvo XV–XVII vekov,* 269, 273–75, cited in *Goroda podmoskov'ia v trekh knigakh,* kn. 2 (Moscow, 1980), 83.

8. *Dmitrovskii krai,* 28.

9. Galloon is gold or silver braid (or other trim) made for military or civil service uniforms.

10. See excerpt from F. I. Tokmakov, *Istoriko-statisticheskoe i arkheograficheskoe opisanie goroda Dmitrova,* chap. 2 (Moscow, 1893), 9, cited in *Dmitrovskii krai,* 50–51; figures also given in N. I. Pavlenko, "I. A. Tolchenov i ego 'Zhurnal'," in *Zhurnal ili zapiska zhizni i prikliuchenii Ivana Alekseevicha Tolchenova,* ed. N. I. Pavlenko (Moscow, 1974), 6.

11. Excerpt of Müller's text from F. I. Tokmakov, *Istoriko-statisticheskoe i arkheograficheskoe opisanie goroda Dmitrova,* chap. 2 (Moscow, 1893), 9, cited in *Dmitrovskii krai,* 50–51.

12. A. I. Aksenov, *Ocherki genealogii uezdnogo kupechestva XVIII v.* (Moscow, 1993), 64–65. B. N. Mironov, *Russkii gorod v 1740–1860-e gody* (Leningrad, 1990), 166–69.

13. The protocols were discovered in the Dmitrov archives by V. Kh. Bodisko and are reported in Pavlenko, "A. I. Tolchenov," 7.

14. *Zhurnal ili zapiska zhizni i prikliuchenii Ivana Alekseeva Tolchenova,* Rukopisnyi otdel Biblioteki Akademii nauk, shifr 34.8.15. kn. 1, ll. 2–3. The diary document is the product of a compilation by the author of notes (now lost) taken in the course of his daily life and work, which he began assembling in the 1790s in a clean draft ultimately consisting of three separate books. This compilation took place over the course of many years and included occasional reflections by the diarist on his past actions. A portion of the diary, mostly the first book, was published in 1974 in a small rotoprint edition of 300 copies by Pavlenko (see earlier citation). Citations in this paper are to the archival copy and will be typed (using this note's citation as a model) as follows: *Zhurnal,* 1:2–3.

15. Aksenov, *Ocherki genealogii uezdnogo kupechestva,* 77.

16. In 1774, he declared a capital of over 35,000 rubles. The next wealthiest merchant (not counting the combined declaration of his brothers) was Stepan Loshkin with declared capital of 10,000 rubles. *Zhurnal,* 1:49.

17. Pavlenko, "A. I. Tolchenov," 7–8.

18. Aksenov, *Ocherki genealogii uezdnogo kupechestva*, 11, 91.

19. *Zhurnal*, 1:32.

20. *Zhurnal*, 1:139. This record of child death leaves little doubt that Ivan's mother was not nursing her children but using a local or household wet nurse.

21. *Zhurnal*, 1:4.

22. I am going to begin this subsection and subsequent ones with excerpts from the diary to give a flavor of the source, as was the practice of Laurel Ulrich in her book *The Midwife's Tale*.

23. The precision with which Tolchenov often records time raises interesting questions about temporal consciousness and its meaning in this period and social group, which I plan to treat in coming work on this family.

24. *Zhurnal*, 2:271.

25. Aksenov, *Ocherki genealogii uezdnogo kupechestva*, 76.

26. *Zhurnal*, 1:5–6.

27. Aksenov, *Ocherki genealogii uezdnogo kupechestva*, 86–87.

28. It is, however, possible that his entry on the marriage choice may be repeating the accepted form for recording such events.

29. This date is mistranscribed in the rotoprint edition as 18th.

30. *Zhurnal*, 1:15.

31. *Zhurnal*, 1:152.

32. *Zhurnal*, 1:262, 1:357, 2:32–33.

33. See the entries for 1783 in vol. 1 of the *Zhurnal*.

34. See the list of recipients of nobility patents by merchants, industrialists, and tax farmers in Arcadius Kahan, *The Plow, the Hammer, and the Knout: An Economic History of Eighteenth-Century Russia*, ed. Richard Hellie (Chicago, 1985), 278. Also comments by Alfred J. Rieber, *Merchants and Entrepreneurs in Imperial Russia* (Chapel Hill, 1982), 37–38.

35. *Zhurnal* 1:147 to end of volume, passim.

36. Even if, as we know, merchants did not always declare their full wealth.

37. I want to thank my colleague Nina Perlina for observations on this point. In his final work, Iurii Lotman looks at related issues: *Besedy o russkoi kul'ture: Byt i traditsii russkogo dvorianstva (XVIII–nachalo XIX veka)* (St. Petersburg, 1994), especially "Zhenskii mir," 46–74.

38. The names and birth (and death) dates of Ivan's children are appended to book 2 of the diary.

39. *Zhurnal*, 1:208.

40. *Zhurnal*, 1:235.

41. *Zhurnal*, 2:20–22.

42. *Zhurnal*, 2:23–24. These and other stories of children in the diary provide material for the continuing historiographical debate on the past emotional relationship and behavior of parents toward their offspring. For a recent review of the debate, see Karin Calvert, *Children in the House: The Material of Early Childhood, 1600–1900* (Boston, 1992), Introduction.

43. P. M. Maikov, *Ivan Ivanovich Betskoi: opyt ego biografii* (St. Petersburg, 1904), 412–15. Also, Hugh D. Hudson, Jr., *The Rise of the Demidov Family and the Russian Iron Industry in the Eighteenth Century* (Newtonville, Mass., 1986), 104.

44. *Zhurnal*, 1:2.

45. *Zhurnal*, 1:5.

46. Arcadius Kahan, "The Costs of 'Westernization' in Russia: The Gentry and the Economy in the Eighteenth Century," *Slavic Review*, 25:1 (March 1966).

47. *Zhurnal*, 3:192. See also Hudson, *Rise of the Demidov Family*, 104.

48. Ivan penned this comment in 1796 when he was assembling his notes for the year 1786 and writing them up in a clean draft.

49. *Zhurnal*, 2:64–65.

50. *Zhurnal*, 2:202.

51. *Zhurnal*, 2:226–27.

52. *Zhurnal*, 2:236–37.

53. *Zhurnal*, 2:322.

54. Ibid.

55. Credit operations in eighteenth-century Russia were notoriously weak. Significantly, the chapter on banking and credit in Kahan's huge study of the period is the shortest in the book, running to only eight pages and treating mostly grants to nobles. Only at the very end of the century, with the establishment of the Assignat Bank in 1797, was some form of state-regulated credit provided for the commercial classes. Kahan, *The Plow, the Hammer, and the Knout*, 311–18.

56. Aksenov, *Ocherki genealogii uezdnogo kupechestva*, 10.

57. Aksenov, *Ocherki genealogii uezdnogo kupechestva*, 11.

58. A. I. Aksenov, *Genealogiia moskovskogo kupechestva XVIII v.* (Moscow, 1988), 61. For similarly high turnover in Russian merchants active in foreign trade at the ports of Archangel and St. Petersburg, see Mironov, *Russkii gorod*, 166–68.

59. Aksenov, *Genealogiia moskovskogo kupechestva*, 85 (table 5).

60. Aksenov, *Ocherki genealogii uezdnogo kupechestva*, 11.

61. Aksenov, *Genealogiia moskovskogo kupechestva*, 62 (table 2).

62. N. I. Pavlenko, "Odvorianivanie russkoi burzhuazii v XVIII v.," *Istoriia SSSR* (1961), no. 2, 71–87. Iu. R. Klokman, *Sotsial'no-ekonomicheskaia istoriia russkogo goroda: vtoraia polovina XVIII veka* (Moscow, 1967), 111–19.

63. A point first argued by a contemporary, Prince M. M. Shcherbatov, "Razmyshleniia o ushcherbe torgovli proiskhodiashchem vykhozhdeniem velikogo chisla kuptsov v dvoriane i v ofitsery," *Chteniia v imperatorskom obshchestve istorii i drevnostei rossiiskikh*, no. 1 (1860), 135–40.

64. I have written about this general issue in earlier works, especially, *The Politics of Catherinian Russia* (New Haven, 1975), and "Character and Style of Patron-Client Relations in Russia," *Klientelsysteme im Europa der Frühen Neuzeit*, ed. Antoni Maczak (Munich, 1988), 211–31.

11

Freemasonry and the Public in Eighteenth-Century Russia

Douglas Smith

————◁∞▷————

ONCE PRIMARILY THE province of its official chroniclers and conspiracy theorists of various stripes, Freemasonry has gained increasing scholarly attention in the past several decades. While numerous studies have been devoted to the history of the lodges in Western and Central Europe—focusing particularly on their importance for early modern political culture—Russia's significant Masonic movement composed of over 3,000 members active in more than 135 lodges in the eighteenth century has long been ignored and remains poorly understood to this day.[1]

By raising a series of new questions about Russian Masonry, this essay seeks to reexamine some of the traditional interpretations not only of the Masonic movement but the history of imperial Russia as well. To assess adequately Freemasonry's historical significance necessitates laying bare its connections to a host of comparable institutions and practices that were then emerging to form a new Russian public sphere, one not unlike those taking shape in other parts of Europe. Not the sole refuge for those men seeking conviviality and purposeful social interaction with like-minded compatriots, Russia's lodges were but part of a developing network of social spaces including theaters, clubs, salons, and similar sodalities that served as meeting places for educated society or, to use the then common appellation, *publika*. So as its title suggests, this article examines two distinct yet tightly interconnected topics—Freemasonry and the Russian public. And it attempts, by viewing Freemasonry within the broader framework of the public, both to offer a new interpretation of the former's historical meaning and to suggest the latter's overlooked importance for our understanding of eighteenth-century Russia. Before turning to the discussion of Masonry and its relationship to the Russian *publika*, however, a few words on the established historiography are in order.

I.

Although the history of the lodges has been little studied for most of the past seventy years, Russian scholars working in the second half of the nineteenth and the beginning of the twentieth century did produce a sizable body of literature on the subject.[2] It is not at all surprising, therefore, that given the lack of any substantive reinterpretations, this literature continues to shape greatly our understanding of the Russian Masonic movement. By adopting the existing interpretive framework, one which, as I discuss below, is deeply flawed methodologically, the handful of recent studies fails to rethink Freemasonry and its importance for Russian history and uncritically reiterates the outmoded assumptions that inform the earlier works.[3]

Traditionally, scholars have relegated Freemasonry to the domain of intellectual history. More specifically, it has been problematized as a component in the history of the intelligentsia. According to this historiography, the pervasiveness of Voltairianism (*vol'terianstvo*) and free-thinking (*vol'nodumstvo*) in eighteenth-century Russia's intellectual climate and, others sometimes add, the social tensions with which society was rife combined to produce a flight on the part of some of the educated élite into the lodge's sanctuary of quietist self-contemplation and a more secularized religiosity. Historians' interpretations of this flight, however, have varied and can generally be divided into two opposing camps.

For most positivist and Marxist historians, both pre- and postrevolutionary, Masonic membership marks the dividing line between progressive action and reactionary withdrawal. Thus, in his multivolume study of Russian social thought, Georgii Plekhanov (1856–1918), the "father of Russian Marxism," saw Russian Masonry as an expression of a broader "reaction against liberating philosophy (*osvoboditel'naia filosofiia*)" coming out of France that characterized the socially "backward" countries of Eastern Europe. Equating Russian Masonic ideology with mysticism, Plekhanov attributed its popularity to Russians' intellectual immaturity vis-à-vis the West which, according to him, accounted for their shock and psychological discomfort when confronted with the age's "most progressive ideas" and their ensuing "flight from our sinful world" into the *Jenseits* of the lodge.[4] The influential Soviet literary scholar G. P. Makogonenko expressed a similar view in the 1950s, arguing that, unlike the intelligentsia who remained socially and politically engaged, the Masons represented those who "simply ran from the world of reality into an inner universe, into a moral world."[5]

The opposing interpretation has perhaps been best articulated in the writings of the historian and leading figure in Russia's Constitutional Democratic Party, Pavel Miliukov (1859–1943). For Miliukov, Voltairianism was homologous to the court, the sphere in which it had most currency: while it initially attracted the literate classes with its sparkle and brilliance, Voltairianism's charms, like those of court society, were artificial, superficial, fleeting, and ultimately rejected. In his view, many educated Russians floundered in a spiritual and intellectual no-man's-land between Voltairianism and the traditional religious world view of their fathers, which they had earlier renounced but now felt lost without. Therefore, the "vanguard of the Russian intelligentsia," those who composed the most intellectually prepared of their generation, turned to Masonry, a movement in which they discovered a new "faith, a faith, however, enlightened by reason." While agreeing with the assertion that Masonry shifted Russians' attention away from the political realm toward a spiritual examination of their inner selves, Miliukov maintained that Masonry, through its explicit disregard for conventional norms of social distinction, played a "huge role" in the nation's social development and in the history of the intelligentsia.[6]

The pervasive focus on the history of the intelligentsia—the search for its ideological origins and initial estrangement from the state and the concern with charting the path that led from this "parting of ways" to the eventual and "inevitable" rise of revolutionary ideologies and parties—has been at once inherently teleological and anachronistic.[7] It has led to the projection of late-nineteenth- and twentieth-century social categories and intellectual constructs back onto the eighteenth century. Neither the Masons nor those opposed to the movement thought of themselves as members of an "intelligentsia"; nor did they construct their world on a distinction between a personal, moral sphere, on the one hand, and a social, political sphere, on the other. The opposition between progressive intellectuals and conservative state upon which these readings are based also bears little resemblance to the realities of eighteenth-century Russian society. Clearly, such distinctions belong to a later period.

By emplotting Freemasonry into the larger narrative of the history of the intelligentsia, historians have adopted an interpretive strategy that fails to capture much of the movement's complexities and that overlooks its usefulness as an entry point into an examination of the local logic of élite life in eighteenth-century Russia. For not only were the intellectual concerns that informed Masonic ideology more widely shared than has usually been recognized, but the practice of sociability the Freemasons exhibited was more widespread as well. As will be shown below, the lodges were not some sort of conventicle—the prototype of future revolutionary cells—but part of the larger network of new spaces and practices shared by the growing public in eighteenth-century Russia. Any attempt to account for the very existence and popularity of Freemasonry must locate the lodges within this broader social topography.

II.

In 1786 three anti-Masonic plays penned by Catherine II were staged at the Winter Palace's Hermitage Theater: *The Deceiver, The Deceived,* and *The Siberian Shaman.* The tsarina intended her satirical depictions of the Masons, however, for a much broader audience than simply the highly circumscribed court élite attending these performances. That very year the Academy of Sciences published anonymous editions of these plays in Russian (both *The Deceiver* and *The Deceived* went through two printings) and two private publishers printed German translations as well. The weekly *Mirror of the World* for February 9, 1786, included a glowing review of *The Deceiver*—every page of which the reviewer characterized as marked by the "spirit of the *great Molière*"—and the February and March editions of the *Growing Vine* were largely devoted to praising this play and to denigrating further the image of Freemasonry and its practitioners.[8] According to one historian, this last example was an obvious attempt by Catherine and her court menials to manipulate public opinion about the staging and publication of her plays and to garner the public's support in her distrust of Masonry.[9]

At first glance this interpretation seems odd: what sort of public opinion was there at the height of Russian absolutism and why would Catherine have felt it necessary or desirable to influence it? Certainly we must be faced with the introduction of a thoroughly contemporary concept into a context in which it simply does not belong. But as a large and growing body of historical work has shown, our modern notions of "the public" and "public opinion" arose under the Old Regime in general, and during the eighteenth century in particular. Building on the pioneering studies of Reinhart Koselleck and Jürgen Habermas, published over thirty years ago, scholars have been engaged in a broad examination of Old Regime politics, society, and culture in their various local contexts; the result has been the development of new approaches in conceptualizing the changes that took place in eighteenth-century Europe. Among the topics taken up—such as the emergence of voluntary societies and associations and the changing forms of sociability and civility—perhaps the most important has been the development of the public.[10] Recent research into the function and numerous manifestations of the public and publicity has shed new light on the changing practices of power under the Old Regime as emerging groups and institutions began to discuss and to define issues over which traditional political and religious authorities had once held a monopoly and as "the public," in its various guises and locations, was increasingly invoked as the only objective, metasocial arbiter capable of judging claims made not only in the cultural but even the political sphere.[11]

To assume, however, that these discussions have any direct bearing on our understanding of eighteenth-century Russia, that Russia too had a comparable public sphere, initially appears untenable. On one level it seems anachronistic; on another it suggests an overly simplistic and unwarranted comparison with the rest of Europe. While the idea of a public comfortably fits within the more highly differentiated social, political, and intellectual settings of England or France, in Russia, with the dominance of the tsarist court in political—and to a large though lesser extent cultural and intellectual—affairs, the comparatively low level of literacy, and the complete lack of any significant middling classes, it seems unwarranted. Moreover, it has been a long-standing truism that it was Russia's total lack of any public sphere, or civil society, that characterized its (usually regrettable) "uniqueness" vis-à-vis the West.

But none of this should distract us from the fact that the public was a central term in Russian élite culture. In the famous polemics of 1769 carried out between the satirical journals *All Sorts of Things* and the *Drone*, for example, the *Drone*'s editor, the young publisher and critic Nikolai Novikov, not only recognized his obligation to "the public," but even gave the final word in their disputes to the "judgment of the public (*na sud publike*)," understood to be a "sensible" and "impartial" social body.[12] Of course, the existence of the public in Russia has been acknowledged before. Yet even though many academic works on the period incorporate some idea of the public in their discussions, most simultaneously deny it any significance for Russia's social and political order.[13] Thus, even if admitted as a historical reality, the public as a subject of inquiry with its own particular genesis, various institutions, and functions, has been largely overlooked until only very recently.[14] The aim here is to put forward some possible ways of envisioning and describing this public and to suggest how its inclusion in the historiography can offer new insights into the age.

The concept of the public employed here refers to two spheres: one purely immanent, or discursive, the other concrete, or physical. As might be expected, the term first entered the Russian language during the Petrine period in the beginning of the eighteenth century.[15] By the end of the century, as Novikov's words demonstrate (and it is possible to supply countless similar references), the public had become a constituent element of educated Russians' mental framework. Throughout the first half of the century, the public, as a discursively constructed body defined by certain shared traits, attitudes, and habits, is largely absent from contemporary discourse. What is evident is the notion of public *acts*. In 1728, for example, the *St. Petersburg News* directed its readers' attention to the "ceremonial public entrance" of Peter II into Moscow and to the "public assembly" and "public meeting" held in the new capital in honor of Peter's coronation.[16] Lacking from the reports is the sense of a public involved in these activities. Rather, the status of those involved, the tsar and a handful of noble personages, conferred upon their actions an aura of publicness.

This "representative publicness," in which, as defined by Habermas, the function of publicity was to display the power and authority of the autocracy and the social order upon which it was based before an audience of subjects, continued to be an important component in Russian political culture throughout the eighteenth century.[17] Nonetheless, by the reign of Catherine the Great a different public sphere, one constituted by and located in recently emerged practices and spaces, had taken shape.[18]

Unlike the earlier notion of the public, the new public sphere was a literate one and literacy to a great extent determined one's ability to participate in it. With the dramatic spread of learning and the concomitant expansion of the book and periodical market, formerly disparate and unassociated Russians became connected through the medium of print.[19] This development is demonstrated by the list of subscribers for the *Mirror of the World* in 1786 which ranged from the empress to a peasant—one Zakhar Vasil'ev Kislov—and included several high-ranking courtiers, state and church officials of various levels, and merchants. In addition to joining persons traditionally segregated by considerable social distance, this and other periodicals brought together Russians also separated by geography. The *Mirror of the World*, for example, was subscribed to in dozens of localities, extending from Reval in the west to Perm' in the east and Astrakhan in the south. In the second half of the century, the print market reached a level of density able to produce a sense of shared identity among those with access to it. Through the joint acts of subscription and reading of journals and books, these individuals came to see themselves and their relationship to each other in a new fashion, i.e., as members of a new community, that of the reading public.[20]

The "honorable public," as this discursive entity was usually called in the press, was connected by more than print. Equally important in its formation was the growing number of *physical* sites where sociable interaction was possible. According to one historian, the eighteenth century was for Western Europe the "sociable century" and this holds true for Russia as well—at least for its two capitals (St. Petersburg and Moscow) and a number of provincial cities.[21] In Catherinian Russia, the public was busy gathering in a series of newly formed venues, including theaters, clubs, societies, circles, coffeehouses, libraries, as well as Masonic lodges.

Perhaps best known among such newly formed institutions was St. Petersburg's English Club, established in 1770 with thirty-eight members. During the reign of Catherine the Great, the club, which maintained its own quarters and provided its members with a convivial setting for playing cards and billiards, reading, dining, and conversation, was one of the most esteemed and popular clubs in St. Petersburg. The capital city was home to several other clubs such as the Schuster Club (also known as the Large Burgher Club), founded in 1770 and composed of state officials, wealthy Russian and foreign merchants, prosperous craftsmen, and various artists, and the American Club, founded in 1783 as an outgrowth of the Burgher Club, which counted 600 members by 1800. Of a somewhat different nature were St. Petersburg's two dance and three music clubs or societies, which put on regular concerts, masquerades, and balls for their hundreds of members. St. Petersburg, however, did not hold a monopoly on these new sodalities. Moscow possessed its own English Club and a Nobleman's Club (later revived as the Moscow Noble Society), while in Kronstadt Admiral S. K. Greig established the Maritime Society and the city of Reval was home to the Harmony Club, to name but a few.[22]

Although the role of these clubs and societies in Russia's social and cultural life remains largely unexamined, their growing significance during the second half of the century is suggested by the rapid growth in their membership. Faced with an expanding pool of prospective members, St. Petersburg's English Club, for example, decided to limit its numbers to 300 in 1780. What is noteworthy is that the club chose to restrict access at the *upper* end of the social scale: all future members, it was decided, could not possess a rank (*chin*) higher than brigadier in the Table of Ranks.[23] Those who held higher ranks were not deterred, however, and continued to seek admission. In 1801 the club finally repealed the ruling—a fact that attests to the importance Russia's élite placed on membership in such clubs.[24]

While primarily established as social gatherings, some clubs were also actively involved in various charitable and benevolent enterprises. St. Petersburg's English Club created in 1772 a "special cash-box for the poor," the contents of which were to be distributed yearly, and the Large Burgher Club set aside a considerable portion of its resources for charity, part of which was used to support over 100 pensioners.[25]

Sodalities with a more utilitarian and narrowly defined purpose were established as well. Examples of this sort of association are St. Petersburg's Mercantile Society (*Kommercheskoe obshchestvo*), founded in 1784 in order to provide the city's merchants an arena for exchanging news necessary for the conducting of business (and for engaging in friendly discussions and card games) and the Mortality Society (*Obshchestvo na smertnye sluchai*), created in 1775 and open to "people of any rank or profession (*vsiakago zvaniia liudi*)" as a vehicle for members to provide financial support for their families upon death.[26]

The eighteenth century also witnessed the creation of several learned societies and circles. The first and most prominent was the Free Economic Society, founded in 1765 upon the initiative of several eminent courtiers and scientists as a patriotic society dedicated to furthering Russia's agriculture and economy. Similar societies appeared not long after. In 1771 the head of Moscow University, I. I. Melissino, created the Free Russian Assembly modeled after the French Academy and composed of the university's professors, famous scholars, and poets; and in 1779 Johann Georg Schwartz, a professor at the university and a central figure in Moscow's Masonic circles, helped establish the Friendly Learned Society whose goal was to spread enlightenment through the publication of useful books, the dissemination of the principles of proper upbringing, and the training of Russian educators.[27]

Finally, the Masonic lodges represented another important institution in the new landscape of the Russian public sphere. Brought to Russia by travelers from England, Germany, and other parts of Europe before the middle of the century, the lodges reached their heyday in the 1770s and 1780s when almost one hundred lodges were in operation. While the country's two capitals served as the major centers of Masonic activity with over sixty lodges between them, slightly more than half of the lodges were located outside these two dominant urban centers in over forty cities, towns, and villages spread throughout Russia's provinces.[28] As in the rest of Europe, the Masonic movement in Russia exhibited a heterogeneous and protean nature characterized by various Masonic systems, frequently in competition with one another, and by a wide range of intellectual orientations and traditions.[29]

In addition to these organizations, the Russian public met in numerous other locales as a cursory perusal of two periodicals demonstrates. In 1780, for example, the *St. Petersburg News* carried advertisements and announcements for, among other things, several concert series, including one to be held in the home of Prince Grigorii Potemkin and another put on by a Society of Italian Actors in the house of the Free Economic Society; a performance of the Russian comic opera "The Good Soldiers" at the German Theater; and the sale of tickets in the Summer Garden's coffeehouse for an upcoming fireworks display. Two issues of the *Moscow News* from 1756 contain an advertisement for a weekly series of concerts to be held in the home of the wife of General Litskin in the German Quarter and an announcement that the library of Moscow University would henceforth be open to the public every Wednesday and Saturday between 2:00 and 5:00 P.M.[30]

The unpublished diary of a young senate clerk, Aleksei Il'in, offers a par-

ticularly vivid glimpse into the sociability of the age. For Il'in, whose diary records his activities and thoughts as a young man in Moscow and St. Petersburg
in the mid-1770s, life revolved around social affairs. The great bulk of his entries
are devoted to chronicling the time spent in pleasant pursuits: strolling with
his male acquaintances in Moscow's Golovinskii Garden admiring the young
females they encountered there; attending masquerade balls, concerts, and one
of St. Petersburg's musical clubs; dining out several times a week; reading and
discussing the journal the *Painter* in the company of close friends; and making
frequent visits to different Masonic lodges.[31] The predominance of these events
in Il'in's diary attests to their centrality in his self-perception as a figure active
in public life and intimates their broader import as constituent elements of élite
life in this period.

The new spaces visited by men like Il'in were public in a very real sense of
the word.[32] Balls, concerts, masquerades, clubs, and theaters were not the exclusive reserve of the court élite or of the nobility. Rather, admission to these and
similar events and spaces was determined to a large extent by one's ability to
pay. Just as the market of print brought together representatives of various social
classes and helped to forge a new social identity, so too did these sites of sociability where people from different social stations and professions—merchants,
musicians, doctors, actors, and officials from practically all levels of the growing
state apparatus—mingled with notables and mighty courtiers.

Naturally, not everyone was permitted to share these spaces, and the borders of the public sphere were not left unguarded. On one level, literacy represented one criterion for membership; on another, social standing frequently operated as an additional requirement. What is surprising, however, is the wide
social breadth of this sphere. On May 19, 1780, the *St. Petersburg News* published
an announcement from the Imperial Academy of Sciences informing the "honorable public" of the opening of the Kunstkamera (the academy's museum,
which grew out of Peter the Great's collection of art and curiosities) to visitors
at the end of the month. Readers were instructed to pick up their admission
tickets a day before their planned visit. The only groups specifically excluded
from this invitation were "livery servants and the lowest ranks of the common
people (*prostaia chern'*)" for whom entrance was prohibited.[33]

As in other parts of Europe in the eighteenth century, the public in Russia
was not constructed in opposition to the political and social élite; rather its distinction from the "common people" largely determined its meaning.[34] As the
right to participate in the public sphere was not founded upon corporate notions of hierarchy, or upon the Table of Ranks, a different set of criteria, based
in part on new norms of deportment and on certain physical markers (e.g.,
clothing), was used to distinguish members of the public from the *prostaia*

chern'. Thus, admission tickets to a theater erected on St. Petersburg's Palace Square on July 11, 1765, were handed out to the most distinguished personages of both genders, to all civilian and military officials, as well as to all those who were properly attired.[35] The fact that the new public sphere was constructed around the existing élite meant that the older logic of representative publicness was not fully undermined; rather its field of operation was expanded through its transference into this new sphere. To be a member of the public was to possess and, more importantly, to exhibit one's superior social status as a participant in this sphere. Vladimir Zolotnitskii's *Society of Various Personae, or Discourses on Human Actions and Manners*, with its harsh condemnation of those who seek to acquire the aura of power that comes with being "an esteemed member of the public," reflects this aspect of the public sphere.[36]

While the public was defined as a symbolic space by its distinction from the common people, this space was not, as Vladimir Zolotnitskii's remarks indicate, uniform. Rather, it was thoroughly riven with tensions, divisions, and rivalries, and publicity was used increasingly as a weapon in the numerous struggles among the groups and alliances that made up the public. If at the beginning of the century, power was sought through the more opaque means of personal influence and patronage within the confines of the court, by the time of Catherine II the nature and the arena of power had changed. Although court intrigue maintained much, or perhaps most, of its former significance, now power and status were also being negotiated through public debate and in the new institutions that made up the public.

Which brings us back to Catherine's tactics in her criticism of Freemasonry. Her staging of these anti-Masonic plays at the court theater reflects the logic of absolutism. Power is centered at court, and, more specifically, in the autocrat who authors the scripts—in this instance both figuratively and literally. The plays were intended for a highly circumscribed audience whose role was to receive them uncritically, to learn quietly the lessons they were meant to teach, and to act accordingly. The publication of Catherine's plays, on the other hand, points to a different logic, one in which decisions are reached through the consensus born of critical reasoning. Presupposed in this process is both an expanded sphere of participation and the relative equality of its participants; what is decisive is not the height of one's social position, but the depth of one's ideas. Catherine's decision to publish her anti-Masonic writings anonymously, as though they were the work of an anonymous member of the public, demonstrates her recognition of the new public sphere's unwritten rules. Even though the idea of equality within the public sphere was a fiction, the sphere's important role in the political culture of late-eighteenth-century Russia was recognized by all.

III.

Catherine was neither the first nor the only one to reprove Freemasonry publicly. Her polemical writings were part of a much broader public debate on the meaning of the Masonic movement in Russia.[37] Prior to 1770 anti-Masonic satires circulated among Russian readers in unpublished form.[38] The publication of "A Psalm Denouncing the Freemasons" in N. G. Kurganov's *Universal Russian Grammar* in 1769, which went through five more printings before the end of the century and enjoyed great popularity, introduced the subject of Masonry to the entire public and helped to keep it in the public eye.[39] This poem, and similar denunciations, did not go unanswered. Just as the publication of anti-Masonic literature grew, so did the published defenses, reaching their greatest numbers in the 1780s.

But why was so much attention devoted to Freemasonry? Why was it perceived as such a threat by its detractors, and why were adherents so adamant in its defense? Part of the answer lies in the fact that the lodges were secret. Masonic secrecy has proven especially difficult to explain and has prompted various interpretations of its supposed purpose. What needs to be stressed, however, is that the Masons were less concerned with keeping the lodges' *existence* secret than on shrouding their lodge *activities* in secrecy. The lodges' sense of mystery distinguished them from other new institutions: secrecy was anathema to the logic of the public sphere which was grounded in the principles of openness and inclusiveness.[40] This tension raises the question of Masonic secrecy's function. The most widely accepted theory, forcefully argued in Koselleck's *Critique and Crisis*, maintains that given the totality of the absolutist state's claim to political authority, the Masons could only exist and operate by hiding behind a veil of secrecy.[41] The view of state and Masonry as necessarily opposed and antagonistic, however, is highly problematic. Upon closer examination of the Russian case, for example, it becomes quite apparent that the two were completely entwined: the court and state apparatus were heavily populated by Masons and the lodges drew the bulk of their membership from the ranks of the court notables and state officials of virtually all levels.[42] The case of Il'in, who was at once a state official, member of the public, and Freemason, highlights this fact and the inadequacies of the state-versus-Masonry opposition. But if Masonic secrecy was not designed to be a shield against the state, then what purposes did it serve?

One key (for there are undoubtedly many) to unlocking the riddle of secrecy is to be found in the concept of virtue which occupied a prominent position in the Masonic creed.[43] Discordant and competing concepts of virtue permeated Enlightenment discourse, and any attempt to reconstruct the mental framework of the Russian public must address the centrality of virtue in its world view. The intense focus on virtue was neither limited to the Masons nor can it be depicted as an expression of a rejection of the "real world" for a sphere of quietist introspection. On the contrary, educated Russians perceived virtue as a fundamental necessity for the betterment of the social order. The Russian poet and high government official Gavriil Derzhavin, who was not a Mason and even poked fun at them on more than one occasion, expressed this sentiment in his poem "Virtue":

> Instrument of benevolence and might,
> Daughter of the Lord, His very likeness,
> In which He wisely combined
> Steadfastness, mildness, intellect, gentleness
> And love for the common weal,
> Oh, mortal's valor, oh, Virtue![44]

Just as Enlightenment discourse placed special value on the social worth of virtue, it also evinced a strong conviction in the ability of human beings to improve themselves, to make themselves more virtuous, and, thereby, to make society better. The path to virtue lay in the inculcation of morals and manners or, as it is called in Russian, *nravouchenie*. Again, *nravouchenie* was not solely the Masons' concern; indeed, it occupied the minds of the Russian public as a whole. One of the most widely published works of the century, the textbook *On the Duties of Man and Citizen*, begins with a section devoted to the "education of the soul," which details the vices to be avoided, the attitudes and behavior that reflect proper morals, and their importance for oneself and society.[45] A 1783 advertisement in the *Moscow News* from that city's gentry boarding school informed the parents of prospective pupils that one of the school's chief goals was to "inculcate good behavior (*blagonravie*) in students' hearts and thus to make them into truly useful, that is, honorable and virtuous fellow-citizens."[46] Children were not the only ones for whom good morals were thought to be of the utmost importance. Both Catherine II's *Instruction to the Legislative Commission of 1767* and the *Order of Procedure for the Legislative Commission*—the guidelines by which it \ as to operate—stress the necessity of morals for the effective maintenance of the empire.[47] Finally, it is especially worth noting the Russian public's love of moralizing literature (*nravouchitel'naia literatura*), comprising books with titles like *The Honorable Man's Pocket Book or Useful Maxims for Every Place and Every Occasion* or *Duties of the Honorable Man*.[48]

As these examples suggest, although virtue resided within the soul beyond the limits of sight, its presence could be communicated through proper conduct—understood as a propensity to perform good deeds, a "natural" sense of modesty, and greater self-control over one's physical desires.[49] Deportment, then, became a sign of one's inner state and was read by those one encountered as a means of determining both whether one belonged to the public and one's status within it.

The Masonic lodge marks another expression of these widely held attitudes. Just as members of the public sought self-improvement in *nravouchitel'naia literatura*, so did they also look to Masonry as an important vehicle for attaining virtue through *nravouchenie*. This was depicted as the main objective of Masonic practice, and it was only by "working the rough stone"—as the Masons characterized their activities—that one could ever hope to become virtuous. As S. I. Gamaleia noted in a speech on April 3, 1783, in the lodge Deucalion: "No, dear brothers, one cannot attain virtue simply with words, one must work and toil day and night and spare nothing if one truly wants to be a student of the Freemasons."[50] The lodge functioned, therefore, as a school of *nravouchenie* where through a variety of exercises (including numerous rituals, rites, speeches, readings, etc.) virtue was inculcated.

The Masons felt themselves to be involved, however, in more than a disinterested quest for moral improvement. As Gamaleia's words make clear, only those fully devoted to the task could ever hope to attain virtue. And in the eyes of his fellow brothers, only they, as Freemasons, possessed such devotion and, therefore, only they possessed virtue. The Masons emphatically proclaimed this fact in one of their many songs:

> Know, that he who knows
> the honored law is a Freemason,
> > that the one who maintains virtue,
> > who runs from the wicked,
> > who helps his friends,
> > who lives by the law,
> Know, that he is a Freemason.[51]

It is worth reiterating the public nature of virtue: far from a simple personal attribute or empty mark of fashion, virtue was a constituent and highly contested element of political discourse and held to be an indispensable ingredient for the perfection of the social body.

The lodge, therefore, occupied a privileged place in the social landscape of the public. Its inhabitants claimed both to possess the secret knowledge required to attain virtue and to be the personification of virtue. This, less than the danger of state repression, accounts for the main function of Masonic secrecy. For through their actions, the Masons attempted to establish a hierarchy within the public based not on the nobility of one's family, or on one's rank (*chin*), status at court, or wealth, but on one's proximity to virtue, having placed themselves at its pinnacle. Access to virtue was not extended to all; it was to be controlled by the Masons, who claimed to be virtue's guardians intent on protecting it from the harmful influences of the wicked and vicious. It was this move to turn a public concern into their own private domain and possession that provoked public criticism of Freemasonry.[52]

The exposés came in various forms and from various authors. Nevertheless, what they all held in common was the intention of making the activities of the Masons public, to remove the curtain of secrecy behind which they acted. To those within the public but outside the lodges, the Masons' perceived lack of virtue and polluted nature made the cover of secrecy a necessity. According to "A Psalm Denouncing the Freemasons," the ways of the Freemasons led to the birth of "all vices," and whereas those who exhibited "real virtue" were visible to all, only those who were ashamed of their deeds hid from sight.[53] Another common element of public criticism centered on the social utility of Freemasonry. In several tracts and plays the Masons' foes depicted them either as crafty swindlers or as wealthy and naive fools showing no concern for the common good and merely caught up in satisfying their own private vices.[54] Perhaps the best known work in this vein, P. S. Baturin's *An Investigation of the Book 'Des Erreurs et de la Vérité'*, went even further in its criticism, claiming that the Masons not only diverted the public's attention from serving the general good, but even propagated radical political and social ideas aimed at undermining the existing order.[55]

Equally aware of the importance of public opinion, the Masons sought to defend themselves against their various detractors through numerous publications. According to the preface to the *Masonic Journal*, a collection of speeches, discussions, and songs published in Moscow in 1784, the Freemasons printed such works so that "members of the Order as well as outsiders might be able to gather at least some basic ideas about true Freemasonry and put out of their heads highly erroneous conclusions and prejudices that false brothers and haters of the Order have for a long time been sowing into gullible and insufficiently steadfast hearts in order to harm the Order."[56] Central to such defenses was the desire to portray the Masons as the real and lone representatives of virtue in contrast to the supposed depravity of the rest of society. In "A Letter to Mr. G***," also printed in the *Masonic Journal*, the author notes that ever since ancient times the most honorable and virtuous men have gathered in small societies in order to "separate themselves from the vicious and corrupt." The activities of the Freemasons, he proposes, were no different: "While closing their doors [i.e., to the lodges] to the weak, the evil, and the depraved, they open them without exception to all meritorious and distinguished men and particularly to the man of virtue."[57] Even when the Masons' own shortcomings were admitted to, this was usually done in such a way so as to suggest the brothers' superior self-awareness and sensitivity. *The Pocket Book for F[ree] M[asons] and also for Persons Who do not Belong to Their Number*, for example, divides society's members into those who are highly cognizant of their moral failings and thus actively seek self-improvement [i.e., the Masons] and those who, largely indifferent to their imperfect state, are content to spend their lives mired in spiritual darkness and ignorance not unlike small children covered in filth blithely frolicking in the dirty street.[58]

Of perhaps greatest significance among published defenses is I. P. Turgenev's *Who can be a Good Citizen and a True Subject?*, first published in French in 1790 before going through three Russian editions by the end of the century.[59] Turgenev's short piece is especially useful since it is one of the few defenses written by a Russian and thus allows us a clearer view of the meanings with which Russians invested Masonry. The key to its interpretation lies in the title itself: Turgenev and his fellow Masons perceived their activities as an expression of their deep-seated concern with making themselves into "good citizens." For them, this required, above all, being good Christians since only those with a fully developed moral conscience would act in accordance with the laws when out of sight of their superiors and the authorities. The good citizen is contrasted with that "considerable number who condone and excuse depravity of all kinds" and who, unrestrained by a greater moral authority, find no shame in committing all sorts of dishonest acts. Only those who have looked deeply into themselves (i.e., worked the rough stone) and replaced vice with virtue can be considered useful, honorable, and trustworthy.[60]

The question posed by Turgenev's title occupied the minds of the entire Russian public. Just as the boundaries of this new structure were far from exact and appear fluid, so too were the newly developing identities of its inhabitants far from clearly set. There was no deed that one could produce on demand to identify oneself as an *honorable man* or *good citizen*. Rather, claims on these identities could only be made and negotiated through the public sphere of print and by one's relation to groups within the public like the Masons.

IV.

This essay has sought to put forward a new interpretation of Russian Freemasonry by bringing out some of the lost meaning and significance that its members (and detractors) attributed to Masonry and by suggesting its importance as an expression of larger social and cultural changes then remaking eighteenth-century Russia. Not only were the forces that attracted men to the lodge greater in number and more complex than has generally been recognized, but the popularity of the movement in no way reflects a rejection of the social and political realities of the age. Quite the contrary. The Masons saw themselves as engaged in nothing less than the construction of a new man, a virtuous man of proper morals and manners who possessed the traits necessary for the maintenance of the social order and the betterment of the common weal. While often found at court, the Mason generally moved within the more expansive social landscape of the public sphere with its own unique rules of social interaction and economy of status.

Although their provisional character must be borne in mind, these findings are important for several reasons. First, they add to our growing knowledge of Russian élite society, which was more dynamic and complex than previously thought. The eighteenth century witnessed a significant transformation as a new public sphere, in the discursive as well as physical sense, took shape and gradually began to subvert the court's once undisputed position as Russia's cultural, social, and political center of gravity. Second, they point to the usefulness of incorporating this public as a constituent element of imperial Russia's institutional landscape into our general interpretive framework. This incorporation offers us a new angle of vision onto Russian society as well as a rich and powerful vocabulary with which to describe and examine this society. At issue is not whether Habermas's model of the public sphere can be slavishly adopted to imperial Russia, but the extent to which the questions and areas of research explored by Habermas, and, subsequently, by numerous other scholars, provide fruitful avenues for future study that promise to illuminate important yet overlooked aspects of Russia's past. Finally, these findings serve to integrate further Russia into the history of the West and force us to reconsider her relationship to other European states by highlighting the degree to which the transformations then reshaping the rest of Europe had a corresponding though still little appreciated and largely unexplored impact on the structures and practices of Russian élite society.

Notes

Research for this article was supported in part by a grant from the International Research & Exchanges Board (IREX), with funds provided by the National Endowment for the Humanities, the United States Information Agency, and the U.S. Department of

State, which administers the Russian, Eurasian, and East European Research Program (Title VIII). Further funding was provided by the Fulbright-Hays Doctoral Dissertation Research Abroad Fellowship and the UCLA Center for Russian and East European Studies. This article was first published in slightly modified form in *Eighteenth-Century Studies* 29, no. 1 (1995): 25–44. I wish to thank the participants of the SSRC workshop for which this paper was originally written and the two outside readers of *Eighteenth-Century Studies* for their constructive comments and criticisms. I am particularly grateful to Peter Pozefsky, Peter Reill, Hans Rogger, and Kevin Tyner Thomas for their helpful advice and encouragement with this article.

1. The literature on European Masonry is too immense to be listed here in any detail. The most useful discussion in English is Margaret C. Jacob, *Living the Enlightenment: Freemasonry and Politics in Eighteenth-Century Europe* (Oxford, 1991). The broader implications of the recent work on French Masonry are discussed in Roger Chartier, *The Cultural Origins of the French Revolution*, trans. Lydia G. Cochrane (Durham, 1991), 162–67. On the Masonic movement in Germany and central Europe, see Helmut Reinalter, ed., *Freimaurer und Geheimbünde im 18. Jahrhundert in Mitteleuropa* (Frankfurt, 1983). The movement's beginnings are discussed in David Stevenson, *The Origins of Freemasonry. Scotland's Century, 1590–1710* (Cambridge, 1988). These figures on Russian Masonry come from an exhaustive, multivolume biographical dictionary recently compiled by Andrei Serkov of the Russian State Library. "Rossiiskoe masonstvo. Entsiklopedicheskii slovar'. tom I. Masony v Rossii (1731–1799 gg.)," unpublished manuscript, n.d.

2. Most significant are M. N. Longinov, *Novikov i moskovskie martinisty* (Moscow, 1867); P. Pekarskii, *Dopolneniia k istorii masonstva v Rossii XVIII stoletiia* (St. Petersburg, 1869); A. N. Pypin, *Russkoe masonstvo XVIII i pervaia chetvert' XIX v.* (Petrograd, 1916); T. Sokolovskaia, *Russkoe masonstvo i ego znachenie v istorii obshchestvennago dvizheniia (XVIII i pervaia chetvert' XIX stoletiia)* (St. Petersburg, 1907); S. P. Mel'gunov and N. P. Sidorov, eds., *Masonstvo v ego proshlom i nastoiashchem*, 2 vols. (Moscow, 1914–1915); Ia. Barskov, *Perepiska moskovskikh masonov XVIII veka, 1780–1792 gg.* (Petrograd, 1915); G. V. Vernadskii, *Russkoe masonstvo v tsarstvovanie Ekateriny II* (Petrograd, 1917).

3. See, for example, In-Ho L. Ryu, "Freemasonry under Catherine the Great: A Reinterpretation," (Ph.D. diss., Harvard University, 1967); or idem, "Moscow Freemasons and the Rosicrucian Order. A Study in Organization and Control," in *The Eighteenth Century in Russia*, ed. J. G. Garrard (Oxford, 1973), 198–232; and Gilbert H. McArthur, "Freemasonry and Enlightenment in Russia: The Views of N. I. Novikov," *Canadian-American Slavic Studies* 14, no. 3 (1980): 361–75. See also Raffaella Faggionato, "La fine di un'utopia. Contributo alla storia della massoneria nella Russia di Caterina II," *Rivista Storica Italiana* 105, no. 1 (January 1993): 36–180.

4. G. V. Plekhanov, *Istoriia russkoi obshchestvennoi mysli*, bk. 3 (Moscow-Leningrad, 1925), 242–43, 263, 282.

5. *Nikolai Novikov i russkoe prosveshchenie XVIII veka* (Moscow-Leningrad, 1951), 284–88. The fundamental weakness of this argument is addressed in Iurii Lotman, " 'Sochuvstvennik' A. N. Radishcheva A. M. Kutuzov i ego pis'ma k I. P. Turgenevu," *Uchenye zapiski Tartuskogo universiteta* 139 (1963): 281–334.

6. *Ocherki po istorii russkoi kul'tury*, vol. 3 (Paris, 1930), 403–407.

7. The expression comes from Nicholas Riasanovsky's well-known study *A Parting of Ways: Government and the Educated Public in Russia, 1801–1855* (Oxford, 1976).

8. *Zerkalo sveta. Ezhenedel'noe izdanie*, pt. 1, no. 1, February 9, 1786; *Rastushchii vinograd*, February and March 1786. Several years before writing these plays, Catherine had already belittled the Masons in a short pamphlet published in French, German, and Russian under the title *Taina protivo-nelepago Obshchestva (Anti-absurde), otkrytaia neprichastnym onomu*. See A. V. Semeka, "Russkie rozenkreitsery i sochineniia imperatritsy Ekateriny II protiv masonstva," Zhurnal ministerstva narodnago prosveshcheniia 39, no. 2 (1902): 343–400.

9. Makogonenko, *Nikolai Novikov*, 6.

10. Reinhart Koselleck, *Critique and Crisis: Enlightenment and the Pathogenesis of Modern Society* (1959; English trans., Cambridge, Mass., 1988); Jürgen Habermas, *The Structural Transformation of the Public Sphere: An Inquiry into a Category of Bourgeois Society*, trans. Thomas Burger, with the assistance of Frederick Lawrence (1962; English trans., Cambridge, Mass., 1989). For a useful discussion of these works and their impact on the study of eighteenth-century Europe, see Anthony J. La Vopa, "Conceiving a Public: Ideas and Society in Eighteenth-Century Europe," *Journal of Modern History* 64 (March 1992): 79–116.

11. On the development of the public in the artistic and musical spheres, see, for example, Thomas E. Crow, *Painters and Public Life in Eighteenth-Century Paris* (New Haven, 1985); James H. Johnson, "Musical Experience and the Formation of a French Musical Public," *Journal of Modern History* 64 (June 1992): 191–226; and David H. Solkin, *Painting for Money: The Visual Arts and the Public Sphere in Eighteenth-Century England* (New Haven, 1993). See also Thomas Nipperdey, *Gesellschaft, Kultur, Theorie*, Kritische Studien zur Geschichtswissenschaft 18 (Göttingen, 1976), 174–205.

12. See the excerpts from Novikov's *Drone* in Harold B. Segel, ed. and trans., *The Literature of Eighteenth-Century Russia. A History and Anthology*, vol. 1 (New York, 1967), 264; and *Satiricheskie zhurnaly N. I. Novikova*, ed. P. N. Berkov (Moscow-Leningrad, 1951), 68. See also W. Gareth Jones' insightful reexamination of these events in "The Polemics of the 1769 Journals: A Reappraisal," *Canadian-American Slavic Studies* 16, nos. 3–4 (Fall-Winter 1982): 432–43.

13. The classic example is Richard Pipes's *Russia under the Old Regime* (New York, 1974), which, even though it is predicated on the assumption that in Russia, unlike in the West, "society" remained a complete captive of the "state," admits to the birth of a literate public in the late eighteenth century. See especially pages 255–56.

14. One article that takes up the subject of the public, although largely in the context of Russia's relations with Western Europe, is Erich Donnert's "Öffentliche Meinung und Pressepolitik unter Katherina II," *Zeitschrift für Slawistik* 18 (1973): 886–91. More recent works on both the eighteenth and nineteenth centuries mark a growing interest in the development of the Russian public and civil society. For the earlier period see Gary Marker, *Publishing, Printing, and the Origins of Intellectual Life in Russia, 1700–1800* (Princeton, 1985); and Marc Raeff, "Transfiguration and Modernization: The Paradoxes of Social Disciplining, Paedogogical Leadership, and the Enlightenment in 18th Century Rus-

sia," in *Alteuropa—Ancien Régime—Frühe Neuzeit. Probleme und Methoden der Forschung*, ed. Hans Erich Bödeker and Ernst Hinrichs (Stuttgart-Bad Cannstatt, 1991), 99–115.

15. See N. A. Smirnov, "Zapadnoe vliianie na russkii iazyk v petrovskuiu epokhu," *Sbornik otdeleniia russkago iazyka i slovesnosti Imperatorskoi Akademii nauk*, vol. 88, no. 2 (St. Petersburg, 1910), 248–49.

16. *Sanktpeterburgskie vedomosti*, February 17, 20; March 5, 1728.

17. Habermas, *Structural Transformation*, 5–12.

18. This essay makes no attempt to account for the specific dynamics behind this development. Some useful observations on the development of the public sphere in Russia are made in Robert Wuthnow, *Communities of Discourse: Ideology and Social Structure in the Reformation, the Enlightenment, and European Socialism* (Cambridge, Mass., 1989), 291–302. On the applicability of Habermas's discussion of the public sphere to Catherinian Russia, see also Andreas Lawaty, "Kulturpolitik und Öffentlichkeit im Zeitalter Katharinas II," in *Handbuch der Geschichte Russlands*, Band 2, Lieferung 11, ed. M. Hellmann, K. Zernack, and G. Schramm (Stuttgart, 1991), 807.

19. Between 1755 and 1775 the number of books and journals published yearly increased from approximately fifty to almost 200. By the mid-1780s, 400 Russian-language books and journals were produced each year. Within a brief twenty-five-year span (1776–1800), 8,000 separate titles were published in Russia, more than *three* times the number printed in the prior *two centuries*. The dramatic growth in published titles paralleled the development of the reading public. As Gary Marker has observed, by the 1780s Russia's "reading public had become large enough to provide an audience for nearly every kind of book for which an audience existed in the West." Marker, *Publishing, Printing, and the Origins*, 71, 105, 202.

20. *Zerkalo sveta*; see note 8. Here a case can be made that as print technology, in conjunction with other forces, helped to create the "imagined community" of the nation, it also served to fashion among fellow-readers a sense of common identity as members of the public. See Benedict Anderson, *Imagined Communities: Reflections on the Origin and Spread of Nationalism*, rev. ed. (New York, 1991), 32–36, 44.

21. Ulrich Im Hof, *Das gesellige Jahrhundert: Gesellschaft und Gesellschaften im Zeitalter der Aufklärung* (Munich, 1982).

22. *Stoletie S. Peterburgskago angliiskago sobraniia. 1770–1870* (St. Petersburg, 1870); M. I. Pyliaev, *Staryi Peterburg* (1889; Leningrad, 1990), 222–29; *Entsiklopedicheskii slovar' Brokgauz-Efron*, s.v. "Klub," vol. 29; N. B., "Znachenie fran-masonstva [sic] dlia flota," *More* 11–12 (March 1907): 315; *Zakony ustanovlennago v 1792 goda sentiabria v 1 den' v gubernskom gorode Revele Kluba Soglasiia* (St. Petersburg, 1792).

23. Promulgated in 1722 under Peter the Great, the Table of Ranks, consisting of fourteen corresponding ranks in military, civil, and court service, reflected the tsar's desire to link social status with state service by supplanting hereditary title with service rank. The military rank of brigadier corresponded to the fifth class or position in the table (one being the highest class).

24. *Stoletie*, 6.

25. *Stoletie*, 25–26; *Entsiklopedicheskii slovar'*, vol. 29.

26. Pyliaev, *Staryi Peterburg*, 226–28; J. C. Grot, *Uchrezhdenie osnovannago v Sanktpeter-burge na smertnye sluchai obshchestva*, 2d ed. (St. Petersburg, 1780), 1–2.

27. On the Free Economic Society, see A. I. Khodnev, *Istoriia Imperatorskogo vol'nogo ekonomicheskogo obshchestva s 1765 do 1865 goda* (St. Petersburg, 1865); on the Free Russian Assembly, see *Istoriia Moskovskogo universiteta*, vol. 1 (Moscow, 1955), 65–66; and on the Friendly Learned Society, B. I. Krasnobaev, "Eine Gesellschaft gelehrter Freunde am Ende des 18. Jahrhunderts. 'Druzheskoe uchenoe obshchestvo,' " in *Beförderer der Aufklärung in Mittel- und Osteuropa. Freimaurer, Gesellschaften, Clubs*, Studien zur Geschichte der Kulturbeziehungen in Mittel- und Osteuropa 5, ed. E. H. Balázs et al. (Berlin, 1979), 257–70; and Longinov, *Novikov*, 180–85, 04–09.

28. On the origins and early development of Freemasonry in Russia, see Vernadsky, *Russkoe masonstvo*, 1–10; and Pypin, *Russkoe masonstvo*, 80–103. The information on the numbers and locations of Russia's lodges is drawn from Serkov (see note 1).

29. On the various Masonic systems operative in Russia, see T. Sokolovskaia, "Masonskiia sistemy," in *Masonstvo v ego proshlom*, vol. 2, 52–79. The literature on the intellectual and ideological content of Russian Freemasonry is immense. Useful introductions include V. Tukalevskii, "Iz istorii filosofskikh napravlenii v russkom obshchestve XVIII veka. (Opyt kharakteristiki ideinykh techenii v russkom masonstve)," *Zhurnal Ministerstva narodnago prosveshcheniia*, n. s., 33, no. 5 (1911): 1–69; McArthur, "Freemasonry and Enlightenment in Russia"; and Andrzej Walicki, *A History of Russian Thought: From the Enlightenment to Marxism*, trans. Hilda Andrews-Rusiecka (Stanford, 1979), 14–26.

30. *Sanktpeterburgskie vedomosti*, February 25, 1780, no. 16, *Pribavlenie*, 201; March 24, 1780, no. 24, *Pribavlenie*, 310–11; May 26, 1780, no. 42, *Pribavlenie*, 565; *Moskovskie vedomosti*, May 31, 1756, no. 11, n.p.; July 2, 1756, no. 20, *Pribavlenie*, 3.

31. Otdel rukopisei Rossiiskoi Natsional'noi Biblioteki (Manuscript Division of the Russian National Library) [Hereafter cited as OR RNB], fond 487, opis' 2, chast' 2, 0.87 and 0.88. Most of the few diary entries that deal with Il'in's Masonic activities were published by V. I. Savva, "Iz dnevnika masona, 1775–1776 gg.," *Chteniia v Imperatorskom obshchestve istorii i drevnostei rossiiskikh* 4 (1908): 1–15.

32. Of course, this is not meant to imply that these were the sole places that might be defined as public or as being the sole public sphere. As is evident, the focus here is on élite culture and thus this essay makes no attempt to address what has been referred to as the plebian public sphere.

33. *Sanktpeterburgskie vedomosti*, May 19, 1780, no. 40, *Pribavlenie*, 529.

34. See Lucian Hölscher, *Öffentlichkeit und Geheimnis. Eine begriffsgeschichtliche Untersuchung zur Entstehung der Öffentlichkeit in der frühen Neuzeit* (Stuttgart, 1979), 81–117. Hölscher characterizes the eighteenth-century German "Publikum" as a new "sozialer Gemeinschaft" of the educated constructed in opposition to traditional notions of "die Gemeinde" or "das Volk."

35. Pyliaev, *Staryi Peterburg*, 214.

36. Vladimir Zolotnitskii, *Obshchestvo raznovidnykh lits, ili Razsuzhdeniia o deistviiakh i nravakh chelovecheskikh* (St. Petersburg, 1766), 29.

37. Catherine's views on Freemasonry have long fascinated Russian historians. Of

particular interest has been the importance of these views in precipitating the arrest of Nikolai Novikov and the suppression of a group of his fellow Moscow Masons in 1792. While Catherine's initial attitude toward Masonry was largely tolerant, following the crackdown on the Illuminati in Bavaria in the mid-1780s and the outbreak of the French Revolution, she came increasingly to share the European-wide fear of societies like the Freemasons as politically subversive. This fear, combined with other important factors such as the Moscow Masons' links to the Prussian court of Frederick Wilhelm II and to Grand Duke Paul, the heir to the Russian throne, eventually led to Novikov's arrest. For Catherine's views on Freemasonry, see Pypin, *Russkoe masonstvo*, 262–81, 295–312; and Semeka, "Russkie rozenkreitsery," 369–400. The most recent discussion of the Novikov affair is K. A. Papmehl, "The Empress and 'Un Fanatique': A Review of the Circumstances Leading to the Government Action against Novikov in 1792," *Slavonic and East European Review* 68, no. 4 (October 1990): 665–91.

38. For example, "Iz"iasnenie nekotorykh izvestnykh del prokliatago zborishcha frank mazonskago" in the Nauchnaia Biblioteka Gosudarstvennogo Ermitazha (State Hermitage Scientific Library), No. 150554, ll. 230ob.–233. See I. F. Martynov, "Rannie masonskie stikhi v sobranii Biblioteki Akademii nauk SSSR (k istorii literaturno-obshchestvennoi polemiki 1760-kh gg.)," in *Russia and the World of the Eighteenth Century*, ed. R. P. Bartlett et al. (Columbus, Ohio, 1988), 437–44; idem, "Masonskie rukopisi v sobranii Biblioteki AN SSSR," in *Materialy i soobshcheniia po fondam otdela rukopisnoi i redkoi knigi BAN SSSR* 2 (Leningrad, 1978), 243–53; and the discussion of the anti-Masonic manuscript "Otvet masonam" in Pypin, *Russkoe masonstvo*, 98–99.

39. N. G. Kurganov, *Rossiiskaia universal'naia grammatika, ili Vseobshchee pismoslovie, predlagaiushchee legchaishii sposob osnovatel'nago ucheniia ruskomu iazyku s sedm'iu prisovokupleniiami raznykh uchebnykh i poleznozabavnykh veshchei* (St. Petersburg, 1769), 325. On this work's great popularity with the Russian public, see I. E. Barenbaum, *Istoriia knigi*, 2d ed. (Moscow, 1984), 55.

40. Habermas, *Structural Transformation*, 37.

41. For a discussion of Koselleck, see La Vopa, "Conceiving a Public," 83–98. The origins of this interpretation of secrecy can be traced back to Kant. See "On the Common Saying: 'This May Be True in Theory, but It Does Not Apply in Practice,' " in *Kant's Political Writings*, ed. Hans Reiss, trans. H. B. Nisbet (Cambridge, 1971), 85–86.

42. Four of the eleven members in Catherine's Imperial Council in 1777, for example, were Masons. In the same year, eleven of her thirty-one court chamberlains were Masons. See Vernadsky, *Russkoe masonstvo*, 86–90. According to one study of Russian Masonry, approximately half of those active in Russian lodges in the eighteenth and first quarter of the nineteenth century were state officials. Tatiana Bakounine, *Le répertoire biographique des franc-maçons russes (XVIIIe et XIXe siècles)* (Paris, 1967), XXIII. The fact that Masons operating outside the absolutist states of Europe, like those in North America, for example, also veiled their activities in secrecy makes this interpretation even more problematic. For an insightful reading of the role of secrecy among some American Freemasons, see Dorothy Ann Lipson, *Freemasonry in Federalist Connecticut* (Princeton, 1977), 238–44.

43. The multiple functions and uses of secrecy in societies like Freemasonry are masterfully discussed in *The Sociology of Georg Simmel*, trans., ed. Kurt H. Wolff (New York, 1950), 345–76. For further observations on the complex role of secrecy in social interaction with direct bearing on understanding groups like the Masons, see Erving Goffman, *The Presentation of the Self in Everyday Life* (New York, 1959), 67–75, 141–45.

44. *Sochineniia Derzhavina*, vol. 1 (St. Petersburg, 1851), 111.

45. *O dolzhnostiakh cheloveka i grazhdanina, kniga, k chteniiu opredelennaia v narodnykh gorodskikh uchilishchakh Rossiiskoi imperii, izdannaia po vysochaishemu poveleniiu tsarstvuiushchei imp. Ekateriny Vtoryia* (St. Petersburg, 1783), 7–68. See also Max J. Okenfuss, "Education and Empire: School Reform in Enlightened Russia," *Jahrbücher für Geschichte Osteuropas* 27, Heft 1 (1979): 57. It is also worth noting that *nravouchenie* occupied an important position in the curriculum of Moscow University in the eighteenth century.

46. Quoted in N. V. Sushkov, *Vospominaniia o Moskovskom universitetskom blagorodnom pansione* (Moscow, 1848), 7.

47. In the Instruction, see especially chap. VII, §76; chap. VIII, §83; chap. X, §247 and 248; and chap. XXI, §553 (2.), *Documents of Catherine the Great: The Correspondence with Voltaire and the "Instruction" of 1767 in the English Text of 1768*, ed. W. F. Reddaway (Cambridge, 1931); *Obriad upravleniia kommissii o sochinenii proekta Novago Ulozheniia* (Moscow, 1767), 10.

48. *Karmannaia knizhka chestnago cheloveka, ili Nuzhnyia pravila vo vsiakom meste i vo vsiakoe vremia* (St. Petersburg, 1794); August Witzmann, *Dolzhnosti chestnago cheloveka* (St. Petersburg, 1798).

49. Virtue, as defined in Novikov's journal *Morning Light*, was first and foremost "the art of keeping one's passions in balance." Quoted in *N. I. Novikov i ego sovremenniki. Izbrannye sochineniia*, ed. I. V. Malyshev (Moscow, 1961), 193. The importance educated Russians ascribed to the interconnected notions of morals, manners, and virtue reflects the degree to which they shared in the broader European discourse of civility. From the growing literature on civility in early modern Europe, see, most recently, Daniel Gordon, *Citizens without Sovereignty: Equality and Sociability in French Thought, 1670–1789* (Princeton, 1994); and Lawrence E. Klein, *Shaftesbury and the Culture of Politeness: Moral Discourse and Cultural Politics in Early Eighteenth-Century England* (Cambridge, 1994).

50. OR RNB, f. 550, O.III.160., l. 5ob. The importance of virtue and moral self-improvement in the mental world of the Masons, especially as expressed in the literary works of M. M. Kheraskov (1733–1803), is discussed in Stephen Lessing Baehr, *The Paradise Myth in Eighteenth-Century Russia: Utopian Patterns in Early Secular Russian Literature and Culture* (Stanford, 1991), 90–111.

51. OR RNB, Titovskoe sobranie, No. 4419, l. 22.

52. This correlates well with Goffman's notion of "inside" secrets, the possession of which "marks an individual as being a member of a group and helps the group feel separate and different from those individuals who are not 'in the know.' Inside secrets give objective intellectual content to subjectively felt social distance." *Presentation*, 142. A similar understanding of the function of secrecy informs Wolfgang Hardtwig's insightful essay on secrecy in Freemasonry. See "Eliteanspruch und Geheimnis in den Geheimgesell-

schaften des 18. Jahrhunderts," in *Aufklärung und Geheimgesellschaften: zur politischen Funktion und Sozialstruktur der Freimaurerlogen im 18. Jahrhundert*, ed. Helmut Reinalter (Munich, 1989), 63–86. See especially 66–68 and 80–84.

53. Kurganov, *Rossiiskaia universal'naia grammatika*, 325. Similar ideas are expressed in "Iz"iasnenie nekotorykh izvestnykh del" (see note 38).

54. Some of these published works, most of which were translations, attacked Freemasonry in general, while others focused their criticisms on specific individuals, groups, or ideas common among the Masons. Works that could be placed in the former group include Thomas Wilson's *Mason bez maski, ili Podlinnye tainstva masonskie* (St. Petersburg, 1784); "Razsuzhdeniia o nachale Vol'nykh kamenshchikov ili Farmasonov," *Rastushchii vinograd*, October 1786, 44–72; December 1786, 62–76; January 1787, 35–46; and the poems of Derzhavin "Felitsa" (1782) and "Na schast'e" (1789). Among the latter group, the adventures of Cagliostro and similar types of "deceivers" who were frequently seen as using the lodges as a cover for their own nefarious purposes were exposed in works such as Charlotte von der Recke, *Opisanie prebyvaniia v Mitave izvestnago Kaliostra na 1779 god* (St. Petersburg, 1787); A. F. Moshinskii, *Kalliostr poznannyi v Varshave, ili Dostovernoe opisanie khimicheskikh i magicheskikh ego deistvii, proizvodimykh v sem stolichnom gorode v 1780* (Moscow, 1788); *Alkhimist bez maski, ili Otkrytoi obman umovoobrazhatel'nago zlatodelaniia, vziatoi iz sochinenii G. Professora Gilboa* (Moscow, 1789); *Karmannaia knizhka, dlia razmyshliaiushchikh iunoshei, sluzhashchaia k priiatnomu i poleznomu ikh uprazhneniiu* (Moscow, 1800), 339–51; and the Russian comedy by N. F. Emin, *Mnimyi mudrets* (St. Petersburg, 1786). The fashionable curiosity for mysticism and magic—especially prevalent among many Masons—was the subject of A. I. Klushin's short play *The Alchemist*, in *Russkaia komediia i komicheskaia opera XVIII veka*, ed. P. N. Berkov (Moscow-Leningrad, 1950), 465–83. Other works include *Mops bez osheinika i bez tsepi ili Svobodnoe i tochnoe otkrytie tainstv obshchestva imenuiushchagosia Mopsami* (St. Petersburg, 1784), a translation of the first section of G. L. Pérau's *L'ordre des francs-maçons trahi, et le secret de Mopses révélé*.

55. P. S. Baturin, *Izsledovanie knigi o Zabliuzhdeniiakh i istine. Sochineno osoblivym obshchestvom odnogo Gubernskago goroda* (Tula, 1790). The book referred to in the title, *Des Erreurs et de la Vérité*, by the French theosophist Louis Claude de Saint-Martin, enjoyed great popularity in the Russian translation among some Masons who became known as Martinists. Catherine the Great made fun of the Martinists in the short anonymous piece "Domovaia zapiska o zaraze novomodnoi eresi i o sredstvakh iztseliaiushchikh ot onoi," *Rastushchii vinograd*, July 1786, III–VII. Also worth noting is "Kratkoe opisanie zhizni perveishago osnovatelia sekty Martinistov, Postella," *Rastushchii vinograd*, March 1786, 6–13. Although Baturin claimed that the Martinists' ideas were politically subversive, there is no direct reference in his work nor in the others listed here to the outbreak of the French Revolution.

56. *Magazin svobodno-kamen'shchicheskoi*, vol. 1, pt. 1 (Moscow, 1784), I–II.

57. *Magazin svobodno-kamen'shchicheskoi*, vol. 1, pt. 1, 46–51.

58. *Karmannaia knizhka dlia V.[ol'nykh] K.[amenshchikov] i dlia tekh, kotorye i ne prinadlezhat k chislu onykh* (Moscow, 1783), 45–46. This work was originally published as *Zapisnaia knizhka dlia druzei chelovechestva* (St. Petersburg, 1781?). Other publications in-

clude William Hutchinson, *Dukh masonstva* (Moscow, 1783); Stanislav Eli, *Bratskiia uve-shchaniia k nekotorym Bratiiam SVBDN KMNSHCHKM* (Moscow, 1784); and J. A. Starck, *Apologiia, ili Zashchishchenie ordena Vol'nykh kamen'shchikov* (Moscow, 1784). The latter two texts were published twice in Moscow that year. The journals *Utrennii svet* (1777–80), *Moskovskoe ezhemesiachnoe izdanie* (1781), *Vecherniaia zaria* (1782), and *Pokoiashchiisia trudoliubets* (1784–85) also figured as important organs for the dissemination of Masonic ideas. Finally, Masonic songs were published in the works of the writers Mikhail Chulkov and Aleksandr Sumarokov. See M. D. Chulkov, *Novoe i polnoe sobranie rossiiskikh pesen*, pt. 4 (Moscow, 1780), 1–2; and A. P. Sumarokov, *Polnoe sobranie vsekh sochinenii*, pt. 8 (Moscow, 1781), 323–24. On the circulation of Masonic texts in Russia, see D. D. Lotareva, "Nekotorye istochnikovedcheskie problemy izucheniia masonskoi knizhnosti v Rossii v kontse XVIII-pervoi polovine XIX v.," in *Mirovospriiatie i samosoznanie russkogo obshchestva (XI-XX vv). Sbornik statei*, ed. L. N. Pushkarev et al. (Moscow, 1994), 142–63.

59. I. P. Turgenev, *Qui peut être un bon citoyen et un sujet fidèle?* (Moscow, 1790); *Kto mozhet byt' dobrym grazhdaninom i vernym poddannym?* (Moscow, 1796; 1798; n.d.).

60. Turgenev, *Kto mozhet byt'* (1796 ed.), 10–12, 32–33.

12

Constructing the Meaning of Suicide

The Russian Press in the Age
of the Great Reforms

Irina Paperno

————··◁∞▷··————

I N THE 1860s suicide—for the first time—became an object of vigorous discussions in Russia, addressed by science, law, fiction, and, above all, by the periodical press, which presented these areas of knowledge to the general public
and mediated between them.[1] In the mid-1860s, basing their impressions on
newspaper chronicles and statistical data, Russian publicists noted that the suicide rate, considered to be on the rise in major European countries, was also
increasing in Russia. The issue became a matter of general alarm. Journalists,
hygienists, police authorities, social scientists, writers, and the general public
were all united in the belief that Russia was experiencing a suicide epidemic. It
was also a matter of common opinion that the suicide epidemic was both "a
mark of the age" (*znamenie vremeni*) and a product of the age, thought to have
been caused by the contingencies of the reform era—a time of dissolution of
social and intellectual order.

In the 1860s, when a suicide epidemic allegedly hit Russia, regular coverage
of suicide in Russian newspapers and efforts to gather and publish statistical
data were new developments, closely connected to the reforms. As a result of
the reforms, local administrations in towns, cities, and provinces (the reformed
municipal organs and the newly created *zemstva*) were to assume responsibility for the public welfare and public health. Judicial reform (1864) opened legal
proceedings to the public. The new censorship statute (1865) offered limited
freedom of the press and created conditions for expanding press coverage and
for a greater quantity of publications and increased circulation. Due to the policy of *glasnost'* ("openness"; literally, "voicedness"), the workings of the social
mechanism as well as the daily lives of ordinary people were opened before the

305

public eye. Daily life became a matter of social responsibility and public concern.[2]

In the 1860s a new intellectual and political radicalism came into being. It was the age of positivism, which—in the words of a contemporary—was a rebellion against "eighteen centuries of the rule of metaphysics."[3] Joining their European cohorts in a belief that the only reality was the world accessible through the senses and science—the world of fact and matter, which is subject to natural laws—Russian positivists frequently carried these ideas to the extreme. Radical positivism, or nihilism, was closely linked with political radicalism. Confrontations between the radicals and the government punctuated the reform years. It was a violent age.

A coherent symbolic vocabulary developed in literature and the popular press for the description of these sociocultural processes. The key concepts were the "reconstruction" (*perestroika*) or (in a pessimistic vein) "decomposition" (*razlozhenie*) of the social order and everyday life. Many regarded the moment as a time of difficult transition: "we are living through a difficult *transitional time* [*trudnoe perekhodnoe vremia*]; "a transitional time between the old and new, between idealism and positivism."[4] Analogies were drawn between Russia in the 1860s and the dissolution of the Roman Empire, when "the former psychological world of man had entirely collapsed," giving way to Christianity.[5] Suicide was treated in this context and linked to these historical processes (these quotations come from discussions of suicide).

With the new age came the "new man" (a Pauline concept appropriated by the atheistic radicals). No longer living under the dispensation of Christian principles, the new man, a man possessing neither immortal soul nor free will, was prepared (in the words of Ludwig Büchner), to "readily submit to the jurisdiction of fixed physical laws."[6] Based on science, the new intellectual order relied on materialistic physiology as the source of knowledge about man. Medical metaphors pervaded the discourse of the press and belles lettres. But the new scientific symbols and the old Christian symbols were interchangeable, with science frequently functioning as the agent of salvation. Literature offered a paradigmatic "new man" in the "nihilist" Bazarov, an image created by the collective efforts of novelist Ivan Turgenev and critic Dmitry Pisarev. A medical student, an atheist (whose bible is Büchner's *Kraft und Stoff*), and, as the reader suspects, a political radical, Bazarov views nature as a "laboratory" in which man is "the worker." Emblematic of these beliefs is his preoccupation with anatomy—a standard symbol of positivistic knowledge—and with the dissection of frogs, which he deems to be made in the same way as men. Overwriting Christian symbolism with the symbolism of science, Pisarev made the frog, used in experiments on the reflexes of the brain, into a new icon, claiming that "it is here, in this frog, that the salvation and renewal of the Russian people lie."[7]

In Russia, as elsewhere in Europe, in the 1860s and 1870s, the natural sciences competed for predominance with the social sciences. The main instrument of the nascent social sciences, statistics, was considered a major source of knowledge about society and, therefore, about man. Russian reformists focused their efforts on collecting objective, reliable facts about society to provide a "key to future change and reform."[8] In the meantime, statistics, along with medicine, provided a key to knowledge about human action, such as crime and suicide. Thus, statistics showed that, when treated collectively, human beings exhibited remarkable regularity in their actions. A philosophical conclusion was drawn: human actions are the result not of individual free will, but of immutable social laws, which govern the aggregate of society in the same way as physical laws govern the human body (a matter for later comment).

Contemporaries frequently saw the social sciences as the successor to the natural sciences. One author described these developments in the following terms:

> It was becoming clear that frogs and test-tubes do little to move the Russian people to actions for the general good. Intellectually developed people [*razvitye liudi*] have taken a moment to think and have decided to change the educational curriculum. The social sciences, rather than the natural sciences, will save the Russian people. . . . The salvation of the Russian people, it has been found, depends on the propagation of sociology. The social sciences talk about the *narod* [the nation, or the people], about its well-being. . . . The new men have pointed . . . to the *narod*.[9]

From the vantage point of today, the process looks different: the concepts of natural science did not displace, but rather overlay those of social science. The social sciences provided a key metaphor—the social organism.

The metaphor of the social organism, derived from the age-old analogy between the living organism and society, was prevalent in the discourse of nineteenth-century West European social science (in the writings of Comte, Spencer, Lilienfeld, Schäffle, and others). In Russia, the organicist discourse of the social sciences appeared concomitantly with the development of populism, with its ideal of collectivism. It was in the Russian peasant commune (*obshchina*), with its collectivist spirit and attachment to the land, that populists found salvation from the chaos brought about by the dissolution of social structures in Russia and from the alienation that capitalism had brought to the West. For the individual, the road to salvation lay in submerging one's personality to the collective desire ("*kollektivnym zhelaniiam russkogo naroda*"[10]).

In Russian cultural mythology of the 1870s, the collective man played the role of a newer and better "new man." Statistics ascertained that the collective man (that is, society) complied to the laws of science. The collective man was immortal, and a true equal to God:

> Birth, marriage, reproduction, death—this is the cycle of the individual person's external existence; but while individual people are born, live and die, the human race—mankind—continues to live, developing as a whole according to definite, regular and immutable laws.[11]

Whereas the earlier ("nihilist") variant of the "new man" was codified in novels, the collective "new man" of the 1870s and early 1880s was created largely in the publicistic and scientific writings appearing in the so-called "thick journals," a genre that combined belles lettres, literary criticism, social commentary, and popularized science.

In the symbolic network outlined above, suicide came to occupy an important, if not the central place. It became a symbol that absorbed many of the social and intellectual concerns of the age, some shared by European thinkers and some specific to postreform Russia. In this chapter, I will trace the process by which the symbolic meanings of suicide were constructed in the Russian press, focusing on what historians view as a distinct period, the age of the Great Reforms (roughly from the late 1850s to the early 1880s).

But before proceeding to analyze the interpretive strategies of the press, I will review what the Russian reading public knew about the views on suicide held by Western science and what Russian science knew about suicide in Russia.

Science on Suicide: What Russians Knew

In the nineteenth century (at least in the first half of the century) the Russian readers relied on West European sources for their understanding of human action. It was in the 1860s that knowledge of Western scientific studies on suicide, known to experts since at least the 1840s, reached the general reader. The popular press of the left-wing persuasion, concerned as it was at the time with constructing a new model of man, paid much attention to the investigations of human action undertaken by the natural (medical) and social sciences. These works reached the public mainly in the form of book reviews and articles popularizing science, published regularly in the "thick journals."

Considered medically, suicide was thought to be a disease, a form of insanity. This widespread view is associated with the name of Etienne Esquirol and his *Des maladies mentales* (Paris, 1838), in which he claimed to have proven that "man only makes attempts upon his life, when in a state of delirium, and that suicides are insane persons."[12] Striving "to fix upon the seat of suicide,"[13] Esquirol considered the data of postmortem reports. If suicidal pathology were to be located inside the body, thus grounding the mental in the physical, the question of the causation of suicide would be settled. Moreover, a larger question would also be illuminated: the nature of human action. But a definitive answer was not to be found. Esquirol had to admit that "the opening of the dead bodies of suicides, has shed little light on this subject"; the changes (mostly in the brain) were "so varied, that we could infer nothing from them."[14] Nevertheless, attempts to fix the seat of thought, sentiment, and action in the body continued, and many scientists were inclined to see them as successful. Though the exclusiveness of the medical explanation came under attack already in the 1840s, the view of suicide as a form of insanity was not entirely abandoned.

The first edition popularizing Western views on suicide to appear in Russia, P. M. Ol'khin's *O samoubiistve v meditsinskom otnoshenii* (St. Petersburg, 1859), relying largely on Esquirol, emphasized a view of suicide as a medical phenomenon. Ol'khin's publication, however, left no traces in periodical press.[15]

Beginning with the 1830s a social science called "moral statistics" (the statistical study of human action) also took upon itself the investigation of suicide. In 1865 and 1866, translations of L. Adolphe Quételet, the father of moral statistics, published in France in the 1830s, appeared in Russia,[16] giving rise to a vigorous polemic. Discussions focused on the philosophical and social implications of statistical regularities, specifically on the issue of the freedom of the will versus determinism—a cornerstone in the dispute between positivism and the Christian worldview.

In 1867, reviewing a compilation of the works of the contemporary Western statisticians A. M. Guerry, Adolph Wagner, and M. W. Drobisch,[17] a publicist from the left-wing *Otechestvennye zapiski* presented the "new science" in this vein:

> among its tasks is one of the most important and fundamental problems for each individual and all humanity: the relation of the law of necessity to an individual's actions, which people customarily view as arbitrary, independent, and free.[18]

The debates around this issue fell on ground prepared (in the early 1860s) by Henry Buckle's *History of Civilization in England* (1857), the book that elaborated the philosophical implications of moral statistics. According to Buckle, statistical evidence revealed in "mathematical language" that human actions "are the result of large and general causes, which, working upon the aggregate of society, must produce certain consequences, without regard to the volition of those particular men of whom the society is composed." The laws governing human action are "more capable of being predicted than are the physical laws connected with the disease and destruction of our bodies."

The logic of this argument implied not that suicide was a disease, but that it was *like* a bodily disease: it called for a metaphor. This metaphor was the "body social," or "social organism," society treated as one man. The metaphor helped a transition between two areas of knowledge by allowing the transfer of medical notions to the study of society. Thus, Buckle suggested that only science, by performing "the anatomy of nations," can lay bare those objective, immutable laws that govern individual and collective actions.[19] Moral statistics was viewed as such a discipline. Some twenty years later, Enrico Morselli, in his magisterial *Il suicidio. Saggio de statistica morale comparata* (Milan, 1879), turned to the same heuristic strategy. As a positivist and medical doctor, Morselli shared the view that human actions are nothing but manifestations of the organic functions of the brain, no different from reflexive actions.[20] But as a social scientist, he believed that even "the most positive" mode of study, when applied to individual cases, would not suffice to reveal those numerous influences to which such seemingly arbitrary actions as suicide and crime are subject collectively, influences that are universal and perpetual.[21] Morselli used the metaphor "the social organism" as his central concept. In Morselli's words, the examination of every single case would not suffice, making it essential to study not the individual body (a subject of psychological medicine), but "the whole of society . . . in the functions of its complicated organism."[22] Moral statistics, by carrying on the investigation of society's internal organization, performs a "genuine process of social autopsy."[23]

Thus, the transition from the medical to the social model of man was achieved by transfering notions that were traditionally used for describing the individual body to the collective body of society. Social science did not replace but engulfed medical science.

One of the main proponents of positivist science in Russia was a prominent radical publicist, Varfalomei Zaitsev. Reviewing the Russian translations of Quételet, he emphasized that the main conclusion made by moral statistics ("that method that created Buckle") was the subjugation of man to a positive law:

> In all of his actions, from the most important to the least significant, the individual obeys statistical laws. . . . Fateful figures, . . . like Fate in ancient times, govern the destinies of man and do not allow him to move even one step away from their mathematical conclusions.[24]

In an attempt to find the exact cause and locus of human action, Zaitsev appealed to the authority of German physiologists who incorporated Quételet's argument on determinism into a radically materialistic view of human nature. Following Karl Vogt, Zaitsev connected the propensity to crime to "the quality and quantity of the constituent parts of the brain, blood, and the nervous fibers."[25] Thus, in the wake of moral statistics, the medical view on the causation of suicide made its appearance in the Russian press.

But most of Russian positivists subscribed to the view that suicide was caused by the social environment (*sreda*)—that is, forces outside the individual. Thus, like their West European counterparts, Russian readers received mixed messages from "science" about the immediate cause and exact locus of human action. Did the cause lie in the body or in society? Did suicide fall under the jurisdiction of medical or social science? But in contrast to Western Europe, in Russia, where science had occupied a peripheral place,[26] the conflict between the disciplinary discourses or disciplinary authorities was far less important than the conflict between the radicals' discourse of (popular) science and the authority of the autocratic regime. In the Russian context—where Orthodoxy was closely associated with the government policy and positivism with political radicalism—moral statistics, along with materialistic physiology, became an argument not only in the debate between positivism and the Christian worldview, but also in the conflict between the radicals and the government.

The following episode serves as an illustration. The first issue of the radical journal *Delo* (January 1866) contained the article "Suicide Statistics (a propos of Wagner's *Statistik der Selbstmorde*" subtitled "Article One" (*Stat'ia pervaia*). It was signed N. Radiukin. This extensive summary of Wagner's treatise was written by Nikolai Shelgunov, a major political activist and radical publicist. Shelgunov emphasized the same point as Zaitsev: statistical science, which had proven that suicide is an involuntary act, questioned the freedom of will (and, by implication, the Christian view of man).[27] However, unlike Zaitsev, Shelgunov sought the cause of human action not in the body, but in the society surrounding the individual. The censorship found this article offensive, and the second part was banned, with the following comment:

> In the present article the author explains the causes of suicide. First, he considers it necessary to mock *ancient philosophies* in which man is considered a privileged creature governed by special laws independent of earthly forces. . . . Examining suicide from this point of view, he tries to prove that suicide, like all other phenomena of human life, is not an arbitrary action but arises exclusively as the result of oppressive circumstances and abnormal conditions in the surrounding environment in which one lives. . . . What follows is a series of vignettes of suicides during

the French terror. The author's goal is to show that political persecution
in particular increases the number of suicides.[28]

The reading provided by the censor indicates that the far-reaching implications of moral statistics were quite clear to the authorities (and to the contemporary reader in general): discussions of suicide in the context of moral statistics signified "antireligious views" as well as aspirations for social and political
reform.

Two comprehensive studies of suicide in Russia appeared in the 1880s: an
extensive article that approached suicide as a medical phenomenon, N. V.
Ponomarev's *Samoubiistvo v Zapadnoi Evrope i Rossii v sviazi s razvitiem umopo-
meshatel'stva* (1880),[29] and a moral statistics, A. V. Likhachev's *Samoubiistvo v
Zapadnoi Evrope i Evropeiskoi Rossii. Opyt sravnitel'no-statisticheskogo issledovaniia*
(St. Petersburg, 1882). Both were reviewed in the popular press.[30] The views of
the two Russian authors on the nature of suicide differed. For Ponomarev, suicide was a phenomenon that belonged entirely to the domain of medicine (his
argument repeated that of Esquirol). Likhachev, following Morselli, viewed suicide as an object of sociology. (Indeed, he fashioned himself as a Russian
Morselli: to formulate his theoretical position, he paraphrased the introduction
to *Il suicidio*.) Following his Western predecessors, Likhachev offered the explanation of the difference between the two approaches, medical and social, based
on the metaphors "the body social" and "autopsy": while psychiatry investigates individual thought, sociology investigates collective thought, or the psychology of the collective man; "developing statistics, society, as it were, subjects
itself to a medico-legal autopsy."[31]

In Russia, attempts at gathering statistical data on crime and suicide had
been made in the 1830–1840s,[32] but systematic efforts started in the 1860s.[33] In
his 1882 study Likhachev gave a comprehensive survey of statistical sources on
suicide in Western Europe and in Russia.[34] Practically all of Russian statisticians
commented on the inadequacy and unreliability of their sources, ranging from
a complaint on the scarcity of data to the affirmation that the available data were
simply "unusable" (*neprigodna dlia raboty*).[35] Nevertheless, they reached a general conclusion: in the nineteenth century the suicide rates in Russia were pro-
gressively increasing. Likhachev arranged the Russian data to show that in the
period between 1803 and 1875 the rate of suicide in Russia had doubled. Though
he had to combine scattered data derived from vastly diverse sources, he was
encouraged by the fact that the tendency for increase in Russia corresponded in
its general configurations to that already noted for other European countries.
(In terms of absolute figures, Russia occupied the last place among developed
European nations, confirming a popular view that the increase of suicide was

the result of civilization, still sadly lacking in Russia.) Still, Likhachev maintained the validity of the general conclusion: Russia was experiencing a suicide
epidemic. Most of his colleagues shared this belief. But it was not science, but
the periodical press that took upon itself the task of interpreting the meaning
of the suicide epidemic for the public.

Suicide in the Press

The first reports of suicides appeared in Russian newspapers in the late
1830s, but regular coverage started only in the 1860s, when Russian newspapers
started to play an important role as a source of information and a vehicle of
public opinion. In 1866 major newspapers started regular coverage of the proceedings of the new, open courts, making crime (for the first time in Russian
history) one of the central topics. It is at that time that reports of suicide grew
in frequency and prominence; major Petersburg newspapers and the so-called
"small press," aimed at popular readers, published several reports of suicide in
each issue, relating the circumstances in considerable detail.[36] Newspapers also
published comprehensive surveys of statistical data.[37]

Initially appearing in the chronicles, selected suicide cases were discussed
in reviews of current social events in newspapers and journals, which offered
social commentary and interpretation. Interpretation of suicide was mostly the
prerogative of the liberal and left-wing or outright radical organs. Among the
daily newspapers, the liberal *Golos* and *Sankt-Peterburgskie vedomosti* devoted
considerable attention to suicide in their weekly feuilletons. Suicide figured
prominently in the "reviews of internal affairs" in the weekly populist newspaper *Nedelia* and in the left-wing monthly journal *Otechestvennye zapiski*. Oppositional organs also featured reviews of scientific treatises on suicide. By contrast, the moderately liberal journal *Vestnik Evropy* devoted little attention to the
topic and the conservative *Russkii vestnik* ignored it altogether. An exception to
this rule was *Grazhdanin*, a weekly newspaper published (beginning in 1872)
by the arch-conservative Prince V. P. Meshchersky who made it his goal to counteract the harmful effects of the liberal press. In the year 1873–74, during
Dostoevsky's tenure as the paper's editor, *Grazhdanin* featured periodical reviews and discussions of crime and suicide, treated as evidence of the social
and "spiritual" pathology for which the nihilist spirit was held responsible.[38]
M. N. Katkov's conservative *Moskovskie vedomosti*, another newspaper that com-
batted nihilism, also commented on suicides in this manner.[39]

Most of the oppositional journals launched in the late 1860s went out of circulation by the late 1880s.[40] With their demise, the prominence of suicide diminished: although suicide reports continued to appear on the pages of the peri-

odical press, suicide lost its status as a central symbol of society. Thus, the rise and fall of the suicide theme parallels the rise and fall of the media forms. The very fact that the public became aware of suicide can be (and was) seen as a product of *glasnost'*. As one journalist put it: "Nowadays, as "openness" (*glasnost'*) is becoming more widespread in our society, one continually hears of new cases of mental derangement and suicide." He continued: "Such cases, of course, are one of the most unfortunate signs of the unhealthy condition of our society."[41] With increased exposure to information came the impression that social pathology was on the rise.[42]

The Suicide Epidemics

Beginning in the early 1870s newspapers and journals started presenting suicides as a regular and anticipated event: "Suicide after Suicide in Petersburg" (*Sankt-Peterburgskie vedomosti*, 24 May 1872); "another suicide attempt was discovered last night" (31 May 1873). In the fall of 1873, drawing on newspaper chronicles, Nikolai Demert from *Otechestvennye zapiski* described the incidence of suicide as an "epidemic":

> In the last few years in Russia, suicide has definitely become a sort of cholera that has gotten into a rotten place expressly created for its proliferation. In cities special weekly accounts of suicides have become a permanent news item.

What the press did, he claimed, was to provide "living illustrations" for statistical figures.[43] By the early 1870s, the notion of the epidemic became a stable part of the newspaper vocabulary. The "Chronicle of Internal Affairs" (*Vnutrenniaia khronika*) section of *Nedelia* even occasionally included a column called "Suicide Epidemic" (*Epidemiia samoubiistv*). Sometimes all the newspaper reported was that the epidemic was running its course. In 1884 the journalists were still reporting a suicide epidemic. It was on the pages of *Nedelia* (one of the few organs launched in the 1860s to survive into the 1880s) that the epidemic raged with special force.[44] In 1886 *Nedelia* commented that the newspaper reporters now commanded a special language:

> Suicide long ago became an ordinary event in Russian life. Nowadays, no one is surprised to see several reports of suicide in every issue of the newspaper: this man or that woman has put a bullet into their skull, taken some kind of poison, thrown themselves under a railroad train or by some other means has settled their score with life. Special expressions have even gained currency, attesting to the permanency of this sad affair and to the wide extent to which it has spread: rare is the correspondence on suicide

in which we do not come across the expressions: "the usual spring or autumn epidemic of suicides has already begun," or: "the victims of this season of suicides are . . . " and so forth.[45]

This terminology was a compromise. In the early 1870s, soon after it started regular coverage of suicide, the press announced the "suicide epidemic"; in the 1880s, the metaphors were adjusted: suicide was presented as an annual, seasonal epidemic (on the model of influenza, not cholera).

Discussing a Case: The Public Dramas of Intimate Life

In 1873 the Russian press was preoccupied with a crime committed in a fashionable hotel in St. Petersburg: a murder followed by a suicide. Although it was a double crime, and one provoked by passion, the so-called Hotel Belle Vue case became a focal point for debates on suicide, its causes and social implications, as well as the implications of making such cases public.

On September 19, 1873, in Hotel Belle Vue, a young man shot a woman, the object of his unrequited passion, and then killed himself. The perpetrator, Timofei Komarov, was a candidate in law at St. Petersburg University. The victim, Anna Suvorina, the author of books for children, was the wife of the prominent journalist A. S. Suvorin, who then worked for the liberal newspaper *Sankt-Peterburgskie vedomosti*, where he published a popular weekly feuilleton, "Sketches and Vignettes" (*Ocherki i kartinki*) signed "Neznakomets" (*Stranger*). The connection of the heroes of this drama to the press heightened public interest in the incident. In its own right, the death of Suvorina had all the characteristics of a sensation: a thirty-three-year-old mother of five children, she was sharing supper with Komarov, in a hotel room, when the shots were fired at about midnight. Her husband, who was supposed to join the couple, arrived at the scene shortly after, having just completed an urgent report for his newspaper.

It is hard to say what shocked the public more—the crime, the revelation of the unconventional mores of men and women of letters, or the very fact that intimate details in the lives of the members of educated society were revealed to the public. The theme of publicity, or *glasnost'*, figures prominently in the accounts of the drama; what *glasnost'* meant in this case was exposing the private to the public eye. The article in *Nedelia* was entitled "Public Dramas of Intimate Life" (*Glasnye dramy intimnoi zhizni*); signed E. K., it was written by a left-wing woman journalist E. Konradi.

Exposed to the public eye in numerous accounts in many organs, from serious political journals to the "yellow" press, were not only the circumstances of the Suvorins' personal drama, but also the woman's body, whose condition, as well as that of the suicide's disfigured body, was described in the papers in considerable detail. A reporter from the gossipy *Novosti*, which published its coverage of the case on the front page, claimed that he saw the body in the morgue and described "a large lacerated wound" in the terms of a postmortem report.[46] *Golos* gave a similar description.[47] *Sankt-Peterburgskie vedomosti* found it essential, speaking for Suvorin, to announce that the victim's husband (contrary to the reports of the rival newspapers) did not object to the autopsy of his wife's body.[48] In itself the operation performed by the press—opening the intimate and the physical to public view—was tantamount to an "autopsy" (*vskrytie*). In this context, the name of the hotel—Belle Vue—acquired an emblematic quality.

Members of the press were clearly ambivalent about such practices. A publicist from *Delo*, B. Ongirsky, after reviewing various newspaper accounts of the Suvorin case in his "Statistical Results on Suicide," reproached the journalists from *Sankt-Peterburgskie vedomosti* for sounding the alarm "throughout the entire liberal camp" (*na ves' liberal'nyi okolotok*) rather than relieving their colleague's grief "in the family circle."[49] The sensationalist newspaper *Novosti* preceded its revelation of the scandalous details with a disclaimer:

> When describing the bloody drama in Belle Vue in yesterday's issue, we found it necessary, out of a completely understandable feeling of delicacy and respect for the honor of the family of Mr. Suvorin, to be silent on one important fact. . . . This fact consists of the following: as told to us by the owner of the hotel Belle Vue, Mr. Lomach, everything in the hotel room that had been occupied by Mr. Komarov was found exactly in place, and the bedding had not been touched.[50]

The socially minded *Nedelia* reported the scandalous fact that this detail was exposed:

> One newspaper had even voluntarily taken on the role of forensic investigator and triumphantly reported to the public that, according to inquiries conducted by the newspaper, the hotel room where the event occurred had been in perfect order and the bedding had not been crumpled![51]

But social language and social argument prevailed over everything. Even *Novosti* concluded their graphic description of the dead woman's body with an appeal to the social significance of the event, treating it as a part of a series and the sign of a social pathology characteristic of the age:

> The frequent repetition of such facts, in part, points to the abnormal condition of the developed sector of our society, and the causes for this con-

dition, in our opinion, lie in the changes that our society has undergone in the last decade.[52]

Publicists writing in "thick journals" followed the same strategy: indecent exposure could be counteracted by passing from the discussions of "personalities" (a product of "our homemade *glasnost'* ") to the "general meaning of events."[53] Since in their weekly and monthly reviews, these journalists addressed a number of cases, they indeed passed from the individual to the collective. For the journalist from *Delo*, "the romantic death of Suvorina killed by Komarov in hotel Belle Vue" was a part of a continuum that extended to "the prosaic death of a poor peasant woman who had hanged herself from a city streetlight near the Mytninsky dvor."[54] As such, these events became social phenomena and, therefore, a matter of social concern. *Nedelia* attributed the two Hotel Belle Vue deaths to an "epidemic" of violence. And of such epidemics "it is hardly possible to doubt that they obey known laws with the same fatefully undeviating regularity as do phenomena of the physical world."[55] Appeals to science and its laws made the procedure appear legitimate.

About a year later, in his feuilleton in *Sankt-Peterburgskie vedomosti* Suvorin himself alluded to his wife's death, along with three similar cases that he witnessed in the course of the year. He compared contemporary young men to the serf owners of the old times, who punished the serf girls for rejecting their amorous advances, and he appealed for judgment to his progressive readers.[56] The journalist made far-reaching social conclusions from his private drama.

The status of the event was clear, but there was no consensus on the cause. The confusion became painfully obvious in the debate between *Nedelia* and *Delo*. The *Delo* publicist, Ongirsky, bitterly lamented the fact that the public, alerted to the issue of murder and suicide by the Hotel Belle Vue case, subscribed to widely diverse views: "some, as usual, saw the root of evil in nihilism and atheism"; some looked for an explanation in the pages of a psychiatric study; and some would not look for the cause at all, attributing the events to fate. Much to Ongirsky's dismay, E. K. from *Nedelia* turned the power of her pen against herself, suggesting that the suicide epidemic was a product of *glasnost'*. She argued that newspaper coverage of crime and suicide provoked those who desired to appear in the spotlight to imitate such acts.[57] To give "the real reason," Ongirsky from *Delo* turned to "facts"—that is, to statistical data. The figures, in his opinion, hardly required comment, "clearly" indicating that poverty was the real cause of the private dramas behind the numbers.[58] A social law was at work. That poverty was not actually an issue for Komarov did not trouble the journalist, but he was troubled, as were many others, by the contradiction between the social explanation of suicide and the traditionally accepted medical view.

He tried to combine the two paradigms: perhaps, poverty caused mental aberration, which then led to suicide? The issue remained unresolved.

In her retort, Konradi gave a penetrating analysis of her colleague's difficulties, pointing out that, like many others, a publicist from *Delo*, confused by knowledge derived from several Western sciences, passed from the social argument to the medical, "simply changing horses midway":

> statistics are cast aside, and another fashionable horse is saddled—the laws of the human organism and psychology. . . . [S]ince we first learned about the existence of statistics as a science and also of several other sciences that study the laws of organic and inorganic nature . . . the number of such articles in Russia has greatly multiplied.[59]

Indeed, there were many such articles. Shaken by the collapse of the absolute authority of the Christian worldview, caught in the contradiction between social and medical explanations of human action (which also troubled Western scientists), bewildered by the novelty of publicity and by the contingencies of the historical moment, Russian publicists—like the Russian public—were profoundly confused. The confusion involved the general frame of reference (Christian and scientific), specific disciplines (medical and social science), and basic categories of social thinking, public and private, individual and social.

Discursive Strategies: Man's Two Bodies

Possible solutions to conceptual confusion were found in the very discourse used to discuss suicide. In the 1860s–80s, a discourse that invested body images with an array of symbolic meanings—a discourse pervaded by intended and unintended metaphors—was prevalent in the Russian press. Fed by organicist trends in Western social theory and the phraseology of Russian populism (adopted even by those who did not subscribe to the populist program), this discourse abounded in metaphors of society as a collective body. The pathology of the social body was a common theme. In the words of Petr Lavrov (in a populist manifesto serialized in *Nedelia* in 1868–69), "the present social order is a pathological order."[60] Autopsy was a common metaphor, used to comment on the power, limitations, and dangers of knowledge and exposure. The idea of pathology was also articulated in the images of the disintegration of the social body. Presented as a consequence of this disintegration, individual suicides were implicated in the destiny of Russian society. Metaphoric categories of science were correlated with political metaphors and suicide acquired a political twist. Various specific explanations of suicide were offered: suicide was connected to atheism and nihilism, growing poverty, development of civilization, social alienation brought by capitalism, or mental illness. What united those who held divergent views was a common language—a set of metaphors and rhetorical strategies derived from the image of the disintegrating social body. This metaphor offered solutions to many contradictions: created by conflation of the two concepts, individual and society, the metaphor encouraged the conflation of the two points of view, the individual and the collective, the medical and the social, the public and the private. It also encouraged the confusion of direct and metaphoric meaning.

In many texts, it was metaphor alone that provided an (implicit) explanation for the suicide epidemic. A journalist from *Otechestvennye zapiski* (in 1872) topped a long list of suicides and crimes with the comment that a society under reform is a victim of vivisection, in danger of losing its limbs.[61] An author from *Nedelia* (in 1873) described a healthy society as a well-integrated organism and lamented that this condition was not currently to be found:

> In vain would you search for that life-giving stream of powerful, fresh, and bold thought that in other epochs runs like an electric current from individual to individual, branching out along various layers of the social formation, as if making up the collectively thinking and feeling whole in which the individual worlds of thought and feeling fuse together.[62]

At present, he thought, the individual "detaches himself from the solidarity of general interests": it was the morbid overgrowth of individual interests and passions that accounted for murder and suicide, such as the Hotel Belle Vue case.[63] The reason for the suicide epidemic was also clear to a journalist from *Otechestvennye zapiski* in 1882: it was brought about by the "decomposition [*razlozhenie*] of communal principles" in Russian society.[64] Another author, writing in *Slovo* in 1880, offered a philosophical explanation of suicide, connecting the epidemic to the Buddhist ideal of nothingness ("nirvana") derived from Schopenhauer. The metaphor, and with it the social argument, however, took over the metaphysical one. Being sucked into the "abyss of nirvana" was not a danger to the individual who was firmly connected to a larger whole, society, the source of life: "when this is the case, a person feels beneath him the firm ground from which he extracts his living juices and his living energy."[65] Severed from the social body, the individuals lost their vitality and naturally succumbed to death by suicide: "Because they do not take nourishment from the flow of the life force in society, their energy weakens and becomes exhausted, and day by day the person unnoticeably approaches a psychological state in which further toiling becomes completely impossible."[66] Adapted to a national context, the image of the social organism resembled the Russian folk symbol of moist mother earth.

In their discussions of suicide, publicists from the anti-nihilist camp also focused on the relationship between the individual, body and soul, and a larger entity. In their case, this larger entity was not only society, but also God. The author of the Christian pamphlet *Our Time and Suicide* (*Nashe vremia i samoubiistvo*), A. Klitin, claimed that as soon as man loses faith, thus severing his connection with "the source of life—God," he is already dead.[67] In *Grazhdanin*, Meshchersky reasoned that because a nihilist gives up the immortal soul (a particle of God within his body), and becomes matter alone, he is subject to total annihilation: "Our young generation is *nihil*, and nothing more [*nichto i nichego bolee*]."[68] The end for a nihilist is, inevitably, suicide; what remains is "smoke and a dead body." Meshchersky discussed the situation in terms of its effect not only on the individual body, but also on the society: "we are all headed for suicide by a rapid or slow process of self-deception and self-decomposition (*samorazlozheniia*) . . . nihilism is the common plague of our society."[69] Like an individual without faith, a society without religion is a body without a soul—a suicide's body in a state of (self)-decomposition.[70] Thus, two antagonistic languages—Meshchersky called them "the language of the spiritual Russia" (*Rossii dukhovnoi*) and "the language of the realistic Russia" (*Rossii real'noi*)[71]—used metaphors built on the same pattern: conflation of the two bodies.

The Suicide's Body as a Locus of Meaning

Most newspaper accounts of suicide followed a standard pattern: a brief description of the location, victim's identity (which was frequently unknown), method of self-destruction, and a detailed description of the suicide's body. The report concluded with a remark: "causes unknown," or "an investigation is being conducted." By far the largest part of the account was frequently devoted to a description of the body. This information was usually taken from official police bulletins, which quoted the postmortem reports—hence the emphasis on the body. As might be expected, images of corporeal disorder (dismemberment, disfigurement, and decomposition) dominated these descriptions. From the newspaper reports, these images made their way to the reviews of suicides in monthly journals. In the following example, from the October 1873 issue of *Otechestvennye zapiski*, the reader is invited to view the body with the eyewitnesses. On a Volga ship approaching Samara, a passenger had leaped into the ship's engine:

curious onlookers saw a kind of bloody pulp, not at all like any living being. . . . the upper part of the unfortunate man's body was already ground up into a solid bloody pulp. An official report has been filed, of course. Apparently, the suicide was from the city of Samara. It is not known what caused him to take his own life.

A list of similarly described cases concludes with a reference to numerous other suicides, such as suicides of common peasants, which are not committed "in such a prominent [*vidnom*] place as a hotel on Nevsky or a passenger ship," and which lack witnesses:

> In several months to a year, when the spring waters subside, a miss-ing person's corpse will be found accidentally. They will write about this event briefly: "the completely rotten body of a man or a woman was found. . . . " Another time, someone's decapitated head will simply be fished out of the water near the steamship bureau, but whose head is it? To what poor fellow does it belong? Who knows! Who knows him, where is he from, what kind of person is he to have lost his head so carelessly?[72]

A case of a severed head appeared in the newspaper *Golos*, which, in its turn, borrowed it from the bulletin of the provincial government, *Samarskie gubernskie vedomosti*. This is what *Golos* reported:

> On August 2nd at 2 p.m. on the Volga River near the bureau of the steam-ship company "Samolet" *a severed head was extracted from the water*. The head belongs, it seems, to a man. There is no hair on it. The outer covering of the head, the face and what remained of the neck are of a dirty green color. They have swelled up and are covered with slime. The membranes of the eyes are wrinkled. The nose, lips, and ears show signs of decompo-sition. A total of eight teeth are missing, four from each of the upper and lower mandibles. The places where the teeth were located are not covered over by gums. The skull bones are intact. Only half of the neck is attached to the head; it ends with the fourth cervical vertebra. On the lower part of this vertebrae, a piece of bone was severed in a horizontal direction. The soft tissue surrounding the cervical vertebrae terminate parallel to the fourth cervical vertebra. Despite the decomposition, it is still possible to determine that they were cut through by a sharp cutting implement.[73]

Since nothing was known about the victim or the circumstances of his death, the newspaper account was largely limited to a forensic report on the condition of the only remaining part of the body, the head. The author of the journal re-view (Demert from *Otechestvennye zapiski*) turned the image of the severed head taken from the autopsy report into an explicit metaphor: a folk idiom *poteriat' golovu* [to lose one's head], which means "to die recklessly." The reader was thus invited to ascribe symbolic meaning to the whole picture: it could be read as an emblem of the decomposition of the postreform Russian society, the result of self-destructive social policies, which the press exposed to the public eye. And the very fact that the journalist chose to discuss death by decapitation (a violent act more likely to have been murder) among suicides, testifies to the symbolic power of the image of suicide.

In conclusion, a note on the mechanism of meaning. Newspaper accounts, in which the information on suicide originated, did not call for developed interpretations. In the absence of interpretation, descriptions of the body borrowed from forensic reports—an essential part of newspaper accounts of suicide—became the locus of textual meaning and carried the weight of explanation. The implied explanation relied on possible metaphoric readings: images of the disintegrating body of a (frequently unidentified) victim could be seen as symbols of the disintegration of the Russian society. On another plane of meaning, these pictures of corporeal disorder, almost always followed by the statement "cause unknown," stood as symbols of the tragic inaccessibility of knowledge about man and society. The reader well versed in this discourse received poetic license to read statements about the physical body metaphorically, as statements about society and as comments about knowledge. Other genres often made such metaphors explicit and used them deliberately. With the newspaper reports, it was the formal requirements of the genre that transformed the descriptions of disfigured bodies into a symbol—the medium created the message.

Between the Metaphoric and the Literal Meaning

Constructed in this manner, discussions of suicide in the press were pervaded by intended and unintended conflations of direct and metaphoric meaning. In one article, "On One Death" (*Po povodu odnoi smerti*),[74] published in the populist monthly *Ustoi* (in 1882), the process of metaphorization itself is literalized in the image of the body of a suicide dissolving in the body of Russia. First, the author presents the reader with a vivid picture of suicide: "before you lies a disfigured corpse." The journalist wants to show death "in the form of a shattered skull, of bloodied integuments, of the brains which have dried stuck to the wall"[75]—the way it would be presented in a forensic report. But at the next stage, the writer takes over the medical examiner, suggesting that the bones of the honest young Russian men who have died by suicide—"the salt of the earth"—"are spread on the face of our earth" (*rasseiany po vsemu litsu nashei zemli*, a folk idiom applied to fallen warriors). Further, we see the bodies "buried in the humid earth" (*skhoronennye v syroi zemle*). And a year later, "the lonely graves will be level with mother earth, and next summer no one will notice or remember that here have decayed the best hearts and the best brains that Russia has ever produced."[76]

From a graphic description of the disintegrated bodies (couched in medical terms) the text progresses, by way of a sequence of idioms evoking the folk symbolism of Russia as mother-earth, to an image that merges the body of the suicide with the body of society. The metaphor is literalized: the individual and the social body converge physically.

Although journalists took recourse in metaphor, they were, nevertheless, deeply concerned with "reality." According to *Delo* (in 1868), scientific data (statistics), in itself, lacked reality, but in the hands of a journalist "that raw material can be put to good use."[77] True to the journal's name (which means "deed"), one author argued for the deed, not the word. Taking statistics as his starting point, he chose to enlarge on the relationship between such environmental influences as "the decay of the atmosphere and the rottenness of the soil" (*gnilost' atmosfery i isporchennost' pochvy*) and the high morbidity in the capital. He explains that it was recently revealed (in *Arkhiv sudebnoi meditsiny i obshchestvennoi gigieny*, "the best and most useful of all the periodical publications in Russia"[78]) that in Petersburg waste is not removed through sewers, but absorbed into the soil. Petersburg's soil is nothing but a repository of decaying matter that poisons the air: "the soil of Petersburg is bit by bit turning into a common garbage pit emitting miasmas." This circumstance is responsible for the epidemics of infectious diseases and the birth of unhealthy children in families who live in basement apartments, in direct contact with the poisonous soil. This "murderous" soil is also responsible for suicides: "a statistician would make a tremendous error, if, while discussing, for example, suicides in Petersburg, he did not consider such circumstances as I have just mentioned."[79]

How is this connection established? Looking through statistical data, the journalist notes a considerable number of cases under the heading "students." He speculates on the cause of high mortality among students, specifically, among medical students. The cause lies in their "material environment." Given the cold, dark, humid cells ("frequently, with cracks in the floor") in which students live, scarce food, intense daily studies, and, moreover, working with decomposed corpses in the hospital, "the soil would be prepared for developing pulmonary tuberculosis" (*vy budete imet' prekrasno podgotovlennuiu pochvu dlia razvitiia legochnoi chakhotki*). The journalist concludes: "Is it any wonder, given the circumstances, that the number of student suicides is a sizable figure?"[80]

Guided by a sequence of rhetorical figures, the reader comes to accept suicides among medical students as no surprise. Central among these figures is the image of the "soil" that "prepared" the development of disease. In this case, no real soil is involved; "soil" is purely a metaphor, a part of the common idiom *podgotovit' pochvu*. But the author also evokes images of the physical, not metaphoric, soil: the miasmic soil soaked in the city's wastes, whose "murderous" influence is reinforced by the decomposing bodies with which medical students deal in the anatomical theater. At the start of his project, the journalist declares that his goal was to discover "the root causes" (*korennye prichiny*) of suicide.[81] Were they to be found, the figures would serve not only as material for moral statistics, but also as "positive data," of practical use to society. In searching for this "positive data," the text vacillates between the literal and the metaphoric meaning of the word "soil," conflating the two. The procedure (looking for the "root cause") is directed by the metaphor: the "root" of the matter is found in the "soil."

The persuasive power of the journalists' arguments seems to lie in the rhetorical connections and symbolic associations. The lull of familiar idioms (such as "to prepare the soil") as well as, for a well-informed reader, the story of Turgenev's character, the medical student Bazarov whose death resulted from contact with a corpse during an autopsy, all contribute to the general impression that the causal connection between the "soil" (a product of decomposing matter) and social ills such as suicide has been positively established. The project of making word into deed undertaken by *Delo* turned into a rhetorical operation of realizing metaphors and metaphorizing scientific concepts.

Two Autopsies

In the popular press as well as scientific publications, "autopsy," understood literally and metaphorically, figured as a predominant method of determining the cause of suicide. The idea of autopsy as an operation aimed at uncovering material manifestations of mental phenomena was consonant with contemporaries' desire for positive knowledge. The symbolic connotations of *glasnost'*, the practice of exposing the workings of social mechanisms to the public view, also added to the metaphor's meaning. The image of a medico-legal autopsy, which combined the authority of science with that of law, doubled, as it were, the symbolic power of penetration. (It was in this context that the journal *Annals of Forensic Medicine* was judged to be the most reliable and effective organ among the Russian periodicals.) Journalists and popularizers of science who wrote in popular press and medical scientists who actually performed autopsies frequently fell victim to the power of this metaphor.

One such scientist was Ivan Gvozdev, professor of forensic medicine in Kazan University, author of the brochure *On Suicide from a Social and Medical Point of View* (*O samoubiistve s sotsial'noi i meditsinskoi tochki zreniia*). Published in

1889, this book summarized the results of twenty years of practice, beginning in the late 1860s. On the whole, Gvozdev subscribed to Büchner's views, claiming that the "force of matter," a concept "used at present to explain all phenomena of the visible world," can also serve as an explanation for the normal and abnormal functions of mental capacities, including suicide.[82] As a scientist, Gvozdev limited his material to "positive data," that is, to evidence of mental activity deposited within cerebral matter. As a positivist, he relied exclusively on his own life experience, "[using] only what we have personally experienced in the course of life in general, and from the data of forensic medical dissections of suicides in particular."[83] On the basis of over one hundred autopsies performed by Gvozdev and his students, he claimed that the adhesion of the dura mater (the outermost of the three membranes covering the brain) to the skull was "one of the characteristic features of death by suicide as such." Though he admitted that the exact role played by the dura mater in mental activity was unknown, Gvozdev argued that its fusion with the skullcap could not have left molecular movement in the brain (that is, mental activity) unaffected.[84] It proved harder to pinpoint the material manifestations of suicidal disposition in the pia mater (the inner membrane), that is, in deeper, and softer layers of matter:[85]

> Although the brain ought to display physical changes corresponding to any mental disorders present, including suicide, these changes are sometimes so elusive or ephemeral that even with acute forms of insanity, they often evade appropriate detection.
>
> With suicide, physical changes in the brain tissue itself are ephemeral and elusive to detection; this is an almost constant phenomenon, especially when we are dealing with people of apparently good mental health who have made an attempt on their lives.[86]

Despite the lack of hard evidence, Gvozdev stood firm in his beliefs, assuming that the physical changes in the brain tissue merely eluded the scientist. He struggled with the two entities that defied the principles of positivism—people who were "apparently" (*po-vidimomu*, literally, "visibly") mentally healthy and brain tissue which had no visible manifestations of pathology. In both cases, the perception was declared to be false: suicides were known to be mentally ill (an axiom going back to Esquirol); mental was known to be inscribed in matter (a tenet of positivism). (In Büchner's words, "there must have been material pathological alterations, though they were not visible."[87]) "Reality" was believed to lie beneath the deceptive surface of appearances, even though it constantly eluded appropriate detection.

A central symbol of positive knowledge, anatomizing was also used as a symbol of positivistic education. Gvozdev, who approached suicide not only from a medical, but also from a social point of view, devoted a chapter to the role of education in causing (or failing to prevent) suicide. Statistics showed that the propensity for suicide increased within the educated classes of society and was higher among the young than among the general population. "Can contemporary education be a reason for suicide, if only a remote one?" asked Gvozdev. In approaching this question, he remained true to the principle of basing conclusions on his own experience and trusting the evidence provided by autopsies. Because he had seen students mainly over the bodies of suicides as he supervised them in performing autopsies, he based his judgment about the quality of education on the quality of the students' autopsy reports.[88] (His sample included about 2,000 student reports, accumulated over twenty years of teaching, beginning in the late 1860s.) Gvozdev was struck by mistakes in spelling, grammar, and diction in these reports and surprised to discover ignorance about the basic principles of physiology. But "nothing has made such an impression [on him] as did the almost complete ignorance of the classical languages among the majority of students finishing their medical education."[89] For Gvozdev, the fact that a typical student allowed his knowledge of Latin to fall into oblivion amounts, in the long run, to a mockery of life itself:

> In our opinion, this is nothing but a direct insult to Latin and an indirect insult to the time spent learning this language—and after all, time is life![90]

With this argument, Gvozdev comes closest to establishing a connection, albeit a symbolic one, between education and suicide (rejection of life). Of the two types of autopsy, a medical procedure and a metaphor, the metaphor seems to have had a stronger explanatory power.

The Writer on Suicide

Writing in "thick" journals, under the same cover with publicists and popularizers of science, writers laid their claim to finding the truth about suicide. Such a claim was put forward by the literary critic and publicist Nikolai Mikhailovsky, one of the main ideologists of populism, in a review written for *Otechestvennye zapiski,* "Zhiteiskie i khudozhestvennye dramy" (January and February 1879). His starting point is, again, an impression (derived from the newspapers) that the incidence of suicide had increased. Echoing newspaper reports, Mikhailovsky cites case after case, capping them with a conventional phrase "the cause of suicide is unknown."[91] The critic turns to letters left by suicides as a potential source of knowledge, but finds no illumination: "in their suicide notes, which are often very sincere and touching, the motives behind the decision to put an end to their lives nearly always remain in a kind of fog through which a stranger cannot discern anything."[92] Apparently Russian suicides, unlike their Western counterparts, are not capable of "publicly baring their souls."[93] According to Mikhailovsky, they themselves do not know the reasons that led them to suicide.[94] While in Europe "the sphere of the unconscious is, in general, not as broad"; a Russian suicide just does not know: "in the depths of his soul, something is stirring, but he can find neither completely conscious thought nor, consequently, the words [to express it]."[95]

Mikhailovsky turns to science, but science is also not of much help. Statistics establishes correlations between the number of suicides and external factors, but because it cannot trace the intermediate links between the two events, statistics fails to uncover the working of the internal mechanism. Rejecting the authority of science, be it statistics or psychology, Mikhailovsky claims that it is the artist who has the power of penetrating into the hidden depths of the human soul: "Where is one to find skillful people? Of course, among artists. No where else. One must still await the successes of scientific psychology."[96] The writer is called to take over both the subject and the scientist in uncovering the mysteries of the human soul.[97]

Concluding Remarks

The Russian press of the 1860s–80s made suicide into a metaphor of the age. Indeed, the concept of suicide contained rich symbolic potential, consonant with the social and intellectual concerns of the time. Different themes converged in this image; different ideological groups invested it with symbolic meaning. The body of the suicide, presented in vivid images of corporeal disorder, stood as a symbol of the disintegration of the body social—the Russian society after the reforms. For positivists, suicide was a test case for the issue of freedom of will versus determinism (and a strong argument for the latter). The autopsy of the suicide was an image that suited the age's preoccupation with the penetrating power of scientific knowledge and the current Russian concern with openness. For those troubled by the advance of positivism and scientism, suicide was both a consequence and a symbol of the atheistic society (the body without a soul). It was also the positivist's worst nightmare: the evidence of man's inability to determine what causes observable phenomena. The obvious inability to determine causation put a heavy emphasis on the discourse itself. Amalgamation of discursive sources (Western organicism, Christian symbolism, and Russian populism) contributed to the widespread conflation and confusion of categories (the individual and the collective, the medical and the social, the body and the soul, the people and the land, etc.), and, ultimately, of the metaphoric and the literal plane of meaning. In this context the real body of the suicide assumed a second existence as a symbol.

Notes

1. Material adapted from Irina Paperno, *Suicide as a Cultural Institution in Dostoevsky's Russia*. Copyright 1997 by Cornell University. Used by permission of the publisher, Cornell University Press. In addition to material in this chapter, the book includes chapters on the treatment of suicide in science, law, and fiction as well as private documents left by suicides.

2. Paraphrasing W. Bruce Lincoln, *The Great Reforms: Autocracy, Bureaucracy, and the Politics of Change in Imperial Russia* (Dekalb, Ill., 1990), 143.

3. From E. Likhacheva's review of Morselli's *Il suicidio, Otechestvennye zapiski*, No. 7, 1881, 22.

4. From the review of suicides in the chronicle "Nashi obshchestvennye dela" (signed D.) in *Otechestvennye zapiski*, July 1872, 83, and E. Likhacheva, 31.

5. Anonymous review of A. V. Likhachev's *Samoubiistvo v Zapadnoi Evrope i Evropeiskoi Rossii* (St. Petersburg, 1882), *Otechestvennye zapiski*, no. 9, 1882, 133.

6. Ludwig Büchner, *Force and Matter* [1855] (London, 1870), 226.

7. D. I. Pisarev, "Motivy russkoi dramy," in his *Sochineniia*, 4 vols. (Moscow, 1955–56), 2:392.

8. Richard Wortman, *The Crisis of Russian Populism* (Cambridge, Mass., 1967), 28.

9. From "Pessimizm nashei intelligentsii" (published anonymously) in *Nedelia*, no. 42, 1880, 1337–38. Written by I. Kablitz [I. Iuzov], the author of *Osnovy narodnichestva* (1882).

10. From "Pessimizm nashei intelligentsii," 1338.

11. From E. Likhacheva, 23.

12. Quoted from J. E. D. Esquirol, *Mental Maladies. A Treatise on Insanity*, translated by E. K. Hunt (Philadelphia, 1845), 301 and 312.

13. Ibid., 307.

14. Ibid.

15. The second edition, entitled *Poslednie dni samoubiits*, appeared in 1863.

16. A. Ketle, *Chelovek i razvitie ego sposobnostei. Opyt obshchestvennoi fiziki* (St. Petersburg, 1865) and *Sotsial'naia sistema i zakony eiu upravliaiushchie* (St. Petersburg, 1866). The original: L. Adolphe Quételet, *Sur l'homme et le dévelopement de ses facultés*, 2 vols. (Paris, 1835).

17. *Nravstvennaia statistika v sviazi s istorieiu prilozheniia chisel k naukam nravstvennym*, published by N. I. Lamansky (St. Petersburg, 1867). The book included material from

A. M. Guerry, *La statistique morale de la France* (Paris, 1933), Adolph Wagner, *Die Gesetzmäs-sigkeit in den scheinbar willkürlichen menschlichen Handlungen vom Standpunkte der Statistik. Statistik der Selbstmorde* (Hamburg, 1864), and M. W. Drobisch, *Die moralische Statistik und die menschlichte Willensfreiheit* (Leipzig, 1867).

18. *Otechestvennye zapiski*, January 1868, 76.

19. Henry Thomas Buckle, *History of Civilization in England*, vol. 1 (London, 1873), 19–27.

20. Quote from the English translation, Henry Morselli, *Suicide: An Essay on Comparative Moral Statistics* (New York, 1882), 6–7 and 9.

21. Ibid., 10.

22. Ibid.

23. Morselli, *Il suicidio*, 18. The section that contained this statement was omitted from the English translation of 1882.

24. V. A. Zaitsev, in "Bibliograficheskii listok" of *Russkoe slovo*, 1865, no. 3, 83–85. Quote from V. A. Zaitsev, *Izbrannye sochineniia*, vol. 1 (Moscow, 1934), 154–55.

25. Ibid., 72 and 83. In the May 1863 issue of *Russkoe slovo*, Zaitsev reviewed the Russian translation of Vogt, K. Fogt, *Estestvennaia istoriia mirozdaniia* (Moscow, 1863).

26. See Alexander Vucinich, *Science in Russian Culture*, vol. 2 (Stanford, 1970), 7.

27. N. Radiukin, "Statistika samoubiistva (po povodu sochineniia Vagnera "Statistik der Selbstmorde")," *Delo*, no. 1, 1866, 312–13. On Shelgunov's authorship, see N. I. Sokolov, " 'Delo'," *Ocherki po istorii russkoi zhurnalistiki i kritiki* II, Leningrad, 1965, 311.

28. Censor F. P. Elenev; quote from Sokolov, 315.

29. Published in volume III of *Sbornik sochinenii po sudebnoi meditsine* (1880).

30. Ponomarev's study was reviewed by E. Likhacheva (along with Morselli); Likhachev's book was reviewed in *Otechestvennye zapiski*, no. 9, 1882, *Nedelia*, no. 40, 1882, and *Vestnik Evropy*, September 1882.

31. A. V. Likhachev, *Samoubiistvo v Zapadnoi Evrope i Evropeiskoi Rossii. Opyt sravnitel'no-statisticheskogo issledovaniia* (St. Petersburg, 1882), 4 and 6.

32. See "Recherches sur le nombre des suicides et des homicides commis en Russie pendant les années 1819 et 1820" par Ch. -Th. Herrmann, *Mémoires de l'Académie impériale des sciences de St.Petersbourg*, VI série, Tome 1: Sciences politiques, histoire et philologie (St. Petersburg, 1832) and K. S. Veselovsky, *Opyty nravstvennoi statistiki Rossii*, in *Zhurnal ministerstva vnutrennikh del*, pt. 18 (1847).

33. See Iu. Gübner's "Samoubiistva v St. Peterburge s 1858 po 1867 god," Arkhiv sudebnoi meditsiny i obshchestvennoi gigieny, vol. 3, 1868; an official survey in *Pravitel'stvennyi vestnik*, no. 100, 1876; I. Pasternatsky, "Statisticheskoe issledovanie samoubiistv v Peterburge za 1870, 1871 and 1872 gody," *Meditsinskii vestnik*, no. 34, 36, 38, 41 for 1873. Between 1873 and 1882, statistical data on suicide also appeared in A. S. Suvorin's popular *Russkii kalendar'*.

34. The Russian data covered the span from the 1830s to the 1880s; Likhachev could not find any data for the years 1841–1858.

35. M. N. Gernet, *Ukazatel' russkoi i inostrannoi literatury po statistike prestuplenii, nakazanii i samoubiistv* (Moscow, 1924), 228.

36. On suicide in the "small press," see Louise McReynolds *The News under Russia's Old Regime: The Development of a Mass-Circulation Press* (Princeton, 1991), 66 and passim.

37. See, for example, *Golos*, no. 215 for 1872, and *Vedomosti S.-Peterburgskoi politsii*, no. 7 for 1870 and no. 43, 44, and 118 for 1873.

38. For coverage of suicide see *Grazhdanin*, 1873, no. 2, 13, 18, 19, 21, 23, 38–40, 43, 49; 1874, no. 1, 2, 11, 12.

39. See, for example, *Moskovskie vedomosti* for April 28, 1873.

40. *Golos* (published since 1863) was closed in 1881; *Sankt-Peterburgskie vedomosti* abandoned its liberal position in 1875; *Otechestvennye zapiski* (which changed hands in 1867) and *Delo* (created in 1866) were closed in 1884; *Nedelia* (published since 1866) abandoned oppositional orientation by the late 1880s.

41. From Orest Miller, "Samoubiistvo ot ekzamena," *Zaria*, no. 6, 1870, 178.

42. For comparative perspective one could draw on Western material. It was in the eighteenth century, when England saw a rapid growth of the periodical press, that the newspaper coverage of suicide created the impression that suicide was a common and specifically English phenomenon. See Michael McDonald, "Suicide and the Rise of the Popular Press in England," *Representations*, no. 22 (Spring 1988) and chap. 9 of *Sleepless Souls: Suicide in Early Modern England* by Michael MacDonald and Terence R. Murphy (Oxford, 1990).

43. "Vnutrenniaia khronika," *Otechestvennye zapiski*, March 1871, 171 and 174.

44. See such publications in *Nedelia* as "Po povodu samoubiistva detei," no. 18 (April 29), 1884; "Maniia samoubiistv," no. 22 (May 27), 1884; "Nash pessimizm," no. 24, 1888; "Otorvannost' ot zhizni," no. 47, 1888. Commenting on the fact that the press noted an increase of suicides for the year 1888, Shelgunov gave an insightful commentary:

> In Russia suicides started occurring neither today nor yesterday. Whether the number of suicides is generally increasing, and whether it has increased in the year 1888, is truly unknown, because there are no exact suicide statistics for Russia. But those who need suicides as "material" [for their interpretations] claim (and this can be done without evidence) that suicide is on the rise.

("Ocherki russkoi zhizni," *Russkaia mysl'*, no. 1, 1889; quote from N. V. Shelgunov, *Ocherki russkoi zhizni*, St. Petersburg, 1895, 654.) Most of his contemporaries did not share his opinion.

45. *Nedelia* no. 18, May 4, 1886, 621.

46. *Novosti*, September 21, 1873.

47. *Golos*, September 21, 1873.

48. *Sankt-Peterburgskie vedomosti*, October 4, 1873.

49. B. Ongirskii, "Statisticheski itogi samoubiistv," *Delo*, no. 11, 1873, 1.

50. *Novosti*, September 22, 1873.

51. E. K., "Glasnye dramy," 1419.

52. *Novosti*, September 21, 1873.

53. E. K., "Glasnye dramy," 1419.

54. Ongirskii, 1. A brief report of the suicide of the peasant (Avdot'ia Nikiforova) appeared in *Vedomosti Sankt Peterburgskoi gorodskoi politsii* on September 27, 1873; on September 22, the police paper printed an equally brief report on the Belle Vue case.

55. E. K., "Glasnye dramy," 1416.

56. "Nedel'nye ocherki i kartinki," *Sankt-Peterburgskie vedomosti*, November 3, 1874.

57. Ongirskii, 1–2.

58. Ongirsky mainly used the data published by I. Pasternatsky, according to which poverty (combined with drunkenness) constituted 53 percent of the cases known for 1870, 1871, and 1872.

59. E. K., "Urok nekoemu publitsistu 'Dela'," *Nedelia*, no. 49, 1873, 1801 and 1803.

60. Quote from P. L. Lavrov, *Istoricheskie pis'ma* (St. Petersburg, 1917), 45.

61. "Nashi obshchestvennye dela," *Otechestvennye zapiski*, July 1872, 83–84.

62. E. K., "Glasnye dramy," 1414.

63. E. K., "Glasnye dramy," 1414.

64. From the review of A. V. Likhachev's study on suicide published in *Otechestvennye zapiski*, no. 9, 1882, 131.

65. D. Kulikovskii, "Samoubiitsy i nirvana," *Slovo*, no. 11, 1880, 178.

66. Ibid.

67. A. Klitin, *Nashe vremia i samoubiistvo* (Kiev, 1890), 3.

68. Vera N. [V. P. Meshcherskii], "Pis'ma khoroshen'koi zhenshchiny," *Grazhdanin*, no. 7, 1874, 208.

69. "Mysli vslukh (Priznaki vremeni)," *Grazhdanin*, no. 19, 1873, 557 and 559.

70. Peter Pozefsky makes insightful observations about the representation of the nihilist's body in the writings of the anti-nihilists, noting the predominance of images of rape, incest, and suicide. Guided by the idea, formulated by Mary Douglas (*Natural Symbols: Explorations in Cosmology* [New York, 1970]), that the human body is often used as a metaphor for society as a whole and that certain social situations engender certain types of body imagery, Pozefsky interprets these images as a metaphor of the disintegration of society as a whole. See Peter C. Pozefsky, *Dmitrii Pisarev and the Nihilist Imagination: Social and Psychological Origins of Russian Radicalism (1860–1868)*, Ph.D. diss., University of California, Los Angeles, 1993, 293–322.

71. M. [V. P. Meshcherskii], "Dve Rossii," *Grazhdanin*, no. 1, 1874, 7.

72. All quotes are from section "Nashi obshchestvennye dela," *Otechestvennye zapiski*, October 1873, 261–64 (written by N. A. Demert).

73. *Golos*, September 1, 1873.

74. "Po povodu odnoi smerti," *Ustoi*, July 1882. The case involved the double suicide of two young officers, Schultz and Khrzhanovsky. Suspected of being "politically disloyal," they were put under arrest. Although nine months later the investigation determined that the accusation was groundless, both chose to resign from the military and retired to their estates. Khrzhanovsky soon shot himself; his friend committed suicide several months later. (Some letters pertaining to the case were published in *Nedelia*, no. 33, 1882.)

75. "Po povodu odnoi smerti," 43.

76. Ibid., 43–44.

77. "Vnutrennee obozrenie," *Delo*, no. 10, 1868, 82–83.

78. "Vnutrennee obozrenie," *Delo*, no. 10, 1868, 84.

79. Ibid., 88–89.

80. Ibid., p. 90.

81. Ibid., 85; reiterated on 91.

82. I. Gvozdev, *O samoubiistve s sotsial'noi i meditsinskoi tochki zreniia* (Kazan', 1889), 5.

83. Ibid.

84. Ibid., 42.

85. In his view of the brain Gvozdev was guided by Wilhelm Griesinger, the author of a standard work on mental pathology (1845), translated into Russian in the 1860s.

86. Ibid., 42–43.

87. Büchner, *Force and Matter*, 120.

88. Gvozdev, 21.

89. Ibid., 23.

90. Ibid., 25.

91. Quoted from *Sochineniia N. K. Mikhailovskogo*, vol. 4, St. Petersburg, 1897, 641.

92. Ibid., 643–44.

93. Ibid.

94. Ibid., 644.

95. Ibid., 648.

96. Ibid.

97. The challenge was taken up by Dostoevsky. Suicide was a central theme in Dostoevsky's private journal, the *Diary of a Writer*, and in the novels written in the late 1860s and 1870s. Judging by his notebooks, the writer closely followed newspaper reports. (For the treatment of Dostoevsky and suicide, see my *Suicide as a Cultural Institution*.)

In Place of a Conclusion

Jane Burbank

———·◁∞▷·———

A N ATTENTIVE READER will have noticed that while this book is organized
by topic, it also preserves a familiar historical attention to chronological
ordering within each section, and in the placement of the first and final articles
as well. We began on a positive note, with Valerie Kivelson's redemption of the
provincial nobility from the charges of political incapacity; we moved across
time and space to address cultural and material practices of individuals and
institutions; we ended with Irina Paperno's depiction of a public that insists
that it is sick, even unto death. Is there a meaning in this sequence?

Our intention in this volume was exploration, rather than production of an
authoritative map. The pictures presented here are in most cases only sections
of larger landscapes.[1] For those concerned with questions of representativeness
or typicality, this volume suggests a great deal of future work. Each of the essays
could be set against—if not tested by—fuller studies of, to take a few examples,
other issues in the press, other imperial institutions and their designs, life in
other borderlands. Here we provide only glimpses of particular settings.

More small-scale studies would constitute appropriate continuations of the
collective project of this volume, but in addition, the question of how to put imperial Russia back together again,[2] how to frame hypotheses and organize research about history over a long time and large space, remains critically important. As noted in the introduction, studies with a thesis about the imperial
period as a whole are remarkably scant on library shelves.[3] Perhaps one unintended consequence of the relentless politicization of the historiography of the
late imperial period was to diminish interest in long-term conjectural thinking
altogether. This is not a desirable development, particularly in the post-Soviet
context when myths about the past have popular resonance and political effects.
This volume draws no conclusions of its own, but ends with questions for further study and with suggestions of the kinds of pictures that our pieces of imperial history, matched with missing segments, might in time evoke.

How would a new history of imperial Russia take shape? Part of the answer depends on the debatable proposition that historians can identify and address long-term processes. It would be a mistake just to replace narratives of failure with narratives of success, a practice that gained popularity, especially in Russia, during the collapse of historiographic conventions in the late *perestroika* period. One problem with the old story of decay was its very structure. Narratives of imperial failure (or success) rely on an episodic illusion: the actions of individuals (*intelligenty,* state bureaucrats) and groups (peasants, gentry) in particular settings become installments of movements, struggles, and conflicts that appear to continue over enormous space and time. But there is no a priori connection between small-scale stories and large-scale historical processes. Did it make a difference to David Ransel's merchant-protagonist that he was only twenty-five years old when his father died? Yes. Did this event make a difference to the strength or weakness of the imperial economy? Not much. Are we still interested in merchant Tolchenov and his fate, as Ransel narrates it? Yes, but not because he proves a point about whether the empire would survive or not.[4] The question of how small stories relate to larger narratives has drawn attention from historians working in many world areas, as poststructuralist, feminist, and colonial studies have displaced the confident interpretions of earlier philosophies of knowledge.[5] Historians of Russia should share this theoretical concern, and speak to it, if they want to extend their interpretations beyond specific settings.

A second problem with earlier narratives of "failure" was how they defined success. To take another example from our volume, focused directly on politics, Kivelson tells the story of 1730, again. This time she tells it to redeem the lesser nobility from historiographic charges of political incompetence that have accumulated over more than a century. She shows that the nobility gained what it wanted from the "constitutional" crisis, and that what it wanted was not a constitution, but to preserve its accustomed familial ways of passing on property, its access to status and wealth, and its informal, flexible means of influencing the autocrat. How does Kivelson change a story of national failure into evidence of class strength? By removing 1730 from the anachronistic frame of political reform in Western European style. In those confines, 1730 became a lost chance, a failure to set legal limits on autocracy, the end of the beginning for Russian democracy. However, when events of the succession—not the "succession crisis"—are told in Kivelson's way, we see that the Russian nobility succeeded yet again in setting limits on the monarch, not through a constitution, but by gaining practical concessions to the nobility's values and interests. Exposing how elites got their ways and in what causes tells far more about the operations of the empire than imposing constitutionalism as a measure of its progress.

Progress, or setbacks to progress, after all, have been the underlying theme of Russian historiography. Whether in pursuit of episodes of class struggle—stations on the way to socialism—or in searches for elements of successful capitalist development, historians have usually measured imperial Russia against their own ideas of what a society should be or at least should be becoming. Such teleology is refreshingly absent from most articles in this collection, but one historian attacks it head on. Steven Hoch insists that we reconceptualize our analysis of the social economy of Russian peasants. Instead of accepting development, especially variants of capitalist development, as the normative measure of peasant (and other) societies' strength or weakness, Hoch points out that there are other standards for comparison and appraisal. His essay shows that peasant society was oriented not toward accumulation, but survival. If historians change their questions, and ask about a society's ability to organize its endurance under particular economic and environmental conditions, Russian peasants do quite well, over a large space and a long time. This leap over the varieties of modernization theory that saturate the field is essential, if we are to recover rural history on its own terms. For some, survival was enough.

If we are to accept the challenge of writing long-term histories and also break with the familiar framework of capitalist development according to its ideal and idealized types, what materials can we use to structure new narrations? For those who want to ask "so what?" "why does this matter?" without falling into the trap of reading failure (or success) onto every institution and moment of imperial Russia, the essays presented here provide suggestions and provocations about when and where to look for significant evidence. First, is there meaning in the time frame? *Imperial Russia: New Histories for the Empire* focuses primarily on the pre-reform period, because this period was understudied in the 1980s when many scholars turned toward the revolution and the Soviet era. But just such a focus on the century and a half before the great reforms raises questions about both what came before and what followed imperial history as we have bounded it.

Answers about continuities and transformations across chronologically labeled "periods" depend, as usual in historiographic controversies, on the questions asked. Earlier debates about whether Petrine Russia represented a qualitative break with Muscovy inform Kivelson's lead essay, but she attempts to shift the nature of the query itself. Rather than accepting a strong divide between two kinds of governance—"Western" rational, meritocratic politics and Russian clan-based, status-seeking practices—Kivelson employs a definition of political culture that embraces both ideas and interest. Defenders of family interest could incorporate meritocratic ideas into their defense of noble privilege, a highly rational stance from the perspective of the nobility. Kivelson's rendering of the political undermines the notions of a Petrine break with Muscovite tradition and an eighteenth-century turn toward Western rationalism, in part by redefining each term of opposition.

Culturalist interpretations of politics work against the concept of sharp breaks in practices of government. Several other essays in this volume should provoke inquiries as to whether "imperial Russia" can be defended as a distinctive period.[6] If so, what were the fundamental transformations that defined the material, institutional, and ideological origins of the imperial system? Hoch suggests the centrality of Russian serfdom to the political economy of the empire. Thomas Barrett emphasizes the strong social impact of extending imperial frontiers. The conventional periodization with its emphasis on Peter I might also be challenged in interpretations that emphasize the long-term practice of incorporation of non-Russian elites into the ruling class as well as shifts in the international context of Russian state power. From these perspectives, was the seventeenth century not a period of imperial state construction? Should we then move our boundaries back in time?

At the other end of this volume's chronology is Paperno's provocative analysis of public discourse about suicide in the era of reforms. Writers concerned with Russia's political institutions—liberals and marxists, contemporaries and historians, in Russia and abroad—have set their alarm clocks to exactly the period Paperno discusses, the 1860s to 1880s. Depending on what future was thought to lie ahead, 1861 has been regarded as either the beginning of the end of the old regime or the birthday of Russian democracy.[7] Does Paperno's article reinforce this timeline of Russian development or call it into question?

One way of reading Paperno's essay is to take the pessimism of journalistic commentary on suicide at face value, and to register its challenge to the notion of a robust and functional imperial society. Perhaps the empire was sick or sick of itself, as the social commentators of the 1870s—from many perspectives—seemed to agree. But even if we accept their reading of their present, there are still chronological puzzles to figure out. What were the reasons for the public's self-despair? Had something happened to disrupt profoundly the affective and economic sources of civic confidence? Had the imagery of autocratic family harmony, introduced in the romantic period, lost its hold?[8] What happened to the survivalist economy of the peasants after the emancipation changed the formal arrangements of authority and land?[9] Suicidal preoccupations may indeed reflect a breakdown of the condominium of gentry and monarchy, sustained by serfdom, that shaped social discourse before 1861.[10]

A more optimistic interpretation of Paperno's contribution might note that a society that examines its ills is in good mental health and interpret the extensive discussion of suicide as a laudable achievement of the Russian public.

Cynthia Whittaker's essay on autocratic ideologies exhibits the differentiated, cosmopolitan, and lively public discourse of the eighteenth century. The multiple images of autocracy produced at that time were directed toward a public that saw itself as a participant in sustaining state institutions. One could draw a line forward from Douglas Smith's essay on eighteenth-century discourses on Masonry and marvel at the ways in which Russian journalism had succeeded in opening up topics of widespread meaning to extensive audiences, not to mention the heterogeneity of the points of view expressed. As in the aftermath of 1991, pessimists and optimists who engage Paperno's discussion of nineteenth-century *glasnost'* journalism will argue over whether to wring their hands over what Russians said about themselves or to celebrate the circumstances that allowed them to say it.

Paperno herself is less concerned with revising conceptions of the reform era and its place in Russian development than with the issue of how public thought was formulated. Her focus is on the metaphoric logic with which Russians imagined their social being. If we are inclined to define historical periodization according to modes of thought, we would want to extend investigations along these lines both back in time and forward. Why—and when—did Russian commentators make the heuristic leap between individual suicides and the sickness of the social body? Paperno suggests that organicism as an interpretive strategy was not unique to Russia; a fusion of statistics with the concept of a social whole was characteristic of Western European social science since the 1830s. But her strong conclusion that suicide became a "metaphor of the age" in Russia from the 1860s to the 1880s provokes inquiry into other symbolisms, and other ways of thinking, in their specific contexts—inquiries that could help us discover the distinctions, if there are any, of these three decades as a critical breakpoint in Russian history.

A second set of questions would take space, not time, as its initial framework. This volume did not presume to "cover" the polity, but included both centrally and peripherally located narratives and set them side by side. This placement was designed to emphasize the connection of practices on the periphery to the Russian social arrangements in the center, and to underscore the ways that, even in central Russia, mainstream institutions—the Orthodox Church in Gregory Freeze's article—had to engage a diversity of cultural understandings. In other words, the center was a site for "civilizing missions" that we frequently associate with the periphery, and the periphery was a site of economic and social construction integral to the preservation of imperial society. This suggestion, however, cries out for elaboration and empirical research over the large map of empire. Is it possible to discover a set of general principles of governance or social organization that were applied throughout the realm? If not, what were the significant particularities—meaningful for both contemporaries and historians—among regions of the empire?

One approach to these questions has been taken up with enthusiasm since 1991; this is the analysis of Russia and the Soviet Union as empires, usually in comparison with the noncontiguous empires of the European powers.[11] The rich historiographic and anthropological literature on third-world societies and the exuberant theoretical debates about colonialism have informed articles in this volume and can be useful in other explorations of imperial Russia. Recent scholarship on the overseas colonial projects of modern European states has moved away from binary and, usually, Manichean oppositions of colonizer and colonized. The old unmatched sets have been rejected for different reasons by different scholars, but the general shift is toward a thicker description of the practice of colonialism, a description that accords agency to a variety of actors, and emphasizes their interactivity and its unpredictable results. In this volume, Barrett's and Willard Sunderland's articles replace the sharp distinction between ruler and ruled with accounts of interactive processes that complicate, productively, the representation of imperial rule.

Another new direction in the study of "Western" imperialism has been renewed attention to ideology and an investigation of its significance for the various agents of empire. While earlier studies were concerned to expose exploitation of colonies as an evil masked by paternalistic doctrine, newer scholarship sees ideologies as entering into and shaping politics and life. One line of reasoning emphasizes the limitations that European ideologies placed on both the conception and the carrying out of colonial projects. Rather than dismissing the rhetoric of universal rights, civilization, and development as bourgeois hypocrisy, some scholars of European empires have addressed the ways in which imperial agents and subjects enacted these notions, as well as the uncontrollable and unintended results of the introduction of colonial discourses into local vocabularies.[12] A similarly nuanced exploration of the principles and rhetoric of Russian empire and their intended and unintended consequences could inform new histories of Russia. One suggestion along these lines would be to investigate the impact of the progressivist autocratic ideologies described by Whittaker on the lives and aspirations of imperial subjects associated in the wide range of "publics" that populated the empire.

Both these tendencies in colonial studies—the move away from a stark opposition between imperialists and natives, and the attention to the power of imperial discourses in both localities and metropoles—would seem to undermine the representation of fixed and separate cultures as the building blocks of empire. Historians of Russia, however, have to take the discourse of fixed ethnic identity seriously, because as Kevin Thomas and Nathaniel Knight show, the idea of multiethnicity was promoted with enthusiasm by the scholars who established ethnographic traditions and information about the empire in the early nineteenth century. A challenging task awaiting future historians is to sustain a separation between the discourse of fixed ethnicities and the social practices of people, practices that cannot be accurately represented with totalizing and limiting notions of national identity.

A deficiency of scholarship on western colonialism is its attempt to bring everyone and almost every area of life into the politics of imperial rule and domination. As most of the essays in this volume suggest, in the Russian empire all of the people weren't concerned with empire all of the time. Not every aspect of life was constituted by imperial relations, and not all the unconstituted parts can be forced into a narrative of relationship to empire. This is not to argue that life was just lived, so much as to suggest that it was lived for a variety of purposes, some distant from colonial projects. The description of those purposes and the discovery of central organizing principles of Russian imperial society could be another way of pulling imperial history back together.

A third kind of macro-historical project would explore the motivations of Russian people and the social structures that sustained and constrained action and imagination. Was there a "Russian" culture, and if so, what were its constituent parts?

One candidate for further study as a central structure of Russian culture is patriarchy, both as a symbol and a system of power. Richard Wortman's work emphasizes that the theatrical performance of filial duty within the imperial family was expected to evoke loyalty and sentiment from imperial subjects. Many of the essays in this volume suggest that the building blocks of Russian society were in fact families, and that power was exercised both within families and among them by male elders. Can these observations about familistic practices be connected to the political and economic trajectory of imperial Russia? In a provocative essay, Edward L. Keenan drew structural connections between the personalized, secret, and collective practices of Muscovite rule and Soviet political culture.[13] Will future investigations of the imperial period see the eighteenth and nineteenth centuries as transmitters of patriarchal culture, or as a time during which its values were significantly challenged?

Cultural historians could pursue a number of specific questions about the qualities and extent of Russian patriarchal practice. For one thing, a commitment to the survival and where possible well-being of one's family, defined extensively and pragmatically, seems to be shared by both major classes of eighteenth-century Russia. The nobles' practice of partible inheritance, including shares for women,[14] is echoed in family-preserving land distributions of the peasant commune. (The peasants, with their principle of allocation according to family size, hit upon a more effective way to keep everyone afloat.) Neither of these two redistributional systems was conducive to sustained accumulation by individuals, and this paucity of resources may provide a clue to the ways the two classes articulated with each other on an estate. Landlords did not ordinarily challenge the patriarchal powers of their serfs; they depended on them to collect what could be gotten from peasant families in order to divide it, in turn, among noble children. Landlords' concerns for their own family members' collective welfare in this way abetted peasant patriarchy.[15]

The studies in this volume also display the vulnerabilities characteristic of family economies in patriarchal care. The wrong man at the patriarch's post could really make a mess of things. This is obvious from the example of various Romanovs at critical junctures, but an incompetent patriarch could disrupt the projects of ordinary families, too. Relatives might try to control the boss's initiatives or renegotiate his status, but the lead man had a heavy weight of tradition on his side. This is one way to look at Ransel's study of the merchant Tolchenov, whose lavish expenditures and lack of managerial oversight led to the precipitous decline of his family's fortunes. The Tolchenov story shows that relatives felt entitled to advise the young man, but ultimately the decisions of the patriarch would make or break the family. Empowered men can go too far, with consequences for many individuals.

Patriarchal power can also be viewed in its relationship to desires, grievances, and ideas of well-being. Kivelson describes the outraged response of nobles to Peter's law on unigeniture. Undoing this invasive law, not leading the polity or making foreign policy, was the nobles' overriding concern. Hoch insists that the power of peasant patriarchs inhibited the development of class solidarity against the lords, as each patriarch made his deal and then extracted it from his subordinates in the household. Peasant patriarchy was in this sense anti-communitarian, but it clearly fostered specific ideas of worth, affection, and power for each member of a peasant household.

The practices of patriarchal power over large family units could be connected to questions about the effectiveness of the several paternalistic ideologies chosen by the autocracy over the imperial period. In particular, one might ask whether the turn toward sentimentalism in the early nineteenth century was at odds with the pervasive values of patriarchal authority. One family—the emperor's—at least had achieved unigeniture and domestic bliss (when in the public view), but the question of whether loyalty to the monarch and his progeny could be extended outside the imperial family through demonstrative representation of filial duty and love is still open.

To turn to even larger questions, did systemic patriarchy set limits on institutional reform, economic transformation, and particularly on capitalist development? Without normalizing capitalism, democracy, or patriarchy, one can still investigate the potentials and constraints that particular kinds of social organization entail. One hypothesis linking cultural practices to economic possibilities is that Russian patriarchal power was better suited to survival than accumulation. Let's return for a moment to Ransel's merchant and his sad decline from prosperity. Tolchenov's disastrous financial actions and their devastating consequences for his family illustrated the vulnerabilities of patriarchal systems of control. Few families could accumulate lasting, consequential, investable wealth if patriarchs had to buttress their authority by spending most of the family fortune and by dividing the remains among all their children. One might investigate the ways in which such practices of patriarchy obstructed the emergence of a bourgeoisie and thus set limits on capitalist development. If such development is regarded as a social good, then the sustained patriarchy of Russia's elites was a disaster for the prospects of the polity in a capitalist world.

From a different, survivalist perspective, however, patriarchal family organization can be seen to have its merits. Tolchenov's relatives played a useful role in protecting the family's diminished resources from his creditors. Reallocation of assets to various kin—uncles, sons, and others—allowed the family to endure, but at lower status. Ransel attributes the Tolchenovs' decline in part to shifts in markets and to competition from nonmerchants; but this saga could be read as a demonstratation of strengths as well as weaknesses of familial agency. One might conclude that the family as a whole was hardy because it could redistribute its resources widely, but that this kind of resilience went hand in hand with strong vertical (including downward) mobility.

It may be going too far to suggest that a Chayanovian pattern of cyclical mobility is observable not just among the peasants but—over longer periods of time, because of greater resources—in the life courses of merchant and noble families. In any case we should ask if the location of significant power in the patriarchal family (overweighing generally the individual, certainly the law, and often the state) is connected with the insistent particularity of economic and social arrangements in Russia. Hoch notes in his summary of estate agriculture that there was "little uniformity in the obligations owed masters." Do the myriad interpatriarchal bargains struck by masters of noble and peasant families account for this important disorderliness? Did this disorder set the brakes against the empire's transit toward a powerful modern economy and a democratic polity?

Finally, in this projection of research projects, we turn to one of the blankest spots in this collection. *Imperial Russia: New Histories for the Empire* has a domestic focus, and omits entirely attention to the international context in which the empire existed. I am not pleading for foreign policy study in its conventional sense, but for the willingness to explore, in new ways, the relationship of Russia's international position to the polity's possibilities. Was maintaining great-power status a choice or an imperative for Russian rulers? Was the extension of the empire a cost or a resource, and for whom? To what extent did foreign conquest endanger or enhance political stability within the country?[16] How did the terms of sustaining the polity in the international arena change over the course of two centuries, in relationship to the transformations of other polities and their political economies? A state is a relational institution, and Russia never existed alone.[17]

Study of imperial Russia as part of a world history can be carried out at several levels—the social geography of political boundaries, the imperatives of economic transformations, the impact of state rivalries and wars, the moving intersections of social practices. At a different conceptual level, a global view of Russian history must engage with the question of the provenance and power of the categories with which scholars work. One of the peculiarities of Russian history that baffles scholarly and other observers is the refusal of the polity to abide by the conventional categories of Western social science (and Western politics). Scholarly response to a "bad fit" into the analytical map generally has not been to jettison the chart, but rather to regard anomalous phenomena or blurred categories as "deviations" from the Western path and *therefore* as explanation for Russia's supposedly erratic and collision-prone historical course. This preservation of Western categories in the face of Russian "deviance" is abetted by the fact that Russian elites for the most part adopted the analytic language of the West, regardless of their acceptance or rejection of a Western future for Russia.

It is the task of scholarship, however, to examine its own categories, even and especially when these categories have played a role in establishing historical possibilities and consciousness. Would the crisis-driven conventions of earlier histories of imperial Russia disappear if we could generate categories of analysis from Russian behaviors, not the postulated behavior of the West? Michael Confino has pointed out that the West itself is a constructed category, based on ideal types that historians routinely and productively interrogate.[18] With respect to theoretical issues that underlie research, the articles in this volume reach out in two directions. One is the analysis of imperial Russia as one of the several European absolutisms, to be investigated with the same scholarly tools and categories—public culture, frontier society, dynastic ideologies—that are used to dissect and visualize the "West." The other direction, implicit in the textured accounts of imperial society or explicit in discussions of political culture and peasant economy, is to challenge quite radically the terms and standards of mainstream—that is, first- and third-world—social science.

Could historians of Russia reverse the direction of the rivers of theory that nourish and confine our thinking? Could new categories emerging from closer readings of imperial Russian history become a part of a more cosmopolitan social science? Future examinations of the uncompleted, ultimately unsuccessful, but all the same long-lasting and socially powerful Russian Empire should inform the study of other areas and become a part of a more worldly history that questions its own categories and its course.

The main purpose of this book has not been to produce a new grand narrative or theory, but to refocus attention on the vitality of the people of the empire acting in their own interests and making their lives in a variety of particular circumstances and possibilities. Conflict is both described and assumed in these essays, but it is not the dominant story. Limitations are part of the picture, however; each essay reminds us that individual striving was always constrained and stimulated by an array of social and ideological conventions. The tsar was far away, but neighbors, business associates, rival scholars, and the like both set powerful limits upon and inspired an individual's or a family's aims and possibilities.

The activities described in these essays—revising the political theory of autocracy, criticizing in print the new secret clubs of which one was not a member, converting to Islam and leading raiding parties against one's former Cossack village—reflect ambitions, worries, and actions that were the history of the empire. The representation of these small-scale triumphs and tragedies may not parallel the rise and fall (if that is what happened) of the empire as a whole, but they do suggest the human connections that held the place together in good times and bad.

Notes

I am grateful to Valerie Kivelson, David Ransel, and Janet Rabinowitch for their attentive readings of earlier drafts of this essay and for their thought-provoking suggestions.

1. See the following monographs in which our contributors develop themes introduced in this volume: Valerie Kivelson, *Autocracy in the Provinces: The Muscovite Gentry and Political Culture in the Seventeenth Century* (Stanford: Stanford University Press, 1997); Richard Wortman, *Scenarios of Power: Myth and Ceremony in Russian Monarchy*. vol. I: *From Peter the Great to the Death of Nicholas I* (Princeton: Princeton University Press, 1995);

Steven Hoch, *Serfdom and Social Control in Russia. Petrovskoe, a Village in Tambov* (Chicago: Chicago University Press, 1986); Irina Paperno, *Suicide as a Cultural Institution in Dostoevsky's Russia* (Ithaca: Cornell University Press, 1997).

2. See Reginald Zelnik's comment on this problem at the SSRC workshop held at the Center for International and Comparative Studies at the University of Iowa in November 1991, cited in Jane Burbank, "Revisioning Imperial Russia," *Slavic Review* 52, no. 3 (Fall 1993): 567.

3. The major exception is Richard Pipes, *Russia under the Old Regime* (New York: Scribner's, 1974). See also Marc Raeff, *Understanding Imperial Russia: State and Society in the Old Regime*, trans. A. Goldhammer (New York: Columbia University Press, 1984).

4. See David Ransel's article in this volume, pp. 256–80, for a discussion of theories concerning the limits of microhistory.

5. For discussions of problems of narrative in European history, see Sarah Maza, "Stories in History: Cultural Narratives in Recent Work in European History," *American Historical Review* 101, no. 5 (December 1996): 1493–1515. On the influence of subaltern studies on historical theory, see the AHR Forum, *American Historical Review* 99, no. 5 (December 1994): Gyan Prakash, "Subaltern Studies as Postcolonial Criticism," 1475–90; Florencia E. Mallon, "The Promise and Dilemma of Subaltern Studies: Perspectives from Latin American History," 1491–1515; and Frederick Cooper, "Conflict and Connection: Rethinking Colonial African History," 1516–45.

6. James Cracraft defended the traditional chronological boundaries of the imperial period at the first meeting of the SSRC imperial Russia initiative; see the discussion in Burbank, "Revisioning Imperial Russia," 565.

7. For Richard Pipes, the police state regime dates from 1881; see his *Russia under the Old Regime*. Many other scholars have studied the late imperial period as an extended crisis for autocratic rule; some outstanding examples are Roberta Manning, *The Crisis of the Old Order in Russia: Gentry and Government* (Princeton: Princeton University Press, 1982); Frank Wcislo, *Reforming Rural Russia: State, Local Society and National Politics, 1855–1914* (Princeton: Princeton University Press, 1990); and Leopold Haimson, *The Politics of Rural Russia: 1905–1914* (Bloomington: Indiana University Press, 1979). For Soviet and many other twentieth-century historians, Lenin's notion that 1861 marked the beginning of the capitalist era in Russia made a strong impact on the dating of imperial decline. On Lenin's impact on understanding of the late imperial period, see Esther Kingston-Mann, *Lenin and the Problem of Marxist Peasant Revolution* (New York: Oxford University Press, 1983). Before 1917, however, the reforms of the 1860s and the advent of capitalism were read by both critics of the autocracy and its supporters as the start of a new era.

8. See Wortman, *Scenarios of Power*, 405–17.

9. See Steven L. Hoch, "On Good Numbers and Bad: Malthus, Population Trends and Peasant Standard of Living in Late Imperial Russia," *Slavic Review* 53, no. 1 (Spring 1994): 41–75, for a critique of the historiography and suggestions for research on this subject.

10. John LeDonne's *Absolutism and Ruling Class: The Formation of the Russian Political Order, 1700–1825* (New York: Oxford University Press, 1991) sets out the structural foun-

dations for dyarchy; in his view 1825 was the beginning of the end for the traditional elite (op. cit., 309).

11. For recent work on imperial Russia as an empire, see Daniel R. Brower and Edward J. Lazzerini, eds., *Russia's Orient: Imperial Borderlands and Peoples, 1700–1917* (Bloomington: Indiana University Press, 1977) and Andreas Kappeler, *Russland als Vielvölkerreich: Entstehung, Geschichte, Zerfall* (Munich: Beck, 1992). For the Soviet period, see Richard Pipes, *The Formation of the Soviet Union*, first published in 1954, and now in its third edition: *The Formation of the Soviet Union: Communism and Nationalism, 1917–1923* (New York: Atheneum Press, 1968); Ronald Grigor Suny, *The Revenge of the Past: Nationalism, Revolution, and the Collapse of the Soviet Union* (Stanford: Stanford University Press, 1993); Helene Carrere d'Encausse, *Decline of an Empire: The Soviet Socialist Republics in Revolt* (New York: Newsweek Books, 1979); and Yuri Slezkine, "The USSR as a Communal Apartment, or How a Socialist State Promoted Ethnic Particularism," *Slavic Review* 53 (Summer 1994): 414–52. For a comparative perspective, see Karen Barkey and Mark von Hagen, eds., *After Empire: Multiethnic Societies and Nation-Building* (Boulder: Westview Press, 1997).

12. See, from a large literature, Frederick Cooper and Ann Stoler, "Between Metropole and Colony: Rethinking a Research Agenda," in their *Tensions of Empire: Colonial Cultures in a Bourgeois World* (Berkeley: University of California Press, 1997), 1–56. This article includes an extensive bibliography on first- and third-world colonialism.

13. Edward L. Keenan, "Muscovite Political Folkways," *Russian Review* 45 (April 1986): 115–81.

14. Lee Farrow examines the law on partible inheritance and its significance for women in her article "Peter the Great's Law of Single Inheritance: State Imperatives and Noble Resistance," *Russian Review* 55 (July 1996) 430–47. On partible inheritance in Muscovy, see Valerie A. Kivelson, "The Effects of Partible Inheritance: Gentry Families and the State in Muscovy," *The Russian Review* 53 (April 1994): 197–212.

15. On the intersection of patriarchs' interests, see John Bushnell, "Did Serf Owners Control Serf Marriage? Orlov Serfs and Their Neighbors, 1773–1861," *Slavic Review* 52, no. 3 (Fall 1993): 419–45, and Steven L. Hoch's monograph, *Serfdom and Social Control in Russia: Petrovskoe: a Village in Tambov* (Chicago: Chicago University Press, 1986).

16. See David Ransel, *The Politics of Catherinian Russia: The Panin Party* (New Haven: Yale University Press, 1975). Ransel points out that the question of expansion or internal development was contested by elites. These debates themselves are evidence of the need to integrate foreign and domestic histories back into a single narrative.

17. John P. LeDonne's new study, *The Russian Empire and the World: 1700–1917* (New York: Oxford University Press, 1997) addresses many of these issues. David McDonald's *United Government and Foreign Policy in Russia, 1900–1917* is an excellent example of the domestic context, causalities, and casualties of foreign policy in the late imperial period.

18. See Michael Confino's "Present Events and the Representation of the Past," *Cahiers du monde russe*, 35:4 (October-December, 1994), 851–53; Burbank, "Revisioning Imperial Russia," 556–57; and Jane Burbank, "The Imperial Construction of Russian Nationality," unpublished manuscript presented at the SSRC workshop in Iowa in 1991.

Contributors

Thomas M. Barrett is assistant professor of history at St. Mary's College of Maryland. He has written articles and essays on the history of Russia's encounter with the North Caucasus.

Jane Burbank is professor of history at the University of Michigan. She is author of *Intelligentsia and Revolution: Russian Views of Bolshevism, 1917–1922* and is writing a book on legal culture in rural Russia.

Gregory L. Freeze is professor of history at Brandeis University. He is author of *The Russian Levites: Parish Clergy in the Eighteenth Century* and *Crisis, Reform, Counter-Reform: The Parish Clergy in Nineteenth-Century Russia*.

Steven L. Hoch is professor of history at the University of Iowa and director of the Project in Russian Population History, 1700–1917. He is currently writing a book, *Land and Freedom: Emancipation and the Rise of a Peasant Economy in Russia*.

Valerie A. Kivelson is associate professor of history at the University of Michigan. She is author of *Autocracy in the Provinces: Russian Political Culture and the Gentry in the Seventeenth Century*.

Nathaniel Knight has taught at the University of New Hampshire and is currently a research scholar at the Kennan Institute. He is preparing a history of nineteenth-century Russian ethnography.

Irina Paperno is professor of Slavic languages and literatures at the University of California, Berkeley. Her publications include *Chernyshevsky and the Age of Realism: A Study in the Semiotics of Behavior* and (with Joan Delaney Grossman) *Creating Life: The Aesthetic Utopia of Russian Modernism*.

David L. Ransel is professor of history and director of the Russian and East European Institute at Indiana University, Bloomington. He is author of *The Politics of Catherinian Russia: The Panin Party* and *Mothers of Misery: Child Abandonment in Russia* and editor and translator of *Village Life in Late Tsarist Russia*.

Douglas Smith has worked with the United States Information Agency in the former USSR. He has written on Soviet affairs for Radio Free Europe/Radio Liberty in Munich, Germany, and is author of *Working the Rough Stone: Freemasonry and Society in Eighteenth-Century Russia*.

Willard Sunderland is assistant professor of history at the University of Cincinnati. He has published articles on issues relating to the history of the Russian empire's eastern borderlands.

Kevin Tyner Thomas studied Russian history at the University of California, Los Angeles. He is executive producer of New Media at Fourth Dimension Interactive in San Francisco.

Cynthia Hyla Whittaker is professor of history at Baruch College and the Graduate School of the City University of New York. She is author of *The Origins of Modern Russian Education: An Intellectual Biography of Count Sergei Uvarov* and *Alexander Pushkin: Epigrams and Satirical Verse*.

Richard Wortman is professor of history at Columbia University. His most recent book is *Scenarios of Power: Myth and Ritual in Russian History, Volume 1: From Peter the Great to the Death of Nicholas I*. He is working on the second volume of this study.

Index

Academy of Sciences, 110, 284
Adelung, Friedrich von, 91–103
Adelung, Johann Christian von, 102
Afanas'ev, Aleksandr Nikolaevich, 126, 139n.80
Agriculture, 152, 153, 154, 203–204
Akhverdov, A. I., 156, 261
Alekseev, A. I., 133n.1, 134n.10
Alekseevich, Fedor (Tsar), 13, 23–24
Alekseevna, Elizabeth (Empress), 64
Alekseevna, Natalie (Grand Duchess), 62
Alekseevna, Sophia, 47–48
Alexander I (Tsar), 223, 225, 240n.40, 244n.85
Alexander II (Tsar), 63–64, 71–74, 77–82, 103
Alpatov, Iakov, 161
Anderson, Benedict, 106–107n.60, 299n.20
Anna Ivanovna (Empress), 6, 7, 15, 19–21, 25–26, 42, 49
Annals of Forensic Medicine (journal), 324
Anthropology, and debate on colonialism, 338–39
Arakcheev, Alexei, 64
Aristocracy. *See* Class; Nobility
Armenians, settlement in north Caucasus, 160–61
Art, and proposals for national museum, 94
Assemblies of the Land, 10
Austria: system of succession, 63; reforms and separation of court and bureaucracy, 66
Autocracy: historiography of imperial period, 3–4; kinship politics and political culture of early 18th century, 5–27; 18th-century historians and idea of, 32–51; imperial family as symbol, 60–83; state and peasant social order, 205–206. *See also* Class

Baddeley, John, 149, 153
Baehr, Stephen L., 53n.13, 83n.5, 302n.50
Baer, Karl von, 108, 112, 114, 116, 117–22, 134nn.4,11, 135n.26, 136nn.36,40,41, 137n.56
Baier, Gottlieb, 52n.3
Bakounine, Tatiana, 301n.42

Balandin, A. I., 139n.82
Barenbaum, I. E., 301n.39
Barkey, Karen, 345n.11
Barkov, Ivan, 37
Barnouw, Dagmar, 278n.4
Barrett, Thomas, xvii, xviii, xxii, 145, 169n.2, 336, 338
Barsov, T. V., 236n.2
Barth, Fredrik, 193n.21
Bashkirs (ethnic group), 180, 182–83
Baturin, P. S., 294, 303n.55
Baumeister, F. C., 238n.18
Bayle, Pierre, 53n.13
Bazin, Germain, 104n.8
Becker, Seymour, 195–96n.38
Behavior, Church and regulation of lay conduct, 223–24, 225–26, 243–44n.79
Beik, William, 30n.42
Bekasova, A. V., 107n.61
Belliustin, I. S., 236n.3
Benckendorff, Alexander, 76
Ber, K. M., 136n.41
Berezin, I., 196n.39
Berg, L. S., 133n.1, 134nn.4,15,16, 139n.80
Besançon, Alain, 61
Beshenkovskii, E. B., 56n.55
Bestuzhev-Marlinskii, Aleksandr, 166
Billington, James, xxiiin.3
Biron, Ernst Johann, 49
Bishops, and institutionalization of Church, 212, 213, 214, 216, 217
Black, J. B., 55n.42
Blagovidov, F. V., 236n.2
Blazejowskyj, A., 237n.12
Bludov, Dmitrii, 76
Blum, Jerome, 204
Blumenbach, Johann Friedrich, 120
Bobrov, A. A., 241n.44
Bogdanov, A., 140n.98
Bolshevik Revolution (1917), xiii
Boltin, Ivan, 33, 35, 42–43, 45, 46, 49, 50, 53n.13, 54n.41, 57n.69, 58n.90
Bossuet, Jacques, 36